l m

s t

x y z

17TH CENTURY

aa bb cc dd ee

18TH CENTURY

ff gg hh ii jj

The Bettmann Archive Picture History of The World

Illustrations on back endpapers are identified on page 223.

Manley Stolzman, Editor
Fred Czufin, Designer

Random House
New York

The Bettmann Archive Picture History of The World

The Story of Western Civilization Retold in 4460 Pictures

Otto L. Bettmann

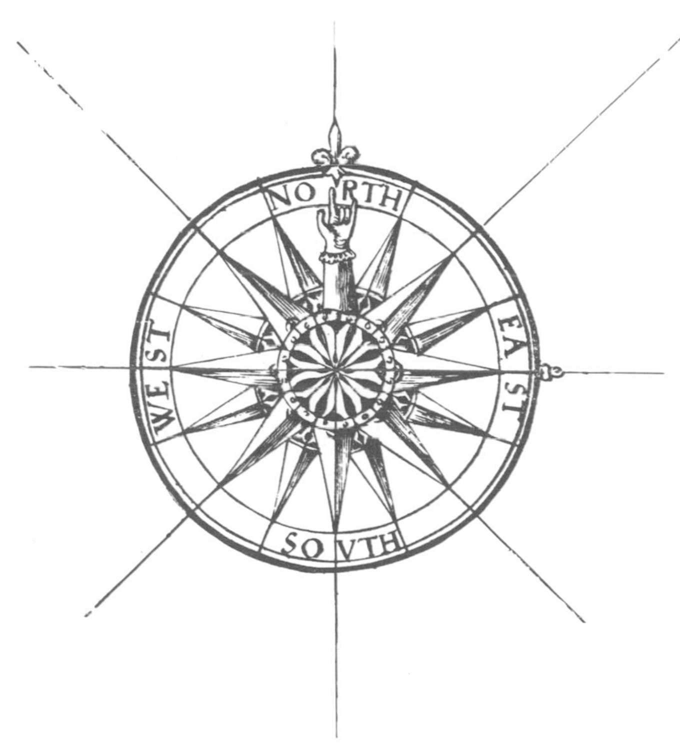

Published in the United States of America by Random House Inc., New York, and simultaneously in Canada by Random House of Canada Limited, Toronto.

Library of Congress Cataloging in Publication Data

Bettmann, Otto

The Bettmann Archive picture history of the world.

1. Civilization, Occidental—History—Pictorial works. I. Title.

CB245.B47 909'.09'821 77-5995

ISBN O-394-41201-X

Manufactured in the United States of America

Produced in collaboration with The Bettmann Archive, Inc. by Picture House Press, Inc., New York.

Editorial Consultant
Dr. Robert Collins

Editorial Assistants
Nancy Jennens
Beverly Mann
Gilda Roberts

Manuscript Development
Joy McLeieer

Art Associates
W.M. Koziolkiewicz
Bruce Wilkins

Production Assistant
Carol Gaskin

Each picture in this book has been given an identification number that appears in parentheses at the end of the caption. Identifications of pictures on Chapter Divider pages are listed on page 222.

CONTENTS

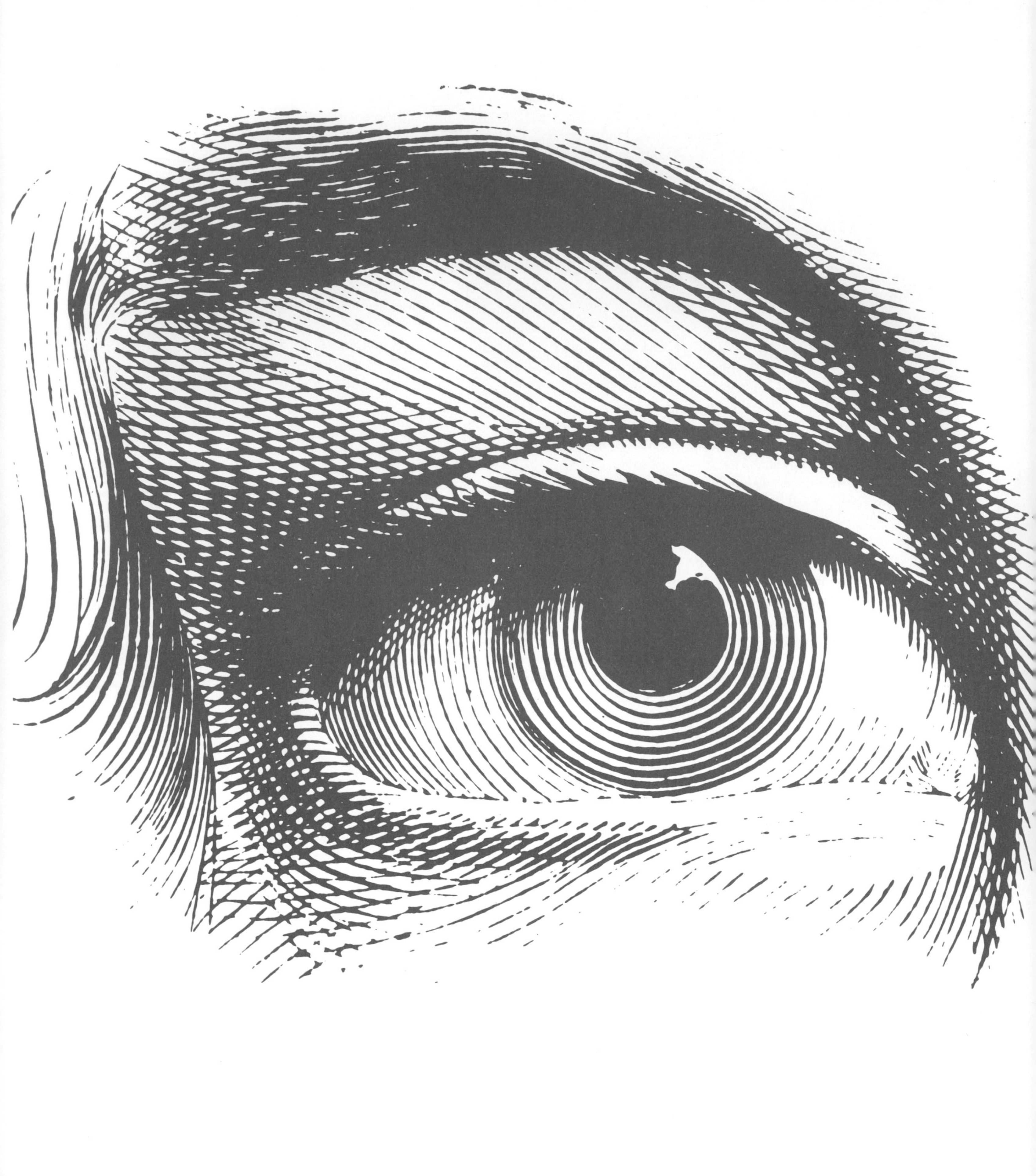

INTRODUCTION

IN AN AGE OF IMAGES, with our ideas shaped and our emotions stirred by television and film, pictures have become a dominant means of communication. Our view of the world today often seems a sort of visual collage which claims us all as eyewitnesses to the present.

The past, also, is increasingly perceived in visual terms: through art, engravings, photographs and vintage newsreels the modern eye may witness a good deal of history. And the collection and interpretation of visual documents has become the work of a new breed of "graphic historians."

In this fraternity I can claim charter membership, for pictures have been at the center of my life work. In 1933, when the onset of the Hitler regime forced me from my position as Curator of Rare Books in Berlin, I began to search out in art centers all over the world graphics recording the public and private lives of ages past. When I reached America two years later, a pair of steamer trunks filled with old prints were my sole possessions.

It was a propitious time for a graphic historian. The great picture magazines were just getting started, and education was turning toward audio-visual methods. In this atmosphere, my collection grew until it became the Bettman Archive, a library of more than three million pictures which represent, in toto, a picture history of Western man.

The idea to put this story between the covers of a book has long fascinated me. Certainly in a generation enamored of the visual media, it is a timely one. When once I mentioned a project of this kind—in a modicum of jest—to my Random House editor, Robert Loomis, he unexpectedly took me up on it. With characteristic panache he set me to work, providing invaluable guidance as we went along. This book is the result.

Recasting an archive into a book is much like trying to fit a giant into the bed of Procrustes, however. From millions of relevant pictures only a small percentage could be chosen. Our story must be told in its boldest outlines, providing an overview of the historical landscape comparable, perhaps, to the foreshortened scene we get of earth when flying at high altitudes. On the other hand, if pictures are to be the main element (thousands of them, more perhaps than ever assembled in a volume this size) they must of necessity be small, and their captions short and pithy.

In departing from conventional methods of picture editing which favor the large picture, the close-up, we had to explore the virtues of miniaturization. I faced the same question besetting the makers of tiny cars, cameras and calculators: will the miniatures perform? I have reason to believe they will: a small picture well reproduced contains as much information as a large one, while the visual sophistication of modern viewers, particularly the young, enables them to "read" pictures easily. The faces of the mighty are now as familiar as family portraits, and we have all learned to recognize images and symbols, at times even without the help of words.

Other features of the book should work in our favor. Unlike conventional illustrations, our pictures do not appear singly, as islands in a sea of text. Rather, they are grouped together thematically, to produce a synergistic effect, and to provide for mutual elucidation. For example, in more conventional usage, a picture of Watt and his steam engine might suffice to suggest the industrial revolution. Here the picture is surrounded with images—of capitalist entrepreneurs, iron and coal resources, inventive craftsmen—all factors which suggest the forces enabling England to lead the world in mechanization. Similarly, positivist philosophers are grouped with pictures of authors and artworks of the mid-nineteenth century, heightening the understanding of the period's jarring shift from romanticism to realism.

These mutually supportive sequences are fitted into a chronological grid, which provides the reader with an immediate impression of coeval events in a given period, and may also suggest fresh relationships: Harvey's discovery of blood circulation, for instance, appears within a context of research on hydraulics, and of the emphasis on elliptical motions in Newtonian physics; Walt Whitman is seen among images of 19th-century expansiveness in the United States, the rise in American self-esteem and the politics of "Manifest Destiny."

In contrast to a textual treatment bound to develop its subject in linear sequence, graphic history as here presented can offer a "synoptic panorama" generated from multiple images. This view is the familiar one generated by television and film in reporting the events of our own day. In a modest way, this book applies the same technique in presenting a glimpse of the past.

No doubt, considering the enormous range of subjects and the limited space available, we have not escaped errors, both of omission and commission. Still, I send my book forth in the hope that it may, in the overall, open up new perspectives, and so add excitement to the study of history.

Otto Bettmann.

PROLOGUE

Creation

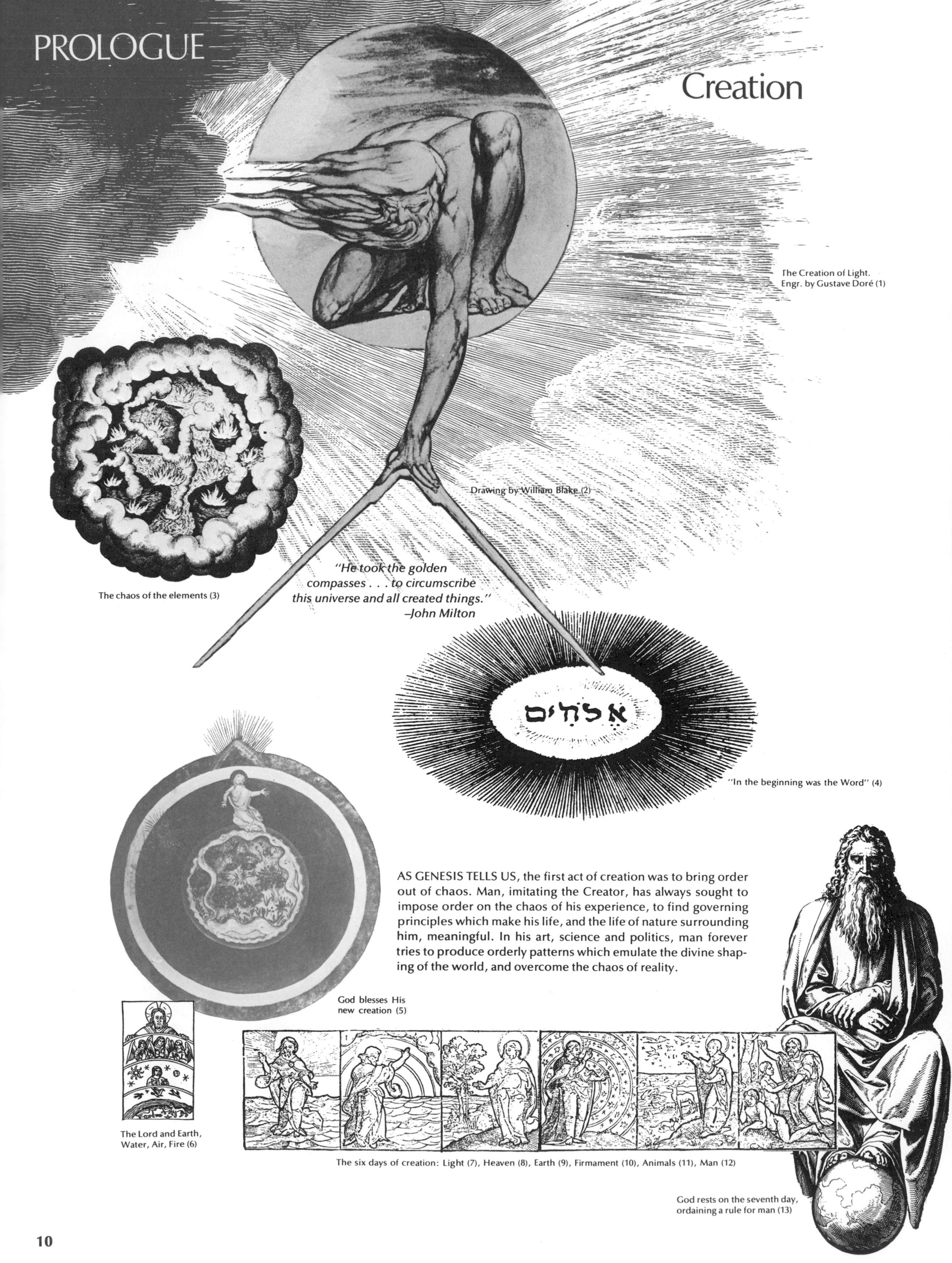

The Creation of Light. Engr. by Gustave Doré (1)

Drawing by William Blake (2)

The chaos of the elements (3)

"He took the golden compasses . . . to circumscribe this universe and all created things."
–John Milton

"In the beginning was the Word" (4)

AS GENESIS TELLS US, the first act of creation was to bring order out of chaos. Man, imitating the Creator, has always sought to impose order on the chaos of his experience, to find governing principles which make his life, and the life of nature surrounding him, meaningful. In his art, science and politics, man forever tries to produce orderly patterns which emulate the divine shaping of the world, and overcome the chaos of reality.

God blesses His new creation (5)

The Lord and Earth, Water, Air, Fire (6)

The six days of creation: Light (7), Heaven (8), Earth (9), Firmament (10), Animals (11), Man (12)

God rests on the seventh day, ordaining a rule for man (13)

Universe

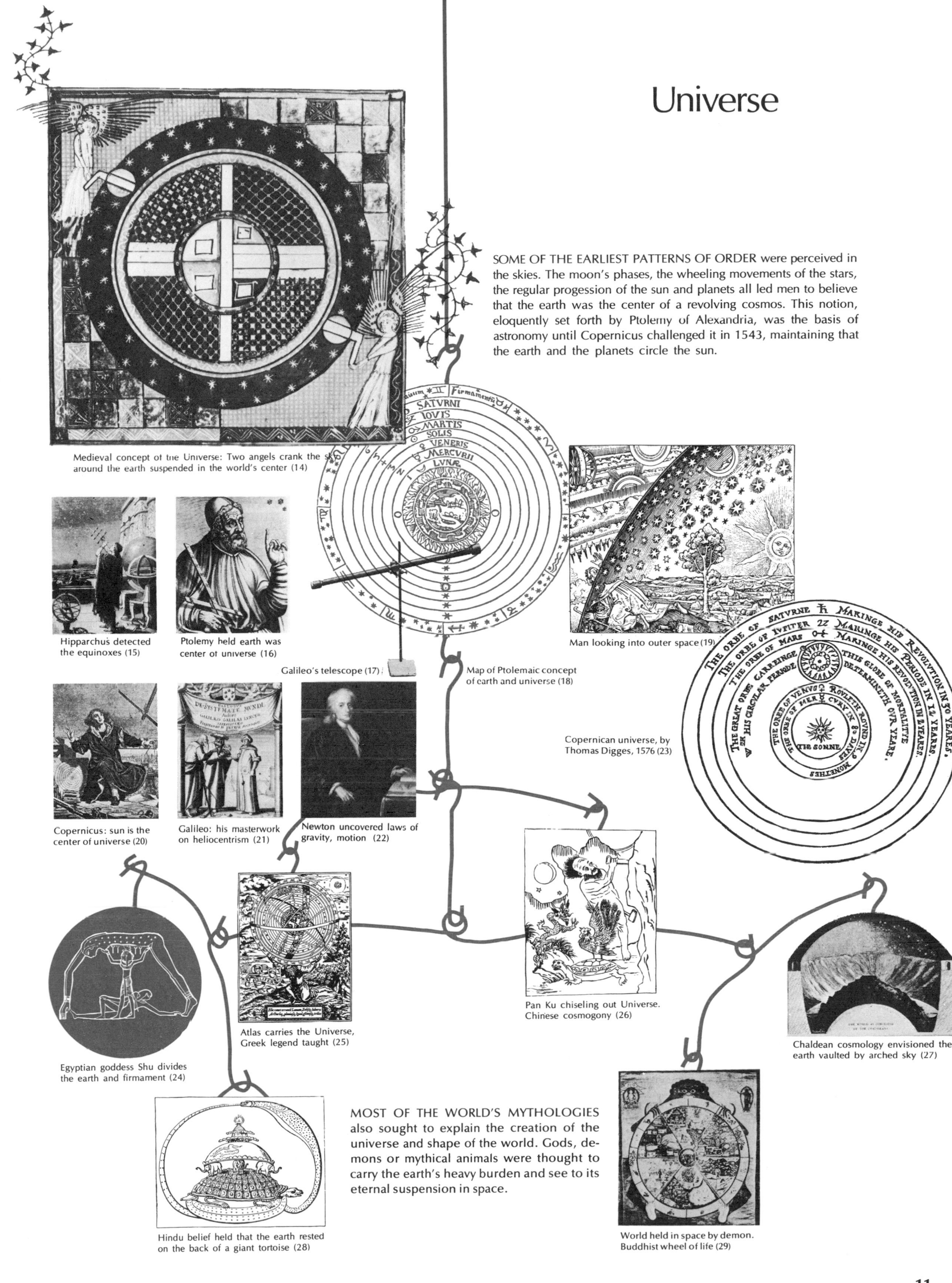

SOME OF THE EARLIEST PATTERNS OF ORDER were perceived in the skies. The moon's phases, the wheeling movements of the stars, the regular progession of the sun and planets all led men to believe that the earth was the center of a revolving cosmos. This notion, eloquently set forth by Ptolemy of Alexandria, was the basis of astronomy until Copernicus challenged it in 1543, maintaining that the earth and the planets circle the sun.

Medieval concept of the Universe: Two angels crank the sky around the earth suspended in the world's center (14)

Hipparchus detected the equinoxes (15)

Ptolemy held earth was center of universe (16)

Galileo's telescope (17)

Map of Ptolemaic concept of earth and universe (18)

Man looking into outer space (19)

Copernicus: sun is the center of universe (20)

Galileo: his masterwork on heliocentrism (21)

Newton uncovered laws of gravity, motion (22)

Copernican universe, by Thomas Digges, 1576 (23)

Egyptian goddess Shu divides the earth and firmament (24)

Atlas carries the Universe, Greek legend taught (25)

Pan Ku chiseling out Universe. Chinese cosmogony (26)

Chaldean cosmology envisioned the earth vaulted by arched sky (27)

MOST OF THE WORLD'S MYTHOLOGIES also sought to explain the creation of the universe and shape of the world. Gods, demons or mythical animals were thought to carry the earth's heavy burden and see to its eternal suspension in space.

Hindu belief held that the earth rested on the back of a giant tortoise (28)

World held in space by demon. Buddhist wheel of life (29)

Prehistoric Life

Primeval Animals

TERRESTRIAL LIFE began in the primeval seas, moved onto land and continued to evolve eon after eon. The dinosaurs, or "terrible lizards," dominated the earth for more than a hundred million years during the Mesozoic era, but apparently were unable to adapt to climatic changes and died out. Smaller, more versatile forms replaced them. The mammalian branch of the evolutionary tree brought forth manlike hominids in East Africa well over a million years ago.

Fighting dryptosaurs during the Age of Reptiles (30)

Stegosaurus ungulatus, about 25 feet long, roamed western United States 185,000,000 years ago. Skeleton (31) reconstruction (32)

Wary dinosaur of the Mesozoic Era (33)

Tricerotops prorsus, about twenty feet long, was last of the dinosaurs (34)

Prehistoric man and wife, 17th-century concept (35)

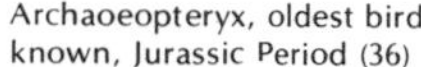

Archaoeopteryx, oldest bird known, Jurassic Period (36)

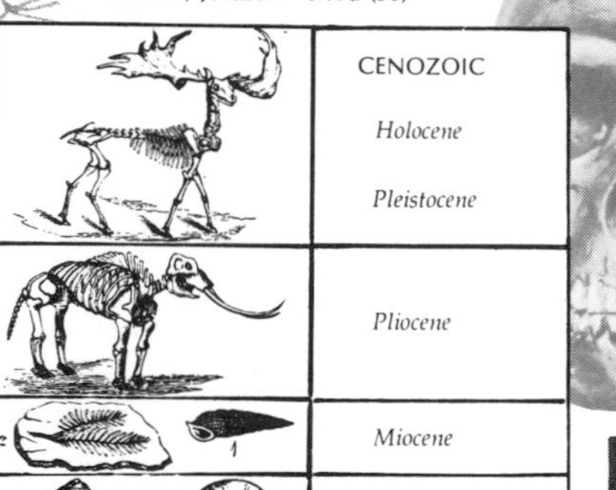

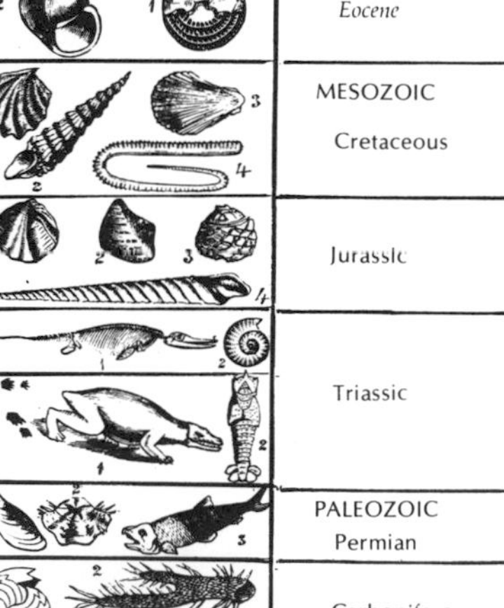

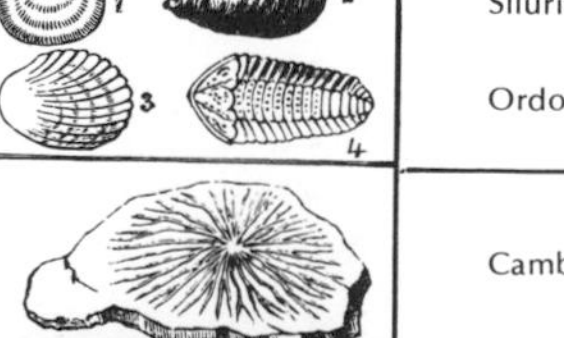

Eras, Periods and Epochs
CENOZOIC *Holocene* *Pleistocene*
Pliocene
Miocene
Eocene
MESOZOIC Cretaceous
Jurassic
Triassic
PALEOZOIC Permian
Carboniferous
Devonian
Silurian Ordovician
Cambrian
ARCHEOZOIC PROTEROZOIC

Geological table showing Eras, Periods and Epochs, and characteristic fossil remains (43)

Emergence of Man

HOMINIDS who stood erect *(Homo erectus)* appeared a half-million years ago, but *Homo sapiens*—the species that includes modern man—appeared only about 75,000 years ago. Some man-like primates, such as Neanderthal man, evidently died out while others flourished, as did Cro-Magnon man, our own nearest ancestor. Cave paintings found in Europe reveal the Cro-Magnon as a hunter and an artist, whose ability to adapt to changing conditions enabled him to survive.

Skull of man of the Neanderthal type (37)

Neolithic hunters shown in cave scratchings (41)

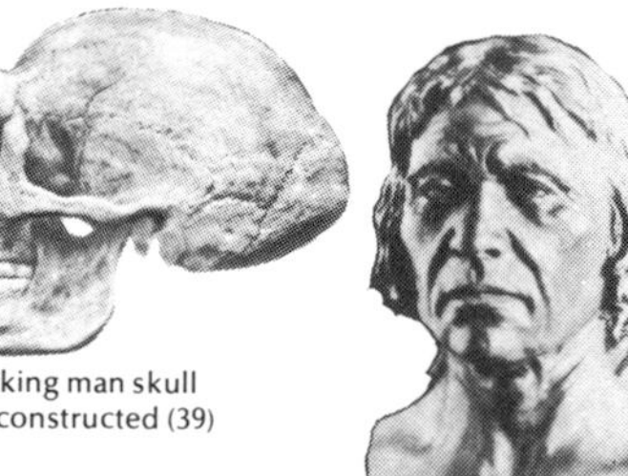

Paleolithic skeletons in the Grimaldi cave (38)

Peking man skull reconstructed (39)

Cro-Magnon man. Reconstruction (40)

Prehistoric hunters corner a mastodon. Painting by Charles R. Knight (42)

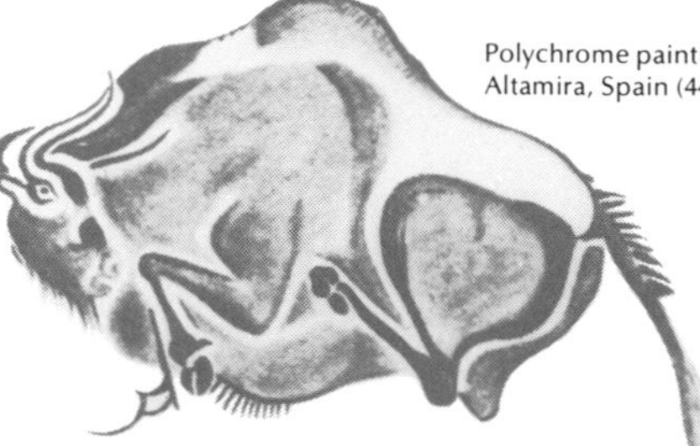

Polychrome painting of bison, Altamira, Spain (44)

Cave artist draws animals to vitiate their spirits (45)

Horses carved on reindeer horn (46)

Art • Magic • Medicine

CAVE ART probably served religious and magical purposes. Magic was also allied with medicine, for primitive man felt that sickness was an invasion of evil spirits that lodged in the head. This belief led to trepanning—drilling a hole in the cranium to allow demons to escape.

Shaman cuts evil from skull (47)

Willendorf Venus (49)

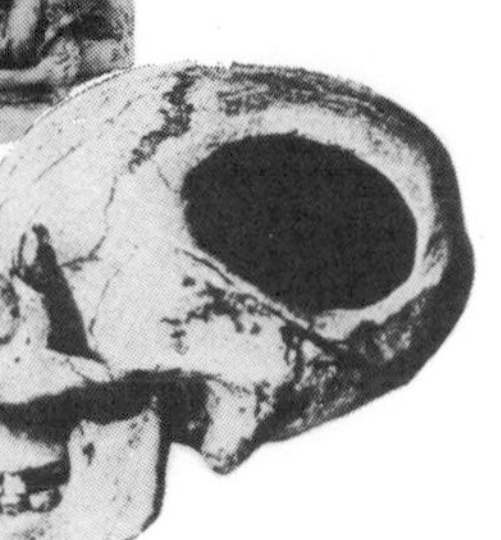

Trepanned skull. Evil spirits gone (48)

Cro-Magnon shaman exorcises pain (50)

Cave man chips flint to make tools, weapons (51)

Man the Toolmaker

DURING THE PALEOLITHIC AGE—the longest human epoch—man survived as a hunter, using flint-tipped weapons. His social evolution may be traced by the development of increasingly sophisticated tools. The appearance of pottery and the plow during the "Neolithic Revolution" made possible the shift from a nomadic to a stable, agrarian way of life—and so modern civilization began.

Pounding kernels with mortar and pestle (52)

Inclined plane enabled man to move heavy loads, establish dolmen (53)

Neolithic dolmen in Kwantung (54)

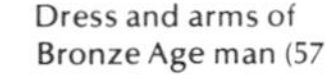

Dress and arms of Bronze Age man (57)

Pots were made for cooking, storage (55)

Bronze Age settlement, England (56)

Tools to cultivate the soil changed man the hunter into a settled agriculturist (59)

Fire-hardened point bound to a heavy shaft made a sturdy mattock that doubled as a weapon 10,000 years B.C. (58)

City Civilizations

THE FIRST OF THE GREAT city civilizations was built by the Sumerians on the Biblical Plain of Shinar, between the Tigris and Euphrates rivers, around 3000 B.C. A non-Semitic people who came from the north or possibly central Asia, the Sumerians worked metals, wrote in cuneiform (incising wet clay with a stylus) and learned to irrigate their fields. Most important, they created the first urban society, building cities like Ur, Eridu, Larsa and Lagash.

The Sumerians were overthrown by Semitic Akkadians, under Sargon I, around 2340 B.C. Fighting was chronic until Hammurabi conquered the Plain of Shinar in 1728 B.C. His forty-two-year reign was distinguished by the legal code he devised—a harsh but just system whose traces are in the pages of the Old Testament.

Sumerian cuneiform tablet with statistical lists (60)

Diorite statue, Lagash, ca. 2400 B.C. (61)

Hammurabi, great king of first Babylonian dynasty, receives the law from Sun God Shamash (62)

Chaldean dairy scene. Figures cut in shell. From an ancient temple (63)

Reconstruction showing workmen building a wall. From Palace at Ur-Nammu (64)

Babylonian seal with sacred bulls and Gilgamesh, epic hero, who sought key to immortality (65)

King Ur-Nammu on the throne of Ur. Third Dynasty, ca. 2300 B.C. (66)

A
B

CHAPTER 1

Antiquity

Egypt
Eastern Kingdoms
Greece and Rome

Egypt

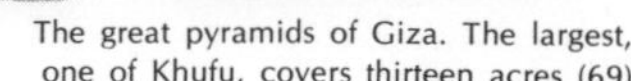

"Egypt" written in hieroglyphics (67)

"Wonders more in number than those of any other land and works it has to show beyond expression great."
—Herodotus

The colossal Sphinx, guardian of the Valley of the Nile (68)

The great pyramids of Giza. The largest, one of Khufu, covers thirteen acres (69)

Camel and driver. Desert travelers (70)

Slaves with overseer move giant lever (71)

THE MONUMENTAL GRANDEUR of Egypt dominates the early history of the world. Dependent upon agriculture, Egyptian civilization produced remarkable achievements in arts and crafts, and nurtured a massive bureaucracy of priests and civil servants. The Pharaohs of the Old Kingdom sought immortality through massive tombs, as at Giza.

Group of Egyptian slaves urged on by overseer pull rope to move heavy building stone (72)

Nile's annual overflow was the source of Egypt's fertility (73)

Surveyors at work. Instruments are much the same today (74)

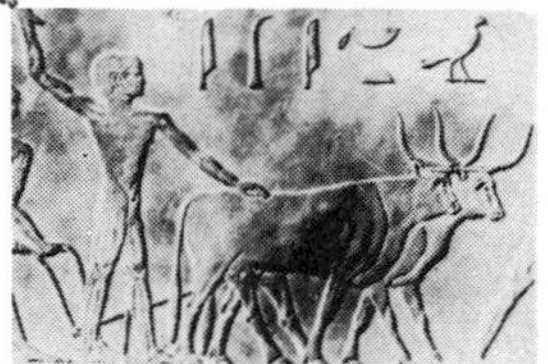

Cattle draw plow for naked farmers. Bas relief from Saqqara (75)

Grain cut by farmer whose wife follows with basket to gather the harvest (76)

Farming and Crafts were Source of Egypt's Wealth

Carpenter uses metal tool (81)

Grinding corn. Stone statue (77)

Egyptian dairy scene: man milks cow. Calf is tied to mother's foreleg (78)

Cleaning and plucking poultry for a Pharaoh's feast (79)

Granaries held surplus grain; tapped in case of famine (80)

Sawing lumber—today as in Pharaoh's time. Photo (82)

Metalworker with blow torch decorates vase (83)

Potter uses giant reamer in jar (84)

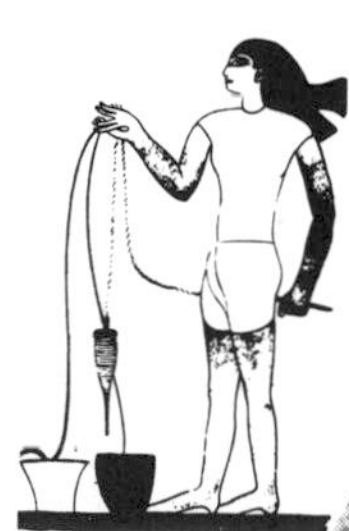

Twisting threads to make twine (85)

THE SCRIBES OF EGYPT, originally keepers of inventories and tax records, soon gained exalted status in the vast governmental bureaucracy. Their skill in writing, along with the development of algebra, sped Egypt's rise as a great power in the ancient world.

Hesira—court official, scribe, 3rd Dynasty (87)

Imhotep—architect, physician, author (88)

◀ Man of Baulak. World's oldest wood statue (86)

Egyptian court officials punish farmer for non-payment of taxes due to royal treasury (90)

Grain inventoried by officials who also record fees and receipts (91)

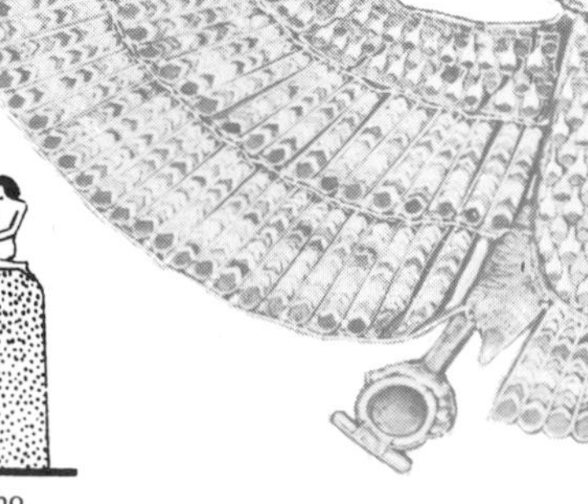

Gold-encrusted breastplate of King Tutankhamen (92)

"The invention of writing and of a convenient system of records on paper has had a greater influence in uplifting the human race than any other achievement in the life of man."

—James Henry Breasted

Scarab—sacred talisman (97)

Papyrus grew in Nile River swamps (98)

Writing

THE MASTERY OF WRITING made possible a record of Egyptian achievement more sophisticated than that of other ancient cultures. The written language evolved by the scribes was made up of pictorial symbols used in rebus-like combinations. As the name "hieroglyphic" (sacred carving) implies, the symbols were at first carved in stone or clay, like the cuneiform characters of the Babylonians. With the discovery that a durable portable writing material could be made from the papyrus plant, Egyptians found the means to accommodate the voluminous records their civilization required.

Scribes recorded all transactions (93)

Dry climate preserved perfectly great mass of papyrus rolls (94)

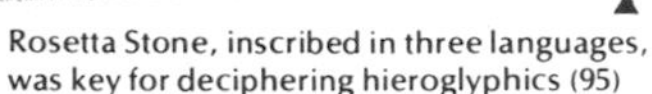

Rosetta Stone, inscribed in three languages, was key for deciphering hieroglyphics (95)

Egyptian priest covered with incantations (96)

Eye of Horus—symbol of well-being, good health (104)

Women in Egypt

Egyptian lady's toilette. Servants perfume hair, color lips, serve healthful foods (99)

Ointment urn held by slave (100)

Carved wooden salve spoon (101)

Coiffure for mother; food for infant. Statuette (102)

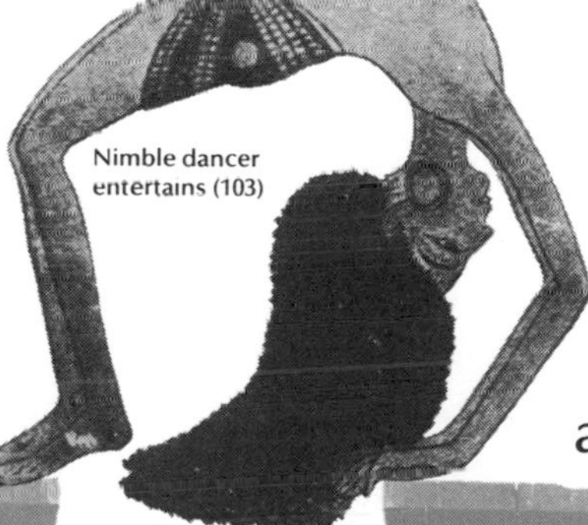

Nimble dancer entertains (103)

Medicine and Embalming

Circumcision—common hygienic practice (105)

Mummy reveals Pott's disease (106)

Sacred Ibis gives self enema (107)

Embalmers wrap mummy as coffin is readied (108)

Mummified head of Pharaoh Ramses II, d. 1225 B.C. (109)

Soul leaves body in form of bird (110)

Kings and Queens

Triumphal arch at Temple of Karnak (111)

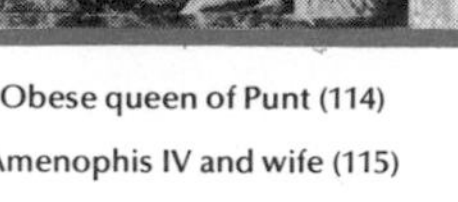

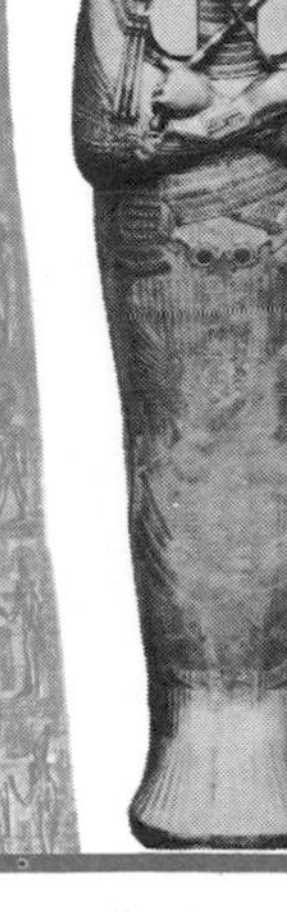

King Chephren (112)

Queen Hatshepsut (113)

Obese queen of Punt (114)

Amenophis IV and wife (115)

Queen Nefertiti (116)

Akhnaton and family (117)

Coffin of King Tut (118)

King Ramses II (119)

Cleopatra in the guise of Isis (120)

Kingdoms of the Middle East

RIVERS WERE THE CRADLE of civilization. Like the Nile-based Egyptians, the people of the Tigris-Euphrates Valley reaped harvests that relieved them of the time-consuming dangerous necessities of the hunt, thus enabling them to develop settled communities. Unlike the inaccessible Nile Valley, however, the Fertile Crescent was vulnerable to invasion.

Victorious Assyrian monarch returns from battle (121)

Croesus, king of Lydia, flaunts his wealth before Solon, Greek lawgiver (122)

Map of the Near East showing the Fertile Crescent (123)

Ashurnasirpal III, king of Assyria, 885-860 B.C. (124)

Hittite warrior with spear, shield (125)

Scenes of life in Ancient Assyria

- **A** Assyrian warrior brings home prisoners of war (126)
- **B** Chaldean phalanx attacking. Stele in tomb of Eannadou (127)
- **C** Slaves haul anthropomorphic colossus of winged god (128)
- **D** Ashurbanipal, Assyria's last great king, dines with wife (129)
- **E** Siege attack on enemy city. Sculpture, Palace in Nimrud (130)
- **F** Officer in tent has nightcap while camels dally outside (131)
- **G** Trainer attends royal horses in Nineveh, capitol city (132)
- **H** Palace of Sargon II (restored) at Dursharrukin, 722 B.C. (133)
- **I** Between wars and rebellions, Ashurbanipal hunted lions (134)
- **J** Night in Nineveh, leading city of ancient world to 612 B.C. (135)
- **K** Babylon died after surrender to Cyrus the Great, 538 B.C. (136)
- **L** Lion brought down by a hunter's well aimed arrow. Bas-relief (137)

Phoenician merchant-galleys probed the seven seas of ancient world (138)

Tyrian purple, foremost royal fabric, a prime Phoenician trade item (139)

The Phoenicians

MEDITERRANEAN-BASED TRADERS who sailed boldly into the Aegean Sea and ultimately the Atlantic, the Phoenicians dotted southern Europe with their trading posts and factory towns. To keep their business records, they developed an ingenious system of phonetic writing whose value to civilization cannot be overestimated: the alphabet.

Phœnician	Greek
𐤀 𐤀	A alpha
𐤁	B beta
𐤌	M mu

Phoenician alphabet started other graphic systems (140)

Phoenicians barter with Britons for artifacts (141)

Prisoners of war were slaves in Phoenician copper mine (142)

The Assyrians

SWEEPING INTO THE FERTILE CRESCENT from plateaus to the north, the Assyrians subjugated the entire Mideast perimeter, from Palestine to Babylonia. They were ruthless warriors who developed an unprecedented arsenal of iron weapons and an overwhelming new strategy of attack, based on fast-moving chariots.

Babylonia

AFTER TWO THOUSAND YEARS OF DECLINE, the metamorphosed Sumerian empire was briefly revitalized in the 6th century B.C. by King Nebuchadnezzar II. His magnificent capital, Babylon, with its wondrous architecture, was famed for its astronomers.

Decorative motif in palace of Nebuchadnezzar, Babylon (144)

Sun worship led Babylonians to discovery of the calendar (145)

Demon of disease inspired fear (146)

Overseer uses megaphone to amplify commands (147)

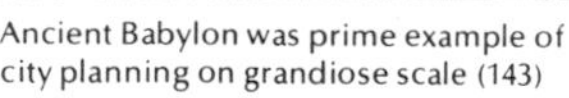
Ancient Babylon was prime example of city planning on grandiose scale (143)

Babylon's library of clay tablets incised in cuneiform rivaled Nineveh's (148)

Sacred Dragon of Babylon. Relief from Ishtar Door (149)

Handwriting on the wall prophesies doom at Belshazzar's feast (150)

Persia

◂ Persian horseman with elaborate bow (151)

WHEN THE CHALDEAN EMPIRE COLLAPSED after Nebuchadnezzar's death, the Persians, an Indo-European people, swept over the "cradle of civilization" with meteoric swiftness and brilliance. Superb equestrians and bowmen, the Persians proved to be competent administrators as well.

Darius the Great, 521-485 B.C. (152)

King Xerxes holds court while slaves use cooling fans (153)

Tiered temple of Anu Adad with towering ziggurats, 1000 B.C. (154)

Persian woman spins, servant holds yarn (155)

The Jews

ORIGINALLY A TRIBE OF HERDSMEN from the Tigris-Euphrates Valley, at about 1600 B.C. the Jews wandered southward toward the Arabian peninsula searching for their Promised Land. After long travels, they established their own nation, Israel. Its existence was precarious from the outset: driven by internal dissension, it was conquered by one people after another. Yet the Jews maintained their monotheistic religion, while their sacred writings gave European civilization its basic spiritual tradition.

◂ Menorah symbolizes days of Creation (156)

Jacob in Egypt with his wandering tribe (157)

Jews under yoke of captivity (158)

Moses holds up the Tablets of the Law. Rembrandt (159)

Solomon the Wise (168)

Bible records how Jews changed from wandering herdsmen to tillers of the soil, living in villages and towns (160)

Jews also became traders: marketplace in Israel (161)

Joshua's army conquers Canaan. Trumpets rumble, people shout, walls tumble 162)

Splendor of Temple of Solomon (163)

Hebrew scholar studies scrolls of religion, law, customs (164)

Tribute paid to Jehu, king of Israel. Relief, 9th century B.C. (165)

Ezra reads the law, revives faith of Jews after Babylonian captivity (166)

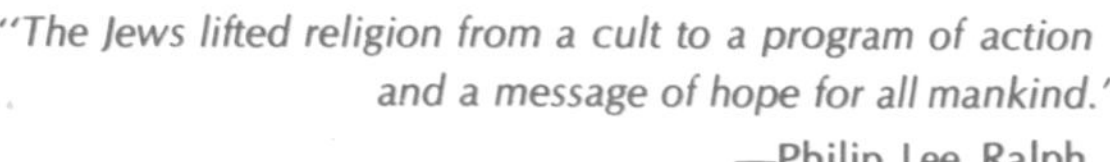

"The Jews lifted religion from a cult to a program of action and a message of hope for all mankind."

—Philip Lee Ralph

A column purported to be from Solomon's Temple (167)

Greece

Mythology: Explaining the Unfathomable

THE GREEKS TAUGHT MAN "the untrammeled use of the intellect," subjecting both natural phenomena and human relations to rational analysis in their desire to find order in existence. They were not only logicians, but poets as well who "explained" the inexplicable through an elaborate mythology centered around Zeus and the gods of Mount Olympus. Combining human traits and divine power, these gods, in art and literature, have been a source of insight and inspiration for all of Western culture.

Zeus and the gods of Olympus dwelt above the clouds, shut off from human view to enjoy bliss, resolve personal jealousies (169)

Helios, God of the Sun. Vase ptg. (170)

Nemesis, Daughter of Night, dispensed justice, rewards, divine retribution (171)

Nectar: gods' drink of immortality (172)

Apollo, God of the Sun and Music (173)

Venus, Goddess of Love, Beauty (174)

Neptune (Poseidon), God of the Sea (175)

Hercules performed 12 great labors (176)

Eros and Psyche, immortal lovers. She symbolized the soul (177)

Satyr, prankish sylvan deity (178)

Divine Wrath

Prometheus gave fire to man (179)

Tantalus suffered from eternal hunger (180)

Sisyphus fated to push a boulder uphill (181)

Homer: Tales of the Heroic Age

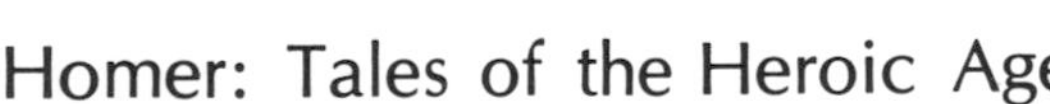

LEGENDS OF GODS AND MEN grew out of local traditions, orally preserved. In the *Iliad* and the *Odyssey,* these disparate elements of folklore appear as a coherent body of legend, providing an epic background for the celebration of Greek culture. Homer's heroes epitomize unfettered individualism and willingness to face life's complexities, representing Greek *ethos* at its best.

Oedipus solves riddle of the Sphinx (182)

King Midas savors his treasures (183)

Centaur was benevolent demigod (184)

Paris abducts Helen: prime cause of Trojan War (185)

Achilles slays Amazon Queen Penthesilia (186)

Homer, legendary epic poet of Greece (187)

Achilles binds broken arm of Patroclus (188)

Menelaus duels Hector, Troy's great hero (189)

Achilles and Ajax play chess. Greek vase (190)

Trojan Horse, Greek stratagem that led to fall of Troy (191)

Laocoön warned Trojans. Crushed by serpent (192)

Odysseus tied to the mast resists sirens' song (193)

Odysseus blinds the giant Cyclops Polyphemus (194)

Achilles slays Memnon, king of Ethiopia (196)

Odysseus sails by Scylla, avoids whirlpool Charybdis (195)

Cretan—Mycenean Civilization

A HIGHLY REFINED CIVILIZATION marked by taste, grace and artistic skill emerged about 2000 B.C. on the Mediterranean island of Crete. One of its rulers, according to legend, was King Minos. When his mountain palace of Knossos was excavated early in this century, Minoan art was found to be far more advanced than contemporaneous work from the Greek mainland.

Minotaur in the labyrinth designed by Daedalus (199)

Head of young girl in palace of Knossos, ca. 2500 B.C. (198)

Minoan vase with fighting and hunting scenes (200)

The Lion Gate, Mycenae, 14th century B.C. (197)

Snake goddess, Mycenaen miniature sculpture (201)

Bullfighter-acrobat—mural in the palace of Knossos, Crete, discovered by Heinrich Schliemann in 1886 (202)

Three beautiful courtesans—wall mural in the Knossos palace (203)

Emergence of Greek Democracy

▲ Meander line, basic Greek pattern (204)

GREEK DEMOCRACY EMERGED against the background of the Persian and Peloponnesian wars. In the first of these, Athens and Sparta joined against the Persian invaders; in the second, they fought each other for the mastery of the Greek peninsula. Meanwhile Athens, under Solon, had made a brief attempt to restrict the power of wealthy oligarchs, to widen the power of the popular assembly and to establish constitutional government. Solon's reforms were curtailed by the coup d'état of the tyrant Pisistratus, but under Pericles the power of the aristocratic party was decisively curbed, and popular democracy achieved.

Athenian warriors on the march. Marble relief, ca. 600 B.C. (205)

Persians defeated the Spartans at Thermopylae, 480 B.C. (206)

Battle of Salamis: Greek fleet defeats Persians (207)

After route of Persians at Marathon, messenger sped to Athens, 26 miles, 385 yards away, the distance of today's marathon race. (208)

Acropolis in Athens, site of magnificent sculpture and sacred architecture (217)

Areopagus was the legislative and judicial council of Athens (218)

Public square in Athens. Speaker could address citizens under the democracy (219)

Pericles during funeral oration honoring dead of Peloponnesian War, 430 B.C. (220)

Themistocles honored for victory at Salamis (209)

- **A** Athena, embodiment of truth, divine wisdom and peace (210)
- **B** Ionian column (211)
- **C** Solon, lawgiver, one of the Seven Wise Men of Greece (212)
- **D** Corinthian column (213)
- **E** Pericles—orator, statesman, general, democrat, Athens' greatest ruler (214)
- **F** Doric column (215)
- **G** Herodotus, savant, traveler, called Father of History (216)

(222)

Ostraka: shards used in voting to exile a person; hence "ostracism" (221)

Trade: Prosperity, Expansion

DEMOCRACY PROPELLED ATHENS to power. Participation in government by the common man freed gifted citizens to exercise their talents, and fostered expansion of trade and political influence. Taxes paid into the Athenian treasury by the nearly 200 cities of the Delian League supported marvelous public works. Athens became antiquity's leading commercial center.

Dionysus in his ship. Red figured vase of Exekias (223)

Fine Greek pottery was in demand throughout the ancient world (224)

Coin shows Athena and symbolic owl (225)

Silphos spice trade brought fame, fortune to Cirene (226)

Woman buys fabric in open market stall (227)

Harvesting olives, delicacy and important Greek export (228)

Ship departs Piraeus harbor loaded with goods (229)

Craftsmen cast bronze statuary in ancient foundry. Vase ptg. (230)

Education Music Dance

GREEK EDUCATION proceeded from the Socratic conviction that all men—women were excluded—possessed a spark "of the divine that can be kindled into flame." The underlying assumption was that wisdom, necessary for self-government, derived from the orderly exercise of the mind. The training of the intellect became a national passion and reached its loftiest heights in the dialogues of Socrates and Plato. But however highly intellectual activity might be esteemed, the Greeks also believed in "a sound mind in a sound body." Exercise in the arena was considered essential to education. Plato maintained that dance and music—the palpable expressions of harmonious thought—were indispensable exercises in a democracy.

Sprint runners in Olympic Games, 6th century B.C. (241)

Teacher recites poetry, plays lyre to inspire, create orderly minds (231)

Body and mind; athletics, philosophy were taught in Greek palaestra (232)

Athletics

Wrestling was important to physical fitness. Relief, ca. 500 B.C. (242)

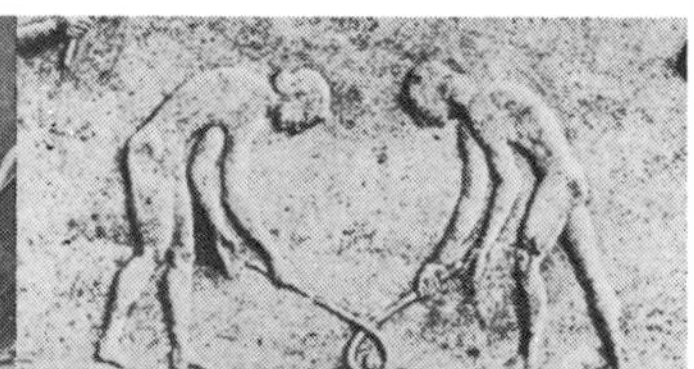

Greek youths build stamina playing game resembling today's hockey (243)

Student writes on wax tablet (233)

5th-century B.C. vase of Duris shows Grecian school life (234)

Writing tools: stylus, wax tablet, ink (235)

Stele of an athlete balancing a ball (244)

Discus thrower, famed statue by Myron (245)

Young men prepare bodies for strenuous exercise (246)

Minerva, Goddess of Wisdom (236)

Plato founded, taught in famed academy (237)

Graceful dancer follows tempo and rhythm of a skilled flutist (238)

World's greatest teachers: Socrates and Plato (239)

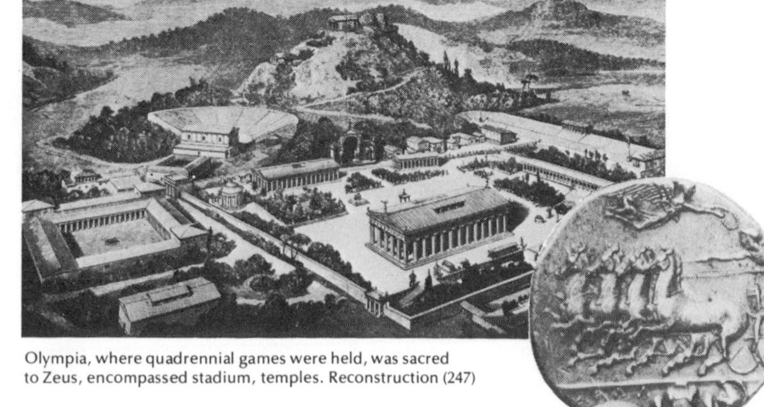

Olympia, where quadrennial games were held, was sacred to Zeus, encompassed stadium, temples. Reconstruction (247)

Cities minted coins honoring their Olympic victors (248)

Tragedy, represented by sculptured mask (249)

Drama Emerges from Dionysian Rites

AN OUTGROWTH of primitive Dionysian rites, Greek drama was a highly stylized art epitomized by the tragedy: a cautionary tale representing man's confrontation with fate, and the arrogance (*hubris*) that must inevitably lead to his destruction (*nemesis*).

Epidaurus theatre as it appears today. Greeks made annual pilgrimages to see plays (250)

Theater of Dionysus in Athens. Performances took all day. Audiences were stirred, freely expressed emotions (251)

Dionysian dance: an orgiastic rite that led to emergence of Greek tragedy (252)

Euripides and Sophocles were Athen's leading venerated dramatists (253, 254)

Furies pursue Orestes: Fate's vengeance for misdeeds is inescapable (255)

Aeschylus, famed tragic poet (256)

Oedipus Rex entrapped by whims of fate (257)

Asclepian Miracles • Hippocratic Wisdom

THE POWER TO HEAL was originally ascribed by the Greeks to Asclepius, a benign god who, with the help of serpents, cured the sick flocking to his shrines. Hippocrates later challenged the mystical concept of disease, treating afflictions as natural phenomena whose causes could be analyzed, and whose cures could be effected through rational therapy. Called the Father of Medicine, Hippocrates produced insights into the nature of disease that are accepted to this day.

Snakes assist Asclepius to effect a cure (259)

Asclepian temple with sacred snakes (260)

A visit to Asclepius. He cured ills of both mind and body (261)

Hippocrates reassures parents after restoring their son to health (262)

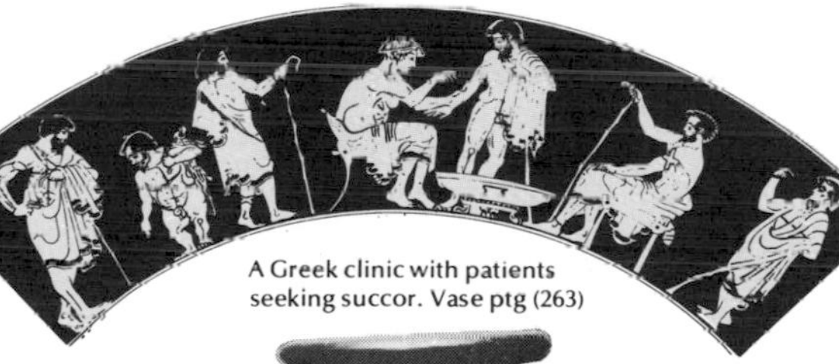

A Greek clinic with patients seeking succor. Vase ptg (263)

Surgeon bandages wounded finger (264)

Women and Slaves

GREEK WOMEN did not take part in running the state. Strangely, their social status declined as the society advanced. Homeric epics treat women with respect, but the otherwise enlightened Age of Pericles saw them imprisoned in domesticity, doomed to early death in childbirth, hardly better off than the slaves.

▲ Asclepian staff (258)

Weaving: women were confined to home and menial chores (265)

Women carry water from town well (266)

Mother humors child in baby chair (267)

Greek girl holds towel folded after bath (268)

Young girl plays the flute (269)

Ancient erotica (270)

"The Loom is woman's work and not debate."

—Menander

War prisoners being sold as slaves at auction (271)

Greek slave carries heavy load (272)

ALEXANDER THE GREAT

Alexander the Great, 356-323 B.C. (273)

BY CONQUERING the fractious Greek city-states, Philip of Macedon imposed upon them a unity they were never able to attain by themselves. The great orator Demosthenes had warned that Philip would subjugate Greece—and so he did, establishing a power base for his plan of world conquest, thwarted by his assassination in 33 B.C.

Alexander's father, Philip II (274)

Aristotle was teacher of young Alexander (275)

Alexander cuts the Gordian knot (276)

Aristotle sees specimens sent by Alexander (277)

Alexander crossed the Granicus River in 334 B.C., defeated the Persians, began his great march (278)

Asked by Alexander what he could do for him, Diogenes responded, "Step out of my sunlight" (279)

Orator Demosthenes opposed Philip and Alexander (280)

Alexander explores sea in a diving bell (281), commands faraway armies with magic horn (282)

ALEXANDER THE GREAT, Philip's son, came to power at the age of seventeen. In the next eleven years he conquered a domain comprising Egypt and Asia Minor and reaching out toward India. Alexander's empire crumbled after his death, but Greek culture remained dominant in the ancient world.

Alexandria: Science Center of the Ancient World

WITH ALEXANDRIA AS ITS CENTER, Hellenism initiated a new scientific age. Scholars converged upon its library, where all the learning of the ancient world was gathered. Here they collated and edited the great writers of antiquity.

Reconstruction of Alexandria, founded in 332 B.C. (283)

◀ King Ptolemy I made Alexandria world's foremost city (284)

Scholars in Library at Alexandria (285)

Papyrus scrolls held ancient lore (286)

Water clock of Ktesibios (287)

Archimedes' screw raises water, astounds people (288)

Archimedes ponders mechanics problem in his garden at Syracuse (290)

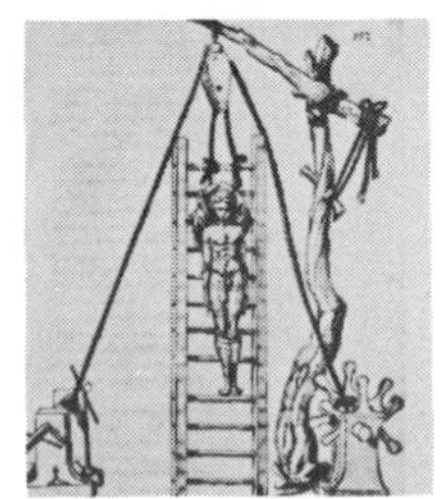

Ancient orthopedic device to redress spine (291)

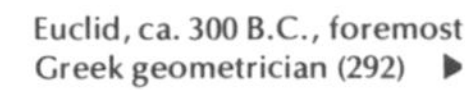

Euclid, ca. 300 B.C., foremost Greek geometrician (292) ▶

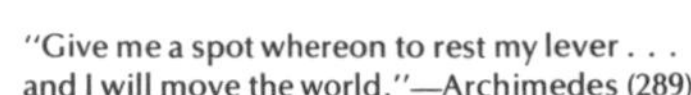

"Give me a spot whereon to rest my lever . . . and I will move the world."—Archimedes (289)

Steam engine described by Hero of Alexandria (293) ▶

SEVEN WONDERS OF THE WORLD

THE SEVEN WONDERS of the ancient world served the same function as today's international lists of tourist attractions. They were one result of Alexander's far-flung conquests, and the popularity of these sights marked the end of Greek provincialism and the rise of a new sense of worldliness.

Lighthouse of Alexandria erected in 270 B.C. (294)

Colossal *Statue of Zeus* by Phidias sat in serene majesty in the Temple at Olympia (295)

Mausoleum of Halicarnassus erected 352 B.C. by Queen Artemisia in memory of husband Mausolus (296)

Temple of Diana of Ephesus admired by Greeks and Romans for its grandeur (297)

The world as the ancients knew it in 500 B.C. (301)

The Pyramids at Giza, the only one of the seven wonders that survives (298)

(302)

The Colossus of Rhodes stood 105 feet high, spanned the harbor entrance (299)

Hanging Gardens of Babylon: travellers marvelled at their vegetation. Terraces were watered via pipes from cistern atop structure (300)

Roma Eterna
A City destined to rule an Empire

Romulus and Remus nursed by wolf (303)

Etruscan warrior, bronze statue (304)

Legendary rape by early Romans of neighboring Sabines (305)

Horatius at the bridge held off Etruscans (306)

Pyrrhus routed Romans. "Pyrrhic victory" (307)

ORIGINALLY A GROUP of modest hill towns, Rome eventually became the power base of an empire that extended from Britain to Asia Minor and ruled millions of subjects—a sizable proportion of the world's population. This incredible rise to world domination resulted from a genius for both military conquest and assimilation of the conquered. Pride in their military prowess led Rome's legions to perform with extraordinary heroism. Their toughness had been developed during a long bloody rivalry with Carthage for control of the Mediterranean, a contest that occupied the Carthaginian military genius Hannibal throughout his career. Though Hannibal brought Rome to the brink of destruction, Carthage was finally destroyed in 146 B.C.

▲ Costume of a consul, Rome's highest official (312)

Hannibal, Rome's greatest foe (308)

Hannibal crosses Rhône River, invades Italy (309)

Rome's first naval victory, at Mylae against Carthage (310)

Romans raze Carthage, become supreme (311)

Orator champions plebs in public square (313)

Tribune Valerian in Senate debate (314)

Going to market. Roman farmers fought against encroaching estate owners (315)

Trials of the Republic

SET ON A COURSE OF CONQUEST, the Roman republic faced nagging problems at home. The survival of the democracy depended upon a fragile balance between the haves—the landowner-senators—and the have-nots—the hard-pressed farmers. Demagogues, driven by ambition to make themselves masters of the city, presented another danger to the state.

Murder of Gaius Gracchus ▼ blocked land reform (316)

Spartacus led slave revolt, 71 B.C. (317)

Catiline conspired against consuls (318). Cicero's oratory foiled attempt to seize power, 63 B.C. (319)

The Army: Source of Rome's Strength, Threat to Its Existence

Signal man and sling-armed soldier (321) ▶

Legionnaire with spear sword and shield (320)

The catapult, used for sieges, helped make Rome invincible (322)

Roman general addresses his men before critical battle (323)

Romans perfected siege technology, introduced catapults, towers, rams, scaling ladders (324)

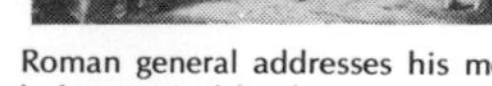

Rome's navy helped army generate overwhelming military power (325)

Pompey consul, general, mighty triumvir (326)

Sulla's proscribed foes see death list (327)

ROME GLORIFIED her generals, but feared their political power. Successful in faraway lands, a military leader might return with his armies to Rome and proclaim himself dictator. To consolidate strength, groups of power-hungry men combined to form triumvirates, but ended up fighting one another. Two men alone jockeyed successfully for power—Caesar and Augustus.

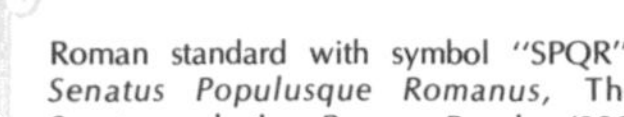

Roman standard with symbol "SPQR": *Senatus Populusque Romanus,* The Senate and the Roman People (328)

"I love Caesar—for he alone united in himself the warrior's will to power with the lonely genius of a sage."
—Mussolini

Triumphal procession of Julius Caesar with prisoners and priceless booty for the state and personal fortune (329-333)

Julius Caesar

WHEN JULIUS CAESAR, backed by the army he had led triumphantly in Gaul and Britain, assumed dictatorial powers in 49 B.C., Roman democracy came to an end. A masterful military tactician (and superb prose stylist), Caesar harbored grandiose plans for Rome, but his assassination in 44 B.C. engendered a bitter power struggle.

Druids were slaughtered in Gallic conquest (334)

Caesar leads army in British invasion (335)

British woman in magic tattoo (336)

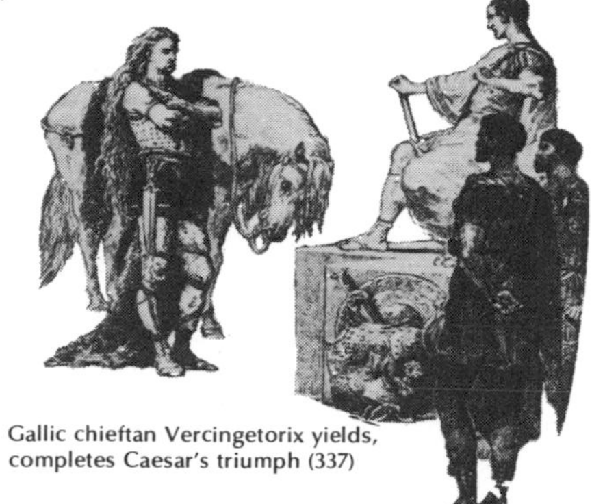

Gallic chieftan Vercingetorix yields, completes Caesar's triumph (337)

Caesar's army pledges its total loyalty (338)

Caesar crosses Rubicon, then conquers Rome, 49 B.C. (339)

Caesar's wife warns of impending tragedy (340)

Caesar murdered in Senate, 44 B.C. (341)

Denarius for Caesar, coined ca. 43 B.C. (342)

Caesar (343)

Augustus Caesar, first Roman emperor (349) ▼

The Augustan Empire

CAESAR'S DUPLICITOUS SUCCESSOR, Gaius Octavius, loudly paid lip service to the democratic ideal, quietly consolidated his hold on Rome, and accepted dictatorial powers with feigned reluctance "to save the republic." In gratitude, a Senate completely under his domination named him imperator in 29 B.C. and Augustus ("the revered") two years later.

The Forum, symbol of Rome's constructive genius, and the global might of the Augustan Empire (344)

A vast government complex, Forum was also used as trade center (345)

Vergil between muses Clio and Melpomene. Mosaic (346)

Maecenas, generous patron of letters, with friends, poets Vergil, Horace (347)

Ovid's *Metamorphoses* his greatest work (348)

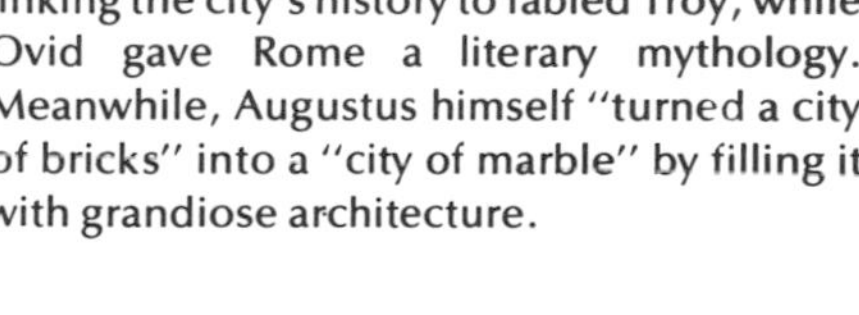

THE GLORY OF THE AUGUSTAN ERA was proclaimed by the emperor's favored poets. Vergil's *Aeneid* fostered Roman pride by linking the city's history to fabled Troy, while Ovid gave Rome a literary mythology. Meanwhile, Augustus himself "turned a city of bricks" into a "city of marble" by filling it with grandiose architecture.

Epochal Events of the First Century, A.D.

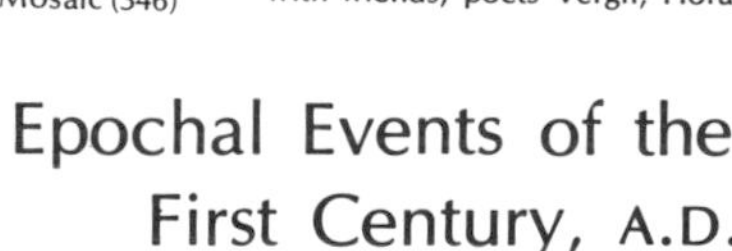

Ancient Roman reading manuscript scroll (350)

Jerusalem destroyed by the Emperor Titus, 70 A.D. (351)

The Jewish historian Flavius Josephus (352)

Eruption of Vesuvius buried Pompeii in 79 A.D. Ashes preserved the city with miraculous completeness (353) ▼

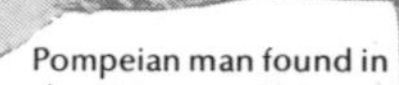

Pompeian man found in sleeping pose (354)

Roman Life

Home • Family • Religion

◄ Pompeian kitchen sink has supply of hot water (355)

THE HOME was the social center for all the Roman people, somewhat of a microcosm of the Roman state. Under the empire, fashionable Roman homes evolved from simple hearth-centered shelters into extravagant showplaces. Following the emperor's lead, trade-rich citizens, the *equites,* built pretentious marble structures with colonnaded *atria,* while the unseen Roman poor huddled in their noisome slums *(insulae).*

Ancient oil lamp with horse head handle. Photo (356) ►

Roman home had central courtyard, the atrium. Social and family life revolved around it (357)

A cultured Roman in his library (358)

Maidservant with tray of food during a banquet. Mural (359)

Lucullus, famed gourmet, with friends at fabulous feast (360)

Noblewoman during her morning toilette (361)

Delivery table speeds Roman childbirth (362)

The columbarium was family sepulcre (363)

Fish mosaic in Pompeii (364)

Pompeian floor mosaic with picture of Death and motto "Know thyself" (365)

Roman altar decoration. Family worshipped domestic gods (366)

Sacrifice in front of a Roman temple (367)

Emperor Commodus shown as Hercules (368)

Augur observes ravens to predict future (369)

Mithra, central figure of popular Roman religion, slays the sacred bull (370)

The Hubbub of the City

THE CITY OF ROME was the empire's nerve center. It grew prosperous from the emperor's vast renovation program that provided employment on an unprecedented scale, and from the introduction of unified coinage, which facilitated trade with the colonies. Prosperity whetted the Roman thirst for life's amenities.

Cobbled street in Pompeii with open-front tavern (371) and water carriers (372)

Social group around a public water well (373)

Chariot races through deep rutted Roman street (374)

Woman pharmacist. Roman relief (375)

Cutler in shop displays his wares (376)

Collecting taxes from settlers in Roman-occupied German province (377)

▲ Baker sells bread from open market stand (378)

Teacher and students. School scene from Roman tomb relief at Trier, Germany (379)

Cleaner's shop. Fuller stomps clothes soaked in urine (380)

Merchants examining fabric. Relief found in Gaul (381)

Loading a Roman grain ship. Fresco painting found in Ostia (382)

"The city, the city . . . . Residence elsewhere is mere eclipse."

—Cicero

Rome's Glory

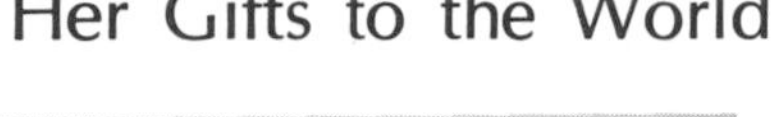

Her Gifts to the World

ROMAN GENIUS was nowhere more evident than in the engineering and architecture of the Augustan era. As many as 80,000 persons could be accommodated in the vast amphitheaters, 3,000 could relax simultaneously in the public baths (*thermae*), and millions of gallons of water were borne to the capital daily by fourteen aqueducts. 87,000 miles of road traversed the empire.

Aqueducts, at times 50 miles long, carried millions of gallons of water to Roman cities (383)

Salus, Goddess of Public Health (384)

Main sewer of Rome: Cloaca Maxima still survives (385)

Baths of Caracalla covered 28 acres (386)

Steam for sweat baths was generated by flow of water over heated stones (387)

A Roman bathing establishment preserved in Bath, England (388)

REMAINS OF ROMAN GRANDEUR

Arch of Titus (393)

Amphitheater Nimes (394)

The Via Appia near Rome (395)

Aqueduct in Segovia (396)

Roman Law

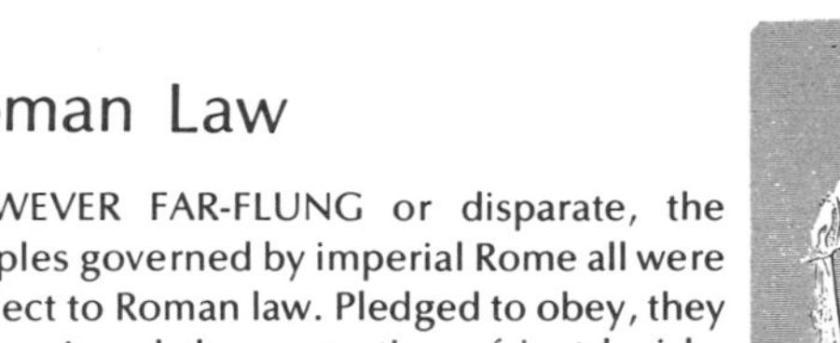

HOWEVER FAR-FLUNG or disparate, the peoples governed by imperial Rome all were subject to Roman law. Pledged to obey, they also enjoyed the protection of just legislation. Roman law provided the basis for legal codes throughout the West.

Themis was Goddess of Justice (390)

Twelve Tables showed code of early Roman law (391)

Emperor Justinian receives codification of law (392)

The Fall of Rome

WITH NO MORE FRONTIERS to conquer, the energy and idealism that drove Rome to empire was shunted into a passion for spectacle, dissipation and display. The impersonal brutality of the gladiatorial games, where many thousands gathered daily to cheer "the upraised dagger plunging into the helpless body," became a symbol of Roman decadence. When even Roman bureaucracy began to fail, paralysis spread everywhere. The end came in A.D. 410.

Nero watches Rome burn (397)

Circus Maximus seated 350,000 Romans (398)

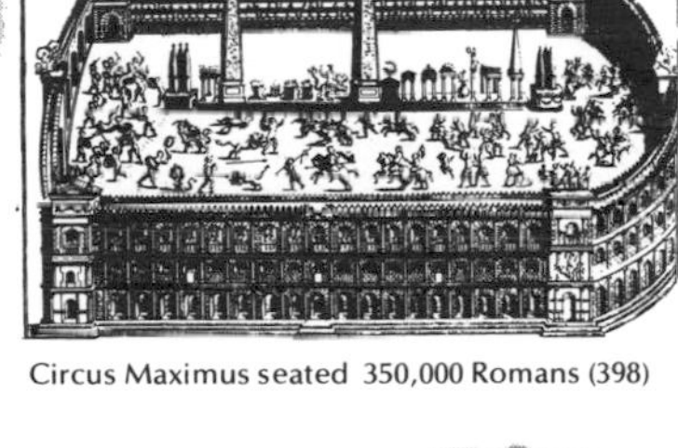

Boxer from Baths of Caracalla (399)

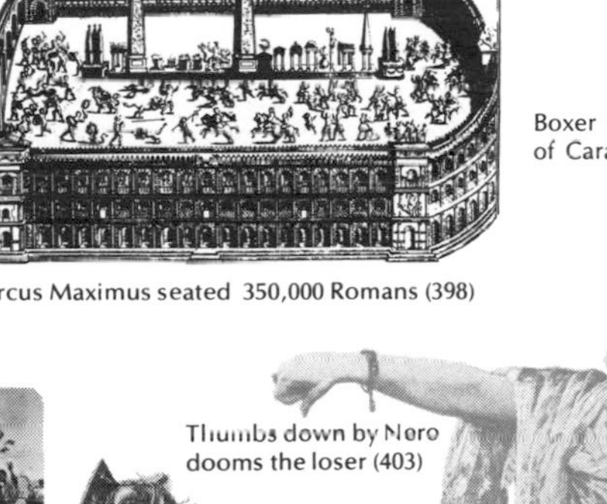

Thumbs down by Nero dooms the loser (403)

Orgy at the time of Rome's decadence. 19th-century painting by G. Simoni (400)

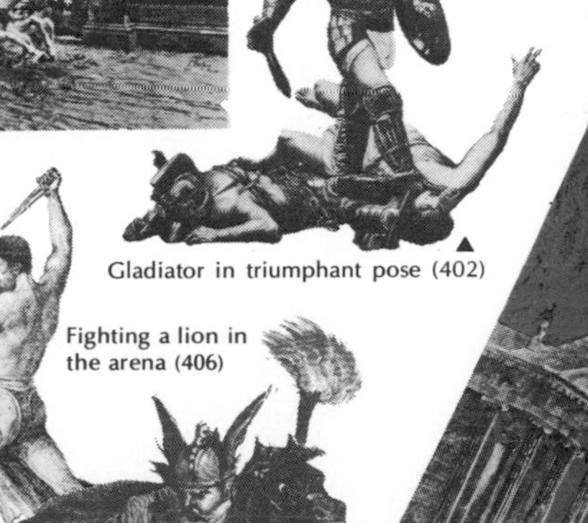

Chariot races entertained and distracted Roman citizens (401)

Gladiator in triumphant pose (402)

Galen, famed Roman physician, treats wounded gladiator (404)

Feasting Romans entertained by hand-to-hand combat (405)

Fighting a lion in the arena (406)

Attila the Hun, called the "Scourge of God" (407)

"The lamp of the world is extinguished and it is the whole world which has perished in the ruins of this one city."
—St. Jerome

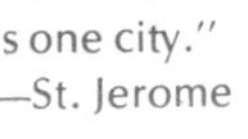

Rome set aflam by the Huns (4

CHAPTER 2

Age of Faith

Feudalism

The Crusades

High Middle Ages

CHRISTIANITY

AS ROME DECLINED, its prestige and efficiency undermined by a series of cruel, indifferent emperors, Roman law gave way to the whims of the powerful, and the quality of Roman life became brutal and capricious. In this atmosphere of gloom the Christian message of hope and love contrasted favorably with the cold, officious state religion. Emperors feared the new faith, and persecuted the Christians, but the heroism of those condemned to die touched the Roman populace, and the Gospel spread. As Tertullian observed: "the blood of the martyrs is seed."

"In Hoc Signo Vinces" . . . "In this sign shalt thou conquer" (409)

The Holy Trinity: Father, Son and Holy Ghost. Miniature from religious encyclopedia by Rabanus Maurus (410)

Eucharist—meal held secretly by early Christians to affirm their creed. Catacomb painting (411)

Roman soldier consigns Christian to death in Circus Maximus (412)

Christians faced martyrdom with courage, gained admiration by many Romans (413)

St. Agatha—patron saint of suffering women (414)

St. Appolonia helps in case of toothache (415)

St. Lawrence was to help those stricken with backache (416)

Constantine the Great

St. Patrick, missionary of Ireland (417)

Nicaea, first Ecumenical Council, 325 A.D. (418)

THE EMPEROR CONSTANTINE adopted the new religion (he was baptized on his deathbed) and moved his capital to the Bosporus to avoid the ever-present threat of Barbarian invasion. Constantinople became a new center of Christian culture, and the main bulwark of empire against the Moslems.

Constantine I (280?-337). Head of statue (420)

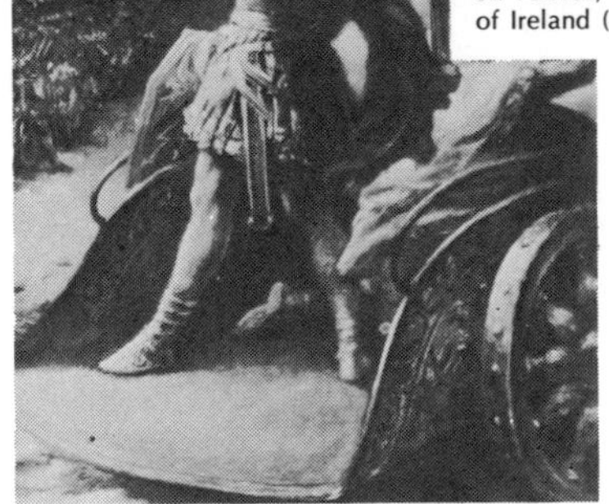

Emperor Constantine, victorius at Milvian bridge in 312 A.D., pledged to become a Christian (419)

East Roman Emperors fought invaders with new weapon called "Greek Fire" (421)

Shapers of a New Faith

EARLY CHRISTIAN LEADERS adapted elements of classical thought, particularly the idealism of Plato, to the doctrines of the new faith. Their scholarship produced a new body of theology which bound together the Christian peoples of medieval Europe.

Christian zealots, eager for salvation, practiced extreme forms of self-denial to demonstrate the moral strength the new faith inspired.

St. Peter was "Prince of Apostles" (422)

St. Augustine wrote "City of God" (423)

Pope Gregory created a new liturgy (424)

Cassiodorus preserved ancient texts (425)

St. Martin: exemplar of human kindness (426)

St. Paul founded churches, spread the gospel to other lands (428)

St. Patrick, saint of Ireland (429)

St. Jerome—scholar in the wilderness (430)

Pilgrim pursued by a peglegged devil (431)

St. Simeon Stylites: 37 years atop pillar in religious devotion (427)

Temptation of St. Anthony. Engr. by Schongauer (432)

Church of St. Michel d'Aiguilhe (438)

Monasticism

RENUNCIATION OF THE WORLD, first practiced by saints and hermits, soon developed into a form of communal life called monasticism. St. Benedict, whose monastery at Monte Cassino set the pattern for living by the "rule," asked his followers to vow perpetual poverty, chastity and obedience. Monks (and later nuns) sought salvation through self-denial, spending their days in prayer, manual labor and care for the sick.

Bishop (433) Abbot (434) Abbess (435) Priest (436) Monk (437)

The monastic hierarchy helped stabilize a world sundered by the decline of Rome.

St. Benedict created rules to govern monastic life (439)

Monte Cassino Abbey, founded in 529, center of the Benedictine Order (440)

Care of the sick, the homeless, the aged one of monasticism's noblest duties (441)

Monk discusses medicinal herbs with novice holding book (442)

Cloistered choristers celebrate Mass (443)

Devoted monk copies holy and ancient tomes (444)

St. Jerome distributes books for monks to copy. Church carried the burden of culture (445)

Monks eating with primitive form of fork from *Cyclopedia* by Rabanus Maurus (446)

Fear of Damnation

HOPE OF SALVATION had a darker side: the fear of damnation. Torn between opposing forces, the devil beneath and heaven above, Medieval man saw the earth as a battleground for the soul.

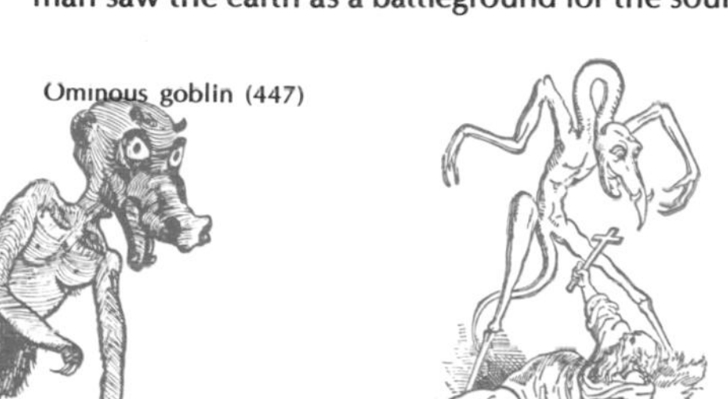

Ominous goblin (447)

Monk with a cross repels demon (448)

The tortured Damned fall into Hell's abyss (449)

Knight flees from a flying dragon (450)

Bishop, monk, scholar, doctor, nun in Dance of Death to oblivion (451)

The Seven Deadly Sins loom everywhere, tempting and threatening man with eternal damnation (452)

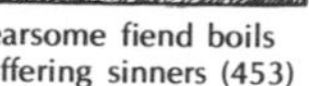

Fearsome fiend boils suffering sinners (453)

Two-faced devil kidnaps helpless virgin (453 A)

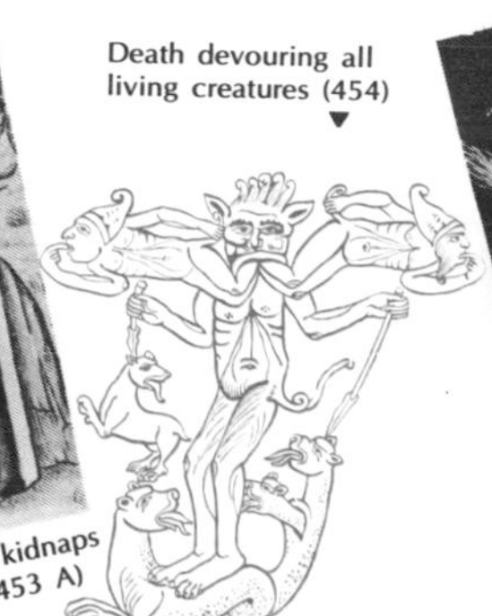

Death devouring all living creatures (454)

Terrible Death on the Pale Horse (455)

Monstrous mouth of Hell. German woodcut (456)

Knight pays homage to his lord (457)

Feudalism

THE BREAKDOWN OF CENTRAL GOVERNMENT, following the fall of Rome, led to the feudal system, in which rigid social classes maintained a fragile network of loyalties based on grants of land. The lords, expanding their holdings through conquest, parceled out land to vassals, who pledged military assistance in return. The serf, in return for protection and service to the lord, was allotted land to cultivate.

King grants land to vassals with royal charters (458)

Vassals render military service to king in return for property, honor (459)

Peasants swear fealty to lord, for protection (460)

Coronation of an English king (461)

King grants land to build monastery (462)

Challenged lord picks up the gauntlet (463)

Feudal life: knights and ladies ride for pleasure; serfs toil in the fields (464)

God spede ye plouz: & sende us korne ynolk

Medieval prayer (465)

Lord and Serf

Messenger delivers sealed envelope (466)

THE MEDIEVAL SERF was virtually a slave. His lord owned both the land and the means of production, and demanded service or tribute for every bushel of corn ground, every loaf baked in his oven. The serf had no hope of advancement, no freedom to move.

Imperious lord sits at war tent (467)

Manorial service: serfs had to work lord's land (468)

Serfs farm land protected by lord's castle (469)

The lord's bailiff punishes serf for neglect in turning millwheel (470)

Rich harvest shared by feudal lady (471)

To pay for farmland, serfs build roads (472)

Harvesting time on a feudal estate, A.D. 1023 (473)

The Law

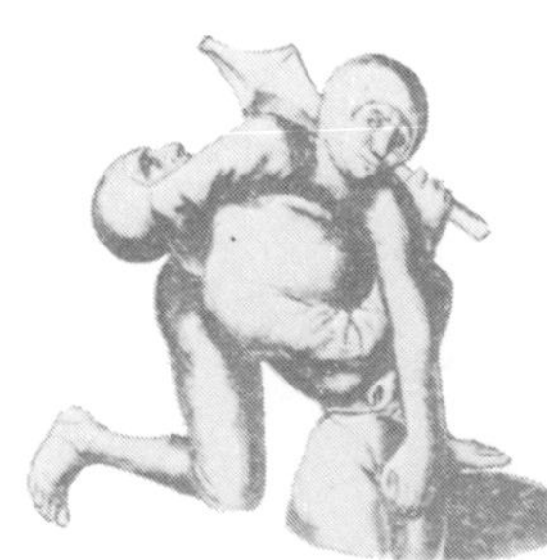
Trial by combat between sexes; woman grabs codpiece (477)

FEUDAL LORDS had absolute power over their subjects, dealing out justice according to whim and local tradition. The slightest misdemeanor might provoke the most brutal punishment—breaking a culprit's bones on the wheel, banishing him to the dungeons.

In addition to providing varied labor to the lord, serfs paid heavy taxes in kind (474)

"The Reaper." Notre Dame, Paris (475)

Peasants carry wood to heat lord's ovens (476)

"Men should work hard so that the earth yields fruit from which the Knight and his horse will live."

Severe punishment was meted out by lord: miscreant's body was broken on wheel (478)

Peasants seek redress in feudal court (479)

Trial by ordeal: walking heated plowshares (480)

Criminal seeks sanctuary at door of a church (481)

Trial of a sow and pigs. Animals were often dragged into court in the belief that they were responsible for their actions, the same as humans. The sow was found guilty and condemned to death; but the pigs were acquitted on account of their youth and the bad example of their mother (482)

Knighthood

THE KNIGHT, the armed horseman who pledged absolute fealty to his lord, stood at the center of the feudal system, which required almost perpetual warfare. Feudal lords were either defending their holdings, or attempting to expand them, and to refill their chronically exhausted treasuries with booty. Though pledged to a chivalric code that paid lip service to gentlemanly virtues, the knight's main business was fighting.

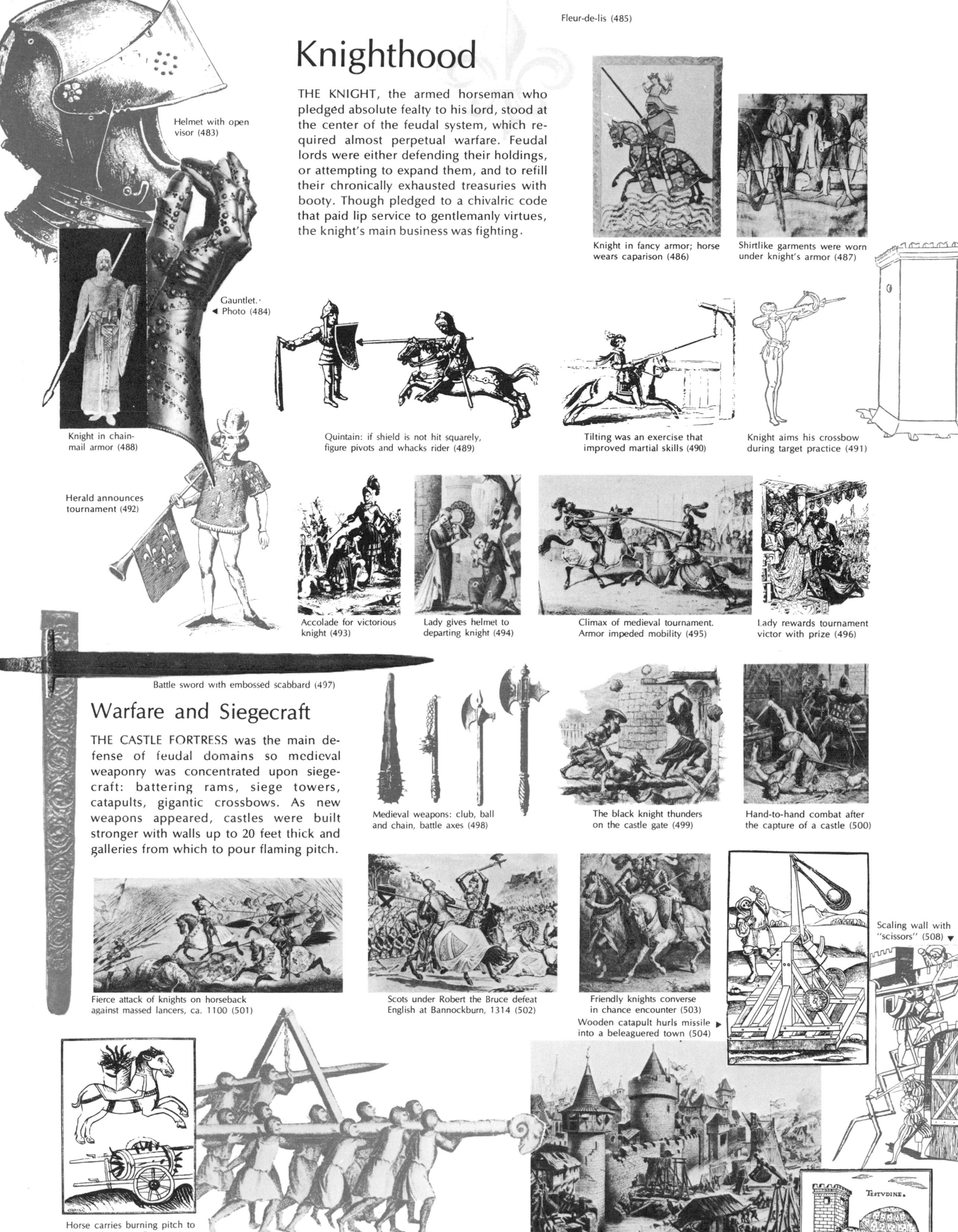

Helmet with open visor (483)

Fleur-de-lis (485)

Knight in fancy armor; horse wears caparison (486)

Shirtlike garments were worn under knight's armor (487)

Gauntlet. ◀ Photo (484)

Knight in chain-mail armor (488)

Quintain: if shield is not hit squarely, figure pivots and whacks rider (489)

Tilting was an exercise that improved martial skills (490)

Knight aims his crossbow during target practice (491)

Herald announces tournament (492)

Accolade for victorious knight (493)

Lady gives helmet to departing knight (494)

Climax of medieval tournament. Armor impeded mobility (495)

Lady rewards tournament victor with prize (496)

Battle sword with embossed scabbard (497)

Warfare and Siegecraft

THE CASTLE FORTRESS was the main defense of feudal domains so medieval weaponry was concentrated upon siegecraft: battering rams, siege towers, catapults, gigantic crossbows. As new weapons appeared, castles were built stronger with walls up to 20 feet thick and galleries from which to pour flaming pitch.

Medieval weapons: club, ball and chain, battle axes (498)

The black knight thunders on the castle gate (499)

Hand-to-hand combat after the capture of a castle (500)

Fierce attack of knights on horseback against massed lancers, ca. 1100 (501)

Scots under Robert the Bruce defeat English at Bannockburn, 1314 (502)

Friendly knights converse in chance encounter (503)

Wooden catapult hurls missile into a beleaguered town (504) ▶

Scaling wall with "scissors" (508) ▼

Horse carries burning pitch to set hostile town aflame (505)

Battering ram shatters sturdy stone wall (506)

Reconstruction of elaborate assault operations on a walled city (507)

Amphibious siege "Tortoise" (509) ▶

Life in the Castle

DESIGNED FOR DEFENSE, the medieval castle was also the center of social life. Space was scarce—only the lord and his lady might have private chambers. But if life was communal, it was often ceremonial—games, dances and banquets enlivened winter months when fighting usually was curtailed.

Turreted French castle designed for defense (511)

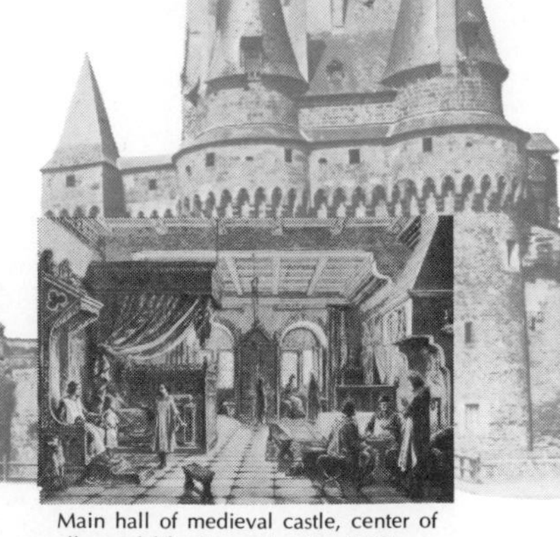

Main hall of medieval castle, center of all social life. Reconstruction (512)

Proud seigneur offers domain to demurring damsel (510)

Knights and ladies leave mountain castle for afternoon sport (513)

Couple playing backgammon (514)

Noble with lady in high hennin (515)

Children play jousting with rope-operated toy (516)

Learning to read with aid of hornbook (517)

Women working with wool (518)

Lady of the castle presides over formal banquet (519)

Carrying in the boar's head—climax of medieval feast (520)

Courtly Love

MEDIEVAL LADIES, officially subservient to their husbands, and in law little better than chattels, found new status in the twelfth century as the code of courtly love spread across Europe. Begun by troubadours in the south of France, the new literature exalted the lady as a goddess whose whim was law and whose wish was every knight-errant's command.

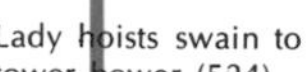

Lady hoists swain to tower bower (524)

Musicians intone for a dance of two young lovers (521)

Christine de Pisan, the middle ages' famed woman writer, dictates to her helper (522)

Man fiddled to sleep by a servant (523)

Knight honored with laurel wreath (525)

Delivering note with bow and arrow (526)

Lady plucks harp at picnic (527)

Two lovers in garden visited by goddess spreading wealth (528)

Dalliance in the bedchamber leaves dog undisturbed (529)

Minstrels and Legends

Minstrel entertains court with news and songs of courtly love (530)

Arthur receives magic sword Excalibur (531)

El Cid meets with the king (532)

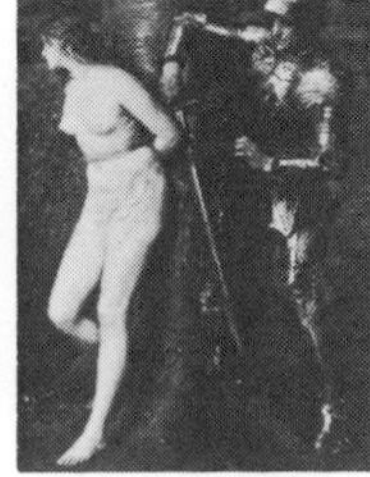

Knight errant freeing damsel in distress (533)

Robin Hood, legendary English outlaw (534)

Spanish knight charges infidel fortress (535)

"Summer is icumen in"—famed seasonal "Cuckoo Song" (536)

Emerging Dynasties

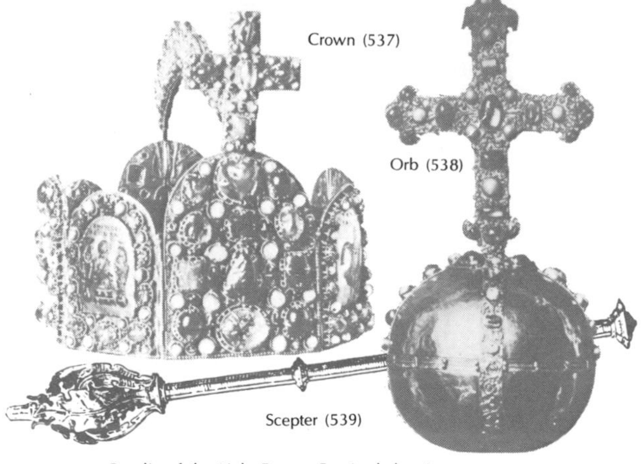
Crown (537)
Orb (538)
Scepter (539)
Regalia of the Holy Roman Empire belonging to German rulers, 12th to 14th centuries.

BEGINNING WITH CHARLEMAGNE in the eighth century, aggressive overlords began to assemble kingdoms out of Europe's scattered feudal domains. Using both conquest and a system of feudal alliances, Charlemagne achieved a semblance of political unity that took in most of central Europe. Otto I, in tenth-century Germany, and William the Conqueror, in eleventh-century England, were the first of these monarchs to give their regions a measure of stability and imperial glory. The new dynastic conglomerates marked a step forward from the anarchic condition left behind when Rome fell.

Alfred the Great (849-889), first king of all England (551)

Lords elect leader, raise him on a shield (540)

Charlemagne. Statue in Cathedral of Metz (541)

Pope Leo crowning Charlemagne on Christmas Day, 800 A.D. (542)

Holy Roman Empire

CHARLEMAGNE'S IMPERIAL DREAM received the official sanction of the Church: he was crowned Holy Roman Emperor by Pope Leo III on Christmas Day, A.D. 800. Though his empire crumbled after his death, future emperors continued the title, and the church-state alignment it implied.

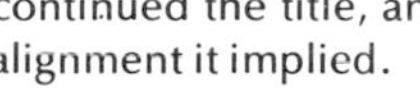

Charlemagne dictates to scholar Alcuin (543)

Emperors

Otto the Great suppressed willful feudal lords (544)

Otto II enthroned, surrounded by Church dignitaries (545)

Emperor and Pope share reign of the world (546)

Investiture of an abbott (547)

Henry IV submits to Pope at Canossa in 1077 (548)

CONFLICT with both Church and barons marked the reign of Emperor Henry IV. The Church insisted upon ecclesiastical supremacy, while the barons resented the emperor's increasing power.

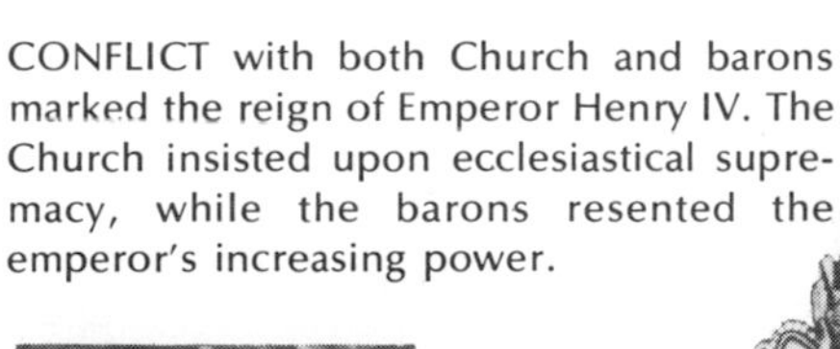

Barbarossa's beard grows under the table (549)

Golden statue of Barbarossa in Dome of Aachen (550)

Decorative column from medieval manuscript (562)

England and France

Trial by jury—an innovation ascribed to King Alfred (552)

Comet forecasts Norman conquest of England (553)

Bayeux tapestry depicts the invasion of England by William the Conqueror (554)

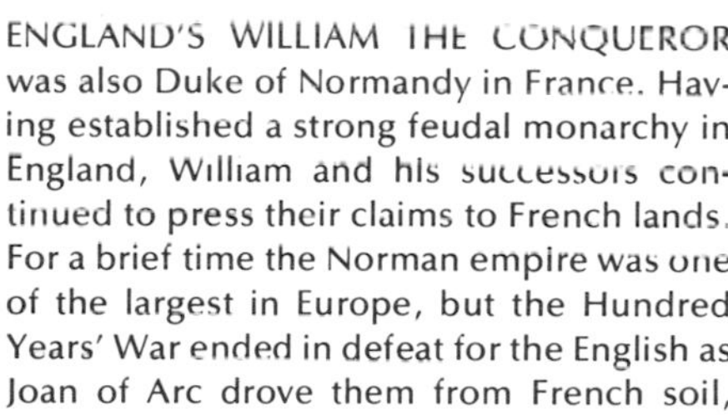

ENGLAND'S WILLIAM THE CONQUEROR was also Duke of Normandy in France. Having established a strong feudal monarchy in England, William and his successors continued to press their claims to French lands. For a brief time the Norman empire was one of the largest in Europe, but the Hundred Years' War ended in defeat for the English as Joan of Arc drove them from French soil, paving the way for French nationhood.

Henry II, tamed feudal lords (555)

Beckett murdered by royal henchmen (556)

King John signs Magna Charta (557)

Johannes dei gra' Rex Angl. Dns Hybn. Dux Normann. Aqnie. & Come

Preamble to Magna Charta that established England's constitutional freedoms (558)

English with longbows beat French, Crécy, 1346 (559)

Joan of Arc takes Rheims, routs the invaders (560)

The Order of the Garter, founded by Edward III (561)

Light from the East

UNIFYING THE SCATTERED tribes of Arabia, the Prophet Mohammed (ca. 569-632) fathered an amazing empire. In the century after his death, Muslim horsemen rode across three continents, conquering Syria and Palestine and pushing eastward toward Persia and the Indus. To the west, they swept into Spain, threatening to overrun all Europe, but were finally stopped by Charles Martel at Tours in 737. The culture they established proved a major factor in Europe's "little Renaissance" of the twelfth century, for Moorish translations of Greek classics, particularly Aristotle, provided the basis of the new Scholasticism, while the "wonders of the East," brought by the Arabs to Europe, stimulated social and economic changes.

Page from 13th-cent. Koran, sacred text of Islam (564)

Moslem Conquerors

The holy mosque Dome of the Rock was built in Jerusalem in 687 (565)

Mohammed with sword and book, symbols of his faith (566)

Mohammed receives mission from Archangel Gabriel (567)

Harun al-Rashid (764?-809) fostered Arabic culture (568)

Preaching the Koran (569)

Science • Trade • Letters

Moorish arch in Spain (563)

Arab cavalryman, from a 10th cent. papyrus (570)

Arab pharmacists mix drugs in the market place (571)

Ancient manuscript shows doctor preparing medicine (572)

Arab astronomers in observatory (573)

Arabian astrolabe made in 1014 (574)

Avicenna and his students (575)

Cautery was Arab's chief surgical instrument (576)

Sick medieval king attended by Arabian doctors, magicians (577)

Rosewater, brought to Europe by Arabs (578)

Eastern star maps revived ancient zodiac signs (579)

Averroes, famed philosopher (580)

Maimonides, Jewish sage at Saladin's court (581)

Jewish scholars receive Arab manuscript (582), deliver Latin version to Christian king (583)

MOHAMMED TAUGHT that war is a holy duty: "He who dies in battle goes to heaven." But the by-products of the Muslim *jihad* (holy war) were far more benign than their swordplay. Besides the intellectual treasures preserved in the libraries —mathematics, medicine, astronomy—the Arabs introduced Europe to a host of new products: silks, dyes, spices, perfumes, and a cornucopia of exotic fruits and vegetables. Their marvelous fables of travel and adventure stimulated development of sagas in French, German and English, and their love lyrics probably inspired the troubadours to sing of courtly love.

Wonder Tales

Arab storyteller enthralls audience at bazaar (584)

Harun al-Rashid, caliph of Baghdad (585)

Sinbad the Sailor fights with the giants (586)

Aladdin and his magic lamp (587)

Ali Baba finds treasure (588)

The Arab legend of Scheherazade (589)

Prince Achmed on the Flying Carpet (590)

Crusaders battle Moslems (591)

The Crusades

THE CRUSADES, one of the most significant events of the Middle Ages, were conceived as a "holy war" to free Christian shrines held by the "infidel." Pope Urban II, who decreed the first of eight expeditions in 1095, probably hoped to counter the dynastic ambitions of feudal monarchs and establish the dominance of the Church. The Crusades were military failures, but they did lead to a cultural awakening in Europe.

Philip II of France and Henry II of England join forces in fight against the infidels (592)

European knights assemble in France prior to embarkation for the Holy Land (593)

Knights aboard crusader ship with cleric at the helm (594)

Arrival of pilgrims in the Holy Land (595)

Louis IX arrives with his army in Egypt (596)

Advance design of landing craft (597)

Godfrey of Bouillon, Crusade leader (598)

Jerusalem, captured in 1099, became the center of Crusaders' "Latin Kingdom" (599)

Baldwin of Flanders, first king of Jerusalem (600)

Frederick Barbarossa, German emperor, leads assault on Moslem fortress in Palestine during Third Crusade (601)

England's Richard I boarding ship (602)

The valiant Saladin, sultan of Egypt (603)

Jerusalem assaulted by catapult (604)

Acre fell in 1291, and Holy Land was reconquered by Arabs (605)

Castle of Kerok became the Jordanian stronghold of Knights Hospitalers (606)

Louis IX (Saint Louis) led Seventh Crusade (607)

The Children's Crusade ended in fiasco (608)

Knight Templar (609)

Wonders of the Orient

AS A NAVAL POWER, Venice served as shipping agent for the Crusades, and her traders foresaw enormous profits to be made from East-West trade. When her most famous citizen, Marco Polo, returned from a voyage to the court of Kublai Khan in 1295, his account of Eastern riches incited Europeans to establish trade routes to the Orient.

Arabic-European trade fair (610)

Marco Polo, traveler to the Far East (611)

Marco Polo with father and uncle set out ca. 1270 (612)

Kublai Khan receiving the western strangers (613)

Pepper harvesting; depicted in Polo's travel report (614)

The Polos bid farewell to the great Khan and his court (615)

"The Crusades opened unknown distances to the European mind and awakened in all the passion for travel and adventure."
—Jacob Burckhardt

A Venetian galley at the time of Marco Polo (616)

HIGH MIDDLE AGES

THE CRUSADES BROUGHT an influx of new ideas into Europe, making the thirteenth and fourteenth centuries a time of fresh departures. Most influential on religious thought were the writings of Aristotle, preserved in Arabic manuscripts. Great theologians like Albertus Magnus and Thomas Aquinas presented Christianity with a new structure by applying the logic of Aristotle to the statement of their faith, attempting to reconcile reason and Biblical revelation.

Sundial, Chartres Cathedral (617)

Cologne Cathedral, epitome of vaulting Gothic spirit (618)

Devotional glass painting (619)

Vaulted Gothic arches, Lincoln cathedral (620)

Albertus Magnus in meditation (621)

Thomas of Aquinas wrote titanic *Summa Theologica*, to resolve conflict of belief and reason (622)

Roger Bacon, Franciscan monk, stressed need for experiment to find truth (623)

Duns Scotus held credo that "God is Love" (624)

Abélard: "Questioning is the key to learning" (625)

New Monastic Orders

THEOLOGICAL REVISIONS brought demands for change in Church structure, particularly closer rapport between clergy and people. New monastic orders (Franciscans, Dominicans, Carmelites) abandoned the ascetic renunciation of the world in favor of direct contact with the people, living among them and assuming practical tasks in society.

Monk in garb of Cistercian order (626)

St. Bernard, dynamic churchman (627), founded first Cistercian monastery at Clairvaux (628)

Newly founded monastic orders abandoned asceticism, encouraged practical work, such as farming (629)

Saint Dominic during burning of heretic writings (630)

St. Hildegard, abbess, famed for her poetic visions (631)

Dominican nun (632)

(633)

A

B

C

ST. FRANCIS OF ASSISI, inspired while hearing mass to go forth and preach, began a calling and a new type of religious order based on humility, poverty and selfless service to Man.

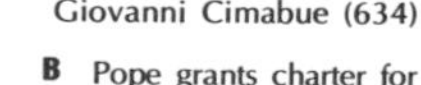

A Saint Francis painting by Giovanni Cimabue (634)

B Pope grants charter for Franciscan order (635)

C St. Francis preaches to the birds (636)

Franciscan monk (637)

Rumbles of Revolt

Papal troops attack the Waldenses, French heretics, in 1487 (638)

Itinerant preacher in makeshift pulpit (639)

Flagellant's whip (640)

Flagellation (641), and the dancing mania (642) of the late Middle Ages exemplified despair and mass psychosis.

Sculptured image of Death (643)

Wat Tyler led English Peasants' Revolt (644)

Wycliff and his lay priests were Reformation trailblazers (645)

Hus, Czech retormer, was betrayed and burned (646)

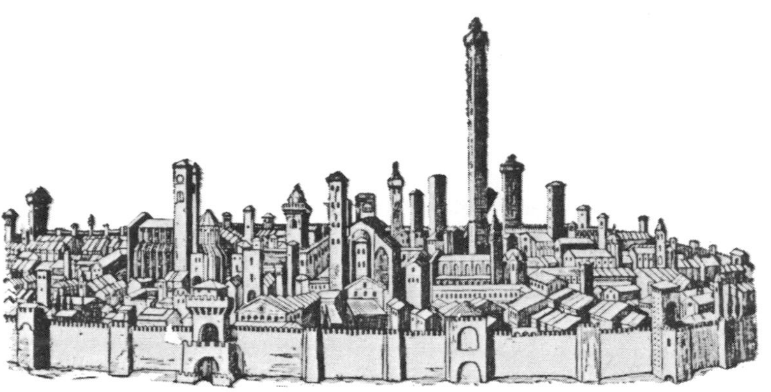

Bologna, seat of university famed for its teachers of law and medicine (647)

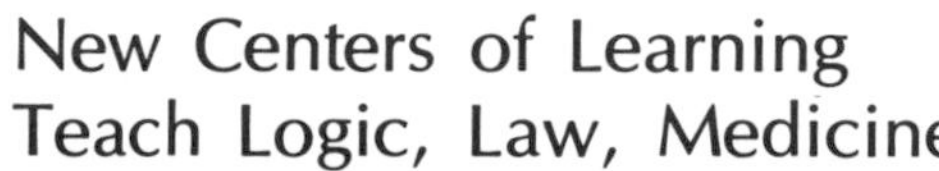

New Centers of Learning Teach Logic, Law, Medicine

Law professor lectures before group of students. Bologna ca. 1400 (648)

Albertus Magnus, venerated scholastic, preached at University of Paris (649)

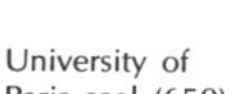

University of Paris seal (650)

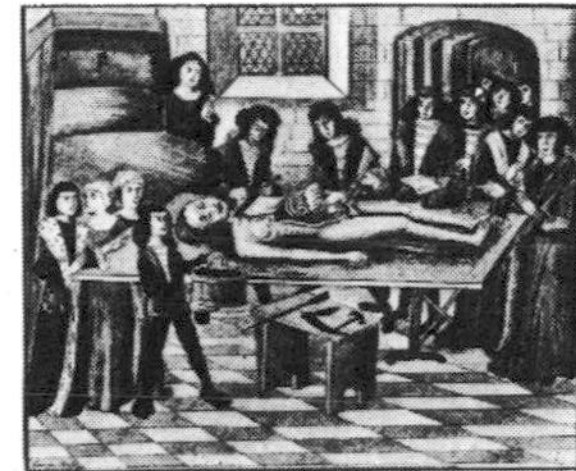

Dissection class at Montpellier (651)

Medical students learn enema's efficacy (652)

AS THE GROWING NUMBER of universities provided centers for the new Scholasticism, the demand for practical training forced them to add secular subjects to their curricula. An increase in disputes over canon law required the training of lawyers, while the rise of Aristotelian logic encouraged science, the arts and medicine.

Seminars involved religious and secular disputes (653)

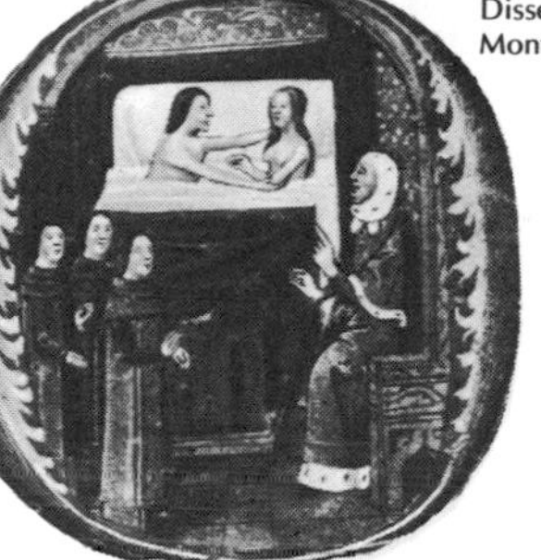

Sex behavior explained. Medieval miniature (654)

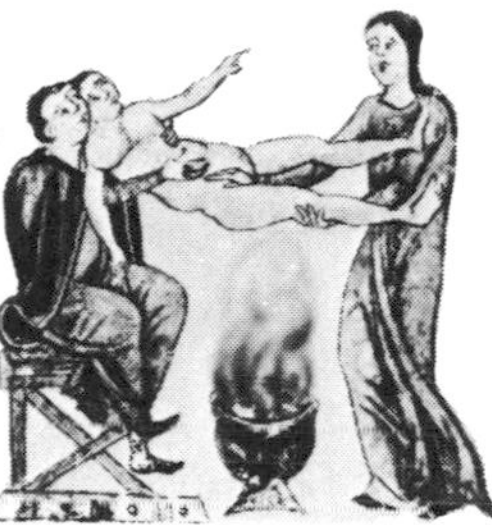

Doctor applies fumigation to cure a woman's uterine trouble (655)

Examining rectum for cancer (656)

Bloodletting to drain body of "morbific" humors (657)

Craniotomy relieves brain pressure (658)

Albertus Magnus' concept of the triune human brain (659)

Anatomical miniature of pregnant woman (660)

MEDIEVAL MEDICINE taught that health and character depended on the humors—the elemental liquids of the human body. The prevalence of one of the four humors—blood, phlegm, black bile, yellow bile—was believed a determining factor in a person's psyche, his or her temperament.

"Four Temperaments Rule Mankind Wholly"

Sanguine: loves music, wine and women (661)

Phlegmatic: lover of sloth and rest (662)

Melancholic: apt to despair (663)

Choleric: violent and full of fire (664)

Medieval Technology

REMARKABLE SKILLS were developed and perfected for the divinely inspired Gothic cathedrals that rose all over Europe. At the same time, burgeoning trade called for new roads, bridges and ships, while cities needed cranes, mills and waterworks.

Glassmaking process. Miniature ptg. (665)

Stamp mill for making of gunpowder (666)

Vehicle propelled by pulling rope (667)

Conveying goods across abyss (668)

Building technology advanced in great age of cathedrals (669)

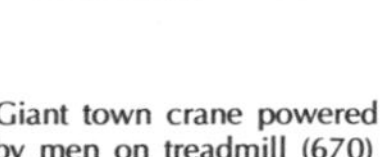

Giant town crane powered by men on treadmill (670)

Metallurgist searches out mercury in cave (671)

Boat propelled by hand-operated paddle wheels (672)

Vision of Technology: Devil turns wheel (673)

Hot-air standard designed to frighten foe (674)

FLORENTIAE·CIVITAS

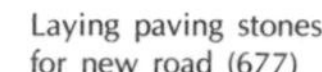

Laying paving stones for new road (677)

(677A)

Rise of Towns

CITIES GREW UP rapidly after the Crusades, serving the new commercial expansion. Often they rose by rivers that carried the flow of goods, and attracted to them the craftsmen needed by the emerging merchant class. "City air makes a man free" went the saying. Most towns were self-governing, and serfs saw them as places to find freedom, and the opportunity to exercise abilities squelched by the traditional demands of feudalism.

Building a road between two towns. 14th-century Flemish miniature (676)

Coat of arms of Florence (675)

City merchants negotiating (678)

Air view of Carcasson, famed fortified town in southern France (679)

Marketplace of town where goods and services were offered (680)

Ferrara, one of Italy's proud city-states (681)

The Guilds

CRAFTSMEN WHO MIGRATED to the cities were not entirely free. Membership in a trade guild was necessary before they could work. Admission to a guild required a rigorous examination, and both working conditions and wages were strictly regulated. Since employers and wage earners were considered members of the same trade, each guild formed a monopoly, restricting competition. But the guilds grew wealthy and powerful, and stood by their members in adversity.

◀ Insignia of Parisian wheelwrights (682)

Quarreling apprentices. Schongauer engr. (683)

Master examines two guild applicants (684)

Silversmith (685) and clockmaker (686) busily working at their crafts.

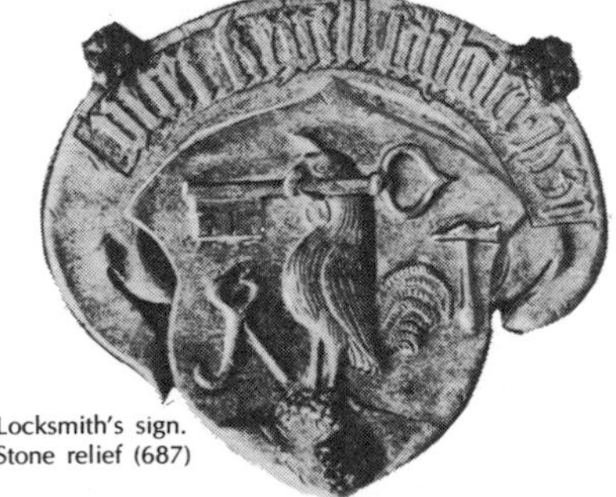

Locksmith's sign. Stone relief (687)

Cheese-maker's shop in old Verona (688)

Testing weights and measures (689)

Artisan casts pewter jars, utensils (690)

Prosperous craftsman with family (691)

Building of cathedral, stonecutters' hut (692)

Trade and Markets

Haggling Hanseatic merchants dicker by bustling harbor (697)

Coat of arms of free city of Bremen, a leading Hanseatic town (701)

Tally sticks used to settle accounts (693)

Armed factor delivers goods to Polish merchant (694)

Weighing goods. Relief from Guildhall of city of Nuremberg (695)

Wine merchants measure casks that are ready for shipment (696)

Medieval fairs, luring merchants from afar, became centers of emerging capitalism (698)

Market stalls outside city gate attract travelers, natives (699)

Peasant family going to town to trade at marketplace (700)

Urban Hygiene

Narrow streets induced fast spread of contagion (702)

Woman spills swill on unwary musicians (703)

Communal bath heated by steam boiler, described by engineer Kyesser, 1405 (704)

Mixed bathing was conducive to prostitution and the spread of venereal disease (705)

Plague was ascribed to astral influence of comets (707)

Prostitutes wash man's hair (706)

THOUGH CITIES WERE the seat of progress, they also became breeding grounds for disease. Crowded conditions and narrow, garbage-filled streets (often nothing more than open sewers) spread contagion. The plague, appearing in Constantinople in 1347, swept across Europe, killing off one third of the population in three years. Public bathhouses, where men and women mixed freely in common tubs, were recognized as sources of infection, though the nature of contagion was hardly understood.

The Black Death

The plague of Florence 1453, made famous by Boccaccio, who with friends fled the city (708)

Doctors were unable to stop disease and death (709)

Lady with attendant carries poodle across miasmic stream (710)

Plague-afflicted couple with buboes (boils). Toggenburg Bible. Miniature, ca. 1400 (711)

Humanism

PROMPTED BY THE REDISCOVERY of classic Greek and Roman writers, a new spirit emerged in literature. The new "humanists," despite the horrors of the plague, focused their attention on the secular life of men and on the pleasures and trials of this world.

Humanists revived study of ancient writers (712)

Dante Alighieri: poet, sage; wrote epic, love sonnets (713)

Vergil guides Dante past horrors of inferno in *Divine Comedy* (714)

Petrarch, first and greatest humanist, poet laureate (715)

Boccaccio, storyteller and author of *Decameron* (716)

Boccaccio narrates piquant stories while away from Florence during plague (717)

Chaucer's Canterbury pilgrims at repast in Tabbard Inn (718)

Start of Canterbury pilgrimage (719). Geoffrey Chaucer (720)

The Old Order Changeth . . .

THOUGH HUMANISM WAS PROMISING, its riches were not readily available as long as hand-written manuscripts were the only means of disseminating literature. But with Gutenberg's invention of movable type—an event of incalculable importance—the spread of Renaissance culture became possible. For the first time, books could be made cheaply enough to reach wide audiences; without them the Protestant movement, based on every man's study of the Bible, would have failed.

Gutenberg: a new age of books, knowledge (721)

Gunpowder's danger feared by scholar (722)

New weapons sealed doom of feudal order (723)

A
B
C

CHAPTER 3

Renaissance

Arts and Letters
The Reformation
Exploration

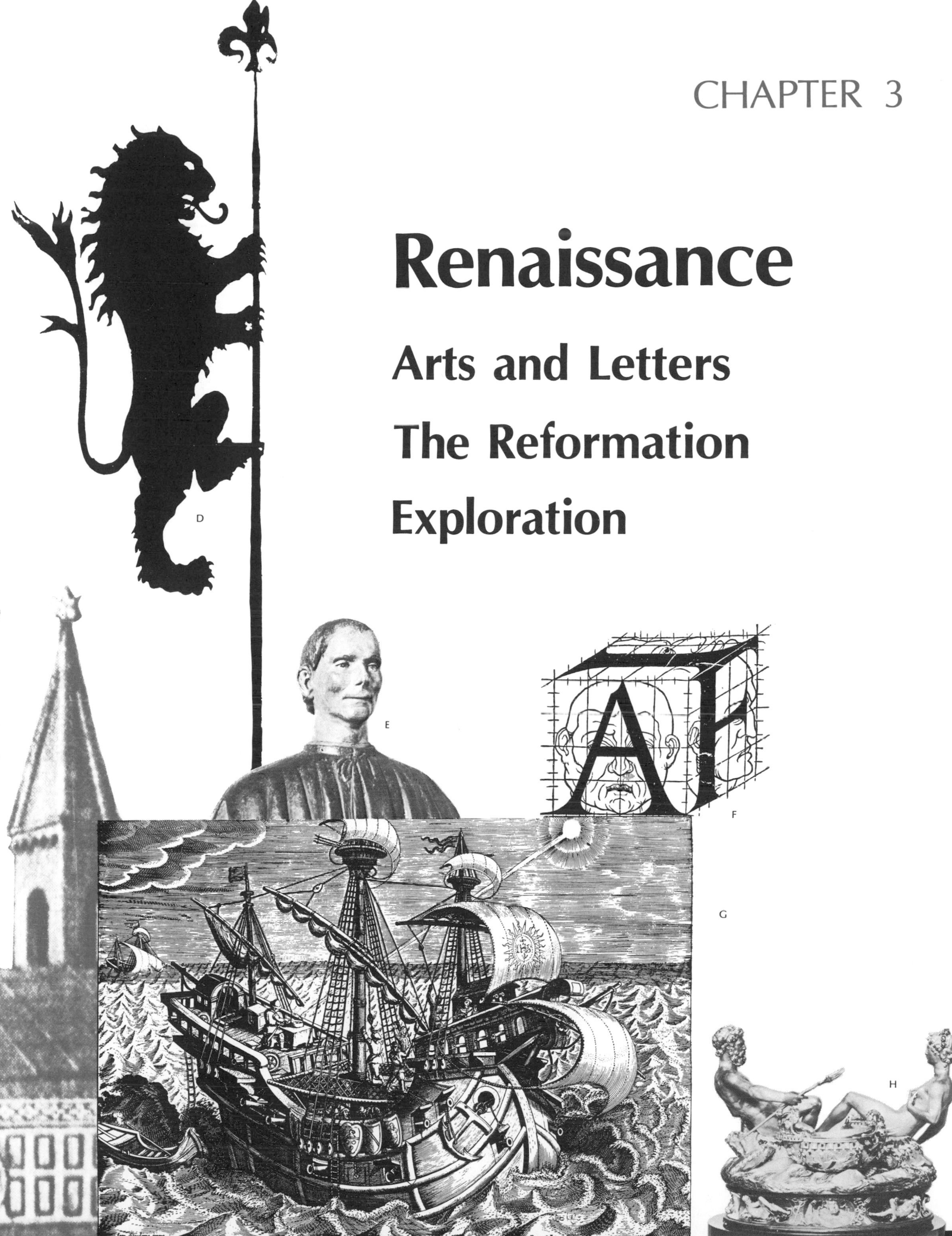

Bounteous cornucopia. Renaissance wdct. (724)

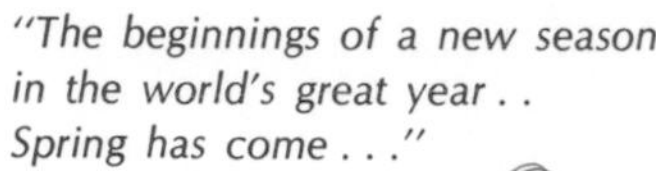
"The beginnings of a new season in the world's great year . . Spring has come . . ."
—Preserved Smith

THE RENAISSANCE

A NEW WAY OF LIFE evolved in Italy within a century, from 1450 to 1550. Turning toward an appreciation of worldy things, Italian culture stressed beauty and pleasure, producing a flowering of the arts and new science of statecraft. Men began to free themselves from domination by the medieval Church, first in the small city-states, than in Rome itself, where the papacy was supreme. The spirit of the Renaissance spread throughout Europe, adding a note to man's yearning to shape his own destiny and exercise the freedom of his own conscience.

Enjoyment and grace of living: A princely outdoor banquet (725)

Sensuality replaces asceticism (726)

Dance expressed best the new *joie de vivre* (727)

Ballet was cultivated as a fine art at the Renaissance courts (728)

Music became an integral part of most social activities (729)

Schembart Runner (730)

Centers of Culture

THE ITALIAN CITY-STATES—Florence, Milan, Mantua, Venice—became focal points of the new culture. Under the Medici, Florence cradled an amazing array of geniuses. Reflecting the ideals of their patrons, they turned the city itself into a work of art. But the greater exercise of men's faculties, the lust for life, also led the power-hungry freely to indulge their baser instincts. The notorious rule of the Borgia family caused their name to become a byword of debauchery and cruelty.

Popes made Rome a resplendent city with powers of a sovereign state (740)

High culture, deep depravity mingle in the new age (741)

Banking: source of Medici wealth, as was global wool trade (731)

Bustle of Florence street during Medici reign (732)

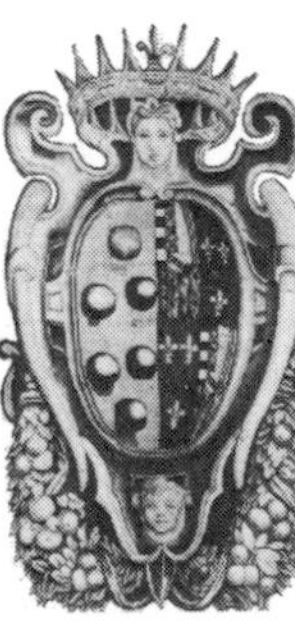
Crest of Medici family (733)

Infamous Borgias: Lucrezia, known for crime, vice (742); Cesare, cruel, treacherous (743); ruthless Pope Alexander II, poisoned accidently (744)

Machiavelli: advice on the pursuit of power (734)

Cosimo de Medici ruled Florence, 1434-1464 (735)

Lorenzo de Medici. Painting by Benozzo Gozzoli (736)

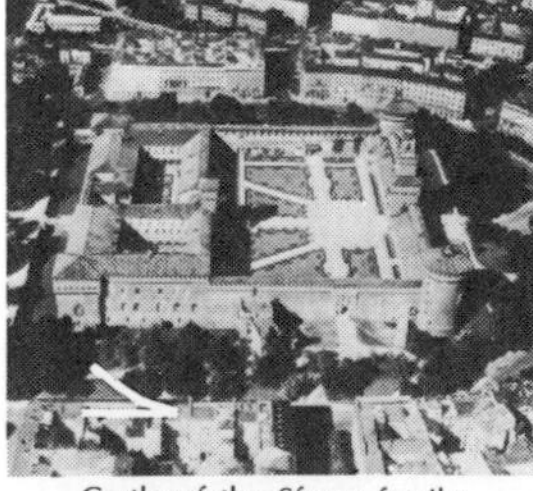
Castle of the Sforza family, rulers of Milan Duchy (745)

Assassination of Galeazzo Sforza, the hated tyrant of Milan (746)

Country seat of the Medici in the Florentine hills (737)

Lorenzo and Platonic Academy (738)

Michelangelo monument in San Lorenzo (739)

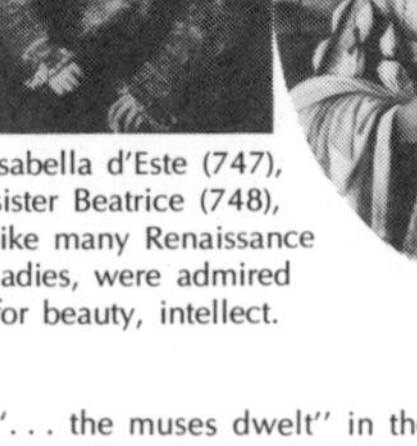
Isabella d'Este (747), sister Beatrice (748), like many Renaissance ladies, were admired for beauty, intellect.

"... the muses dwelt" in the Este palace in Ferrara (749)

Lionelle d'Este (749A)

Florentine lion (750)

Beauty: God's Gift to Mankind

Detail from Botticelli's "La Primavera" (751)

Benvenuto Cellini (752) created gold saltcellar for King Francis I (753)

Emperor Maximilian as patron of artist (754)

Mural painters enhanced beauty of cities (755)

Head of Michelangelo's statue of "David" (756)

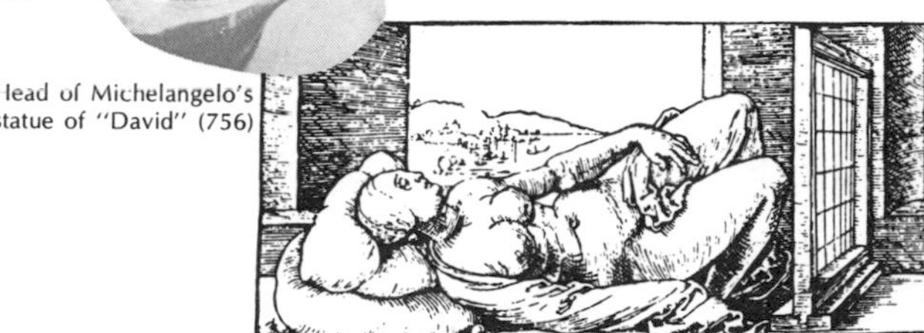

Albrecht Dürer explores beauty of female body with aid of viewing grid (757)

THE REBIRTH OF MAN'S sensuous appreciation of nature, long obscured by the stylized devotional forms of medieval art, was the work of Renaissance painters and sculptors. Michelangelo, Da Vinci, Dürer, Botticelli, Cellini—all studied nature and man afresh, discovering in both natural phenomena and in the human form a unique beauty.

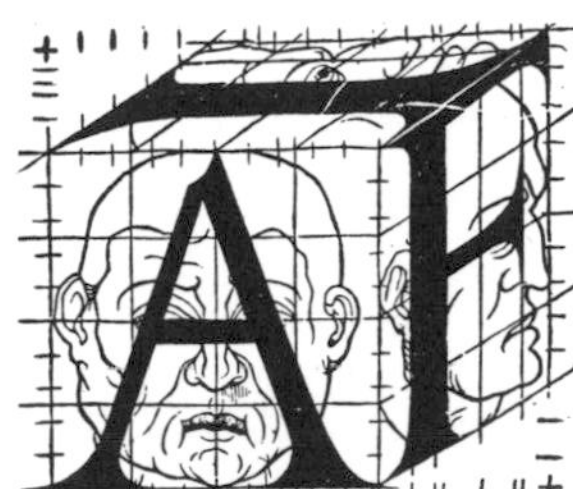

The proportion of letters became subject of intense interest (758)

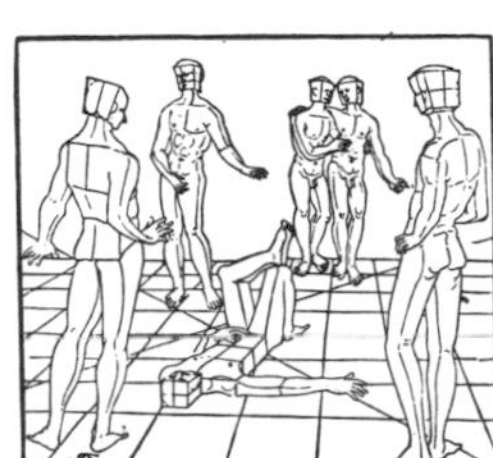

Art and geometry combined in science of perspective (759)

Venetian lady with horned hairdo (760) reveals platform shoes (761)

Use of lipstick is shown in Renaissance wdct. (762)

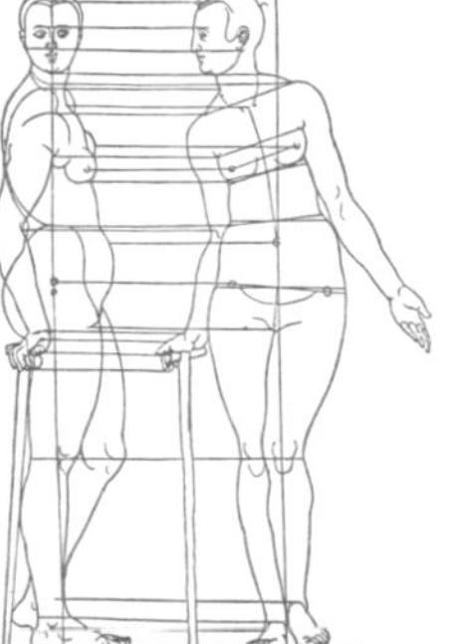

Dürer study of proportions of the female body (763)

Printers allied with scholars gave new wings to Renaissance thought (764)

Artist created first realistic textbook illustrations (765)

Aldus Manutius, master printer, used italics for small-sized books (766)

Aldine printer's mark (767)

Reading spawned new wisdom (768)

Renaissance printer setting type (769)

Flowering of Letters

THE NEW ART OF PRINTING helped disseminate the Renaissance spirit, further weakening the control which the Church, with its monastic scribes, had once exercised over written communication. More books now reached wider audiences, stimulating literature in the native tongue rather than Latin. Tasso and Ariosto wrote romantic epics in Italian, Rabelais gave free expression to the Renaissance *joie de vivre* in French, while in Spain, Cervantes produced one of the world's greatest stories, *Don Quixote*.

Tasso, poet laureate at court of Ferrara (770)

Ariosto wrote comedies, epics and poems (771)

Scholars study science and nature; record results (772)

Rabelais (773); his Gargantua (774) expressed Renaissance ebulliance.

Montaigne (775), wise with felicity of form. His chateau at Dordogne (776)

Cervantes (777). His *Don Quixote* (778), a literary classic, burlesqued the romance of chivalry.

Lope de Vega (779), Spanish dramatist.

DOZE.
COMEDIAS
DE LOPE DE
VEGA CARPIO
COM AS LOAS
ao principio.

Dirigidas ao Senhor Gonçalo Pirez Carualho Prouedor das obras del Rey noßo Senhor.

As que neste libro se conchem vaõ na volta desta folha.

Impreßas com licença da Santa Inquisiçaõ. Por Iorge Rodriguez. Anno de 1605.

(780)

New View of the Universe

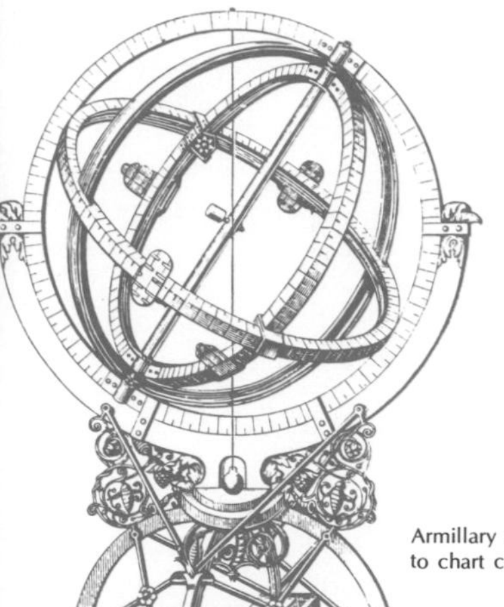

Armillary sphere, a globe used to chart course of stars (781)

Copernicus upset ancient concept of heavens (782)

Tycho Brahe in his observatory. He charted star motion with accuracy (783)

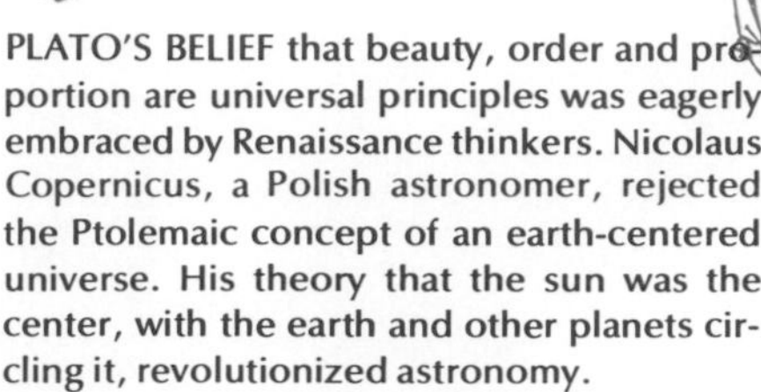

PLATO'S BELIEF that beauty, order and proportion are universal principles was eagerly embraced by Renaissance thinkers. Nicolaus Copernicus, a Polish astronomer, rejected the Ptolemaic concept of an earth-centered universe. His theory that the sun was the center, with the earth and other planets circling it, revolutionized astronomy.

Stellar constellations: Taurus the Bull, Justice, Scales of Justice (784A,B,C)

Man's Body

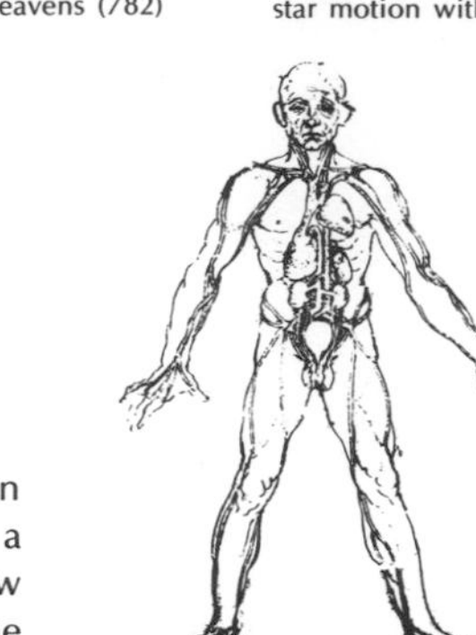

Artists explored anatomy. Leonardo drawing (785)

Studio of a Renaissance scientist surrounded by instruments (786)

IN THE SAME YEAR, 1543, the Italian anatomist Andreas Vesalius published a book in seven volumes that marked a new era in medicine. Based on dissections of the human body, and illustrated with startling woodcuts, *De . . . Fabrica* gave physicians their first reasonably accurate notion of human anatomy. The result was improvement in the art of surgery, as described in the highly successful books of Ambroise Paré. Dissection aroused heated opposition, however, prompting a Swiss physician, Paracelsus, to oppose the new medicine with a metaphysical approach to disease.

Vesalius based his anatomy on dissection of dead bodies (787)

Student finds bones for anatomy study (788)

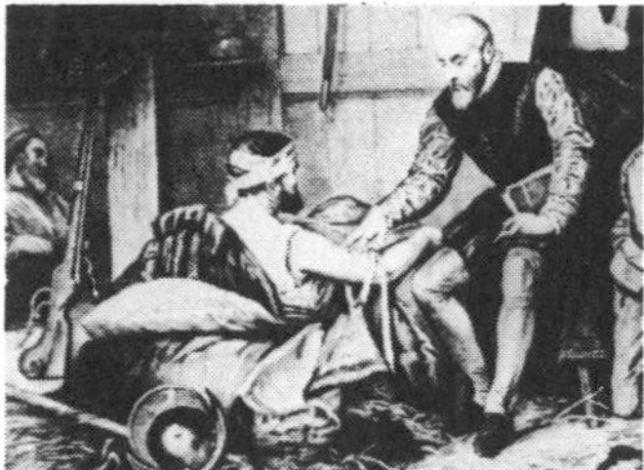

Paré based his surgery on Vesalian insights (789)

Surgeon ties patient to operating table (790)

Plastic surgery practiced by Gasparo Tagliacozzi (791)

Orthopedics, bonesetting, utilized Renaissance technology (792)

Books explored new ways of childbirth (793)

Paracelsus, doctor and magician (795)

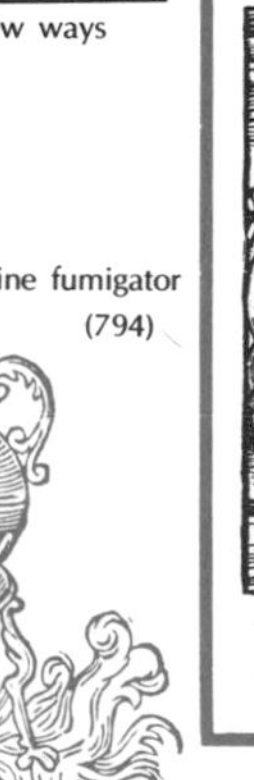

Uterine fumigator (794)

He thought ills caused by stars (796), divided body into metric zones (797)

Metallurgy

THE METAL-BASED ECONOMY, introduced late in the Middle Ages, developed rapidly in the Renaissance. As kings and emperors coined money to finance armies (discarding the old system of feudal allegiances), advancing military technology also demanded more and more iron and steel. Mining and metallurgy flourished, and the search for new sources of ore obsessed the power-hungry.

(798)

Dowser seeks precious metal, useful ore (799)

Air pump facilitated the work in mine's deeper regions (800)

Smelting furnace, from Georgius Agricola's *De Re Metallica* (801)

Minting money, a necessity for monarchs to pay armies (802)

Foreign redoubt, heavily armed to protect traveling traders (803)

Silver coin of Holy Roman Emperor Maximilian I (804)

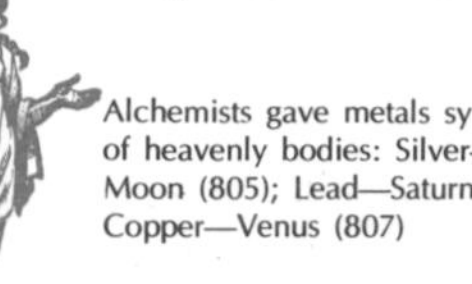

Alchemists gave metals symbols of heavenly bodies: Silver—the Moon (805); Lead—Saturn (806); Copper—Venus (807)

New Money Economy

MONEY, "the root of all evil," was soon the source of all power. International trade produced immense private fortunes, for traders and those who financed them. The Medicis were early merchant-bankers with branch offices in many trading centers. Merchants were freed from carrying large sums of money over unsafe roads by a credit system that soon made European financiers more powerful than kings, at least in raising money. The Fugger family of Augsburg, investing heavily in silver mines as well as trade, rose to become the financiers of Emperor Charles V.

Merchants negotiate deal (808)

Goods are weighed and readied (809)

Accountant posts entries (810)

Merchandise baled and forwarded (811)

Exotic visitors (812)

Settling accounts near wharf (813)

Gangplank down: merchants board with shouldered goods (814)

A successful merchant. Ptg. by Holbein (815)

Venetian merchant-banker with scale and measure, the tools of his trade (816)

Arithmetic lessons mean better accounting (817)

Moneylender at this banking table (818)

New Arabic ciphers compared with old discs (819)

"The Money Changers." Ptg. by Massys (820)

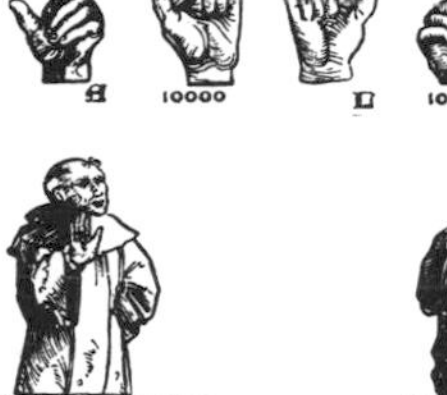

Traders devised private sign language. The practise continues today (821)

Fugger Family

Fugger's cabinet shows branch locations (822)

Charles V's debt canceled out by magnanimous Fugger (823)

Fugger of Augsburg. Wdct. by Dürer (824)

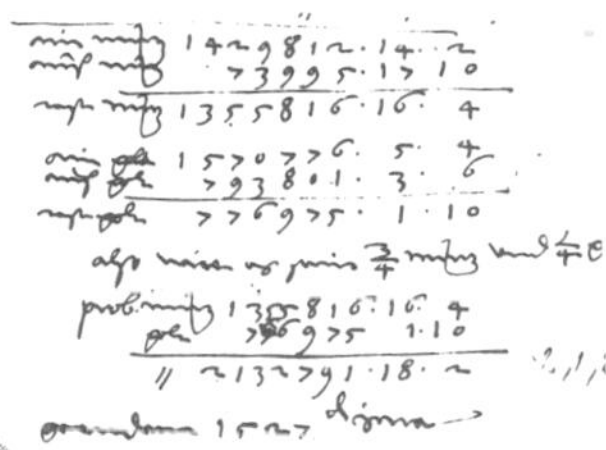
Balance sheet of Fugger enterprises tops 2 million old florins (825)

Venice: Hub of World Trade

STRATEGICALLY LOCATED between East and West, master of the Adriatic Sea, and close to Byzantium and Russia, Venice thrived on the maritime trade. As long as she dominated the rich trade from the Orient, Venice was unequaled in wealth and power, the seat of a far-flung commercial empire that drew the envy of the world. But her monopoly was soon to be broken by the exploration of the new trade routes.

Venetian Lion; La Summa Gloria di Venetia (826)

Doge, oligarchic ruler, under ceremonial parasol (827)

A Venetian tax collector (828)

Rialto Bridge in Venice - meeting place of merchants became a humming international trade center (829)

Verrocchio's *Colleoni*; symbol of might (830)

Venetian diplomat-trader dictates to scribe. Ptg. by Carpaccio (831)

Battle of Lepanto, 1571: Turkish defeat reaffirmed dominance of Venice (832)

Romanticized view of a night in Venice (833)

(834)

Age of Exploration

GREED AND CURIOSITY, aided by newly invented nautical instruments, now encouraged voyages of exploration designed to break the Italian monopoly of world trade. "Henry the Navigator," Prince of Portugal, spearheaded these efforts, first with expeditions down Africa's West Coast. Then, in 1497, Vasco da Gama sailed around Africa to India, establishing Portugal's monopoly of Indian Ocean trade. Spain soon challenged Portugal's successes, however. After Columbus' voyages, Spanish expeditions conquered Mexico, Yucatán and Peru, vanquishing the Aztecs and Incas, and bringing back gold and treasure to finance Spanish domination of the seas.

◄Ship's position checked with jack staff (835)

Fanciful fish cavort on marine charts (839)

Henry the Navigator sighting fleet (836)

Measuring distance of returning ship (837)

Perfected compass by Flavio Giova (838)

Geographers' new maps aid exploration (840)

Columbus with map of his discoveries (841)

Simple! Apocryphal story of Columbus and the egg (842)

King and Queen of Spain, backers of Columbus (843)

Columbus leaves Palos on August 3, 1492 (844)

Columbus' flagship, the caravel *Santa Maria* (845)

(846)

Landing of Columbus in the Bahamas (847)

Columbus received by Ferdinand and Isabella after his return from the New World (848)

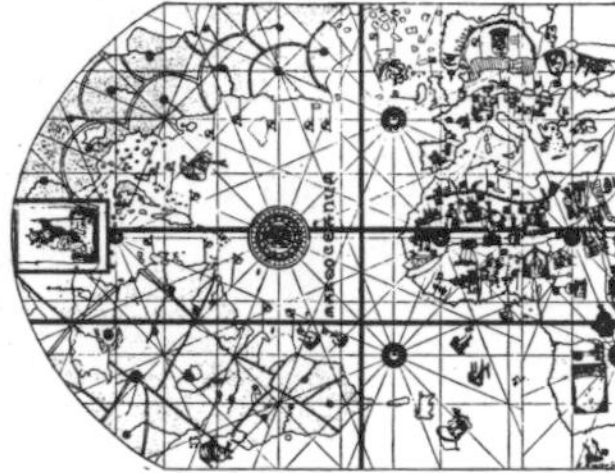

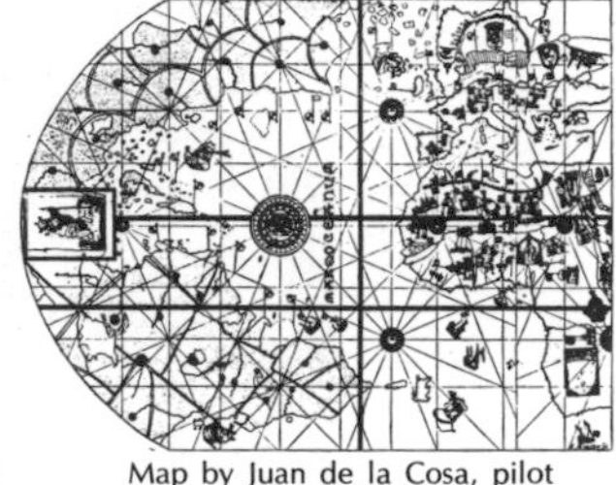

Map by Juan de la Cosa, pilot of one of Columbus' ships (849)

TIMETABLE OF VOYAGES

1497

John Cabot describes his first voyage to King Henry VII (850)

1513

Balboa discovered Pacific Ocean, claimed it for Spain (854)

1498

Amerigo Vespucci, after whom new continent was named (851)

1520

Magellan, first to sail around the globe (855)

1499

Vasco da Gama sailed from Europe around Africa to the East (852)

1534

Jacques Cartier explored St. Lawrence River (856)

1512

Ponce de Leon, governor of Puerto Rico, discovered Florida (853)

1538

De Soto embarking from Spain to explore America (857)

Travel report, 1596 (858) ▼

IOYFVLL NEWES
Out of the New-found
VVorlde.

EXPLORERS ALSO BROUGHT BACK to the Old World wondrous tales of plants and animals never imagined, of mysterious natives with exotic ways and amazing social customs. Early travelers called these natives "Indians," thinking they had landed in India.

New foods (maize, squash, potatoes) and medicinal plants excited Europe. Balm from the weeping tree, quinine from the cinchona plant, quickly became part of the Old World pharmacopoeia. But tobacco caused the greatest sensation, quickly earning a place as a prime New World crop, as pipe smoking became the rage.

Exotic races shown in 1493 chronicle (859)

Indian settlement and stockade (860)

Powwow among the Indians (861)

(864)

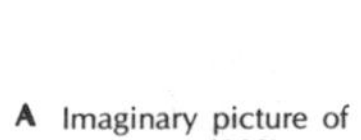

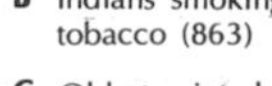

A Imaginary picture of coco tree (862)

B Indians smoking tobacco (863)

C Oldest printed illustration of corn plant (865)

D Florida Indians impale a crocodile (866)

A Spanish master (867)

The Conquistadors

IN ELEVEN SHIPS, with a mere 500 men, Hernando Cortez sailed from Cuba to Vera Cruz, Mexico, in 1519. Burning his ships to prevent his soldiers from escaping, Cortez pushed inland, killing and looting. Montezuma, the Aztec king, tried to appease him but was imprisoned, and after much bloodshed and intrigue, Cortez mastered the land in 1521.

Pizarro was equally brutal in the conquest of Peru. With 180 men and 27 horses (which terrified the natives), he took the Inca capital of Cuzco in 1533, executing Atahualpa, the king. Driving away the natives, the Spaniards seized enormous "land grants" for themselves. Thus arose "New Spain."

Cortez welcomed by Montezuma (Nov. 8, 1519). Spaniards made the Aztec king prisoner (868)

Montezuma attacked by his people (869)

Horses of conquistadors frightened natives (870)

Pizarro crossing the Andes (871)

Coronado discovers Missouri River (872)

Spaniards inflicted cruel punishments on recalcitrant natives (873)

Natives make sugar from cane for Spaniards (874)

Spanish conquerors supervise slave labor in salt mine (875)

South American Indians panning gold (876)

Missionary Las Cassas bewails cruelty (877)

Mining gold in Spanish America. Gold was prize coveted by all conquistadors (878)

Culture of the Conquered

THE SPANIARDS DEFEATED the Aztecs and Incas so easily because neither culture had an adequate defense against horsemen bearing guns. Both peoples were just emerging from the Stone Age, developing the use of metals. They had no plows, and only primitive stone wheels. Nevertheless, they had achieved an astounding cultural level. The Aztecs built vast urban centers, mastering the intricacies of irrigation and food supply with primitive technology. The Incas left impressive monuments to their engineering skill: bridges spanning vast mountain gorges, irrigation systems, grandiose temples.

- **A** Childbirth deity Chiateto. Mexican sculpture (879)
- **B** Aztec calendar stone (880)
- **C** Cultivating and harvesting corn. From Mexican Codex (881,882)
- **D** Aztec warrior chief in full regalia (883)
- **E** Peruvian poncho with cat motif (884)
- **F** Decorative clay jar of the Chohila culture (885)
- **G** Mexican gold pectoral with image of Death (886)
- **H** Giant serpent head on Yucatan temple (887)
- **I** Inca quipu, calculating strings with knots (888)
- **J** Inca family during potato harvest (889)
- **K** Elaborate ceremonial Inca pottery vessel (890)
- **L** Art of weaving shown in Aztec manuscript (891)
- **M** Childbirth. Pottery handle (892)
- **N** Sacrifice to the sun. Cutting out victim's heart (893)
- **O** Chichen-Itza Temple, a Yucatán landmark (894)

The Reformation

Luther. "He threw the apple of discord into Europe" (895)

THE SPIRIT OF THE RENAISSANCE was one of rebellion against old forms, as well as the search for new ones. This defiance was turned with special vigor against the Church. The increasing worldliness of the papacy, accompanied by notorious corruption and nepotism, had greatly weakened the Church's prestige. Onerous taxation of the laity to finance grand public works in the Vatican became increasingly oppressive. Kings and princes resented Rome's constant interference in local affairs, as well as papal control of much of their own nations' wealth. Thus, a break with Rome was building, waiting for an issue.

Pope was defiled as Antichrist, Rome as Whore of Babylon. Wdct. (896)

Monk smuggling woman into monastery cell (897)

Indulgences: sinners to be forgiven by retributive payment to Pope (898)

Monk and nun in bedroom tryst (899)

Devils throw debauched monk into Rome's Tiber River (900)

Erasmus of Rotterdam

SOME VOICES preached moderation. Erasmus of Rotterdam, recognizing the abuses of the Church and the wickedness of some clergy, tried to reform the Church quietly from within, freeing clerical writings from the scholastic commentaries which blocked a return to the Gospel.

Erasmus flayed clerical abuses but was loyal to Church (901)

Caricature of monk from his work (902)

With printer Froben, edited Greek New Testament (903)

His *In Praise of Folly* pilloried foibles of his time (904)

Martin Luther

WHEN LUTHER NAILED his 95 theses to the church door at Wittenberg in 1517, listing abuses of the Church and questioning its power over man's conscience, he sought debate, not rebellion. But the arrogant response of the Church, plus popular outcry against the flagrant sale of papal indulgences to complete St. Peter's Cathedral in Rome, fomented a revolution. Many German princes, perhaps for political gain rather than religious conviction, sided with Luther, making the break with Rome complete.

Posting the 95 theses on the Wittenberg church door (908)

Bulla contra Erro
res Martini Lutheri
et sequatium.

Pope counters with bull (905)

Luther defies Pope by burning bull, precipitating break with Rome (906)

Laity to partake in Lord's Supper (907)

Luther is excommunicated, Diet of Worms, 1521 (909)

Luther hiding in Wartburg where he and Melanchthon translate the Bible (910)

Biblia/das ist/ die
gantze Heilige Sch-
rifft Deudsch.
Mart. Luth.
Wittemberg.
Begnadet mit Kür-
fürstlicher zu Sachsen
freiheit.
Gedruckt durch Hans Lufft.
M. D. XXXIIII.

Title page of first Luther Bible (911)

Protestantism

Pamphlets spread Protestantism, made it a "book religion" (912)

Luther, defying monastic celibacy, led happy family life (913)

Calvin taught stern Protestantism, basis of later Puritanism (914)

Zwingli forbade all rituals, images (915)

John Knox, founder of Presbyterianism (916)

Anabaptists persecuted in Netherlands (917)

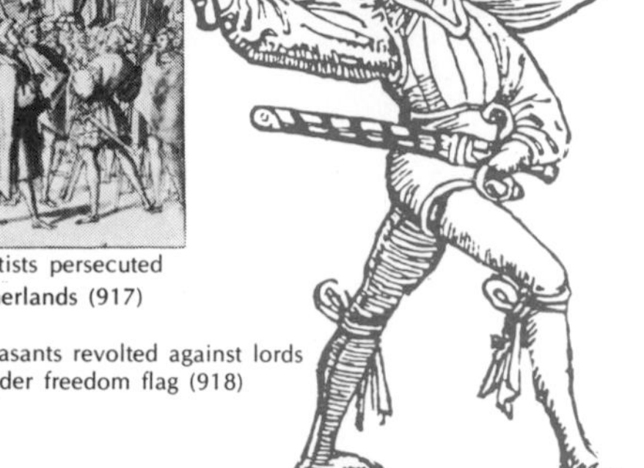

Peasants revolted against lords under freedom flag (918)

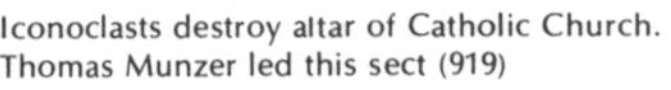

Iconoclasts destroy altar of Catholic Church. Thomas Munzer led this sect (919)

Troubled Church is tossed on the sea of discontent (920)

The Troubled Church—Counter Reformation

STRONG VOICES within the Catholic Church had long called for reform, particularly to end abuses of Renaissance popes. At the Council of Trent in mid-century (1545-1563) these forces sought to inspire a renewed spirituality, a return to the true Catholic faith that would undercut the Protestant Reformation. The art of the Baroque sought to give visual power to this new sense of faith's dynamic mission.

Meanwhile, more radical factions within the Church, like those of Ignatius Loyola and the Society of Jesus, favored a militant approach. Heretics were attacked through a revival of the Inquisition, and an Index of Forbidden Books was set up.

Council of Trent, 1545: the Church fights back, institutes reforms (921)

Ignatius of Loyola receives papal approval for Jesuit order (922)

Ignatius of Loyola preaching. Painting by P. P. Rubens (923)

Francisco Xavier, ardent Jesuit missionary (924)

Matteo Ricci propagated faith in China (925)

Coat of arms of the Inquisition (926)

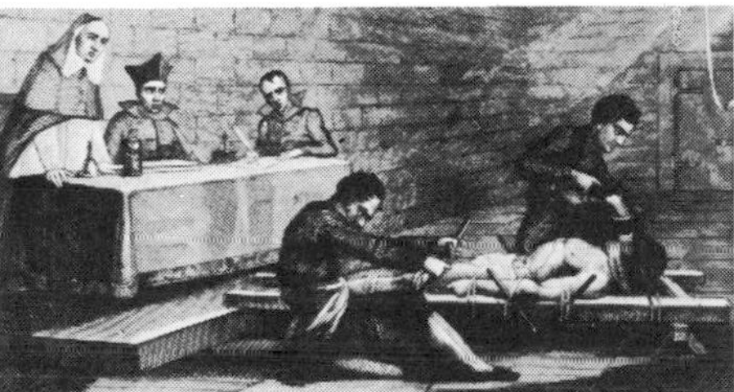

Counter Reformation revived Inquisition to curb defection from Church (927)

Suspects of Protestantism crucified in France (928)

Palestrina hands copy of his Mass to Pope Marcellus initiating reform of Church music (929). This was only one of the attempts to install Catholicism with new vitality and brilliance. Architecture and painting similarly showed the spirit of a resurgent Church, culminating in the art of the Baroque. ▶

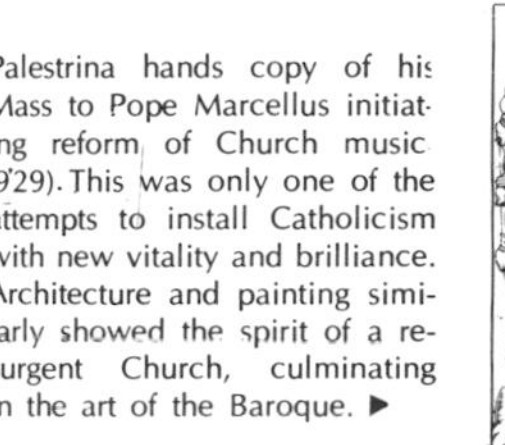

Alva, charged by Spain to reconquer Holland (930)

Egmont, Dutch leader, captured, killed (931)

Mass execution decreed by Alva's Blood Council. 1568 (932)

Seige of Leiden broken, 1574: dikes cut, land flooded, ships bring food (933)

THE COUNTER REFORMATION produced terrible conflicts in Holland and France. The Duke of Alva, sent as Captain General to the Netherlands by Philip II of Spain, convened a Council of Blood which condemned thousands, including the famous Count Egmont commemorated in Beethoven's Overture. An attempt to exterminate Calvinist Huguenots on St. Bartholomew's Night, 1572, plunged France into civil war until the Edict of Nantes (1598) provided some semblance of religious toleration.

Catherine de Medici plots massacre (934)

Death of Admiral Coligny (935)

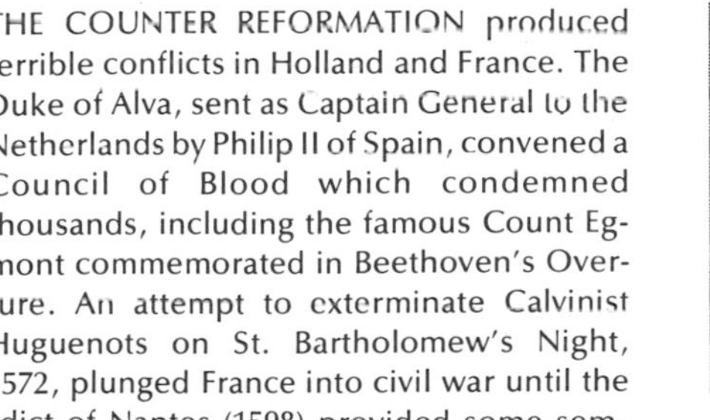

King Henry III, with a vacillating stand in the war between Catholics and Huguenots, was murdered by monk Jacques Clement (936) who was quartered for his crime (937)

Infamy in France

Queen Catherine de Medici inspects victims in Paris street on the morning after the St. Bartholomew massacre (938)

(940)

Henry VIII by Holbein (941)

Catherine of Aragon (942)

Bluff Harry the Eighth
To six spouses was wedded.
One died, one survived,
Two divorced, two beheaded.
(Nursery rhyme)

FOR HIS OPPOSITION to Lutheranism, Henry VIII earned a papal accolade as "Defender of the Faith." Yet when Pope Clement VII refused to sanction Henry's divorce from Catherine of Aragon in 1534, he boldly renounced loyalty to Rome, making himself head of the Anglican Church. Popular dissatisfaction with Rome supported Henry. Opponents were executed, including the great Sir Thomas More, who became a Catholic martyr.

But the confiscated monastic lands and treasure, parceled out to loyal supporters, provided resources Henry needed to strengthen the state.

Mary Tudor, daughter (943)

Anne Boleyn (945)

Elizabeth, daughter (946)

Anne Boleyn executed (944)

Jane Seymour (947)

(952)

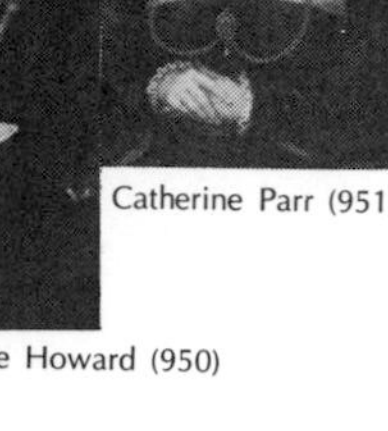
Catherine Parr (951)

Catherine Howard (950)

Anne of Cleves (949)

Prince Edward, son (948)

Title page of More's *Utopia*, 1516. Illustr. by Hans Holbein (953)

Thomas More, "a man for all seasons" (954)

HENRY'S DEFECTION from Rome was an added inspiration to the work of Biblical translators, who sought to provide every Englishman with a text of the Scriptures he could read. Henry saw that an English Bible could heighten national consciousness, and ordered that the Great Bible, the work of Myles Coverdale and William Tyndale, be distributed to every parish church in 1539. These translations helped set standards for English prose.

English Bible presented to King Henry VIII (955)

Tyndale Bibles smuggled into England (956)

Bible translated by Myles Coverdale, 1535 (957)

BIBLIA
The Bible that
is, the holy Scripture of the
Olde and New Testament, faith-
fully and truly translated out
of Douche and Latyn
in to Englishe.
M. D. XXXV.
S. Paul. II. Tessa. III.
that the worde of God maie
sage, and be glorified. &c.
S. Paul Col. III.
de of Christ dwell in you plen
wysdome &c.
Josue I.
boke of this lawe departe
mouth, but exercyse thyselfe
and nighte &c.

Henry VIII grants charter to company of barber-surgeons of London (958)

Conversational group at court ball (959)

Dr. Andrew Borde, "Merry Andrew" (960)

Meeting of Henry VIII and Francis I. Field of Cloth of Gold, 1520 (961)

The *Great Harry* flagship in the fleet of Henry VIII (962)

Sword received by Henry VIII as "Defender of the Faith" from Pope Leo X. After his break with Rome, Henry kept title and sword (963)

"Bloody Mary"

IF HENRY VIII'S TURN toward Protestantism proved popular, Mary Tudor's attempt to restore Catholicism in England did not. Mary was the daughter of a Spanish princess. Her marriage to Philip II of Spain, Holy Roman Emperor and chief defender of the papacy, reflected her sense of religious zeal. During her brief reign (1553-1558) many Anglican churchmen were burned at the stake, earning her the epithet "Bloody Mary."

Mary Tudor with her husband, King Philip II of Spain (964)

Mary welcomed to London, 1553. Her half-sister Elizabeth at right (965)

Thomas Cranmer, Protestant bishop, seized by group of Catholic priests (966)

Burning of Protestants during the reign of "Bloody Mary" (967)

Elizabeth R
(968)

ENGLISH PROTESTANTISM took its final form under Elizabeth I, whose 45-year reign encompassed England's greatest period of national vitality. Elizabeth's womanhood was a great diplomatic asset, allowing her to dangle the prospect of marriage before various foreign contenders, while demanding extreme loyalty from her counselors. She also managed to control both Protestant and Catholic factions.

Coronation at Westminster Abbey in 1559 (969)

(970)

". . . the Queen, very majestic; her face oblong, fair; her eyes small, yet black and pleasant; her nose a little hooked; her lips narrow, and her teeth black. . . . she wore false hair, and that red. . . . her air was stately."
Hentzner's Travels, 1598

Thomas Gresham, Queen at Royal Exchange (971)

The Queen appears at session of the House of Commons (972)

Lord Burghley dominated in foreign affairs (973)

Robert Dudley, Queen's early favorite (974)

"A Royal Picknick." Wdct., 1575 (975)

The Queen goes to a wedding at Blackfriars in a litter carried by six knights (976)

Queen and court during a hawking party (977)

Lord Essex, Queen's favorite (978), accused of treason, imprisoned, beheaded, 1601 (979)

Young Mary Stuart, by Fouquet (980)

Two Fateful Years
1587-1588

Mary, Queen of Scots, playing golf at St. Andrews. She fancied the game (982)

Mary Stuart visits Nostradamus (983)

Mary Stuart executed after prolonged conflict with Queen Elizabeth (984)

Raleigh spreading his cloak before the Queen (985)

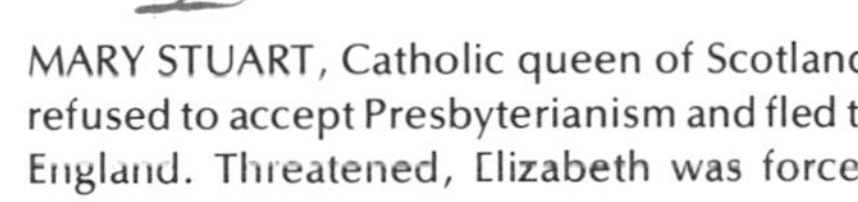
MarieR
(981)

MARY STUART, Catholic queen of Scotland, refused to accept Presbyterianism and fled to England. Threatened, Elizabeth was forced to order her execution in 1587.

THE SPANISH ARMADA, Philip of Spain's final effort to restore Catholicism in England, was defeated (some thought miraculously) in 1588. England soon dominated the seas.

The Spanish Armada coming up the English Channel (986)

The English fleet under Howard, Drake, Hawkins defeats "Invincible Armada," July 1588 (987)

Drake knighted by the Queen aboard *Golden Hind* (988)

Elizabeth the Queen: an apotheosis (989)

OVERSEAS EXPANSION

The English landing in Virginia, 1607 (990)

Raleigh captures Spanish governor of Trinidad (991); Claims region for the English Crown (992)

First potato planted in Ireland (993)

Merchants of Virginia.

Virginia Company coat of arms (994)

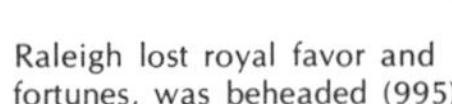
Raleigh lost royal favor and fortunes, was beheaded (995)

Elizabeth: Patroness of Letters

Queen Elizabeth accepts dedication of new opus from poet George Gascoigne (996)

THE EDUCATION OF ELIZABETH was remarkable, even for a princess. She was called "bookish"—for she liked books, even using them as décor in her chambers. Proficient in Latin and Greek, and aware of the maturing Renaissance culture, she encouraged poets to seek favor by literary achievements. The result was a flurry of poems and plays designed to glorify England and its queen. Sidney, Spenser, Raleigh, Donne, Jonson, Shakespeare, all contributed to an efflorescence of English literature.

Francis Bacon outlined a system of the exact natural sciences (997)

Dr. William Gilbert performs electrical experiments before the Queen (998)

Ben Jonson, dramatist, poet laureate (999)

Sir Philip Sidney, brilliant poet, valiant soldier (1000)

The metaphysical poet John Donne (1001)

The Tragicall Hiſtory of the Life and Death of Doctor Fauſtus.
Written by Ch. Mar.

Title page, Marlowe's *Dr. Faustus* (1002)

Chamber players and madrigalists during the Elizabethan Age (1003)

(1004)

THE GENIUS OF SHAKESPEARE was the epitome of literary achievement that represented his age and yet transcended it. His histories, comedies and tragedies reflected popular interests of the day, yet ennobled them with philosophical and poetic perspective. The range of his knowledge encompassed nearly all facets of Renaissance thought, and his verse raised the English language to new heights of power and eloquence. His "pride and joy in the greatness of England" is everywhere apparent.

Edmund Spenser, poet and allegorist (1005A)

The Shepheardes Calendar, high point of Renaissance poetry (1005, 1006, 1007, 1008)

Spenser's *Faerie Queene*, First Edition, 1598, (1009)

Skyline of London seen from across Thames River (1010)

Globe Theatre premiered Shakespeare plays (1011)

Swan Theatre: public sat in circular galleries (1012)

Shakespeare's players at the court of Elizabeth (1013)

Mr. WILLIAM SHAKESPEARES COMEDIES, HISTORIES, & TRAGEDIES.
Published according to the True Originall Copies.
LONDON
Printed by Isaac Iaggard, and Ed. Blount. 1623.

The First Folio, with famed Droeshout portrait (1014)

Richard Tarleton, comic actor (1015)

A PLEASANT Conceited Comedie CALLED, Loues labors loſt.
As it was presented before her Highnes this last Christmas.
Newly corrected and augmented By W. Shakespere.
Imprinted at London by W.W. for Cutbert Burby. 1598.

First title page with author's name (1016)

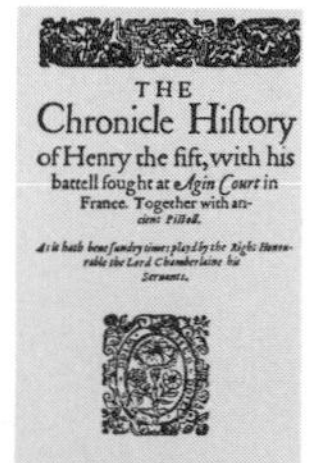
THE Chronicle Hiſtory of Henry the fift, with his battell fought at Agin Court in France. Together with Auntient Pistoll.
Printed for T. P. 1608.

AN EXCELLENT conceited Tragedie OF Romeo and Iuliet.
LONDON, Printed by Iohn Danter. 1597

SHAKE-SPEARES SONNETS.
Neuer before Imprinted.
AT LONDON By G. Eld for T. T. and are to be solde by

Shakespeare's works often appeared garbled. First Folio Edition of 1623 established authentic version (1017,1018,1019)

Memorable Quotes . . .

"The pound of flesh . . . 'tis mine and I will have it." (1022)

"A horse! A horse! My kingdom for a horse!" (1023)

"Lord! what fools these mortals be!" (1024)

Richard Burbage was first actor to play the role of Hamlet (1020)

Shakespeare's tomb in church at Stratford (1025)

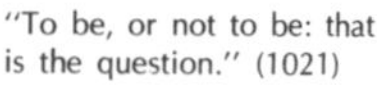
"To be, or not to be: that is the question." (1021)

Epitaph on Shakespeare's grave at Stratford (1026)

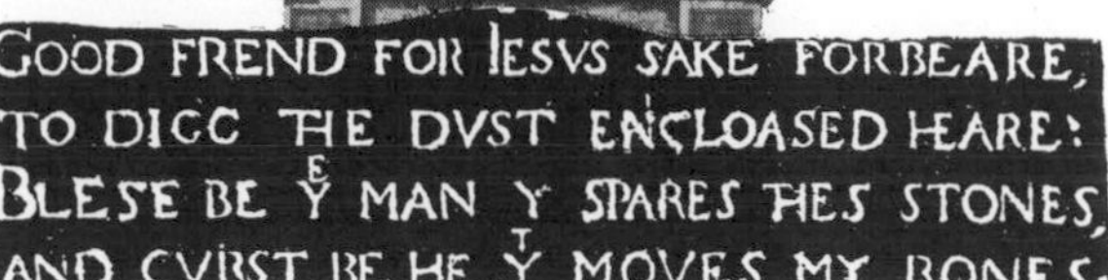
GOOD FREND FOR IESVS SAKE FORBEARE,
TO DIGG THE DVST ENCLOASED HEARE:
BLESE BE Y^E MAN Y^T SPARES THES STONES,
AND CVRST BE HE Y^T MOVES MY BONES.

(1053)

Happy couples join hands in courtyard dance (1027)

Elizabethan People

THE HUSTLE AND BUSTLE of Elizabethan London, easily observed in old prints of the period, show a populace full of vitality, freedom and abandon. Even the peasantry, fettered with social strictures and often bound to the soil, seemed to have a hearty enthusiasm for life. At least part of the spirit of this age stemmed from the knowledge, shared by lord and peasant, that their queen loved them. Elizabeth, who never married, declared herself wedded to her country. "My love is for my people," she said. "I pray to God whoever succeeds me be as careful as I am." Elizabeth was not remote, but highly visible as she made frequent "progresses" through the countryside. Her care for the people, uncommon among European monarchs, helped generate an intense national pride.

- **A** Nonesuch Palace. Queen's favorite residence (1028)
- **B** Courtier (1029)
- **C** Peasant (1030)
- **D** Elizabethan lady (1031)
- **E** Equestrian couple (1032)
- **F** Morris dancer (1033)

(1034)

(1035)

(1036)

(1037)

(1038)

(1039)

(1040)

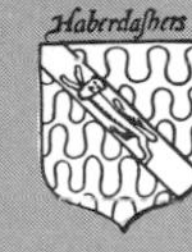

(1041)

(1042)

(1043)

(1044)

(1045)

OF ONE OF THE ABOVE 12 COMPANIES IS THE LO. MAYOR OF THE CYTE COMENLY CHOSEN

Work and Pleasure

London watchman warns to extinguish lights (1046)

A clothes stall, or "frippery" (1047)

Vendor of oysters (1048)

An alehouse with chickens roasting on a spit (1049)

Ratcatcher offers his service (1050)

Elizabethan love symbolism: the smitten heart (1051)

A peddler of notions and nick-nacks (1052)

"Make hay while the sun shines;" 16th century popular saying (1053)

The Women Take Pride

"Theyr breasts they embuske up on hie and theyr round Roseate buds immodestly lay foorth . . ." (1054)

A scold wearing a brank (1055)

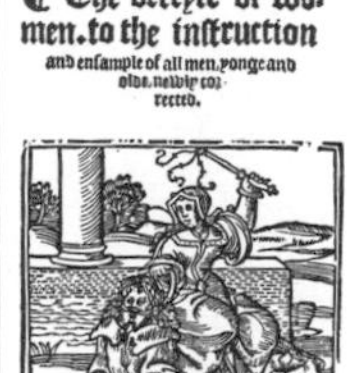

The decepte of women, to the instruction and ensample of all men, yonge and olde, newly corrected.

Bossy women chided in tract (1056)

Death of the Queen—an effigial monument (1057)

ENGLISH WOMEN quite naturally took pride in the sex of their ruler, copying Elizabeth's vanities, and finding in her a new basis for self-assurance and daring. In fashions (unmarried women dressed with chest bare and often exposed their breasts) and in mingling more freely with men, they showed a new independence—or impertinence, according to the men, who complained at the change.

"I commend you to the assured protection of the Almighty who will preserve you safe, I trust in all felicity."

The state carriage of Queen Elizabeth (1058)

A
B
C
53
7
A
B
C

CHAPTER 4

The 17th Century

Absolutism

Rise of Science

The New World

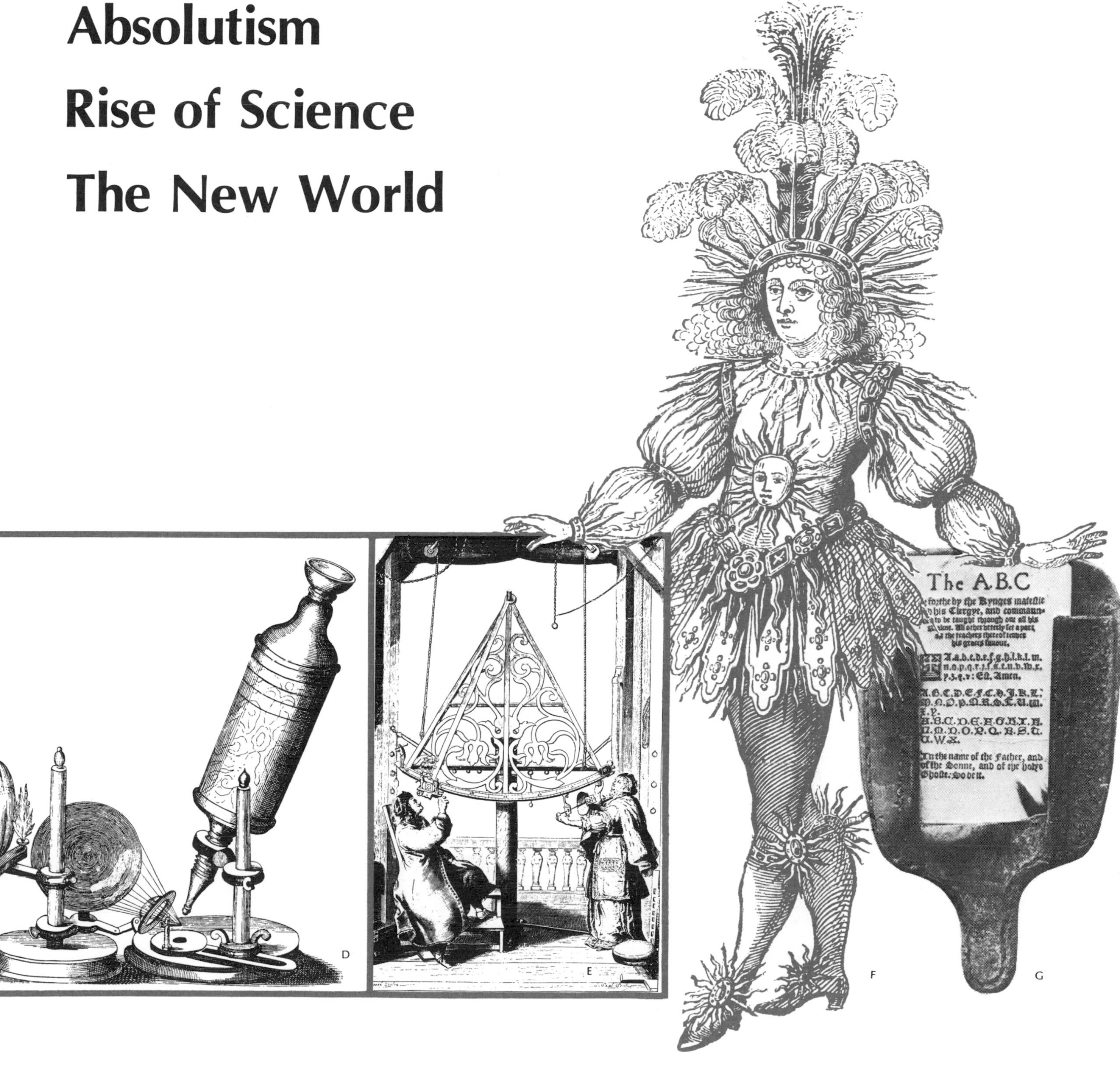

THE 17th CENTURY

Harbingers of doom: stars portend war, famine, death (1059)

BEGUN as a religious conflict between Protestants and Catholics, the Thirty Years' War (1618-1648) soon deteriorated into a power struggle between Europe's monarchies. As French armies attacked their archrivals, the Hapsburgs, whose dynasty linked Austria, Germany and Spain, the Danes and Swedes jockeyed for territory; and even smaller states, only marginally involved, were eager for territory and spoils.

This unsavory contest was fought almost entirely on German soil. For three decades, waves of marauders devastated the German countryside, more intent on looting than fighting. By 1632 a deadlock had been reached. None of the combatants was strong enough to win—weak enough to surrender. Yet sixteen more years of shifting alliances and betrayals followed before a settlement was reached.

THROUGH THE PEACE OF WESTPHALIA in 1648, France emerged as Europe's dominant power, fulfilling Richelieu's dream, while the Hapsburg empire declined. Germany itself, its populace reduced by one-third, its countryside ravaged, was split into more than 300 principalities, and Holland, freed from Spanish rule, prospered anew.

Macabre mood expressed in 17th century engraving (1060)

Closing of church in Branau (1061) and Prague defenestration (1062) signalled war's beginning.

Rennselaerwyck cannon made in 1630 (1063)

Magdeburg after siege was sacked and 25,000 citizens died (1064)

Power-mad Wallenstein, Austrian General (1065)

Death of Gustavus Adolphus set back Protestant cause (1066)

(1070)

Peace of Westphalia, 1648 ended 30 Years War (1067)

Mazarin, France's cunning peace negotiator (1068)

Post rider brings joyful news of peace, but Germany lay in shambles (1069)

Brutality... Demoralization

With no central authority to keep order, robbers roamed highways, killing innocent travelers (1071), pillaging the countryside without mercy (1072)

Pitiful war veterans begging alms (1073)

Conniving war profiteers—Kippers and Wippers—defraud populace with worthless money (1074)

Armies Back Power Politics

THE LONG WAR, aided by the dawning age of science (Galileo first worked out the parabolic trajectory of the cannonball), stimulated both new skills in military tactics and the development of new weaponry. It also gave impetus to trade, since the support of armies needed hard cash and supplies.

Musketeer with weapons and low match (1076)

Ballistic experts test effectiveness of cannon. 17th-cent. engr. (1075)

Ballistics engineers were siegecraft experts (1077)

Amphibious attack vehicle fords streams, moats (1078)

Air-inflated bed to enhance the soldiery's comfort (1079)

Soldier of fortune flaunts lance (1080)

Diagrammed trajectories for 16th-cent. artillery (1081)

Absolutism

The Sun King's motto (1083)

DURING A REIGN of fifty-four years, Louis XIV gathered into his hands as no monarch before the total management of his country. Ignoring challenges from the nobility, he directed all affairs of state—military, economic and social. The King's personal whims governed everything from battle plans to the minutiae of the ballet, and the court revolved around him like a constellation girdling the sun. Although his reign brought economic ruin to France, its artistic heritage was glorious.

Louis XIV sun motif (1082)

The Sun King impersonates himself in ballet (1085)

Louis XIV. Sculpture by Lorenzo Bernini (1084)

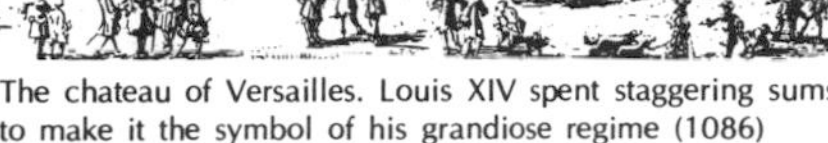
The chateau of Versailles. Louis XIV spent staggering sums to make it the symbol of his grandiose regime (1086)

Court assembles for King's levée (1087)

Nobleman greeted by a subaltern (1088)

Louis XIV conferring with his ministers in house of Madame de Maintenon (1089)

King dances during court ball (1090)

Billiards was Louis XIV's favorite game. He preferred it to cardplaying (1091)

Madame de Maintenon, wed to king in 1783 secret ceremony (1092)

Literature

THOUGH THE MASSES were not involved, French literature and theatre reached new heights under the Sun King. Louis, it was said, devoted half his working day to stagings of dramas, pageants and ballets which were an integral part of the court entertainment. Except for Molière's comedies, most court presentations were stately and rigid.

Moliére as actor in one of his own plays (1093)

Title page of Moliére's published works (1094)

Moliére and troupe during court performance (1095)

Paris bookstore. Engraving by Abraham Bosse (1096)

La Fontaine, whose fables have become classics (1097)

Racine refined tragedy and made it subject to classic rules (1098, 1099)

Comic figure from French stage (1100)

Music

MERGING DRAMA with ballet and music, Jean-Baptiste Lully developed the French court opera to reflect Louis XIV's taste for lavish entertainment. The human voice was now matched with the violin, which became dominant in ensemble music so that the "first violinist" assumed the role of today's conductor.

Royal court violinist for Louis XIV (1101)

Lully, creator of French opera (1102), breaks baton in rage while conducting orchestra (1103)

A musical instrument salesman. Engraving by Lamerssin (1104)

Grotesque violinist: ballet figure (1105)

Title page, Lully ballet (1106)

MERCANTILISM . . .
The Gospel of Hard Cash

LOUIS XIV, holding tightly the political reins of his nation, mastered its economy with equal strictness. Embracing mercantilism, which had been in the ascendancy since the Renaissance, Louis turned the state itself into a giant entrepreneur, setting precepts for money management, export and international trade. Jean Baptiste Colbert, the genius of this planned economy, pursued the acquisition of gold bullion with almost paranoiac abandon. The system depended upon the manufacture of goods for export, and the importation of raw materials, at low prices, from the colonies. These materials were then transformed into marketable commodities and resold at higher prices to the colonists.

Le Diable d'Argent (1107)

Counting money, basis of fiscal power (1108)

Tax payments enforced to finance war machine (1109)

Louis XIV inspects artworks made for export trade (1110)

Colbert created revenue-producing industries (1111)

Typical harbor from which exports to colonies brought influx of money that strengthened mercantile state (1112)

Banks were under state control (1113)

Colonial Markets

WITHOUT FURTHER EXPANSION of France's overseas possessions, Louis XIV's economic policies could not succeed, since the colonists must supply both raw materials and willing markets (later not so willing) for the mother country's products. Spain and England had thus far shown more exploratory zeal than France, but Louis remedied this by building an empire, "New France," across Canada—later challenged by England.

LaSalle, assigned by King to establish new colonies in America (1114, 1115), traveled the Mississippi, claimed land for France. Later went to Texas (1116)

Father Marquette pioneered French colonization (1117)

Quebec, France's first foothold in the new world (1118)

Frontenac, the governor (1119)

Sieur de Cadillac obtained land grant that became city of Detroit (1120)

Father Jogue, missionary and colonizer (1121)

Lord's Splendor — Peasants' Misery

THE COST OF LOUIS XIV'S GLORY was great human misery, among victims of conquests abroad and peasants exploited at home. Taxes nearly doubled in France (from 85 million to 152 million livres annually) to support the extravagance of his court. Farmers suffered double jeopardy, subject both to royal tax collectors and to their feudal lords.

Peasant farmyard with a poor French family (1122)

Hall of Mirrors, Versailles—scene of lavish royal pageantry that cost the state millions (1123)

Coiffure for lady aristocrat (1124)

Beggar woman and children (1125)

"Spider and fly." Imperious lord accepts peasant's taxes (1126)

Farmer struggles for a scant livelihood (1127)

French court feasting at a sumptuous banquet (1128)

A lady of the court (1129)

"The Baker's Family," one of the realistic masterpieces by Jean Michelin (1130)

A courtier (1131)

(1132)

THE RISE OF SCIENCE

First printed map of the moon, from *Selenographia*, 1647 (1133)

Pendulum clock to measure pulsebeat of the sick (1134)

PARADOX MARKED THIS AGE. The senseless intrigue and depravity of the Thirty Years' War was countered by the rise of science and a new spirit of rationalism. As observation and experiment replaced blind reliance on authority, promises only dimly perceived in the Renaissance were fulfilled. Scientists set out to formulate the natural laws governing the universe, while philosophers explored the structure of society.

Amateur scientists banded together to form learned societies, pursue research (1135)

Kepler found the laws of stellar motion (1136)

Hevelius charted moon surface (1137)

Milton visits Galileo in his Padua observatory (1138)

Pendulum used in time studies (1139)

Galileo condemned by Inquisition for advocating Copernican System (1140)

Refracting telescope was improved by Newton (1141)

Newton in garden studies the fall of apples (1142)

Galileo on Pisa Tower studies gravity (1143)

Spectral experiments reveal to Newton deeper insights into nature of light and color (1144)

ON THE POLITICAL FRONT, the power-hungry gave free play to their baser instincts; but scientists began to form non-political fraternities whose only aim was the pursuit of truth and the free dissemination of knowledge. The Royal Society of London, founded in 1662, was the first, but similar groups soon formed in Italy, Sweden and Germany.

Isaac Newton heads Royal Society, leading science group (1146)

Astronomical instrument and sun face (1145)

Otto von Guericke, in public demonstration of Magdeburg hemispheres, proves nature of vacuum, air pressure (1147)

Pascal's giant barometer shown in Rouen (1148)

Experiment by Nicholas Culpepper, herbalist and quack salver (1149)

Robert Boyle, English chemist, paragon of the new interest in natural sciences (1150, 1151)

John Napier invented logarithms, used "Napier's bones" (1152)

Leibnitz investigated the laws of calculus (1153)

At age 19, Pascal invented adding machine (1154)

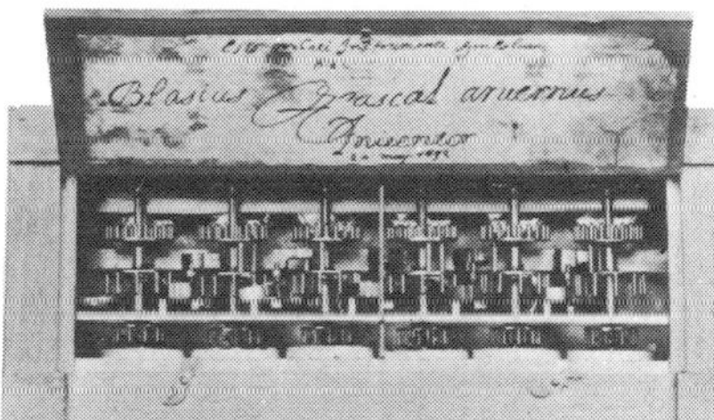
Replica of Blaise Pascal's calculator. Seventy copies were built; some given as royal gifts (1155)

Landscape artist uses camera obscura (1156)

FRANCIS BACON saw the new science as the source of all of man's power. Some of that power became evident in the seventeenth century as science advanced. New instruments (the thermometer, telescope, pendulum), coupled with an experimental approach toward uncovering the laws of nature, gave man a new and reliable power over more of his environment.

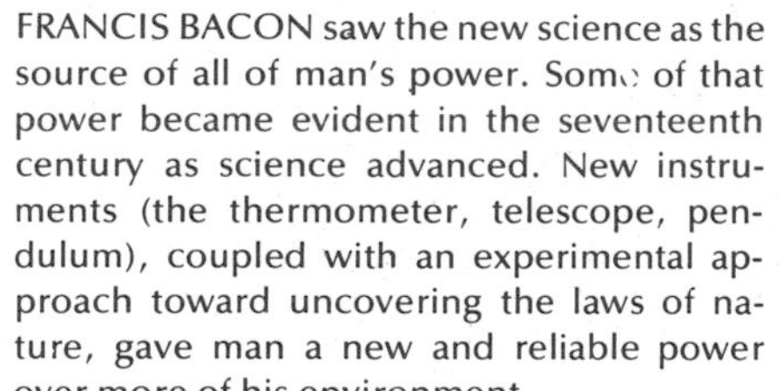
Slide projector invented by Athanasius Kircher, Jesuit scientist (1157)

Torricelli measures air pressure with his mercury barometer (1158)

Papin's "digester," presaging today's pressure cooker (1159)

Newton proposed steam wagon to work by jet propulsion (1160)

Knowledge Expanded by Experiment

AS GALILEO, KEPLER AND NEWTON formulated new laws governing the physical universe, medicine began to re-examine biological and anatomical dogmas. Man, the microcosm of the universe according to Renaissance beliefs, must surely reflect the workings of the cosmos.

Such insights marked a turning point for medicine. The research of Galileo and Newton on gravity pumps and valves enabled Harvey to discover and demonstrate the circulation of the blood, and Sanctorius to demonstrate the effects of metabolism. Although medical dogmas still held sway, the seventeenth century made a fine beginning in experimental medicine.

Metered man: the 17th century was the age of measurement (1161)

Sun thermometer invented by Robert Fludd (1162)

Pancreas secretions of dog were examined by De Graaf (1163)

Anton Leeuwenhoek (1164) used microscope (1165), singlehandedly started science of Bacteriology.

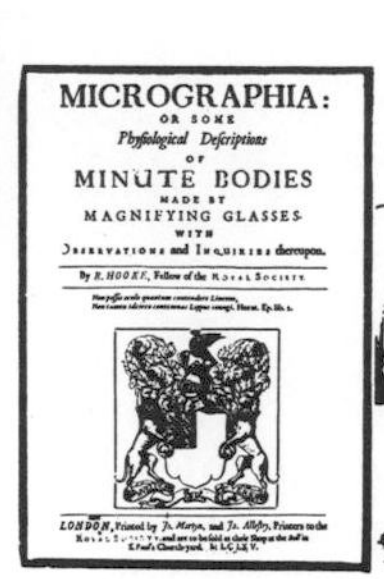

Title page of Robert Hooke's work (1166). With his microscope (1167) he discovered cells (1168) as the basic units of living tissues.

Medicine Advances

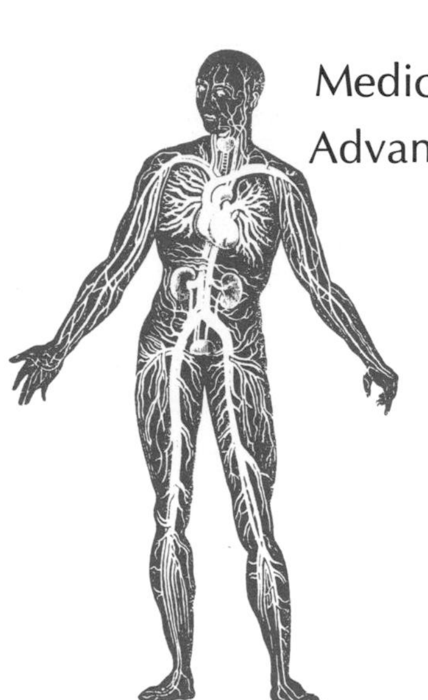

Harvey's circulatory system, the basis of modern cardiology (1173)

Weight watched before and after meal (1169)

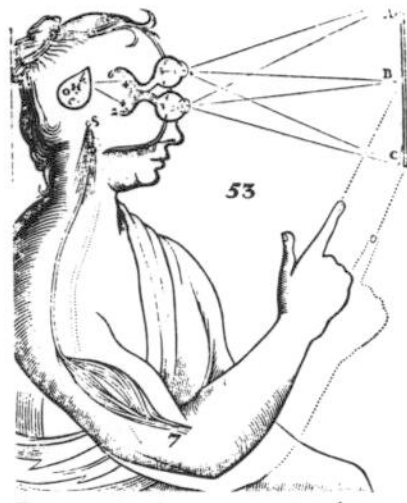

Descartes's concept of how vision works (1170)

Harvey explains his theory to King Charles I (1171)

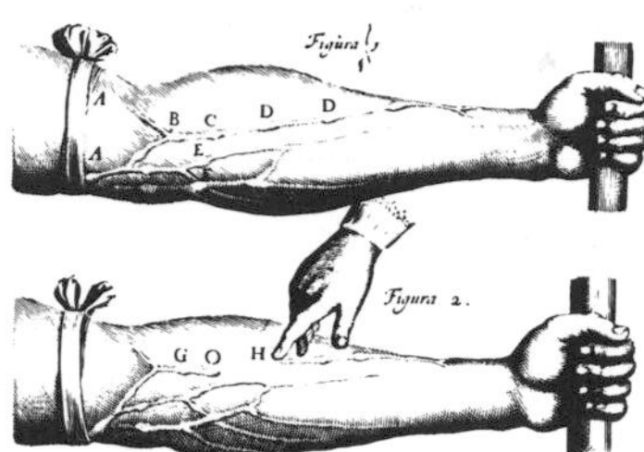

Harvey's treatise *De Motu Cordis* explained valve action (1172)

Dutch anatomists demonstrate the pump action of the heart (1174)

Blood transfusion as a therapy was first explored by Sir Christopher Wren (1175)

17th century surgeon and instruments (1176)

Aneurism treated in a doctor's office (1177)

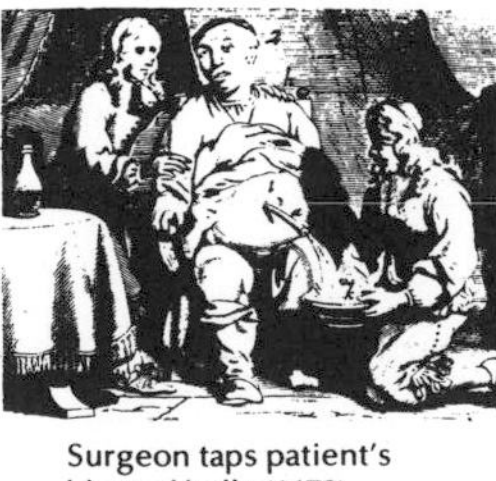

Surgeon taps patient's bloated belly (1178)

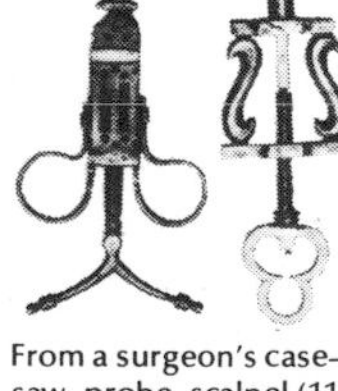

From a surgeon's case—saw, probe, scalpel (1179)

¶ Of *Cancer*, which the Greekes called *Carsinoma*.

Although that Cancer bee comprehended under the schirrous humors, yet there is great difference: for Cancer is a hard tumor, round, unequall, with dolour, punction and pulsation: it groweth sooner than Schir, and hath great baines about it, tumified and swelled, full of melancholicke blood, and doth resist being prest upon. It is sometime taken for the sore of a beast, and is called Cancer, because it sticketh fast to the part as doth the Crabbe-fish to that which it taketh hold on; as also the baines which are about are like unto Crabsfeet. It is of colour livide or blacke, hard, and rough, eating, gnawing, and going, like unto the Crabbe-fish

Pa.li.4.cap.24 Denifinition.

Cel.li.5. ca.28

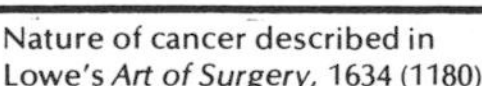

Nature of cancer described in Lowe's *Art of Surgery*, 1634 (1180)

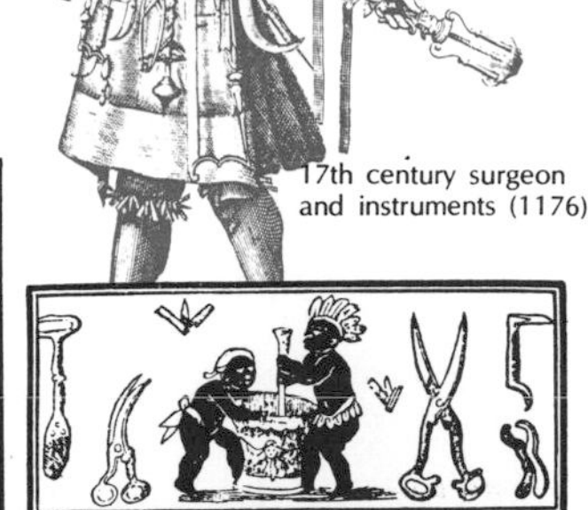

Handbill of Dr. Case, a notorious London quack doctor and charlatan (1181)

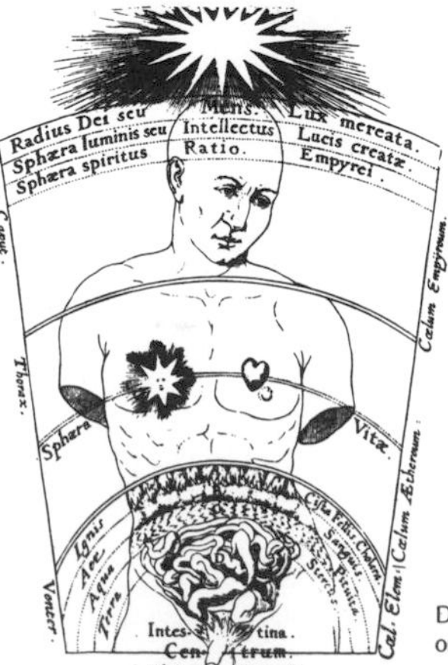

Dr. Fludd's cosmic anatomy relates organs to spheres of heaven (1182)

Removing cancerous breast, 1644 (1183)

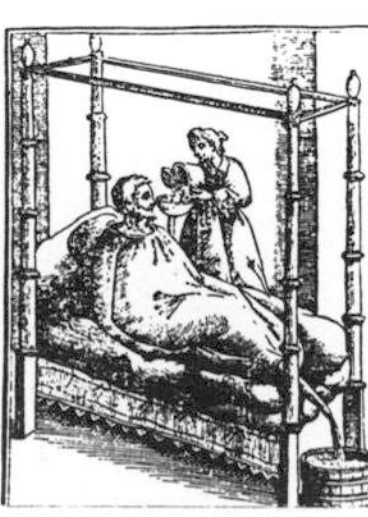

Enema to relieve constipation (1184)

Fever fought with cold-water bag (1185)

Quack pretends to "cut stones" (1186)

Suggestion to distill flighty ideas from patient's head via heat therapy (1187)

All ye that are of *Venus* Race,
Apply your selves to Dr. *Case*;
Who, with a Box or two of PILLS,
Will soon remove your painfull ILLS.

(1181A)

England

Kingly Absolutism Gives Way to Constitutional Monarchy

James I: "The King rules by divine right" (1188)

Gunpowder Plot to kill king at Parliament opening (1189)

Guy Fawkes was caught on Nov. 4, 1605; hanged (1190)

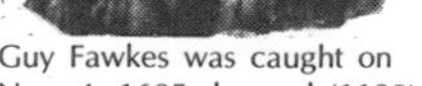

*Our father which art in heauen, hallowed be thy name.
10 Thy kingdome come. Thy will be done, in earth, as it is in heauen.
11 Giue vs this day our daily bread.
12 And forgiue vs our debts, as we forgiue our debters.
13 And lead vs not into temptation, but deliuer vs from euill: For thine is the kingdome, and the power, and the glory, for euer, Amen.

The Lord's Prayer from the King James Bible prepared during his reign (1191)

Puritans, persecuted, left for Holland, then America (1192)

English inn during the Purital period where men met, discussed religion, politics (1193)

Charles I opposed the Commons, lost (1194)

King Charles defies the Parliament (1195)

Royalist pamphlet puns, bemoans King confined to Isle of Wight (1196)

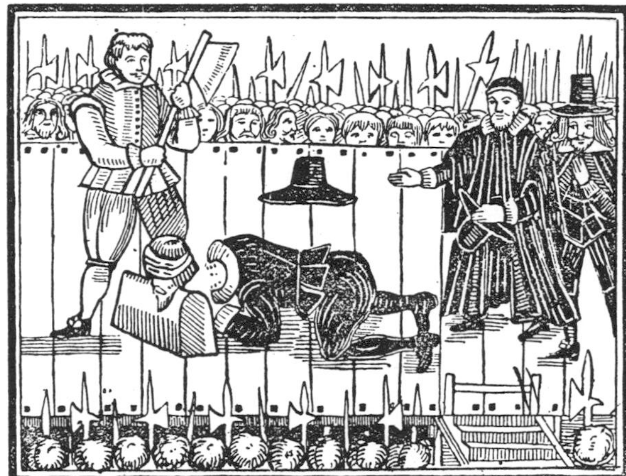

Charles I, condemned by court of 67 judges (regicides) as "Tyrant Traitor, Murderer and Public Enemy," was beheaded in 1649 (1197)

The Protectorate

"Take away that bauble!" Cromwell dissolves Rump Parliament, 1653 (1198)

Oliver Cromwell as Lord Protector of England (1199)

Cromwellian army officer (1200)

AS THE GRIP of absolute monarchy tightened around France, the English across the Channel rejected the doctrine of the "divine right of kings." When James I (son of Mary Stuart) ascended the English throne in 1603, he acted as an absolute monarch. His son, Charles I, dissolved Parliament and tried to rule without it, but the conflict soon burst into open warfare, with the Puritan Oliver Cromwell leading the parliamentary forces. Charles's Cavalier army was defeated; the King was captured, tried and executed.

CROMWELL'S RULE was wise but stern. After his death the English sought a more liberal leader; they found him in Charles II. Charles was witty, fun-loving and too smart to repeat his father's mistakes, but his son James, a Catholic, resumed the battle with Parliament and was forced to abdicate. Parliament then invited James' daughter Mary and her husband, William of Orange, to rule jointly but subject to the approval of Parliament.

Cromwell refuses the crown and title of King offered by Parliament, 1657 (1201)

The Great Seal of England during Protectorate (1202)

The Restoration

Charles II was wiser than his father (1203)

"He rode into the capital with people shouting for joy, roads strewn with flowers, fountains running with wine" (1204, 1205)

Charles II lifted Puritan restraints; gaiety prevailed at his court (1206)

Nell Gwyn, the King's prime paramour (1207)

Scene from Restoration comedy, 1685 (1208)

The Glorious Revolution

Coronation of James II in Westminster, 1685 (1209)

Embattled king escapes to France (1210)

William of Orange was called to England to be a joint sovereign with Mary, daughter of James II (1211, 1212)

The Bill of Rights secured England's constitutional monarchy (1213)

(1214)

LONDON WAS HIT by two natural catastrophes at the time when England was embroiled in political turmoil. In 1664 the Great Plague struck the city killing about 70,000 citizens. Then, a year later, the Great Fire devastated London destroying three-fourths of its buildings. But the city rose again in renewed splendor of brick and stone, thanks to the architectural genius, Christopher Wren.

Meanwhile, doctrinaire disputes between Royalists, Presbyterians, Puritans and other splinter groups acted as fuel to inflame the best literary minds. (The climate of controversy brought about such classics as Milton's *Aeropagitica,* a plea for freedom of the press, and John Hobbes' *Leviathan,* a political tract that accepted the natural depravity of man and sought to restrain his base instincts through an oligarchic government.) But the spirit of the plain people was not neglected: in *Pilgrim's Progress,* John Bunyan gave them an allegory of Christian life, rich in imagery yet simple and full of power. It became a great influence on English speech.

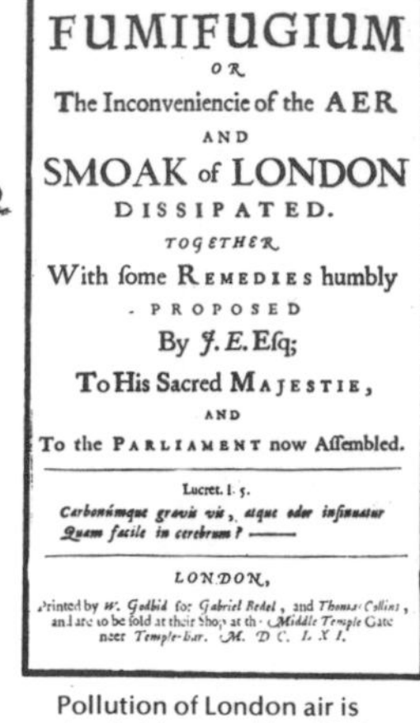
FUMIFUGIUM
OR,
The Inconveniencie of the AER
AND
SMOAK of LONDON
DISSIPATED.
TOGETHER
With some REMEDIES humbly
PROPOSED
By J. E. Esq;
To His Sacred MAJESTIE,
AND
To the PARLIAMENT now Assembled.

LONDON,

Pollution of London air is decried in pamphlet (1215)

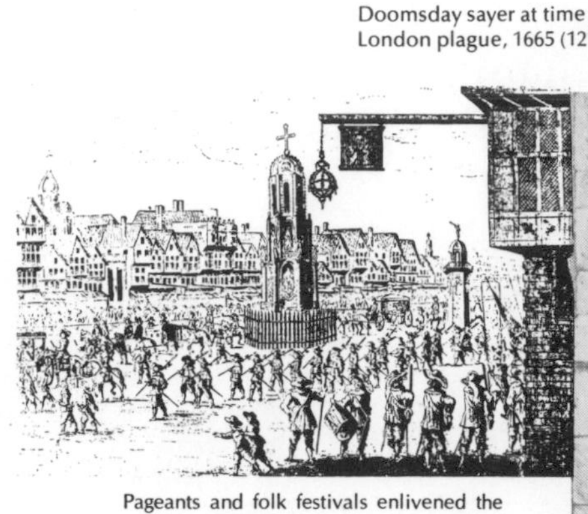
Pageants and folk festivals enlivened the London streets. Cheapside, 1640 (1216)

Doomsday sayer at time of London plague, 1665 (1217)

Doctor wears protective anti-plague garb (1218)

"Bring out the dead"—plague scene. Fires were to fight miasmic air (1219)

Doctors probe for plague's cause (1220)

London ruins after Great Fire, which killed thousands (1221)

LONDON TRADESMEN
Shoemaker (1222)
Box-maker (1223)
Chicken man (1224)
Tailor (1225)
Soap-boiler (1226)
Button-maker (1227)

Coffee served to literati (1228)

Milton pleads for a free press (1229)

Milton, grand stylist—master of abuse (1230)

Leviathan–Hobbes recommended aristocratic government in 1658 treatise (1231)

John Locke founded Empiricism (1232)

John Dryden was England's poet laureate (1233)

From John Bunyan's *Pilgrim's Progress:* The man with the muck rake (1234)

Pilgrim in sight of Heavenly City (1235)

Samuel Pepys, diarist of London life (1236)

Izaak Walton wrote *The Compleat Angler* (1237)

Title page of humorous novel of 1676 (1238)

CHAPBOOKS

For the less literate, printers published chapbooks—small pamphlets that catered to the popular taste, moral tracts, wonder stories. One of their attractions, aside from price, was their woodcuts.

Criminal punished (1239)

Usury condemned (1240)

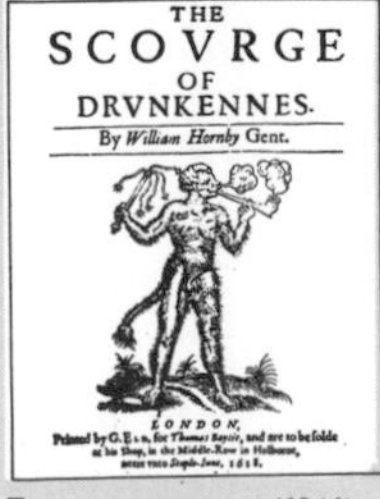
THE
SCOVRGE
OF
DRVNKENNES.
By William Hornby Gent.

LONDON,

Temperance tract (1241)

Witches dancing at night (1242)

The ox turned farmer (1243)

Dutch map-making flourished, combining a mastery of nautical science and the craft of printing (1244)

Holland

Sea Power • Trade • Prosperity

AFTER EIGHTY YEARS of rebellion against Spanish conquest, Holland won its freedom at last in 1648, and soon became a great commercial power. Establishing colonies as far apart as the East Indies, South Africa and the New Netherlands, Dutch merchants acted as international entrepreneurs (we would call them "middlemen"), buying such products as tea, cotton and sugar in bulk, then parceling them out to world markets.

Waerachtigh Verhael
Van de Schip-vaert op
OOST·INDIEN,
Ohedaen
By de acht Schepen, onder den Heer Admirael *Jacob van Neck*, en de Vice-Admirael *Wybrand van Warwijck*, van Amsterdam gezeylt in den jare 1598.
[illegible]
De Voyagie van Sebald de Weert, naer de Straete
MAGALANES.

t'AMSTELREDAM,
[illegible] Anno 1648.

TITLE FROM HARTGERT'S SERIES OF DUTCH VOYAGES. AMSTERDAM, 1648.

East India Company—core of Dutch overseas trade (1245)

Amsterdam became Europe's busiest harbor as Holland vied with England for colonies (1246)

Tulip-mania speculation in flower bulbs which sold for as much as $5200 (1247)

Venturesome merchants primed prosperity. Rembrandt (1248)

Ship (1252)

Salting herring: fisheries flourished, provided work for many (1249)

Amsterdam bourse became important center for international trade (1250)

Draper's shop: textiles were best quality (1251)

Holland trained skippers for its large fleet (1253)

Explorers ride turtle on Mauritius Island (1254)

(1255)

Science and Art Flourish

THOUGH COMFORTABLE in their new-found wealth, Holland's burghers favored an unpretentious way of life clearly reflected in their art. Subjects drawn from daily life in streets, harbors, marketplaces, ghettoes and churches were treated with a "glorious simplicity," and painted on a small scale suitable to the simple homes of the Dutch merchants. By mid-century, Amsterdam alone had 300 painters (Rembrandt among them) but only 70 butchers.

Holland's political climate was tolerant: Descartes and Spinoza found refuge there, and medical students flocked to Leyden University. Holland in the 17th century was a vigorous and progressive center of culture.

Even the lowly showed an interest in foreign lands, geography. Sketch by Rembrandt (1256).

Leyden Anatomical Theater, study center for Dutch doctors and artists (1257)

Rembrandt sketched "Polish Rider" (1258)

Baruch Spinoza, Dutch-Jewish philosopher (1259)

Descartes took refuge in tolerant Holland (1260)

Hugo Grotius explored international law (1261)

Leyden University had one of Europe's great libraries (1262)

Brueghel sketch of theater in village marketplace (1263)

Fruit seller offers wares on frozen canal (1264)

Jovial Dutch burghers enjoy a family musicale (1265)

Rembrandt frolicking with Saskia (1266)

Artist Jan Steen and family enjoy stay in Dutch tavern garden (1267)

Dutch windmills. Drawing by Cornelis Visscher (1267A)

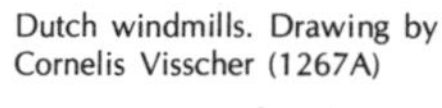

The New World

IN AMERICA, the 17th century was a period of settlement by English colonists, from Virginia to Massachusetts Bay. Widely scattered at first, these settlements prospered and expanded, gradually developing a sense of political and commercial identity, and setting the stage for the emergence of a new nation in the next century.

Virginia

THE BEGINNINGS were not so auspicious, however. The first permanent settlement, Jamestown, was beset by disease, starvation and hostile Indians. Then, John Rolfe's discovery of a method of curing tobacco changed Virginia's fortunes.

The Cataract of NIAGARA some make this Water-Fall to be half a League while others reckon it no more than a hundred Fathom.

First published view of Niagara Falls includes detailed scene of busy beaver colony (1268)

NOVA BRITANNIA.
OFFERING MOST
Excellent fruites by Planting in
VIRGINIA.
Exciting all such as be well affected
to further the same.

LONDON
Printed for SAMUEL MACHAM, and are to be sold at
his Shop in Pauls Church-yard, at the
Signe of the Bul-head.
1609.

Englishmen invited to settle in Virginia colony (1269)

A Virginia Indian warrior with hunting bow (1270)

Jamestown, England's first permanent settlement in North America (1271)

Virginia Co. Seal (1272)

English merchant ships entering Jamestown harbor (1273)

John Smith, explorer of Virginia (1274)

Captain Smith captured (1275). His rescue by Pocahontas (1276) is not fully authenticated.

Rationing corn during winter of 1609 (1277)

Discovery of Roanoke's lost colony, founded by Sir Walter Raleigh (1278)

"Respectable young women" arrive "for wives of settlers"—1621 (1279)

First slaves sold in Jamestown (1280)

Virginia: meeting of first Legislative Assembly in America, 1619 (1281)

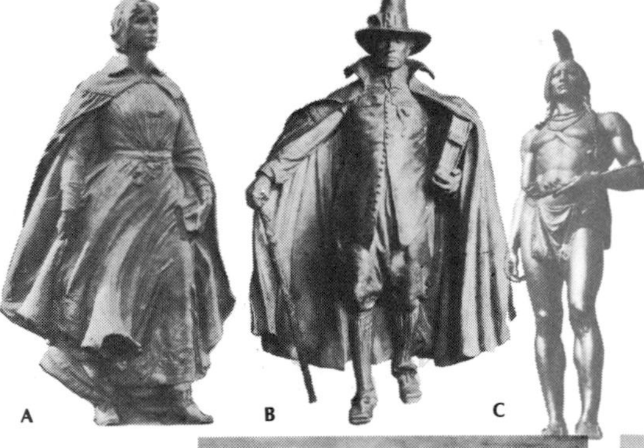

Massachusetts — The Bay Colony

BEFORE DISEMBARKING at Provincetown harbor in 1620, the 102 settlers on the *Mayflower* signed a compact providing for government by the will of the majority. Massachusetts thus became the first American example of democracy. The Bay Colony grew rapidly, yet not all newcomers remained there. The Pilgrim fathers insisted that their church was the only legitimate one, compelling dissenters to seek refuge elsewhere.

Mayflower Compact provided colony with democratic ground rules (1285)

The *Mayflower* lands at Cape Cod in 1620 with 120 passengers on board (1286)

First Thanksgiving, Plymouth, 1623. The Indians stayed three days (1287)

Autocratic Governor John Winthrop (1288)

SEVERAL
Laws and Orders
MADE AT A
GENERAL COURT

Massachusetts laws: 1679 collection (1289)

Reconstruction of first Town House of Boston, 1657 (1290)

Roger Williams (1291), banished from Salem for democratic views, fled and founded Providence, Rhode Island (1292)

Rhode Island

BANNED FROM SALEM in 1635 for his "newe and dangerous opinions," Roger Williams purchased land from the Indians in Rhode Island, naming his settlement Providence.

Connecticut

THOUGH HE OPPOSED Roger Williams' tolerance of religious dissent, Thomas Hooker favored democracy, and he wrangled a charter from Charles II granting Connecticut freedom to manage its own affairs.

The Charter Oak stood until 1856; said to have been 1,000 years old (1295)

Thomas Hooker led congregation of hundred families to settle in Connecticut (1293)

Colonists, fearful that their charter be revoked, hid it in an old oak tree (1294)

A "Pilgrim Maid." Statue in Plymouth, Mass. (1282)
B "The Puritan." Sculpture by Saint-Gaudens (1283)
C Chief Massasoit, friend of the Pilgrims (1284)

Niew Amsterdam - New York

First representation of a native New Yorker (1299)

Henry Hudson receives commission from Dutch East India Co. to find northeast passage (1296). Instead, he went northwest and in the *Half Moon* (1297) found, explored the Hudson River.

Indian Village of the Manhattan tribe as it looked before Dutch colonized Nieuw Amsterdam (1298)

Peter Minuit buys Manhattan island from the Indians for $24 (1300)

Oldest known view of the island of Manhattan with Fort Nieuw Amsterdam, 1651 (1301)

Dutch burgher enjoys life, prosperity (1302)

Dietrich Knickerbocker, father of New York (1303)

A New York night watchman rattles his warning (1304)

Albany with aristocratic Dutch architecture (1305)

Peter Stuyvesant (1306), the harsh, despotic director of Nieuw Amsterdam, had to yield to the English in 1664 (1307)

N.Y. City receives charter, 1686 (1308)

ORIGINALLY SETTLED by the jovial Dutch, New York's early history reflects a certain bonhomie. Established as a trading post rather than a religious refuge, the city surrendered without a fight when the English, under Richard Nicolls, arrived in 1664. Nieuw Amsterdam was renamed New York, honoring the Duke of York, later James II. It was England's must crucial acquisition in the New World.

Seal of the City of New York (1309)

Pennsylvania

WILLIAM PENN received a grant of land (Pennsylvania) as payment for the vast debts owed by the King to his father. An idealist and a Quaker, he considered the new colony a "holy experiment" where persecuted minorities could live in freedom. Philadelphia became a symbol of "America to be."

Wm. Penn signs treaty with the Indians (1310)

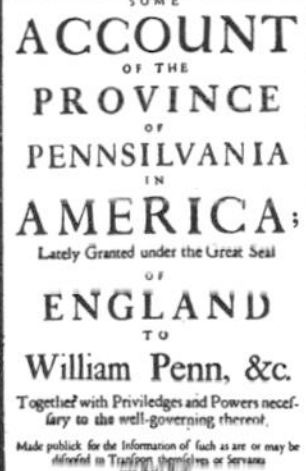

SOME
ACCOUNT
OF THE
PROVINCE
OF
PENNSILVANIA
IN
AMERICA;
Lately Granted under the Great Seal
OF
ENGLAND
TO
William Penn, &c.

A 1681 report on Pennsylvania (1311)

Penn laying out the city of Philadelphia in 1682 (1312)

First Meeting House of Quakers, the Society of Friends (1313)

Colonists & Indians

European traders buy sugar cane from Indians. Engr., Cuba map (1315)

◀The native and the immigrant (1314)

Maize, the Indians' staple food (1316)

Mohawk Indians in daily chores (1317)

Settlers are attacked, massacred by band of vengeful Indians (1318)

The Jamestown Massacre of 1662 almost annihilated the Virginia colony (1319)

A Wampum: Indians' medium of exchange (1320)
B Peace pipe: used to pledge good will (1321)
C Scalp: proudly flaunted victory trophy (1322)
D Tomahawk was buried as peace gesture (1323)
E Fanciful print of Indian queen (1324)

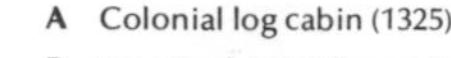

A Colonial log cabin (1325)
B New Engl. brick house (1326)
C Typical salt-box house (1327)
D James River mansion (1328)
E Hand forged hammer (1329)
F Massachusetts ax (1330)
G Rolling pin (1331)
H Spinning wheel (1332)

HUTS, CAVES AND CRUDE LEAN-TOS had to do for the first colonists, until ground could be broken and tools and materials assembled. Log cabins, first introduced by the Scandinavians who settled along the Delaware River in the mid-1600s, used easily available materials and provided both sturdy shelter and protection from hostile Indians.

As the pioneers took root and survived hardship, they began to build more elaborate homes. These reflected the styles of the mother country, be it England, Holland or Germany. Most colonial homes boasted only the barest of necessities, with perhaps a few treasures brought across the sea. Though the wealthy built mansions, in general the American colonists lived in a cultural atmosphere more crude than that of Western Europe.

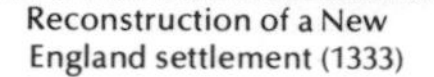

Reconstruction of a New England settlement (1333)

Building of stockade was a communal task (1334)

Housing

Slat-back chair (1335)

Foot warmer (1336)

Fireplace—interior of log cabin. Return from the hunt (1337)

Young lovers communicate via "whispering rod" (1338)

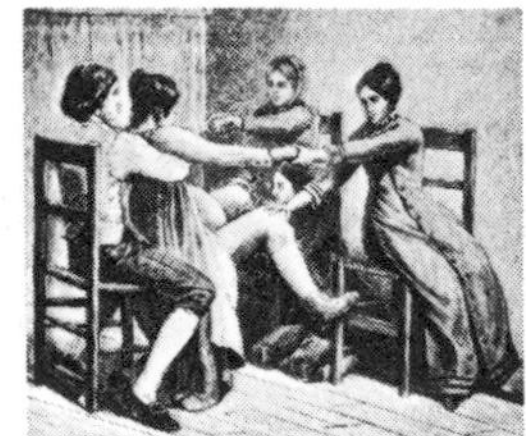

Husband holds wife as neighbors assist with childbirth (1339)

Trundle bed to accommodate mother and child (1340)

Second Plymouth Meeting House, built in 1683 (1341)

Religion

ESCAPE FROM RELIGIOUS PERSECUTION was a prime motivation in settling the new continent, and thus religion remained a dominant force. The New England Puritans believed themselves to be carrying out a divine mission, establishing a community ruled by God's word, with the minister assuming a pivotal position. Often intolerant of others, they persecuted Catholics, Quakers and Baptists with a very un-Christian fanaticism.

Puritans called to church (1342)

Sunday service in New England church, from Hawthorne's *Scarlet Letter* (1343)

Anne Hutchinson, heretic, banned from Boston (1344)

Anne Dyer, a Quaker, led to gallows, hanged for sedition in 1660 (1345)

Quakers opposed Puritan theocracy, were ruthlessly persecuted (1346)

John Bowne's house where Quakers met secretly (1347)

(1348)

Witchcraft

IN 1692, the grim atmosphere of the Puritan village of Salem was shocked by a witch mania. A group of young women had shown fits of hysteria and alleged that witches were the cause. The clergy readily took up the case, and by inflammatory sermons fanned the people's fears. A special court prosecuted hundreds in an atmosphere of terror, and nineteen persons were hanged. Afterward some of those who had been taken in by the "witch delusion" courageously confessed that it had been a tragic mistake.

The Wonders of the Invisible World:
Being an Account of the
TRYALS
OF
Several Witches,
Lately Excuted in
NEW-ENGLAND:
And of several remarkable Curiosities therein Occurring.
Together with,
...
...ON MATHER.

(1350)

Cotton Mather, theologian, and witch hunter (1349)

Arresting a witch. Print by Howard Pyle (1351)

Trial of George Jacobs, witch, in 1692 (1352)

On the way to execution. Nineteen witches were hanged (1353)

He that don't learn his A B C, For ever will a blockhead be:

New England primer, 1690. Estimated sale - three million copies (1354)

Puritan fathers suffered no nonsense (1355)

Dame school taught pre-school children how to read (1356)

Hornbook was carried by children on belt (1357)

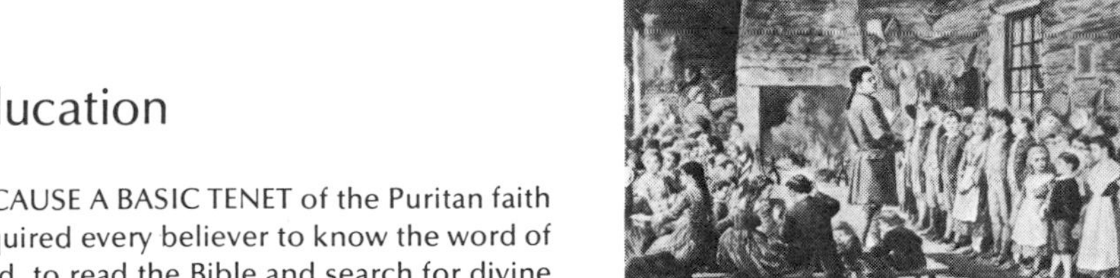

One-room colonial school house. Communities with hundred or more families provided teachers (1358)

Hornbook had transparent horn cover in front (1359)

Teacher gives spanking with hornbook (1360)

Education

BECAUSE A BASIC TENET of the Puritan faith required every believer to know the word of God, to read the Bible and search for divine guidance therein, the Puritans placed a premium on literacy, for literacy meant piety. The young must be taught to read and write, in order to lead a God-fearing and useful life in the community. Education, then, held a high priority, and Massachusetts merely reflected Puritan conviction when, in 1647, the colony decreed that each town of 100 or more households must establish a grammar school at its own expense.

To prepare students for the ministry, three universities were founded in colonial times: Harvard, William and Mary, and Yale.

The first college in America was founded in 1636 (1361), then named for its benefactor, John Harvard (1362)

Conn. Collegiate School, chartered in 1701 (1363), was named after Elihu Yale in 1718 (1364)

Trades • Occupations

Shopkeeper discusses piece goods with a client (1365)

Newly arrived imports are bartered in trade (1366)

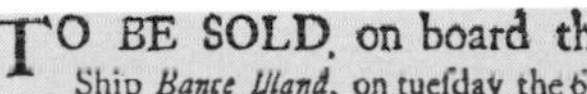

TO BE SOLD, on board the Ship *Bance Ysland*, on tuesday the 6th of *May* next, at *Ashley Ferry*; a choice cargo of about 250 fine healthy

NEGROES,

just arrived from the Windward & Rice Coast. —The utmost care has already been taken, and shall be continued, to keep them free from the least danger of being infected with the SMALL-POX, no boat having been on board, and all other communication with people from *Charles-Town* prevented.

Austin, Laurens, & Appleby.

N. B. Full one Half of the above Negroes have had the SMALL-POX in their own Country.

Poster offers African slaves, most of them immune to smallpox (1367)

Slave dealer auctioning off slaves on coast of Africa for shipment to America (1368)

(1372)

Farmer pounding corn in hollowed trunk. Branch acts as spring (1369)

Due to lack of passable roads, boats conveyed goods (1370)

Tobacco was Virginia's most remunerative crop (1371)

Mail carrier on plank-covered road. The delivery of lett was once a week in summer, fortnightly in winter (137

Drying fish on the coast of Maine (1374)

Town crier chanted news, announced laws (1375)

Candlemaker's shop. Franklin started in this trade (1376)

Simon Willard, skilled clock-maker and inventor (1377)

Iron works were restricted by the English government (1378)

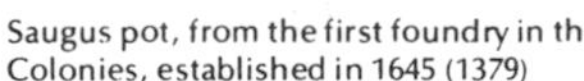

Saugus pot, from the first foundry in the Colonies, established in 1645 (1379)

A

B

C

CHAPTER 5

The 18th Century

Ancien Régime
Enlightenment
Classicism

THE EIGHTEENTH CENTURY

The young Dauphin, soon to be Louis XV (1382)

Philippe, Duc d'Orléans, the pleasure-loving regent (1383)

Mme. de Pompadour, powerful mistress of Louis XV (1384)

Mme. Du Barry was vulgar, wildly extravagant (1385)

Interior of a salon in Louis Seize style (1386)

Medieval strip farming endured in France (1380)

French lord is paid tax by a tenant farmer (1381)

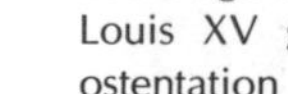

LOUIS XIV had made France a leading power, and his court a paradigm of glory, but his successor, his great-grandson Louis XV, "lacked the talent to use his talent." Inheriting the Sun King's throne at the age of five (under the regency of Philippe II, Duc D'Orléans), Louis XV grew up to devote his life to pleasure, reveling in ostentation and dalliance. Despite its glamour, the French court hovered near financial disaster; and the new king, failing to defend adequately his American possessions, lost them to England in the Seven Years' War, plunging French prestige to its nadir. Whether the king or Madame Pompadour uttered it, the saying "Après moi le déluge" was prophetic.

Mississippi Bubble

THE SPECULATIVE SCHEMES of John Law, a Scottish adventurer, lured thousands of Frenchmen to Louisiana. But when the "Mississippi Bubble" burst in 1720, France's hope for easy prosperity vanished, and the screws of taxation were tightened again.

A Wind merchant and bubbles (1387)
B John Law, wild speculator (1388)
C Hunchback becomes desk (1389)

A Lady's Day

(1390)

Morning call: lady is helped by two maids to arise (1391)

Breast care: a critical look at size of "rosebuds" (1392)

A maid attends her lady emerging from bath (1393)

Hairdresser powders lady's coiffure (1394)

Husband applies force to "tighten up" wife (1395)

Ornate coiffures were maddest whim (1396)

A lady promenades with her lackey (1397)

Rococo couple meets for morning airing (1398)

"Le Souper Fin"—fashionable courtiers enjoy a gourmet repast after a busy, unproductive day (1402)

Aristocratic couple visits stylish shop (1400)

Ceremony of undress at the end of the day (1401)

(1399)

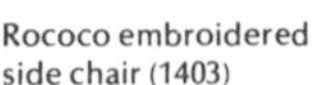

Rococo embroidered side chair (1403)

A Cupid, the reigning deity (1404)

B Messenger of love (1405)

L'Amour Toujours

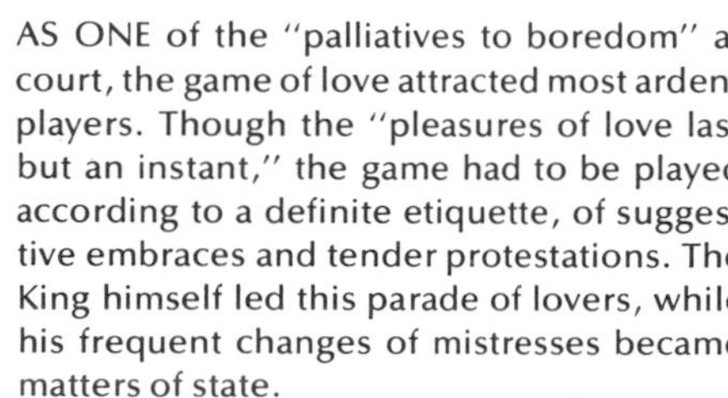

AS ONE of the "palliatives to boredom" at court, the game of love attracted most ardent players. Though the "pleasures of love last but an instant," the game had to be played according to a definite etiquette, of suggestive embraces and tender protestations. The King himself led this parade of lovers, while his frequent changes of mistresses became matters of state.

Elopement via parachute (1409)

"Declaration of Love." Painting by Jean François Troy (1406)

Ardent courtier plays rococo Romeo (1407)

Ce qui est bon à prendre est bon à garder (1408)

Dancing parties on opulent scale filled the evenings of society: Le Bal Paré (1410)

Aristocrat at his toilette, assisted by maids (1411)

Indiscreet intruder caught in lady's boudoir (1412)

Casanova—sensualist, rage of society (1413)

Rococo Art

AMATORY DALLIANCE is pictured with more candor in rococo art than in written chronicles. In gallant genre paintings, lovers were transposed into a world of fable "under the garlands and celestial blues of an eternal spring." To adorn the salons and ladies' boudoirs, there were many fine artists, Watteau their unsurpassed master.

Rococo beau in bucolic setting makes love while strumming the lute (1414)

Camergo, invented ballet slipper (1415)

After-dinner backgammon game. Engr. by Moreau le Jeune (1416)

"The Swing"—Fragonard's famous painting (1417)

Louise O'Murphy, Louis XV's mistress. Ptg. by Boucher (1418)

Shop of art dealer Gersaint. Painting by Watteau (1419)

Watteau—luminary of rococo art, with portfolio (1420)

Apprentices grind paint in artist's studio (1421)

Porcelain (1422)

The Other Side of the Coin

(1423)

Mother with children in French peasant hut (1424)

Itinerant family with *lanterna magica* (1425)

Three orders of French society: cleric robs noble, gives alms to poor (1426)

ONLY THE UPPER LEVEL of French society was mirrored by most artists—a thin veneer covering the wretchedness of France as a whole. The mass of people struggled through a life of hardship, undernourishment and toil. Always in fear of famine or disease, the peasants inhabited filthy, lice-infested hovels, in dramatic contrast to the splendors of the court.

Distribution of the King's bread causes riot (1427)

Traveler's carriage stopped by suppliant beggars (1428)

Peasant lad climbs into a girl's cottage loft (1429)

(1430, 1431, 1432, 1432A)

Enlightenment

VOLTAIRE WAS IN THE FOREFRONT of those who attacked the abuses of the *ancien régime*. In novels, letters and pamphlets he ridiculed the prejudices and cruelties of the absolutist aristocracy. He used the weapon of cynicism with biting skill, becoming the Enlightenment's most powerful protagonist.

The *philosophes* of the Enlightenment held that men had sufficient reasoning power to solve rationally not only their own problems but those of society. As Newton found laws governing the universe, the new "philosophers" believed there were laws governing the social structures of family, town or nation. The challenge was to discover this key to social reform.

The changing moods of Voltaire (1433)

Voltaire. Bust by Houdon (1434)

Voltaire at his writing desk. Porcelain caricature ca. 1773 (1435)

Voltaire leads intellectuals in discussing timely issues (1436)

Voltaire having breakfast and conversation with friends (1437)

Voltaire's dear friend, Mme. Chatelet (1438)

Fernay, Voltaire's château in the South of France (1439)

CANDIDE, OU L'OPTIMISME, TRADUIT DE L'ALLEMAND DE MR. LE DOCTEUR RALPH. MDCCLIX.

Candide: terse satire of optimism (1440)

Montesquieu (1441), in caricature (1442), influenced politics and the law.

Rousseau holding his *Social Contract* (1443)

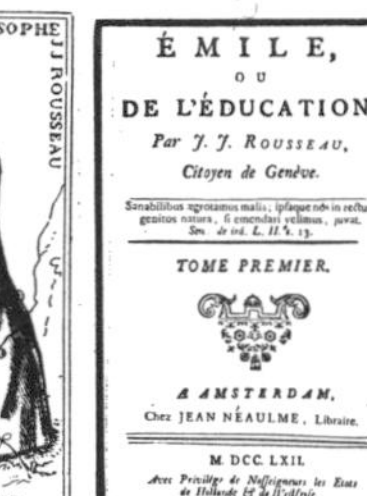

ÉMILE, OU DE L'ÉDUCATION. Par J. J. ROUSSEAU, Citoyen de Genève.

TOME PREMIER.

A AMSTERDAM, Chez JEAN NÉAULME, Libraire.

M.DCC.LXII.

Rousseau's theories on education (1444)

Contrat Social burned by censors in 1763 (1445)

Rousseau in his dying hour once more exults in Sun of Enlightenment: "more light" (1446)

The Encyclopedists

TO FORM A RATIONAL SOCIETY, said the *philosophes,* ignorance and superstition must be replaced by knowledge, authoritarian precepts by rational ideas. With that aim, writers, *philosophes* and amateurs banded together for inspired disputes. Led by D'Alembert and Diderot, a group of writers produced a monumental project—the *Encyclopédie . . . des sciences, des arts et des métiers.* No other work contributed as much to the advancement of the Enlightenment.

Encyclopedists in editorial session plot to produce Enlightenment's masterwork (1447)

Jean Le Rond d'Alembert, (1717?-1783) (1448)

Encyclopédie editor Denis Diderot (1449)

La Mettrie thought man is a machine (1450)

De Holbach, radical materialist (1451)

Baron von Grimm and friend Diderot (1452)

Café Procopé—cradle of Enlightenment (1453)

Marquis de Condorcet died during Revolution (1454)

Argricultural techniques depicted in typical plate from *Encyclopédie* (1455)

Toward Technology

BESIDES THEORETICAL DISCOURSES, Diderot's *Encyclopédie* presented a vast array of factual data, and a unique pictorial inventory of trades practiced in mid-century France. It shows a surprisingly high level of technical knowledge, with pictures of water wheels, mining establishments and machine tools. The detailed, heavily annotated drawings stimulated the development of technology leading to the Industrial Revolution.

Large power wheel turns lathe for pewterware (1456)

Early industrial mechanization in gold purifying mill: mine products are washed, pulverized, mixed with mercury (1457)

Water remained primary power source until advent of steam (1458)

Treadmills utilized the manpower available in prisons (1459)

Grindshop shows laborers compelled to work in precarious position (1460)

Equine power plant in use in a French beer-brewing establishment (1461)

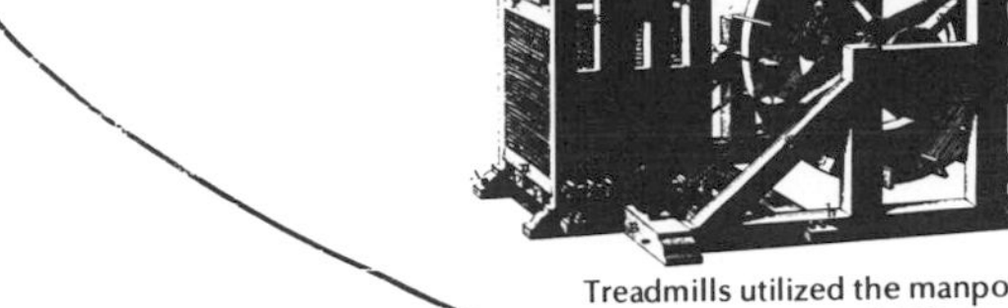

Electrical Discoveries

THE IDEAS OF THE ENCYCLOPEDISTS were eagerly accepted in the American colonies, for much of the New World adventure was powered by the vision of a new, rationally ordered state. The greatest figure of the Enlightenment in America was Benjamin Franklin, a famed experimental scientist whose interests, too, were encyclopedic.

Franklin during kite experiment (1462)

EXPERIMENTS
AND
OBSERVATIONS
ON
ELECTRICITY,
MADE AT
Philadelphia in *America*,
BY
Mr. BENJAMIN FRANKLIN,
AND
Communicated in several Letters to Mr. P. COLLINSON of *London*, F. R. S.

LONDON:
Printed and sold by E. CAVE, at *St. John's Gate*. 1751.
(*Price 2s. 6d.*)

Franklin's electrical research (1463) made him important figure in science (1464)

Coulomb: electrical unit named after him (1465)

Umbrella equipped with a lightning rod (1466)

Luigi Galvani (1467) thought animal tissues produced electrical current (1468). His experiments were ingenious (1469) but his deductions were wrong.

Volta (1470) invented the voltaic pile (1471)

Electric therapy became *au courant* but proved ineffective (1472)

Friedrich Mesmer (1473), father of hypnotism, held séances around table of tubs charged with animal magnetism (1474)

Scanning the Heavens

Nebular hypothesis of origin of the universe (1475), theorized by Kant, was given scientific form by Pierre Laplace (1476)

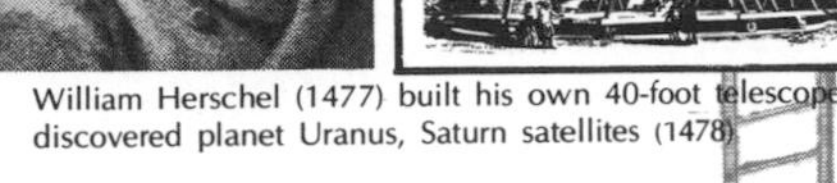

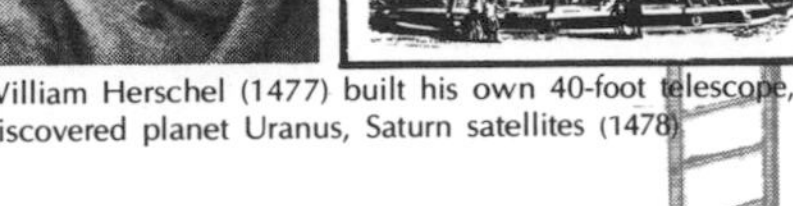

William Herschel (1477) built his own 40-foot telescope, discovered planet Uranus, Saturn satellites (1478)

Astronomer at Greenwich Royal Observatory (1479)

Halley predicted comet's reappearance (1480)

Halley's comet returns every 76 years (1481)

The grand orrery by Rowley (1482)

The Structure of Plants

RATIONAL ORDER was an obsession of the 18th century. The search for ordering principles was pursued everywhere—in the cosmos, in human society, in the kingdom of nature. A generation of dedicated scientist-classifiers evolved viable, practicable methods for identifying and classifying known plants, and the great number of new ones discovered in the New World. Especially important to the life sciences was Linnaeus' binomial nomenclature system.

◀ 18th century microscope (1483)

Observing plant growth in biology laboratory (1484)

Microscope as an aid in research (1485)

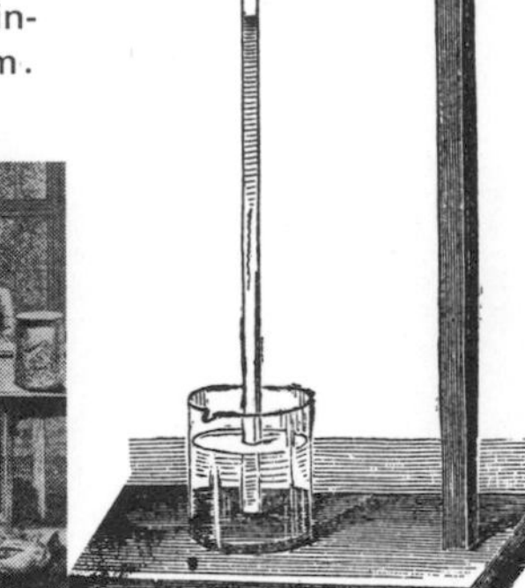
Hales observed movement of the sap in plants (1486)

Botanists on field trip study many plant species (1487)

Hales measured blood pressure in the vein of a horse (1488)

Linnaeus devised plant order (1489)

Buffon wrote 44-vol. *Natural History* (1490)

Withering found digitalis (1491) in the foxglove plant (1492)

Spallanzani explored animal digestion (1493)

Jussieu brings cedars of Lebanon to Paris Jardin des Plantes (1494)

Boerhaave lectures on medical botany to Leyden students (1495)

Erasmus Darwin, evolutionist (1496)

Von Haller studies plants of Alpine region (1497)

Hutton studied earth (1498)

Lamarck theorized influence of environment on rise of plant, animal species (1499)

Expanding Scope of Medicine

MEDICINE, too, came under the sway of the new rationalism. John Hunter, a pioneer in anatomical transplants and an avid student of the laws of human growth, conducted research in the techniques of dissection. Humanitarianism, an outgrowth of the Enlightenment, led medicine to expand its scope—to include the poor, the crippled, political prisoners—and to extend care to children, whose medical needs had long been ignored. In this field Edward Jenner achieved the greatest triumph, by discovering and demonstrating the mechanics of vaccination, freeing children and many adults from the perennial threat of smallpox.

Jenner's discovery of vaccination freed mankind of scourge of smallpox (1500)

Anatomy instruction advanced, spurred medical progress (1501)

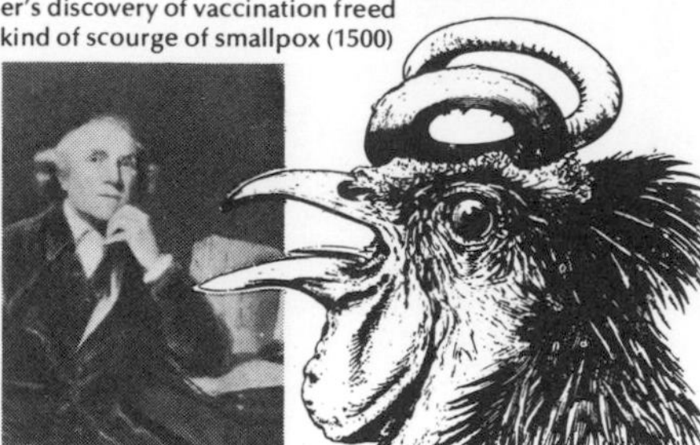
John Hunter, experimental surgeon (1502), first to explore organic transplants (1503)

Rowlandson cartoon: "The Dissecting Room" (1504)

Graverobbers provided anatomy schools with cadavers (1505)

Boerhaave prescribed starvation diet for body's ills (1506)

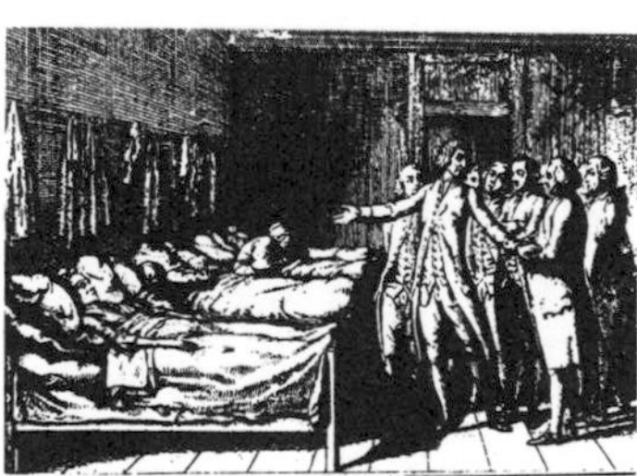
Enlightenment brought better sick-care, bedside teaching (1507)

Dr. J. Lind conquered sailors' scurvy by introducing lemon juice (1508)

Doctors, moved by humanitarianism, gave charity care to the lowly (1509)

Jenner's first vaccination on a boy of six (1510)

Doctor protects patient and defies death with enema syringe (1512)

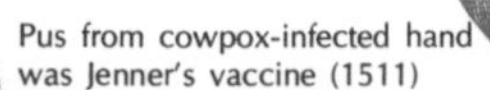
Pus from cowpox-infected hand was Jenner's vaccine (1511)

Chemistry Prime Mover of Science Progress

NEWTON'S DISCOVERIES of laws of physics, demonstrations of principles, and orderly analyses of matter and energy became exemplars for the physical sciences in the 18th century. He also added considerably to the knowledge of mathematics and calculus, and along with inventing the sextant, devised navigational aids to predict the changing positions of the moon and the stars.

A similar course was set in chemistry by Lavoisier, who proved that matter is never lost and that chemical substances react in predictable ways. He drew up a table of known elements and initiated modern chemical nomenclature by providing names, such as oxygen and hydrogen.

Apparatus used for experiments on compression of gases (1513)

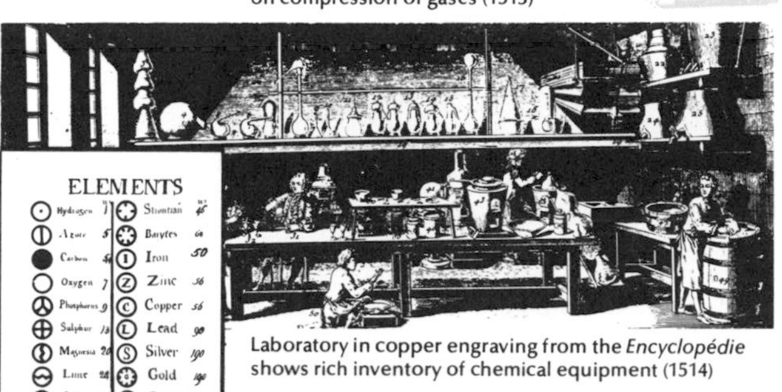

Laboratory in copper engraving from the *Encyclopédie* shows rich inventory of chemical equipment (1514)

◀Dalton's atomic table, basis for atomic theory (1515)

John Dalton, chemist and physicist (1516)

Joseph Priestly (1517), chased from England (1518), came to America; discovered oxygen but did not know this.

Cavendish, hydrogen discoverer (1519)

Lavoisier made chemistry a science, was guillotined in Revolution (1520)

Mme. Lavoisier helps her husband (1521)

Réaumur devised first thermometer (1522)

B. Thompson, Count Rumford (1523)

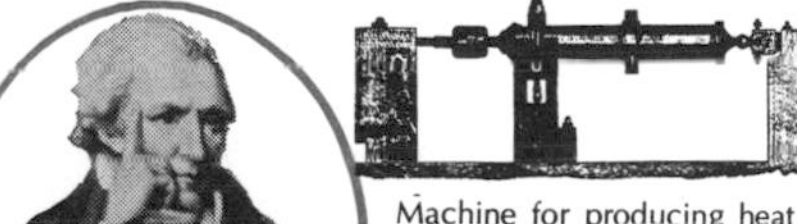

Machine for producing heat developed by Rumford (1524)

Inventions Discoveries

Cugnot first to construct automobile like car. It had three wheels (1525)

Visual telegraph was introduced by Claude Chappe (1526)

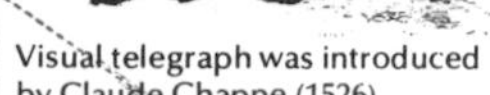

Solar reflector used by Buffon, nature encyclopedist (1527)

Montgolfier bros. tried heat-filled bags (1528)

First balloon ascension was staged at Versailles (1529)

Attempts to fly were widely ridiculed (1530)

Balloon being filled with hydrogen (1531)

Montgolfier's balloon (1532)

THE FIRST PRACTICAL BALLOON, devised by the Montgolfier brothers and filled with hot air, went aloft in 1783, but in the same year J. A. C. Charles launched a balloon filled with a lighter-than-air substance, discovered by Cavendish but named "hydrogen" by Lavoisier.

Two-legged press, prone to dodge censor (1533)

The Spread of Knowledge

NEW KNOWLEDGE was no longer confined to the community of scholars, but spread widely via the printed word. Book publishers supplemented scholarly works with tracts and pamphlets popularizing new discoveries, new insights and social theories. Journals grew in number, with more than 900 founded between 1750 and 1789, while the catalogue at the Leipzig Book Fair tripled in the two decades after 1776. "If error and prejudice have forged the chains of the people," said Baron de Holbach, "science, reason, truth will some day break them."

Magic-lantern show: educational (1534)

Secrets of nature discussed. Teacher uses educational pictures (1535)

Balladeer accompanied by fiddler pleases the newshungry (1536)

Man reads newspaper to attentive friends (1537)

Enlightenment brought bonanza of books (1538)

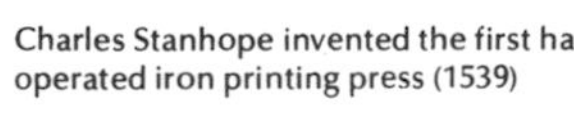

Charles Stanhope invented the first hand-operated iron printing press (1539)

Crown used when Prussia became a kingdom (1540)

Enlightened Despotism

Pageant during coronation of first Prussian king, Frederick I (1541)

ENLIGHTENMENT ALSO CAME to Europe's absolute rulers, who began to think of themselves as servants of the people —"enlightened despots." Prussia moved first in this direction as the Great Elector and later King Frederick William I overhauled the machinery of government, furthered trade and manufacturing and tolerated religious dissidents, particularly skilled artisans.

The Great Elector (1542) was victorious against the Swedes in 1675 at Fehrbellin (1543)

Introduction of potato raised Prussia's living standard (1544)

Giant Guards: the pride of Frederick William I (1545)

Enraged king thrashes a negligent official (1546)

Refugees from Salzburg are welcomed in Prussia (1547)

Frederick William convened "Tobacco Parliament" (1548)

King supervises building of city of Berlin (1549)

Frederick William I was a temperamental king (1550)

Frederick William, noticing his subjects dodging him on the street, struck one of them with his whip and cried, "Damn it! I want you to love me."

Frederick the Great

THE MODEL OF THE ENLIGHTENED despot is Frederick II, a brilliant military tactician victorious against great odds in his drive to expand Prussia. Opposed by Russia, Austria and France in the Seven Years' War, he won the prize he craved—Silesia.

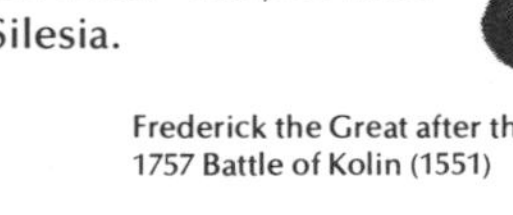

Frederick the Great after the 1757 Battle of Kolin (1551)

Austrians surprised at Lissa Castle (1552)

Victory at Rossbach, 1757, over French, Austrian armies (1553)

Drillmaster enforces army discipline (1554)

Loved by his people, King Frederick was called "Der alte Fritz" (1555)

BUT FREDERICK WON his epithet "the Great" through an unprecedented rapport with his people. Though he sometimes ruled harshly, it was for their benefit. Calling himself "the State's first servant," he labored endlessly to make Prussia a more prosperous and more tolerant state.

Frederick the Great inspects the building of a new dam in Eastern Prussia (1556)

Refugee weavers present their products (1557)

Weaving establishment of Salzburgers visited by Frederick the Great (1558)

Berlin's porcelain was well-known export article (1559)

A MAN OF HIGH CULTURE as well as a military genius, Frederick was sensitive to intellectual currents and intrigued by the philosophy of Enlightenment. He drew Voltaire (at least temporarily) into his entourage, and his court at Sans Souci excelled in music and philosophical discussion.

Frederick and Voltaire (1560)

The Flute Concert at Sans Souci. Frederick was a fine flutist; he also composed (1561)

Bach playing before King in Potsdam castle (1562)

Sans Souci palace at Potsdam where Frederick entertained notables (1563)

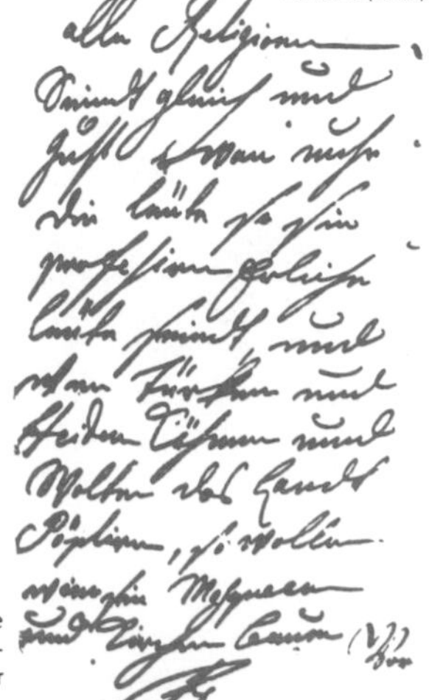

One of Frederick's marginal notes: "All religions are good only if their adherents are good . . . . If Moslems came to my country I would build mosques for them. . . ." (1564)

Austria

Joseph II and his mother, Empress Maria Theresa (1565, 1566)

MOST BENEVOLENT of the enlightened despots was Joseph II of Austria, who tried endlessly to resolve conflicts and remedy injustices pervading the Austrian Empire. He issued 6,000 orders and had 11,000 laws passed during his reign—freeing slaves, abolishing judicial torture, improving the condition of Austrian Jews.

Emperor Joseph visits peasant family (1567)

His experiments with new ways of ploughing (1568)

Count Kaunitz, progressive Austrian minister (1569)

Joseph II encouraged his ministers to institute many reforms (1570)

Russia

Catherine II, Empress of Russia (1579)

EVEN THE HARSH, oligarchic structure of the Russian Empire showed some response to the Enlightenment. Peter the Great's attempts to Westernize it brought a few superficial changes. When Catherine II ascended the throne, she called Voltaire her Master and the *Encyclopédie* her Bible. Catherine purchased Diderot's library and bought quantities of European art, but (as she admitted to Diderot) there was a wide gulf between drafting enlightened charters and instituting the reforms. She was opposed by a reluctant aristocracy, whom she needed to bolster her regime. Her expansionist policies were more successful, resulting in the partition of Poland and gain of the Crimea.

Peter the Great began to westernize Russia (1571)

Cutting beard, introducing Western customs (1572)

Peter studied shipbuilding incognito in Holland (1573)

Czar founded city of St. Petersburg (1574)

Russian peasants live in dismal hut (1575)

Prince Potemkin, favorite of Catherine the Great, wielded great political power (1576)

Village built by Potemkin feigned prosperity (1577)

Russian serf and his wife brutally beaten by estate supervisors (1578)

Pugachev's revolt misfired (1580)

Catherine II converses with Denis Diderot (1581)

Queen encouraged science (1582)

Kosciusko, Polish patriot, came to America (1583)

Two-headed eagle of Russian Empire (1584)

Poland partitioned by great powers (1585)

Orlov, Queen's paramour (1586)

Catherine steps over imperial rivals to Constantinople (1587)

Dashkova headed Academy of Arts, Sciences (1588)

France

Louis XVI saw need for reform (1589)

EARLY IN HIS REIGN, Louis XVI of France encouraged his ministers to introduce financial reforms, but the French economy was near collapse and threats of bankruptcy forced him to retreat before opposition from both court and Queen. Not popular uprisings alone, but the aristocracy's hostility to the crown brought about the Revolution.

King in quest of popular support gives alms to needy French peasants (1590)

Populace in hope of reform acclaims King, Finance Minister Turgot (1591)

Turgot introduced reforms opposed by nobility (1592)

Louis XVI and Finance Minister Necker face coffers emptied by nobles and clergy (1593)

Humanitarianism

"Thus do the useful end their days." Sketch by Francisco Goya (1594)

Rebirth of charity: family feeds beggar (1595)

LOGICAL ANALYSIS and reasoned discussion were not the only aspects of Enlightenment philosophy. Believing in the perfectibility of man, humanitarians attacked social injustice with feeling and passion, directing attention to the miserable plight of the outcast, stimulating a strong surge of compassion for the maligned or neglected. The abject condition of prisoners, the inhumane treatment of the insane, the cruel neglect of the unwed, all found staunch and eloquent spokesmen. Those who considered slavery, of any kind, a blotch on the human conscience, now raised their voices.

Prison Reform

Pamphlet exposing cruelty inflicted in English debtors' prisons (1598)

Prisoner enchained in cell of a London jail (1596)

Beccaria, Italian jurist and prison reformer (1597)

Windmill ventilator invented by Stephen Hales, installed at Newgate Gaol, London, in 1752. It drastically reduced deaths among prisoners due to noxious air (1601)

John Howard, English humanitarian, exposed inhumanity of prisons and sped reforms (1599)

(1600)

The Insane

Bedlam, London's madhouse, epitome of uproar and confusion (1602)

Spasmodic sufferer put in chains (1603)

Dr. Benjamin Rush's tranquilizer (1604)

Madwoman visited in Bedlam Asylum (1605)

Dr. Philip Pinel freed insane at Bicêtre Hospital, Paris, where they were abused, kept in chains (1606, 1607)

Child Welfare

Child is brutally beaten by French schoolmaster (1608)

Tight swaddling caused many infant deaths (1609)

Doctor gives child hefty enema (1610)

ORTHOPÆDIA:
Or, the ART of
CORRECTING and PREVENTING
DEFORMITIES
IN
CHILDREN:
By such MEANS, as may easily be put in Practice by PARENTS themselves, and all such as are employed in Educating CHILDREN.
To which is added,
A DEFENCE of the ORTHOPÆDIA, by way of SUPPLEMENT, by the AUTHOR.
Translated from
The *French* of M. ANDRY,
Professor of Medicine in the ROYAL COLLEGE, and Senior Dean of the Faculty of PHYSICK at *Paris*.
IN TWO VOLUMES.
Illustrated with CUTS.
VOL. I.
LONDON:

Posture of children examined in orthopedics treatise (1611, 1612)

Swiss pedagogue Johann Pestalozzi explored child's psyche, applied Rousseau's theories (1613, 1614)

Thomas Coram started child-welfare movement (1615)

London's Foundlings Hospital, for whose benefit Handel wrote *The Messiah* (1616)

London beggar woman gives up child (1617)

Despondent unwed mother murders her child (1618)

Unwed mother discretely gets rid of unwanted infant (1619)

Religious Revival

*"Do all the good you can
by all the means you can
in all the ways you can
in all the places you can."*
—John Wesley

AN EMOTIONAL NEED not filled by the established church or by the rationality of enlightenment philosophy led to the formation of new religious groups. A longing for spiritual rebirth and a more personal rapport with God characterized the Quakers, the Pietists of Germany, the Moravians of Bohemia. All preached a contemplative religion permitting "every soul to find God in its own way." When John Wesley, an Anglican priest, embraced this belief, he was forbidden to preach in his own church. Wesley preached 40,000 sermons and traveled 250,000 miles to spread "Methodism," formally established as a new church in 1784.

Hell-and-brimstone preachers found ready response (1620)

John Wesley: God is in man's own heart (1621)

Whitefield gave emotion-filled sermons (1622)

Charles Wesley preached to Indians; wrote over 6,500 hymns (1623)

John Wesley made trip to America 1735, visited Georgia (1624)

Two-level Methodist meeting house (1625)

Barbara Heck, New York Methodist reformer (1626)

Mysticism

A SWEDISH THEOLOGIAN, Emanuel Swedenborg, preached a mysterious doctrine emphasizing cosmic consciousness. His work influenced William Blake and other "pre-Romantic" artists. The Freemasons attracted others with a bent towards mystery, including Washington and Mozart.

Emanuel Swedenborg (1627)

Blake drew his own metaphysical prophecies (1628)

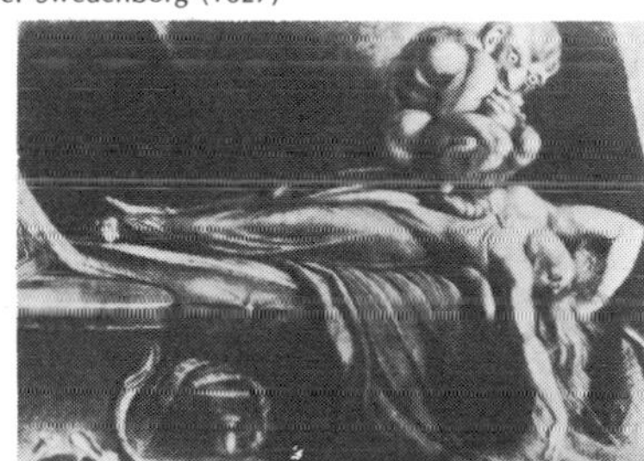

The Nightmare, ptg. by Henry Fuessli, whose work reflects a new tendency towards mysticism (1629)

Freemasonry

Mysterious rites of Freemasons gained many adherents (1630)

Symbols of Free Masonry, First Degree (1631)

Lafayette and Washington, fellow Masons (1632)

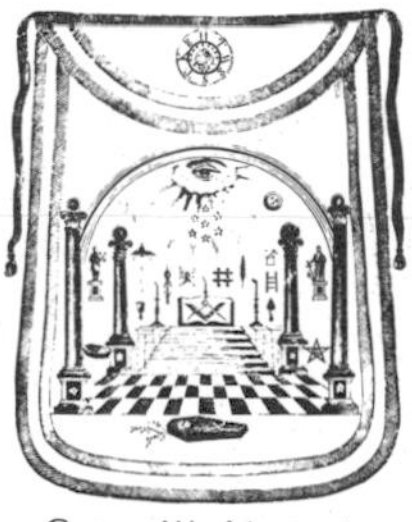

George Washington's Masonic apron (1633)

George Washington shown as a Master Mason (1634)

Symbols of Free Masonry: the working tools (1635)

Quakers—Sects

Quaker Meeting House during a service (1636)

Philip Hermon, Quaker (1637)

Quakers in typical garb of sect (1638)

Philip Spener, leader of Lutheran Pietism (1639)

August H. Francke, founder of German Pietism (1640)

Family in daily religious contemplation (1641)

Francke blessing children of his congregation (1642)

Music expressed the Pietist creed (1643)

Procession during "Great Awakening" of 1740, a Methodist crusade (1644)

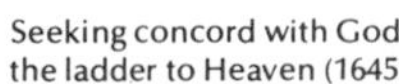

Seeking concord with God: the ladder to Heaven (1645)

Musical Culture

(1647)

Baroque Sonorities

THE REVIVAL OF RELIGION, sweeping through Europe and America, promised (in the terms of a contemporary engraving) "a new ladder to heaven." Meanwhile, musicians, seeking new form and symmetry in their compositions, emulated the mathematical precision expressed in Newton's laws of physics. These trends meet most effectively in Johann Sebastian Bach, who sought to lift man's spirit to a state of grace through cantatas and oratorios, as well as through the mighty sonorities of his organ music. Though his works were charged with the emotion of a true believer, they were also carefully structured along mathematical lines. Handel followed similar principles of composition, and wrote many oratorios, but he was a more worldly man, whose works were designed for court performances and for concert halls as well as churches.

Church music at time of J.S. Bach. Choir, organ, orchestra join to praise God (1646)

Bach at the organ—wonders of structure and sonority (1648)

Monument in Leipzig, a city in which Bach was treated shabbily (1649)

St. Thomas Church where Bach was organist, cantor (1650)

He created concertos for performance in his own large family circle (1651)

Clarinet (1652)

George Frederick Handel (1653) excelled in opera. His oratorios were operas for church (1654)

Water Music was written for George I boat ride down the Thames (1655)

The Handel monument in Westminster Abbey (1656)

The Messiah sung each year to benefit foundlings (1657)

Italian Masters

- **A** Scarlatti wrote piano sonatas (1658)
- **B** Vivaldi: Concerti Grossi (1659)
- **C** Stradivarius: violin maker (1660)
- **D** Pergolesi: chamber opera (1661)

The School of Vienna

Gluck wrote operas in the Italian tradition (1662)

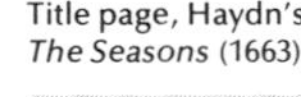

Title page, Haydn's *The Seasons* (1663)

Hadyn put on his best clothes when he composed (1664)

Esterhazy Palace, where Haydn was court composer (1665)

Haydn rehearsing chamber music—group in Esterhazy Palace (1666)

Viola da gamba: violincello's classic forerunner (1667)

Grand piano played by Mozart during stay in Prague (1668)

Mozart, child prodigy, tutored by his father, Leopold (1669)

Don Juan: punishment and damnation (1670)

Figaro: Cherubino discovered (1671)

The Magic Flute: Papageno, the merry bird catcher (1672)

Rebirth of German Letters

AFTER A CENTURY of suffering in the aftermath of the Thirty Years' War, German culture revived. By mid-18th century the spread of Enlightenment, renewed interest in classical antiquity, and a new cult of emotion and sentiment produced a burgeoning of German letters. Most representative was Johann Wolfgang Goethe, whose *Werther* exemplified the sentiment of *Sturm and Drang*, while his *Faust* reflected a turn toward mysticism as well as the utopianism of the Enlightenment. In philosophy, Kant, in a monumental achievement, outlined *a priori* concepts that determine much of what the human mind perceives.

Emotional ebullience was a strong element of *Sturm und Drang* (1674)

Poets—Dramatists

(1673)

Scene from Goethe's *The Sorrows of Young Werther*. Published in 1774, it became a bestseller (1675)

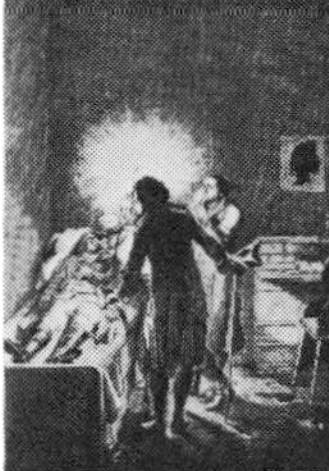

Werther discovered after suicide (1676)

Goethe's journey to Italy converted him to classicism, cult of Greek beauty (1677)

Winckelmann, early archaeologist (1678)

Faust signs pact with Devil, dipping pen in blood (1679)

Homunculus; alembic-made human (1680)

Illustration by Delacroix for Goethe's *Faust* (1681)

Lessing, innovative dramaturge (1682)

Schiller: historical dramatist, poet (1683)

Thinkers

Klopstock, author of Miltonian epics (1684)

Herder, folklorist and historian (1685)

Kant, author of *Critique of Pure Reason*, in discussion with his friends (1686)

Rococo Elegance Bourgeois Solidity

THE ART OF LIVING in the 18th century moved between two poles, aristocratic and bourgeois. As the century began, both style and value were dictated by the extravagant courts of absolute monarchs, whose taste was mimicked by all who could do so. But as the century progressed, an unpretentious, warm and domestic model evolved—the Biedermeier style, focused upon the average middle-class couple: solid, hard-working citizens enjoying family life, comfort and simple pleasures to brighten their leisure time.

Husband welcomed by virtuous wife (1687)

Private postal service of Thurn and Taxis families was helpful to German commerce, sped exchange of ideas (1688, 1689)

Berlin citizens on the way to a country picnic (1690)

German engraver Chodowiecki and family in his studio (1691)

Housewives and maids clean and mend clothes, catch up on gossip (1692)

Skilled craftsmen built elaborate coaches for the aristocracy (1693)

(1694)

England

Queen Anne and the Elder Pitt

WITH CONSTITUTIONAL MONARCHY established and religious turmoil diminished, England was ready, in the 18th century, to build a commercial empire. George I, first of the Hanoverian kings, was involved with his own duchy, and displayed only a cavalier interest in English affairs. Parliament, led by Sir Robert Walpole, thus gained decisive control; Walpole became, in fact if not in name, the first British Prime Minister (1721-1740).

Under the leadership of William Pitt, England drove the French from India and Canada, greatly expanding English colonial power in Asia and in the New World.

Queen Anne (1695), last British monarch to exercise royal veto. In her reign, Scotland joined England in Act of Union (1696)

(1698)

Marlborough wielded power at Queen Anne's court (1697)

George I, first of the Hanoverians (1699)

Walpole holds a meeting with his cabinet (1700)

George II, last English king to lead army into battle — at Dettingen in 1743 (1701)

Pitt the Elder presided over England's expansion (1702)

"The Politician", engraving by William Hogarth (1703)

Beau Nash, arbiter of fashion (1704)

The Rich and The Mighty

WHILE ENGLISH GOVERNMENT alternately favored the interests of newly enriched merchants or the old gentility—the "squirearchy"—the poor suffered greater degradation than ever. Life on the streets of 18th-century London presented a study in contrasts: the elegance of the rich against the wretchedness of the masses.

Society lady carried in sedan chair through London street (1705)

Life of English aristocracy: family meets during the tea hour (1706)

Artist's studio unexpectedly invaded by intruder (1707)

Aristocratic youngsters learn to dance the minuet (1708)

Date descends in elevator carriage. Cartoon (1709)

Fashion's folly: fop in Macaroni outfit (1710)

Profligate company playing for high stakes (1711)

A dandy suffers from tight lacing (1713)

"Music . . . rejoiceth the Spirits and unloadeth Grief from the heart" (1712)

. . . The Lowly

Peddler offering tarts (1714)

" Industry and Idleness:" women confined to workhouse (1715)

The depravity of "Gin Lane" (1716)

Hogarth's "Shop Sign" (1717)

Brawling peasants at Tyburn Gate (1718)

Stagecoach loading at a country inn (1719)

Street life in London: "The Enraged Musician" upset by noise (1720)

WILLIAM HOGARTH held a mirror before London society and found it cruel and selfish. His bitingly satirical engravings often depict the wretched and debased, subjects hardly treated by artists before.

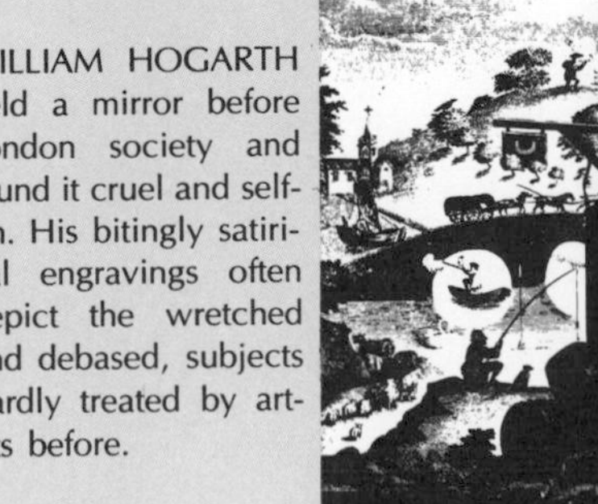

Faulty perspective ridiculed in print by Hogarth (1721)

Dynamic Colonialism

India

Early English trading station had warehouses and church (1722)

Robert Clive, governor of India affirmed British rule (1723)

Tortures of Black Hole, Calcutta outrage (1724)

Battle of Plassey gave Clive possession of Bengal (1725)

Balance of power: England outweighs all states of Europe (1726)

ENGLISH DOMINION over India was energetically pursued by Sir Robert Clive, who represented the British East India Company. Between 1745 and 1760 the French were driven from most of their possessions. Although masses of British soldiers were murdered in the "Black Hole of Calcutta," Clive's victory at Plassey finally established British control in India.

Warren Hastings, Governor-General of India (1727)

Lord Cornwallis as governor of India gets hostages from local ruler (1728)

Canadians found snowshoes essential for travel (1729)

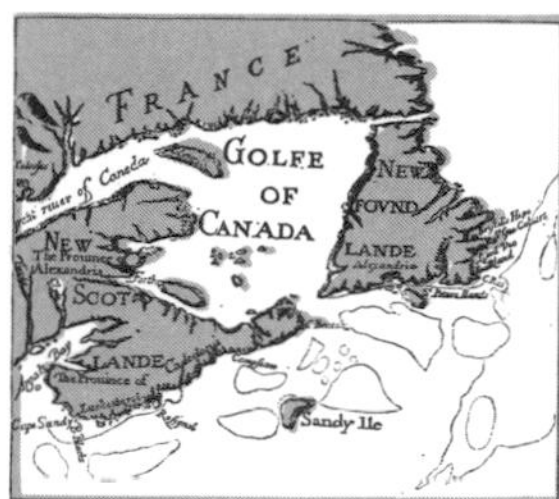

Map of French, English possessions in America: New Acadia (1730)

The English in America

Earliest view of Georgia, established by the English as a refuge for imprisoned debtors (1731)

Oglethorpe, founder of Georgia (1732)

George Washington arrives at Fort Duquesne (1733)

IN AMERICA, too, the British sought, successfully, to drive the French from Canada and the Mississippi Valley. Though young General James Wolfe lost his life in the encounter, the British took Quebec in 1759, and soon controlled all of Canada. Meanwhile, James Cook's discovery of Australia gave England a foothold in the Pacific.

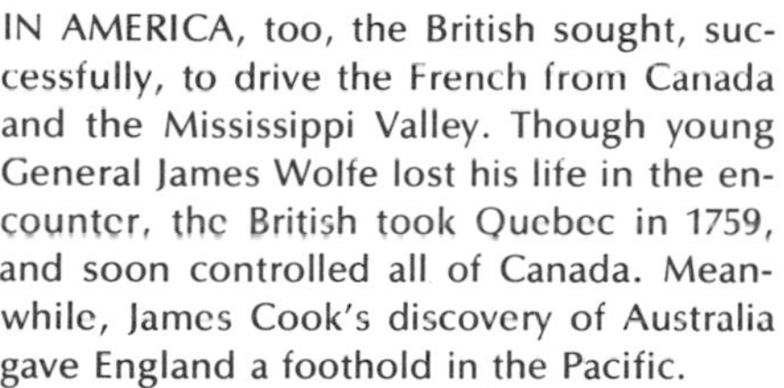

Braddock's confident army moves into French territory (1734)

Louisburg taken by joint forces of English and Colonists (1735)

The English attack Quebec, win New France (1736)

General Wolfe died in assault (1737)

Pacific Possessions

(1738)

Captain Dampier sees first boomerang (1739)

Cook discovered, charted Pacific islands (1740)

Capt. Cook nears New Zealand coast (1741)

Cook sailed around world in the *Resolution* (1742)

Union Jack raised in Australia, making it British possession (1743)

East India House, London (1745)

Merchant's office near busy wharf. England became rich through foreign trade (1746)

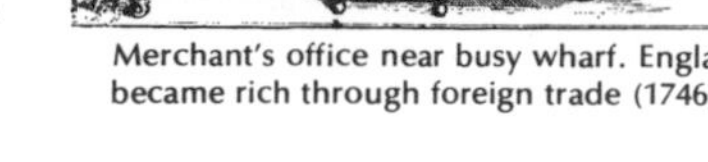

Flag pronounces supremacy of England in world trade (1744)

WORLD-WIDE EXPANSION OF TERRITORY provided England with unprecedented control of international trade. Between 1720 and 1760 British exports doubled, making England the richest as well as the most powerful country in Europe. Demand for British goods increased so rapidly that the need for some means of accelerating production became apparent. British colonial expansion was thus the bellows which fanned the fires of the Industrial Revolution.

England Gears Up for Industrial Age

MOVING TOWARD THE INDUSTRIAL REVOLUTION, England had several advantages over other nations: her colonial empire stimulated demand for goods and brought venture capital which could be invested in new means of production. Iron and coal were plentiful, as were eager craftsmen with inventive skills. James Watt, a Scottish instrument maker, first turned the steam engine into a source of industrial power. Called upon to repair a Newcomen engine, he found a way to convert its vertical pumping action into the rotary motion needed to power machinery. His engine revolutionized industry and social life.

Watt works on Newcomen engine that was used mainly to raise water from mines (1748)

Financiers meet with Watt to discuss the manufacture of new steam engines (1749)

Matthew Boulton (1750) formed partnership with James Watt (1751) to establish engine factory.

Inside Boulton-Watt workshop, where steam engines were built for factories (1752)

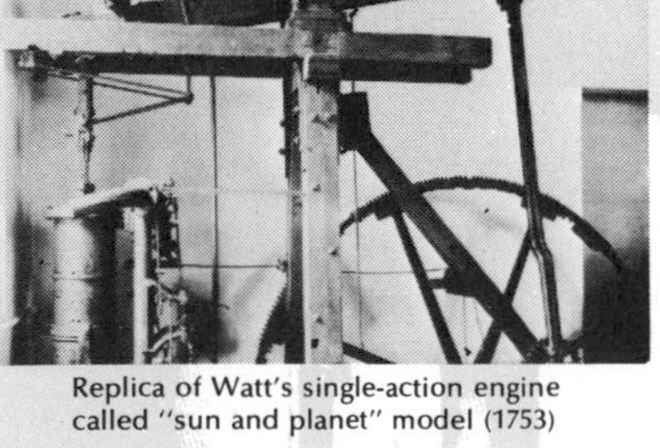

Replica of Watt's single-action engine called "sun and planet" model (1753)

English banker ready to provide capital (1754)

Early foundry used charcoal in smelting of iron (1755)

Abraham Darby discovered coke smelts better (1756)

AT the Old Collier *and* Cart, *at* Fleet-Ditch, *near* Holborn-Bridge, *Are good Coals, Deals, Wainſcote and Beach*, &c. *ſold at reaſonable Rates, by* John Edwards.

London coal cart. Adv. leaflet (1757)

Machine cogwheels were made of wood until iron became more readily available (1758)

Giant bellows aided iron foundry (1759)

James Watt: Coal—Steam—Power

"We sell here, sir, what all the world desires to have: power!"

—Matthew Boulton to James Boswell

Plan of Watt's new improved steam engine of 1784 (1747)

Load of ore rolls down tracks to foundry. Horse will haul wagon back to mine (1760)

Steam wagon by Murdock, 1784—early use of steam in transportation (1761)

Trevithick showed in public display practical use of locomotive (1762)

Textile Making Mechanized

Yarn spinning at home as practiced before the Industrial Revolution (1763)

Hargreaves' spinning jenny, invention that revolutionized textile manufacture (1764)

Arkwright constructs spinning frame (1765)

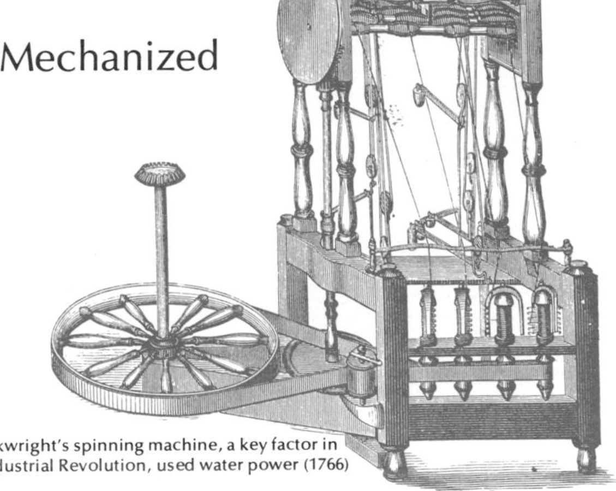
Arkwright's spinning machine, a key factor in Industrial Revolution, used water power (1766)

Crompton (1767), destitute, sold mule spinning patent for £60. Cartwright invented the power loom (1768)

Luddites, fearing unemployment, destroyed machinery (1769)

ENGLAND'S BURGEONING POPULATION, the result of progress in medicine, sanitation and agriculture, now created a great demand for cheaper clothing. Since cotton was produced abundantly in the American colonies, it seemed the ideal staple to fill the need. Inventions designed to accelerate the processing of cotton fiber appeared with chain-reaction speed until the textile industry was mechanized, from spinning the threads to weaving the finished cloth. But as technology expanded, management found it had to revise its economic thinking.

Management Genius

NEW LABOR SAVING DEVICES solved some problems but created others. Machines must be coordinated, the flow of production carefully planned. Laborers must be "induced to unremitting diligence to conform to the regular celerity of the machine." Managing all these factors took a special ability, and it was Richard Arkwright who first made the system work. So poorly educated in his youth that he studied grammar all his life, Arkwright emerged as the management genius of the industrial age.

Smeaton improved water-power in mills (1770)

Arkwright employed 600 In steam-driven factory (1771)

Josiah Wedgwood: potter, management genius (1772)

New Economic Theories

A RADICAL REVERSAL in economic thinking prepared the way for the new age. Adam Smith (following the theory of laissez faire pronounced by Quesnay) redefined a nation's wealth in terms of productive capacity. His *Wealth of Nations* made him the apostle of free enterprise.

Quesnay held land a source of wealth (1773)

Bentham: happiness for all is aim of life (1774)

Type foundry works with division of labor (1775)

AN
INQUIRY
INTO THE
Nature and Caufes
OF THE
WEALTH OF NATIONS.
By ADAM SMITH, LL.D. and F.R.S.
IN TWO VOLUMES.
VOL. I.
LONDON:

Adam Smith (1776) suggested division of labor and free trade; believed competition healthy for economy (1777)

Land and property were thought by physiocrats to be backbone of wealth. Now labor was stressed (1778)

Malthus (1779) thought factory system would tax food supply, lead to over-population (1780)

Industrial mine uses steam, transport, labor (1781)

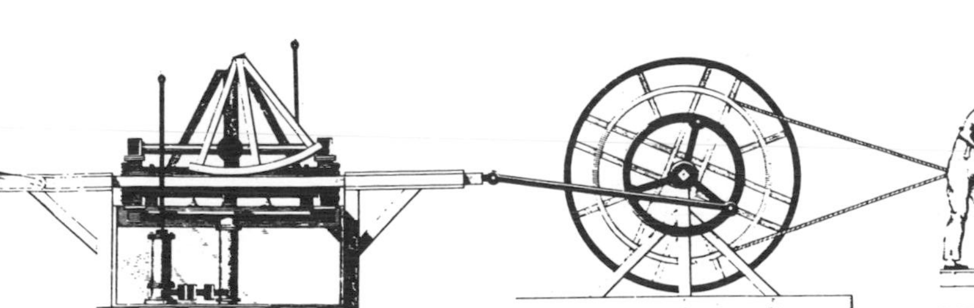
Stream-driven power shaft led to progressive mechanization in all industries (1782)

A Great Age of Literature

ENGLISH LETTERS of the period reflect an air of cosmopolitan self-assurance, with emphasis on style: "What oft was thought but ne'er so well expressed." Delicate satire, provoked by the prevailing smugness of "society," became a dominant mood in poetry, as in the works of Alexander Pope. Some writers ridiculed the optimism of the Enlightenment: Jonathan Swift called mankind "the most pernicious race of little vermin to crawl upon the earth."

ALEXANDER POPE

Alexander Pope: "wicked wasp of Twickenham" (1783)

The Rape of the Lock combined poetic beauty, wit, and lyricism (1784)

Pope was 4' 3" high and crippled (1785)

Cartoon of Pope as the "Pope of Letters" (1786)

JONATHAN SWIFT

Jonathan Swift, master of social satire (1787)

Swift wrote London diary: *Letters to Stella,* his young friend (1788)

TRAVELS INTO SEVERAL Remote NATIONS OF THE WORLD. In FOUR PARTS. By LEMUEL GULLIVER, First a SURGEON, and then a CAPTAIN of several SHIPS. VOL. I. LONDON: Printed for BENJ. MOTTE, at the Middle Temple-Gate in Fleet-street.

Gulliver's Travels—both a children's adventure story and a pungent critique of the follies of humanity (1789, 1790)

The King of the Brobdingnagians looms large over ant-like Gulliver (1791)

The Rage for Novels

APPEALING TO ANOTHER AUDIENCE, fiction writers of the period developed the English novel, spiking tales of travel, adventure and romance with insight, sympathy and caustic wit. A rapidly expanding readership among the middle classes waited breathlessly for each installment of Samuel Richardson's *Pamela; or Virtue Rewarded,* ringing church bells all over England when she finally got her man.

DANIEL DEFOE

THE LIFE AND STRANGE SURPRIZING ADVENTURES OF ROBINSON CRUSOE, Of YORK, MARINER: Who lived Eight and Twenty Years, all alone in an un-inhabited Island on the Coast of AMERICA, near the Mouth of the Great River of OROONOQUE; Having been cast on Shore by Shipwreck, wherein all the Men perished but himself. WITH An Account how he was at last as strangely deliver'd by PYRATES. Written by Himself. LONDON: Printed for W. TAYLOR at the Ship in Pater-Noster-Row. MDCCXIX.

Robinson Crusoe was based on actual island adventure of Alexander Selkirk. Defoe wrote 250 other novelistic tales (1792, 1793, 1794)

ADDISON & STEELE

THE SPECTATOR. VOLUME the FIRST. LONDON: Printed for J. and R. TONSON and S. DRAPER. MDCCLIII.

Joseph Addison (1795) wrote the *Spectator* (1796) with Richard Steele (1797). Their essays on manners, morals and social criticism were exemplary.

SAMUEL RICHARDSON

Samuel Richardson (1798) idealized chastity in multi-volume novels. His *Pamela* (1799) considered first modern novel.

HENRY FIELDING

THE HISTORY OF TOM JONES, A FOUNDLING. In SIX VOLUMES. By HENRY FIELDING, Esq. LONDON: Printed for A. MILLAR, over-against Catharine-street in the Strand. MDCCXLIX. Title-page of First Edition of "Tom Jones"

Henry Fielding (1800) wrote for the theater. In *Tom Jones* (1801, 1802) he created period's most important novel with rambunctious, true-to-life characters.

LAURENCE STERNE

Laurence Sterne (1803) wrote *Sentimental Journey* (1804), a collection of acidly whimsical sketches.

TOBIAS SMOLLETT

Tobias Smollett wrote picaresque novels (1805)

Illustration by Rowlandson for Smollett, *The Expedition of Humphrey Clinker* (1806)

OLIVER GOLDSMITH

Oliver Goldsmith (1807)

Vicar of Wakefield, novel by Goldsmith (1808)

The Literati of London

Dr. Johnson and Boswell in Fleet Street. "When a man is tired of London he is tired of life" (1809)

The literati, with Johnson presiding, dine in London's Cheshire Cheese Inn (1810)

THE GRAND MASTER of London's literary society was Samuel Johnson. Though he produced important works (his *Dictionary* of 1756 the most epochal), it was the force of his personality, his wit and common sense that left their imprint on the age. Clubs and coffeehouses, always popular in England, now became the emporia of wits, with Johnson's literary club the uncontested leader. All of this might have been lost to us, were it not for Boswell's *Life of Johnson*.

The intellectual brilliance nurtured in this atmosphere contrasts favorably with the subdued mood of other European cities. Not all writers made fortunes as did Pope with his translation of Homer. But the presses poured forth books and pamphlets, and the Strand became a "highway of letters." As Johnson observed in 1779: "General literature now pervades the nation . . . every house is supplied with a closet of knowledge."

Johnson, Mrs. Thralle close friends (1811)

Best bet for Scotsmen, Johnson held, was to come to London, as Boswell did (1812)

Johnson in travel costume (1813)

Bonanza for Bookmen

A sandwichman advertises books and popular sheet-music (1814)

Circulating library and bookshop (1815)

Bibliophile makes rare find (1816)

Fat publisher—starving author (1817)

FINGAL,
AN
ANCIENT EPIC POEM,
In SIX BOOKS:
Together with several other POEMS, composed by
OSSIAN the Son of FINGAL.
Translated from the Galic Language,
By JAMES MACPHERSON.
Fortia facta patrum. Virgil.

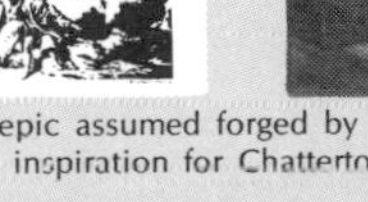

Ossian epic assumed forged by MacPherson (1818) became inspiration for Chatterton's poetry (1819)

The Forgers

RENEWED INTEREST in England's literary past inspired several ingenious forgeries. Thomas Chatterton, undoubtedly a poetic genius, composed his *Rowley Papers* at the age of twelve, presenting them as 15th-century poems. Although even Horace Walpole was deceived for a time, the fraud was proved and the unfortunate Chatterton poisoned himself at seventeen. James McPherson's romantic but fraudulent *Poems of Ossian* also found many admirers.

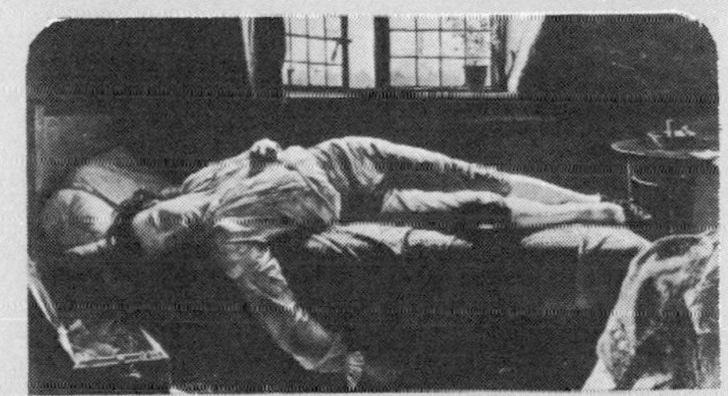

Chatterton killed himself when his Rowley forgeries were discovered (1820)

(1821)

Edward Gibbon, historian of Roman Empire (1822)

Historians and Epistolarians

David Hume: philosopher, historian of England (1823)

Horace Walpole, dilettante, London society gossip (1824)

Lady Montague, brilliant correspondent, wit (1825)

Chesterfield: *Letters to his Son*, a classic (1826)

The Stage

Gay's Beggar's Opera was popular London show—played for two seasons (1827)

Dagger scene from *Macbeth* in costumes of 1763 (1828)

David Garrick, famed actor, friend of Johnson (1829)

Richard Brinsley Sheridan: comedies of manners (1830)

London stage declined in importance as novel-writing flourished (1831)

THE
CONSTITUTIONS
OF THE
SEVERAL INDEPENDENT STATES
OF
AMERIC
THE
Declaration of Independence
THE
ARTICLES OF CONFEDERATIO
BETWEEN THE SAID STATES;
THE
TREATIES between HIS MOST CHRISTIAN MA
and the UNITED STATES OF AMERICA.
Published by order of Congress.
PHILADELPHI
PRINTED BY FRANCIS BAILEY, IN MARKE
M.DCC.LXXXI.

CHAPTER 6

A New Nation

Eve of Revolution

War of Independence

U.S. Constitution

D

E

AMERICAN COLONIES IN REVOLT

THE TREATY OF PARIS in 1763 gave England the vast expanse of America, but the cost of defeating the French was high. To pay the war debt, England enacted a continuous series of taxes and restraints upon trade, designed to enrich the mother country at the expense of the Colonies. Protests from the Colonists, erupting in the Boston Massacre in 1770, prompted a lull in London's demands. But when the Stamp Act provoked open rebellion (the Boston Tea Party), King George III lost his patience. Boston Harbor was closed, threatening American trade with ruin. A common bond of resentment began to unite the Colonists, though few considered an open break with England.

James Otis protests "Writs of Assistance" issued by Crown against recalcitrant Colonists (1832)

THE RIGHTS OF THE British Colonies Asserted and proved. By James Otis, Esq; BOSTON

Pamphlet that voiced grievances (1833)

Stamp issued to mock British tyranny (1834)▶

Bostonians destroy Stamp Act papers (1835)

Merchants protest against curtailment of trade (1836)

New Yorkers tumbling the statue of George III (1837)

Boston Massacre, March 5, 1770. Death of Crispus Attucks (1838)

On the Death of Five young Men who was Murthered, *March* 5th 1770. By the 29th Regiment.

Colonial propaganda sheet showing Boston Massacre coffins (1839)

Providence merchants prevent tea-laden *Gaspé* to land (1840)

The Boston Tea Party Dec. 16, 1773 (1841)

Tax man hanged in effigy (1842)

America forced to swallow a bitter dose of taxation (1843)

First Continental Congress seeks divine guidance in prayer (1844)

MOST OF THE COLONISTS still favored peaceful accommodation. John Adams estimated that fully two-thirds sought only redress of grievances, favoring limited dependence upon the Crown. The remaining third was vociferous, their wrath expertly kindled by that archrevolutionary, Samuel Adams. The antagonism between Loyalists and Patriots was so intense that America was nearly plunged into civil war before the Revolution could get off the ground.

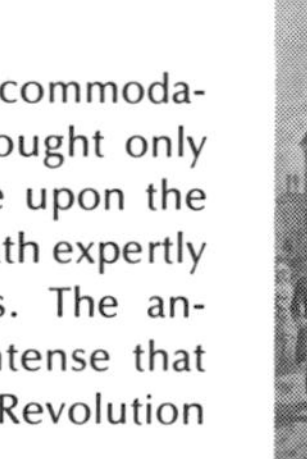

Delegates to the First Continental Congress after a session (1845) held at Carpenter's Hall, Philadelphia (1846)

Patrick Henry famed for "Give me liberty or give me death" (1847)

George III shown perusing *The Rights of Man* (1848)

Poor old England trying to reclaim his wicked American children (1849)

Lord North pursued ruinous colonial policy (1850)

English general compliments Indians for scalping colonial foe. Cartoon (1851)

Loyalist railed and banned from American soil by Patriots (1852)

Hutchinson remained loyal to crown (1853)

Town meeting takes strong action (1854)

Pitt sympathized with Colonial revolt (1855)

CROWN AND PARLIAMENT were far from united in planning the empire's repressive Colonial policies. Supporters in Parliament (including Pitt) overtly or covertly backed the American cause.

Burke defended rights of the colonists (1856)

Toward Independence

In defense of America's liberty: Minuteman (1857)

British fleet occupies Boston Harbor, taking revenge for Tea Party (1858)

South Church—belltower (1859)

Revere's midnight ride April 18, 1775 (1860)

Minuteman leaving his home to join ranks of farmer-patriots (1861)

BRINGING THE COLONISTS to their senses seemed a simple task to England. Fresh from victory over the professional armies of France, the English forces saw the ill-trained, ill-equipped militia of the Colonials as less than formidable. Yet they totally misjudged the spirit of their adversary. English armies might take Boston, New York, Charleston; but on their own soil, using the methods of guerrilla warfare—evasion, escape, surprise—the Colonials could not be beaten decisively.

Revolution's first armed encounter, Lexington, April 14, 1775 (1862)

Battle monument, Lexington (1863)

Minutemen repelling British, Concord Bridge (1864)

With Benedict Arnold, Ethan Allen captures Fort Ticonderoga on May 10, 1775 (1865)

Planning the battle of Bunker Hill (1866)

Patriots fortify Breed's Hill the night before the battle (1867)

Battle memento from Trumbull ptg. shows Gen. Warren's death (1868)

Bunker Hill hairdo sported by patriotic lady (1869)

(1869 A)

Sam Adams, firebrand propagandist (1870)

John Hancock, merchant, agile revolutionist (1871)

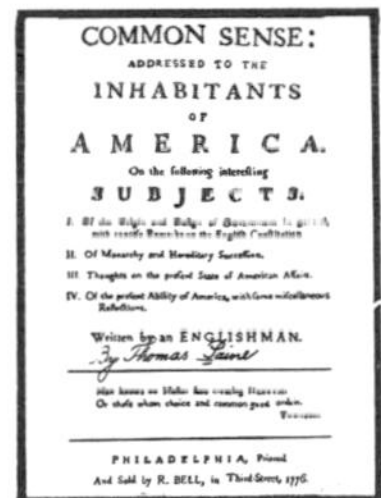
COMMON SENSE;
ADDRESSED TO THE
INHABITANTS
OF
AMERICA,
On the following interesting
SUBJECTS.

Written by an ENGLISHMAN.

PHILADELPHIA, Printed
And sold by R. BELL, in Third-Street, 1776.

Tom Paine's pamphlet sounded clarion call of revolt, sold thousands of copies (1872, 1873)

Printers were active distributing latest revolution news (1874)

Jefferson drafts Declaration of Independence (1875)

"Declaration of Independence." John Trumbull painting (1876)

A defiant John Hancock signs Declaration (1877)

Tolling first peal for liberty - Philadelphia bellringer (1878)

THE SPIRIT OF FREEDOM, a factor no military appraisal could take into account, welded the Colonial forces at last into an effective, united front. The dream of a government based on consent of the governed inspired them. The Declaration of Independence translated into action both this dream and the political thought of the age of Enlightenment.

America throwing her master King George III into jeopardy (1880)

Dec. of Independence printed as the Liberty Bell (1879)

IN CONGRESS, JULY 4, 1776

The unanimous Declaration of the thirteen united States of America.

(1881) When in the Course of human events it becomes necessary for one people to dissolve the political bands which have connected them with another, and to

"The Young Continental"—idealized version. Army was ragged (1882)

Armed Conflict

An Uneven Match

STRICTLY SPEAKING, the Colonies had no army: state militias were committed to local defense. When Washington took command of the "Continental Army" in 1775, it was mostly nonexistent. With an initial appropriation of only $6,000, Washington proposed the hunting shirt as a makeshift uniform. Problems of money and manpower continued to chafe the American leader. Soldiers were apt to pull out at will—some enlisted for only three months at a time.

Minutemen drilling after hours. Engr. by Howard Pyle (1883)

Fife and drum band leads group of Minutemen into battle (1884)

Washington taking command of Continental Army in Cambridge, July 3, 1775 (1885)

Recruiting: privateers enlist, tempted by the promise of rich bounty (1886)

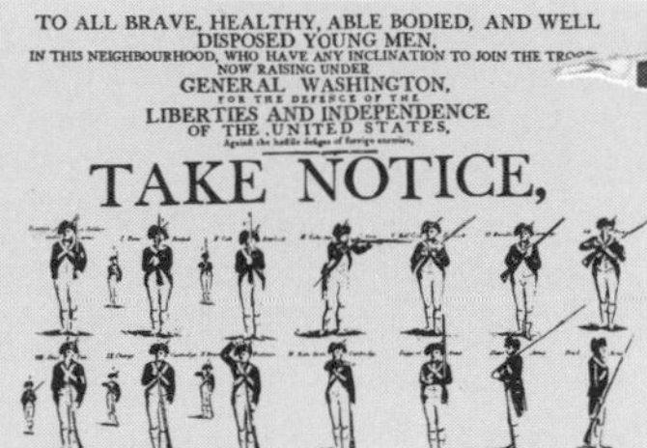

Washington urges young men to join army. Poster with drill instructions (1887)

Revolutionary War uniforms: general (1888), artillery captain (1889), rifleman (1890)

Helpers at Home and Abroad

AMERICA FOUND FRIENDS abroad. Coaxed and prodded by Benjamin Franklin, and partly motivated by their traditional enmity toward England, the French provided loans and equipment to the American rebels. At last they joined the Colonists as full-fledged allies, sending troops under General Lafayette in 1778. Other European generals, experts in training and tactics, offered their services. Eventually a respectable Continental Army was forged, though its core numbered a mere 25,000 soldiers.

Robert Morris helped finance Washington's army (1891)

Paper money issued by Mass. Colony (1892)

Haym Salomon advances cash to American government (1893)

Franklin signing the Treaty of Alliance with France (1894)

French ambassador welcomed by Continental Congress (1895)

Washington and Lafayette meet for first time (1896)

Lafayette ready to join the American forces (1897)

General von Steuben drilling Washington's army; winter at Valley Forge (1898)

A Pulaski, Polish nobleman, created new cavalry corps (1900)
B Kosciusko, Polish patriot; made colonel of engineers (1901)
C Rochambeau commanded French army in America (1902)

A

B

C

LOOSELY JOINED under the Articles of Confederation, the thirteen colonies approved an American flag in 1777. Since the graphic arts were inexpensive to produce, patriot artists like Paul Revere used them extensively to champion the rebel cause. As the war progressed, American mottoes, designs and insignia appeared, providing a symbolic focus for the hopes and aims of the republic.

Franklin's famous cartoon calling for unity (1904)

Clasped hands: an appeal to join union (1903)

Pine-tree flag, adopted in 1776 by Massachusetts (1906)

America challenging British Lion (1905)

Revolutionary motto with picture of Franklin (1899)

Annals of the War

THOUGH ULTIMATELY VICTORIOUS, the American army won few battles. Washington held his ragtag troops together by force of character. An occasional victory, such as the Battle of Trenton, was followed by setbacks in which the American general preserved his army through successful disengagement, avoiding defeat. The British, though, were constantly open to harassment.

Powder horn with design by a Continental soldier (1908)

1776

Nathan Hale hanged as a spy by British on Long Island (1907)

Retreat from Brooklyn Heights, Battle of Long Island (1909)

Washington crossing Delaware to escape pursuit by Cornwallis (1910)

1777

Princeton: Washington beats Cornwallis who had hoped to "bag the fox" (1911)

Liberty Bell leaves Philadelphia as General Howe nears (1912)

Surrender of Burgoyne at Saratoga (1913)

1777
1778

Valley Forge winter encampment (1914)

Washington praying at Valley Forge (1915)

Lafayette leads cavalry attack in Battle of Monmouth (1916)

Molly Pitcher, heroine at Monmouth battle (1917)

George Rogers Clark fights English in West; gained stronghold at Vincennes (1918)

1779

Jones' *Bonne Homme Richard* battles H.M.S. *Serapis* (1919)

Jones defies British call for surrender (1920)

Marines recruited for action in Revolutionary War (1921)

American harbor scene—mariner with sextant (1922)

1780

Francis Marion, "Swamp Fox", harrassed British troops (1923)

Capture of Major André in Westchester, N.Y. (1924)

Pageant shows Benedict Arnold, traitor, on way to be burned in effigy (1925)

Triumphant Finale

"YOU CANNOT CONQUER A MAP!" cried William Pitt, and the British were finally forced to see the justice of his dictum. Tired of being hounded, suffering from poor leadership and poor intelligence, the British army blundered into an American and French trap at Yorktown. Eight thousand redcoats laid down their arms and surrendered, prompting the British Prime Minister, Lord North, to moan, "It's all over." Still, it took two years to negotiate an effective peace (1783), and the British did not evacuate New York until 1784.

1781
1783

Surrender at Yorktown ended the War (1926)

New York hears news of Cornwallis' surrender, hails victory (1927)

Army of Cornwallis, after surrendering arms, sails for England, Oct. 1781 (1928)

Signing of the Peace of Paris; unfinished Trumbull ptg. (1929)

Evacuation of New York. American flag was raised 1784, after British departure (1930)

Reconciliation between Great Britain and her daughter America (1931)

We the People *of the United States*

(1932)

"WE MUST HANG TOGETHER or we will hang separately," Ben Franklin told his fellow rebels, but victory dissipated this common bond. The Articles of Confederation, inadequate in war, were unworkable in peace. Political collapse seemed imminent when fifty-five of America's best public-spirited thinkers assembled in May 1787 to forge a new constitution. This document, though declaring boldly that the people were to govern, at the same time established a strong federal power. With Washington the rallying point between Hamilton and Jefferson, the Federalists won ratification of the new government in 1788.

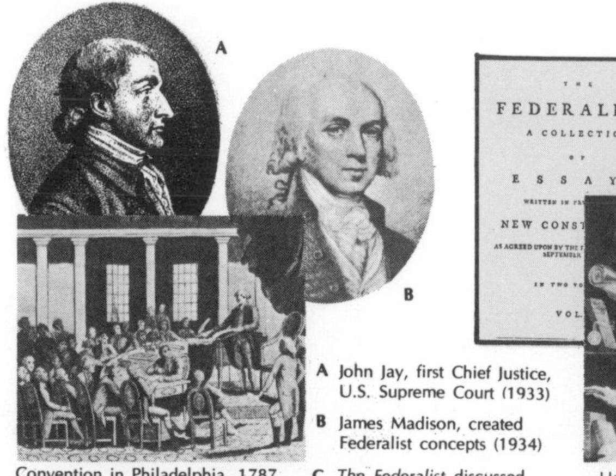

Convention in Philadelphia, 1787, Washington presiding (1936)

A John Jay, first Chief Justice, U.S. Supreme Court (1933)

B James Madison, created Federalist concepts (1934)

C *The Federalist* discussed Constitution (1935)

Hamilton wrote most of *Federalist Papers* (1937)

Shays' Rebellion, caused by financial woe among New England farmers (1938)

Signing of the Constitution. New Hampshire was last state to ratify, in 1789. Government began March 4, 1789 (1939)

Giant float in New York to celebrate ratification of the U.S. Constitution in March 1789 (1940)

Washington the President by Gilbert Stuart (1941)

Washington the President

UNPRECEDENTED EXCITEMENT greeted Washington's inauguration as the first President, for it symbolized the real beginning of a new nation. Washington accepted the office with some doubts, but fulfilled it with honor and an equanimity that withstood regional conflicts and party strife. During his two terms the country was able to structure its government and find its place among nations. But Washington warned against involvement with European politics.

Washington being informed of his election as President of the United States (1942)

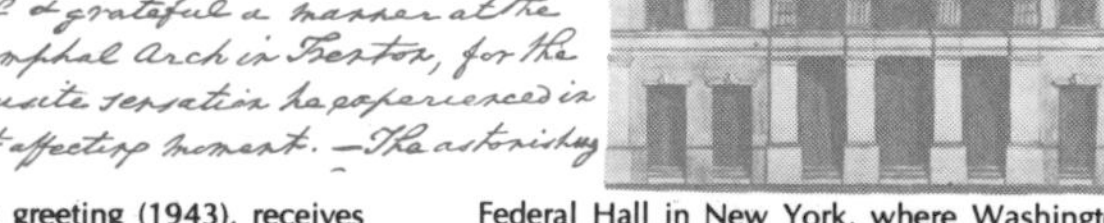

President-elect en route to inauguration accepts roadside greeting (1943), receives triumphal welcome in New Jersey (1944), thanks ladies of Trenton (1945)

Federal Hall in New York, where Washington's tumultuous inauguration took place (1946)

Washington taking presidential oath on his family Bible (1947)

Washington. Sculpture (1948)

First Cabinet: Knox (War), Hamilton (Treasury), Jefferson (State), Randolph (Atty. Gen.) (1949)

Jay burned in effigy for unpopular Treaty (1950)

Alexander Hamilton, spokesman for the moneyed interests of new nation (1951)

Washington leading minuet during reception. He was criticized for "Federal Court" (1952)

Slaves were essential work force at Mt. Vernon estate (1953)

Marquis de Lafayette visits Washington family at Mount Vernon (1954)

Washington drinks a toast to Nellie, his stepdaughter, during her wedding (1955)

Memorial to George and Martha Washington designed by painter John Trumbull (1956)

Post-Revolutionary America

ENGLISH COLONIAL POLICY had forbidden exploration and settlement of the western lands —nothing beyond the Appalachian mountains was open to settlers. But now, freed of restraint, Americans set out like greedy children to explore their new continent. Roads, where they existed, were in pitiful shape, but to gain access to new regions and facilitate trade, there came a flurry of turnpike building. Water traffic also proliferated. Anthony Wayne's victory over the Indians at Fallen Timber, followed by the Treaty of Greenville (1784), soon opened the new Ohio Territory—an alluring prospect for settlers. As population increased, Congress provided a government for each new territory.

American stagecoach leaving western station. Engraving by Weld (1957)

An American saw mill. Engraving, 1790 (1958)

Turnpike road between Yorktown and Baltimore, Maryland. Engraving (1959)

The Lure of the West

Conestoga wagon carried families and freight in frontier expansion (1961)

"Plan of a newly cleared farm" near river front in backwoods Post-Revolutionary America (1960)

Daniel Boone's first sight of Kentucky (1962)

First territorial government, at Marietta, Ohio (1963)

Fraudulent sale of American wilderness land by Anglo-American speculators (1964)

Building log cabin at the frontier was an undertaking by entire community (1965)

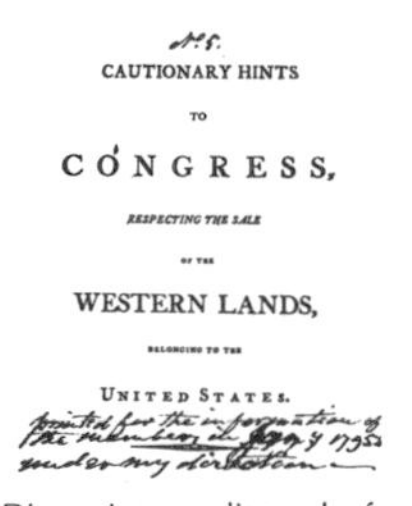
No. 5.

CAUTIONARY HINTS

TO

CONGRESS,

RESPECTING THE SALE

OF THE

WESTERN LANDS,

BELONGING TO THE

UNITED STATES.

Discussion on disposal of free government land (1966)

Johnny Appleseed plants new trees in the Ohio Valley (1967)

Old Ways of the South

KING COTTON brought increasing wealth to the agricultural South, enhancing its traditional aristocratic ways. British cotton mills, their capacity immeasurably increased by new machinery, waited eagerly for American cotton. With the invention of the cotton gin, the South was able to increase its output of cotton fiber eightfold between 1794 and 1804. But more cotton meant more slavery.

John Jacob Astor as a young emigrant buying furs from Indians in Upper New York (1968)

Group of fur traders bribes Indians with liquor (1969)

Robert Gray discovers Columbia River. Name of his ship was *Columbia* (1970)

Old Bruton Church in Williamsburg, Virginia. Painting by A.W. Thompson (1971)

Planter's family on the terrace of their Virginia estate. Wash drawing (1972)

Sunday after church. Congregation of plantation aristocrats (1973)

Formal presentation in a Westover, Va. plantation manor house (1974)

Colonial merchants read *Maryland Gazette* (1975)

Tobacco packed in barrel-like container is rolled to market. Virginia (1976)

Singing Circle. Cover of hymn collection (1977)

Crafts Prevail but Mechanization Stirs

EXCLUSIVE RIGHT to their discoveries was guaranteed American inventors by the new Constitution. Congress implemented this idea in 1790 by issuing the first patent law, and the next decade swarmed with new contraptions. Indeed, inventive genius seemed to be an integral part of the American character. Eli Whitney's invention of the cotton gin revolutionized the textile industry, and the mass-production methods he devised proved seminal to the later industrial growth of America.

Shipwright (1978)

Iron founder (1980)

Copper printer (1981)

Calico printer (1979)

Wood turner (1982)

Separating cotton fiber from seeds by hand (1983)

Whitney inventing cotton gin (1984)

Replica of original cotton gin by Eli Whitney (1985)

Cotton gin introduced on Southern plantation (1986)

Mass production: Whitney introduced manufacture of guns with interchangeable parts (1987)

Eli Whitney. Painting by Samuel Morse (1988)

The Whitney Armory in New Haven, Connecticut (1989)

Samuel Slater, pioneer machine builder (1990)

Rhode Island: water provided power for newly invented textile machines (1991)

View of an early cotton factory: Spinning (1992)

George Washington visits cotton mill in Beverly, Mass. (1993)

Factories

INDUSTRY IN THE COLONIES was restricted and sometimes forbidden by the mother country—England's prosperity depended partly upon maintaining a captive market for British manufactured goods. The new nation was thus industrially backward, but it did not long remain that way. Textile centers in New England soon vied with British producers for Southern cotton; and in other factories as well, the Yankees showed that they excelled in many aspects of industrial design.

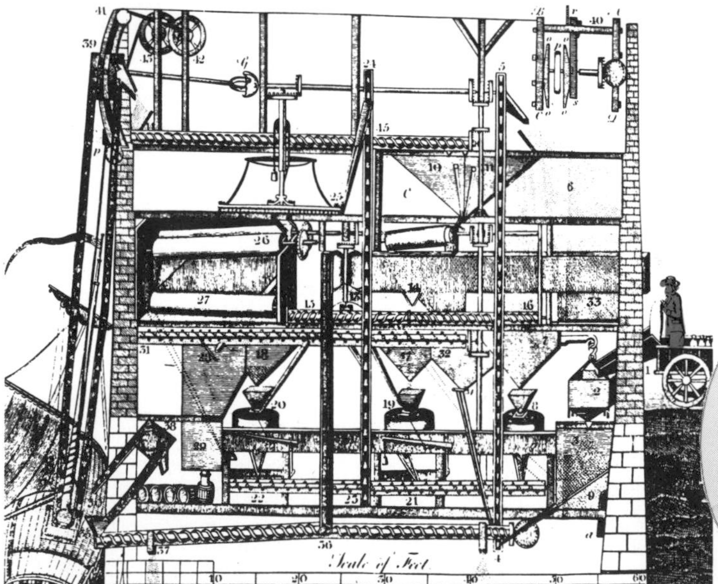

Oliver Evans' improved mill. It was completely mechanized and needed only one operator (1994)

Oliver Evans, American machine builder (1995)

Iron foundry in Salisbury, Connecticut. Water wheel powered its machinery (1996)

Transportation

SPEEDY TRANSPORTATION was a major commercial need in a nation with vast distances between markets, at least by Old World standards. River traffic governed much of commerce, and thus the invention of the steamboat was of major importance. Though John Fitch launched the first steam-driven boat in 1787, it remained for Robert Fulton to design and produce the first workable model. Thereafter, until the age of railroads, rivers filled with splashing paddle wheelers carried the nation's commerce.

John Fitch working on model of his steamboat (1997)

Fulton's steamboat on trial trip up the Hudson River (1998)

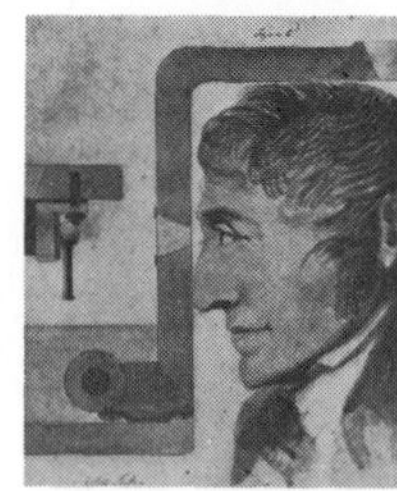
Fulton on periscope of his submarine, 1804 (1999)

John Fitch's first steamboat, launched in 1787 (1997 A)

Oliver Evans' amphibious steam vehicle (2000)

Growing Cities

Street peddlers: "Radishes! Radishes!" (2001) "Fine Rockaway clams!" (2002)

ALTHOUGH NINE TENTHS of the people in America lived on farms in 1789, cities were to play an important part in the growth of the country. New York, favored with natural harbor facilities and the highly accessible Hudson Valley, became the center of finance, shipbuilding, and the leisure pursuits of a land-rich gentry. It served as the first site of the new federal government, later to be replaced by Philadelphia.

Tontine Coffee House: trading center (2006)

New York

New York exporters and shipmasters. Pyle (2004)

View of New York Harbor shortly after the federal government was established (2003)

Meeting of New York Stock Exchange in 1792 (2005)

Tea-water pump in Greenwich Street, New York City (2007)

Laying wooden water pipes, New York (2008)

American counting house, merchant's office (2009)

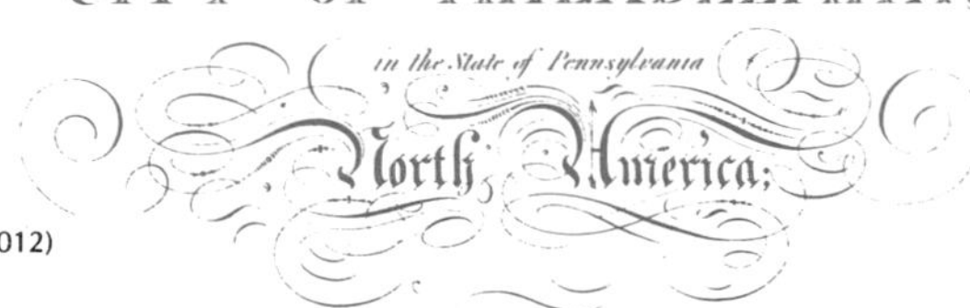

(2012)

THE BIRTHPLACE OF AMERICA and the site of the Constitutional Convention, Philadelphia was a cosmopolitan urban center. The founding here of the Bank of the United States (1791) gave the city dominance for a time in American commerce. Philadelphia's intellectual atmosphere, in the tradition of William Penn and Benjamin Franklin, was conducive to pursuit of the arts and sciences. President Washington's presence added glamour.

Scene near the Brooklyn Ferry. Woodcut, ca. 1790 (2010)

New York's frequent fires were fought by communal bucket brigades (2011)

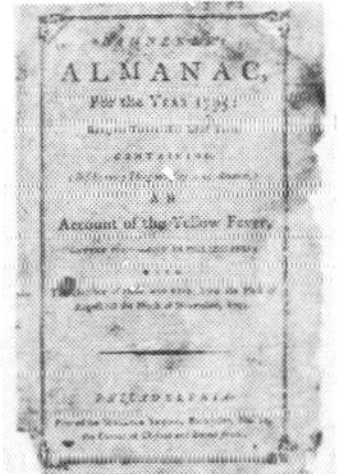

Almanac by Banneker, black astronomer (2013)

Yellow fever ravaged Philadelphia in 1793 and hundreds died (2014)

University of Pennsylvania opened America's first medical school (2015)

Wilson Peale showing his private museum (2016)

Rittenhouse, Philadelphia astronomer (2017)

Phila.: cradle of fire insurance (2018)

Stand of food merchant along High Street (2019)

A butcher's stand on Market Street (2020)

Election Day scene in Philadelphia (2021)

Penn.-Dutch printing establishment (2022)

Building the frigate *Philadelphia* "to defend commerce" (2023)

Quakers near Arch Street Meeting House (2024)

Washington

THE SITE CHOSEN for the new capital, named in honor of General Washington, was a mosquito-infested morass, dotted with ramshackle buildings, and housing about 3,000 persons, a sixth of them black. Once the government was established, however, appearances changed rapidly. A new architectural magnificence soon made it a symbol of the nation's power.

Washington in garb of Freemason lays cornerstone for U.S. Capitol (2026)

Beginnings of Washington D.C. Blodgett's Hotel, ca. 1799 (2027)

Building the President's House. It was still unfinished when Adams arrived (2028)

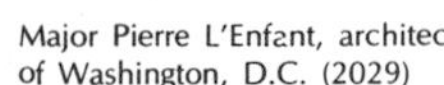

Major Pierre L'Enfant, architect of Washington, D.C. (2029)

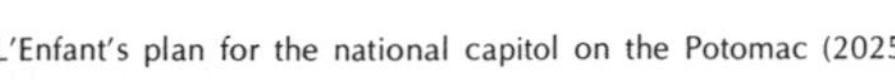

L'Enfant's plan for the national capitol on the Potomac (2025)

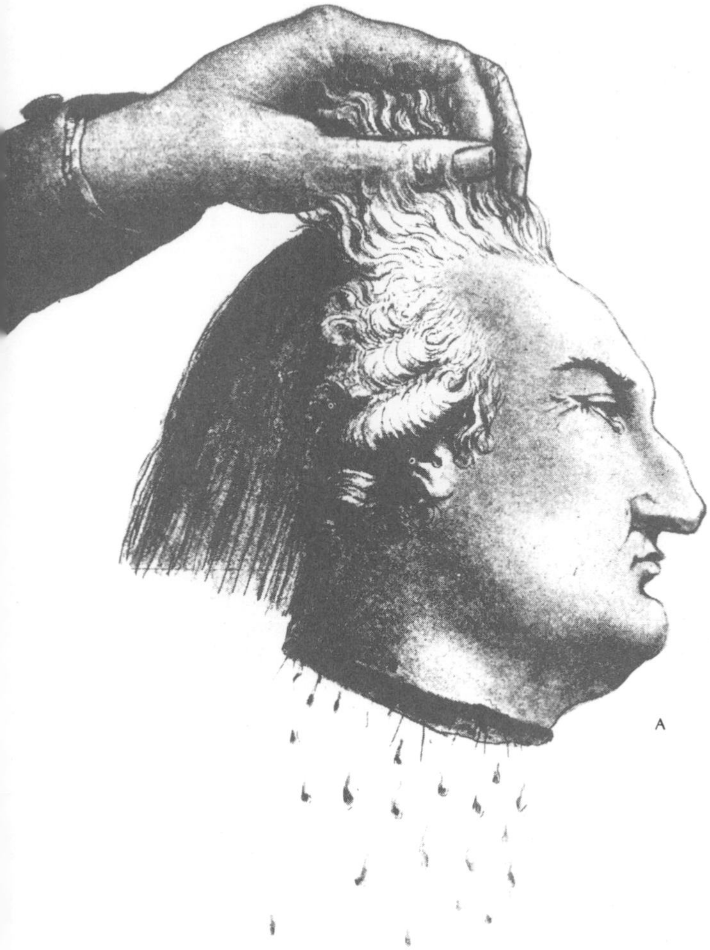

A

C

B

CHAPTER 7

The Age of Revolt

Upheaval in France
New World Alignments
Jacksonian Democracy

THE FRENCH REVOLUTION

Rising Fever

THE BANKRUPTCY of Louis XVI's government forced the King to call together the Estates-General, hoping for fiscal reform. But the Third Estate, the Commons, refused to consider fiscal matters before the redress of grievances. Locked out of the meeting hall at Versailles, they swore an "Oath in the Tennis Court" on June 20, 1789, not to disband until France had been given a constitution. Many Frenchmen still hoped to establish a constitutional monarchy, but Louis XVI reacted unwisely. When he attempted to dismiss Jacques Necker, a popular minister, radical spokesmen so inflamed the people's emotions that mobs stormed the Bastille, setting the prisoners free (July 14). This was the signal for full revolt.

Opening of the Estates-General, May 5, 1789. Third Estate bolted, formed "National Assembly" (2031)

The great abuse; peasant woman supports Church, nobility (2032)

Freedom cap atop liberty tree (2030)

QU'EST-CE QUE LE TIERS-ÉTAT? TROISIÈME ÉDITION. 1789.

Third Estate met at Versailles Tennis Court to give France a constitution (2033, 2034)

Mirabeau, a reasoned revolutionary (2035)

Storming Bastille, July 14, 1789, marked onset of revolution (2036)

Declaration of the Rights of Man, Aug. 26, 1789 (2037)

Noblemen surrender aristocratic badges, join the revolution (2038)

King agrees to rule France as a constitutional monarch (2039)

Louis XVI's attempt to leave Paris secretly was foiled by capture at Varennes (2040)

King wears a freedom cap to soothe the mob (2041)

Louis XVI seized, takes leave from family held prisoner in Temple Tower (2042)

Temple Tower, ancient Paris fortress (2043)

Citizens rally to defend threatened France (2044)

Revolutionary troops win at Valmy, 1792 (2045)

"Marseillaise" sung for the first time by composer Rouget de Lisle (2046)

(2047)

Radicalization

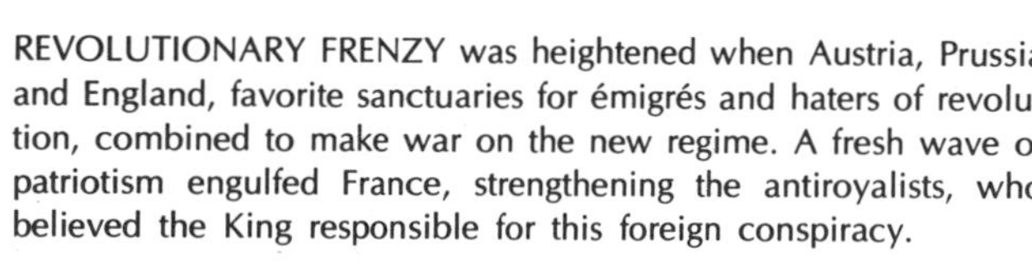

REVOLUTIONARY FRENZY was heightened when Austria, Prussia and England, favorite sanctuaries for émigrés and haters of revolution, combined to make war on the new regime. A fresh wave of patriotism engulfed France, strengthening the antiroyalists, who believed the King responsible for this foreign conspiracy.

Populace was informed of revolutionary events by flood of pamphlets (2048)

Woman fighter (2049)

Sans-culotte (2050)

Dr. Guillotin claimed he could chop off heads speedily (2051)

The guillotine—symbol of Reign of Terror (2052)

Condemned as traitor, Louis XVI was guillotined on Jan. 21, 1793 in front of Tuilleries (2053)

The head of Louis XVI (2054)

Marat stabbed in bathtub by Charlotte Corday (2055)

Imprisoned Corday before her execution (2056)

A friend of liberty and justice (2057)

Reign of Terror

INTERNAL STRIFE and foreign threats moved the National Assembly to confer absolute powers on a council of ten, the Committee of Public Safety. After a bloody power struggle, radicals won control of this committee and began the wholesale slaughter of counterrevolutionaries, real or suspected. Thousands went to the guillotine, but the terror continued, for once their foes were eliminated, the Revolutionary leaders turned upon each other. Robespierre, a man who professed Rousseau's ideal of a benevolent, humanitarian state, ordered hundreds of men executed, including many of France's great intellectuals. Finally he himself was strapped to the guillotine.

Robespierre, the power behind the Reign of Terror (2058)

Heads of noblemen spiked for public display (2059)

Danton was president of the radical Jacobin Club (2060)

Tribunal set up by Danton to liquidate his political and personal foes (2061)

Jacobin, member of extreme wing (2062)

Aristocrats carted en masse to face executioner (2063)

Marie Antoinette on way to the scaffold (2064)

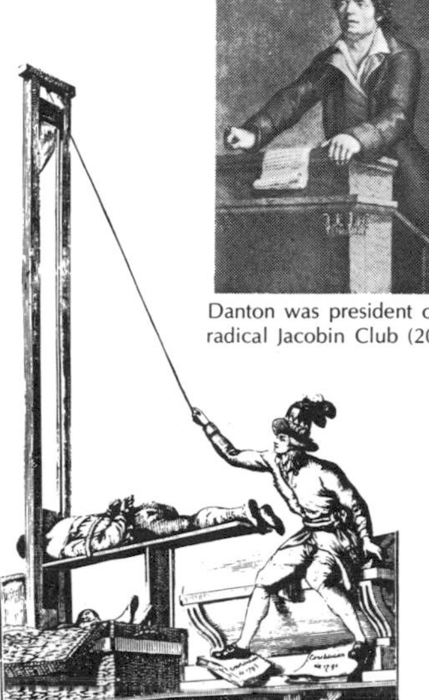

Robespierre, having executed everybody, finally executes the executioners (2065)

Robespierre arrested, victim of mortal power struggle (2066)

Old-fashioned firing squad used where guillotines were unavailable (2067)

Napoleon Takes Over

AFTER THE BLOOD BATH WITHIN, foreign invaders threatened France anew. The Directory, given absolute power by the new legislature, now mounted a successful campaign against Austria. The hero of this war, fought mostly in Italy, was General Napoleon Bonaparte. He was so successful, he soon became a threat. Although his campaign in Egypt, designed to cut Britain's lifeline to India, proved a failure, Napoleon sneaked home and overthrew the bankrupt Directory. On December 24, 1799, Napoleon was elected First Consul by plebiscite.

Member of Directory. Gillray engr. (2068)

Young general Napoleon, ordered by Directory to fight Austrians in Italy, won brilliant victories, showed genius for strategy and diplomacy (2069)

Napoleon leads troops at Arcole Bridge (2070)

Austrians accept armistice at Leoben after his successful Italian campaign (2070A)

At Mantua, French army used reconnaissance balloons (2071)

Napoleon after victory sketched by Gros (2072)

First Consul Napoleon crossed Alps via Saint Bernard Pass, 1800 (2077)

Pointing to the pyramids, Napoleon evokes his historical mission (2073)

Napoleon left Egypt secretly, abandoning his army (2074)

Jaffa plague sufferers seek cure via Napoleon's "King's Touch" (2075)

Acclaimed as First Consul in 1799, Napoleon became dictator (2076)

Master of Europe

PROCLAIMED EMPEROR in 1804, Napoleon saw himself as a second Charlemagne ("my distinguished predecessor") unifying the whole of Europe under his sceptre. At the height of his power Napoleon did, indeed, control most of it—from Italy to Norway, from Spain to Warsaw. His armies trampled kingdom after kingdom in an unprecedented series of battles, alliances, usurpations and betrayals. Still, the Emperor's archenemy, England, defied both his economic blockade (the Continental System) and his armed rage—for while Napoleon's armies seemed invincible on land, Britain still controlled the seas.

Imperial emblem (2078)

Napoleon crowning himself in front of Pope Pius VII. J.L. David (2079)

Afterwards he crowned Josephine as Empress of France (2080)

Napoleon at Austerlitz, where he defeated Russia and Austria, Dec. 2, 1805 (2081)

After vanquishing Prussia, Napoleon enters Berlin through the Brandenburg Gate (2082)

Napoleon meets Czar Alexander I of Russia on raft at Tilsit in 1807 (2083)

Napoleon cast as Roman emperor ruling world like Augustus (2084)

England the Unconquerable

John Bull (2085)

Bonaparte (2086)

French scheme to conquer England via English Channel tunnel (2087)

Nelson annihilated French fleet (2088)

Napoleon "48 hours after arrival in England" (2089)

Impounding of English goods during embargo against England (2090)

Napoleonic throne in the Fountainbleau castle (2091)

Letizia Bonaparte, "La Mère" (2092)

Jérôme, Napoleon's brother, King of Westphalia (2093)

Court and Family

NAPOLEON'S COURT was brilliant. Its privileged nobility, except for the Emperor's relatives, were ranked by merit rather than by birth, but they luxuriated in their estates, titles and incomes. Favors were distributed lavishly and imperial rancor was expressed with swift harshness—as to the twenty-seven cardinals who, because they were absent from the Emperor's marriage ceremony to Marie Louise, were stripped of their great revenues.

The Bee: Bonaparte family symbol (2094)

La Grande Armée

THE SOURCE of Napoleon's might was his army, unmatched in Europe for its dauntless spirit. With gestures of comradeship and the lure of glory, Napoleon inspired his troops with an almost mystical loyalty.

Court pays tribute to Napoleon and Marie Louise after marriage (2095)

Pauline, Napoleon's sister, was a daring society pace-setter (2096)

Napoleon and infant son, the King of Rome (2097)

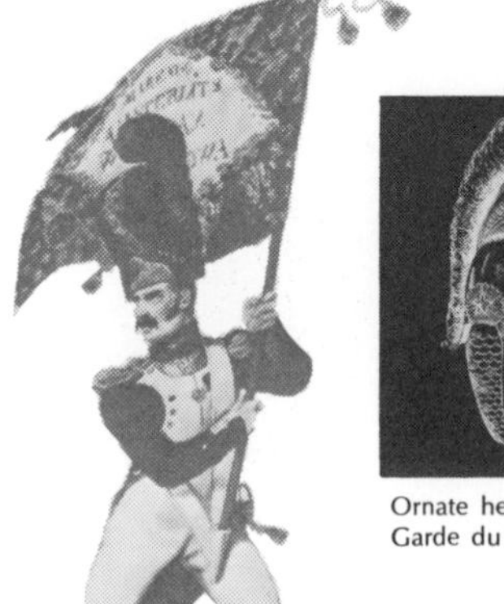
Flag bearer of the Imperial First Grenadiers (2102)

Ornate helmet of Imperial Garde du Corps (2098)

Napoleon studying map of Europe during strategy session (2099)

Napoleon treated his soldiers as comrades in arms (2100)

Napolen directs battle during a hurried camp meal (2101)

Wars of Liberation

WHEN THE CZAR REFUSED to endorse the Continental System (which was ruinous to Russia's economy) Napoleon invaded his country, with the largest army yet gathered upon the continent—500,000 men. The result was a debacle—barely one fifth of those soldiers survived a forced retreat during a Russian winter. Meanwhile, Prussia, secretly armed during her period of subjugation, led in reforging the alliance against France. With Austria and Russia, the Germans defeated Napoleon at Leipzig in 1813. Joined by England and Sweden, the allies encircled Napoleon at Paris, forcing his abdication and exiling him to the island of Elba in April, 1814.

Napoleon's army found Moscow deserted and soon consumed by flames. Facing destruction, he evacuated city on October 19, 1812 (2103,2104)

Napoleon gagged by Leipzig nut (2110)

Solitary Emperor views the desolation (2105)

Retreating soldiers faced Russian winter and a hostile populace. Only 100,000 returned (2106)

Napoleon in flight from Russian winter (2107)

Iron Cross, cast during 1813 War of Liberation (2108)

Allied monarchs observe battle of Leipzig (2109)

Philosopher Fichte as volunteer (2111)

Victorious allies enter Paris—Napoleon's European regime collapses (2112)

Napoleon leaves officers before going into exile on Elba (2113)

Congress of Vienna

THE DIPLOMATS who met in Vienna in 1814 to slice up Napoleon's empire had no interest in democratic reforms. At the behest of Talleyrand and Metternich, France was treated leniently, so that its new king, Louis XVIII, might establish a "butter state" monarchy, while Russia, Prussia and Austria formed the Holy Alliance to halt the spread of democratic government.

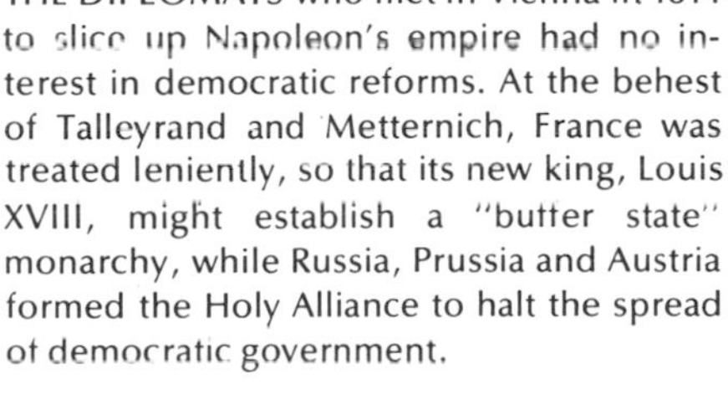

"Cutting up the cake of Kings": dynasts grabbing the spoils of victory (2114)

Metternich; power behind Vienna Congress (2115)

Congress of Vienna where many states played for territory gains (2116)

NEWS OF NAPOLEON'S FLIGHT from Elba in March, 1815 reached the Vienna Congress just as the exiled Emperor, after a triumphant march from Cannes, was entering Paris to begin the last "hundred days" of his rule. The allies left him little time to reorganize his empire. Their vast army under Britain's Duke of Wellington inflicted the final defeat on Napoleon at Waterloo, June 18, 1815.

Wellington victor at Waterloo (2117)

The many faces of Talleyrand (2118)

Holy Alliance of Russia-Prussia-Austria represented powers of reaction (2119)

Napoleon welcomed back from Elba (2120)

Napoleon's end: June 18, 1815 Battle of Waterloo (2121)

Wellington, Blücher join after battle (2122)

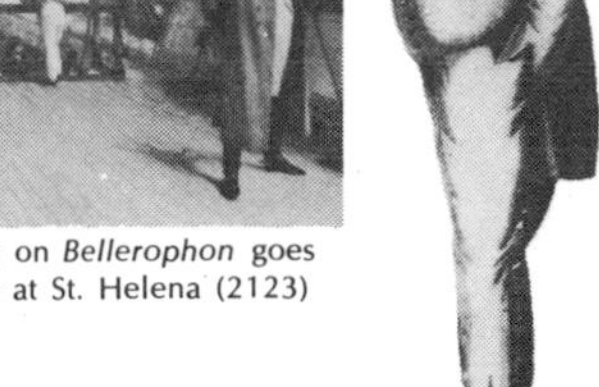

Napoleon on *Bellerophon* goes into exile at St. Helena (2123)

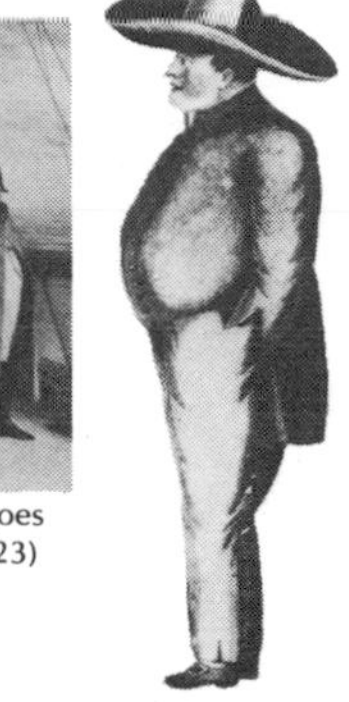

Exile, St. Helena (2124)

He died here in 1821 after bout with stomach cancer (2125)

Empire Life Style

Looser Gowns—Looser Habits

BECAUSE COLORS AND ORNAMENTS were forbidden by the Estates-General in 1789, good republicans avoided the ornate fashions of the old aristocracy, affecting simple coats, and plain long trousers to replace the courtly knee-breeches called "culottes." (The Sans-Culottes were to become a radical party.)

But Napoleon's court affected the mode of the Roman Imperium. Roman fashions, mingled with Egyptian motifs (a reminder of the emperor's Egyptian campaign) permeated all aspects of courtly style—fashion, furniture, decoration and even the Imperial insignia.

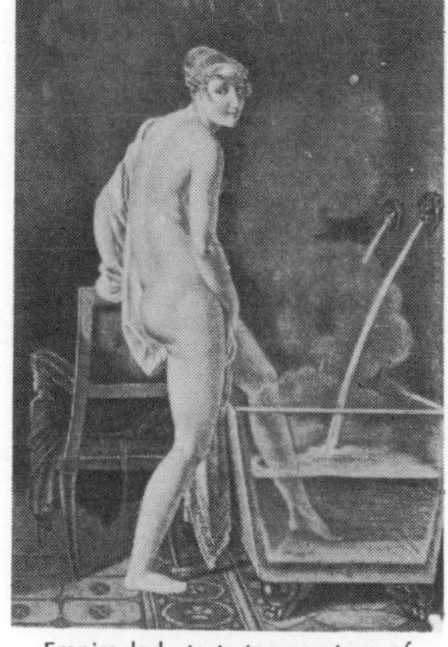

Empire lady tests temperature of transparent crystal bath (2126)

Wide-lapelled dandy, *"merveilleux"* (2127)

Couple sits near a window with Venetian blinds (2128)

Salon of *nouveaux riches* shows décor of Empire period (2129)

Madame Récamier lounging on Récamière she named (2130)

Chess mates in setting of Napoleonic period (2131)

Magic-lantern show projects Paris family life (2132)

Diabolo, played by an amorous couple (2133)

Partying Parisians play kissing game; from *Le Bon Genre* (2134)

Dance expressed gusto of Empire life style (2135)

Parisian parks offered amusement devices for young and old (2136)

Empire couple watching balloon ascent (2137)

Ice cream became the rage. Many exotic flavors were offered (2138)

Female entrepreneur sells hot sausage on a bun (2139)

Ladies congregate in an *atélier des modistes,* chat and try out latest hat fashions (2140)

Le professeur de coiffure uses dummy to create hair style for novelty-craving Parisians (2141)

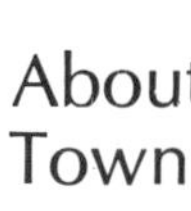

About Town

Empire couple. Lady in simple white gown; gentleman in multicolored outfit (2142)

Houdon is visited in studio while sculpting famed astronomer Pierre de Laplace (2143)

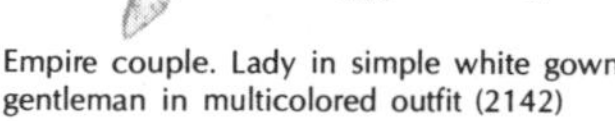

WOMEN'S FASHIONS, rejecting the heavy corsets and crinolines associated with a regal society, turned toward simple, diaphanous (even at times transparent) white gowns, which fully displayed a lady's charms. The spirit of expansive optimism, and the international cast of the Empire, were reflected in an amoral, free-floating society. The upper classes indulged in dancing, gambling and more liberal relations between the sexes (with a decided rise in illegitimate births). On a more subdued level, the middle class enjoyed the same freedoms.

French gourmets meet for food tasting (2144)

Brillat-Savarin, arbiter of gastronomy (2145)

Empire fashion fop (2146)

England's Regency
Dominated by a Pleasure Loving Monarch

DURING HIS FINAL ILLNESS, George III relinquished the government to his son, later George IV. The Regent's scandalous amatory adventures and profligate life style offended the nation. Around his palace of pleasure at Brighton were gathered crowds of loose women, rakes and gamblers. Still, his reign left an imprint upon architecture and men's fashions. The rebuilding of London (of which Regent Street and Regent Park are reminders) was designed by his crony John Nash. Another associate, Beau Brummel, helped him to set foppish standards for male attire.

Beau Brummel, the Regency's famed fop (2147)

George IV in his carriage (2150)

Gluttonous George lampooned by English satirist Gillray (2148)

Scandalous affair of Prince George with divorcée Fitzherbert discovered by Princess Caroline (2149)

(2151)

Dandy dons a corset to gain slick figure (2152)

Prince was addicted to cardplaying, met friends in London clubs (2153)

Thomas Rowlandson, pictorial satirist:

"There is in him a healthy rollicking fatness, a rich amplitude of physical life."
—J.B. Priestley

"A little tighter." Husband in hopeless struggle (2154)

Rowlandson ridicules the gourmet who eats like a glutton (2155)

Romanticism

"The Itch." cartoon by Rowlandson (2156)

Reckless driver has Death riding postilion Ominous warning by Rowlandson (2157)

IN CONTRAST TO the Brighton set, a new mood of high seriousness emerged in English literature. The Romantic poets—Wordsworth, Coleridge, Byron, Shelley, Keats—sympathized with the idealism of the French Revolution, and sought a more imaginative, more personal expression of the human spirit.

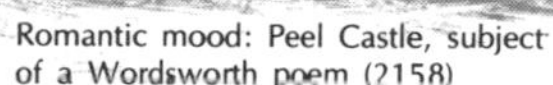
Romantic mood: Peel Castle, subject of a Wordsworth poem (2158)

John Keats died at twenty-six (2159)

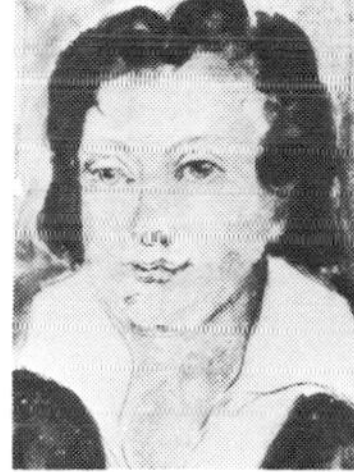
Percy B. Shelley fled to Italy in 1818 (2160)

Shelley drowned near Pisa. His body was cremated in presence of Byron (2161)

William Wordsworth was British laureate (2162)

Walter Scott in castle at Abbotsford (2163)

ILLUSTRATIONS
OF
the ROMANCE of
IVANHOE
ENGRAVED BY FRANCIS KEARNY
from Drawings by
RICHARD WESTALL ESQ. R.A.

Scott's *Ivanhoe;* romantics idolized medieval chivalry, faith (2170)

Jane Austen wrote novel *Pride and Prejudice* (2164)

Charles Lamb; brilliant, incisive essayist (2165)

Thomas de Quincey an opium addict (2166)

William Hazlitt was master essayist (2167)

Samuel T. Coleridge (2168) wrote the brooding, symbolic *The Rime of the Ancient Mariner* (2169)

Lord Byron created the romantic hero and emulated him in his own life (2171), fought for Greece's freedom (2172)

Lionized and frequently scandalized Byron leaves England forever (2173)

America Enters World Politics

John Adams (2174)

The Adams family home in Quincy, Mass. (2177)

DESPITE WASHINGTON'S ADMONITIONS, the United States now took sides in the French-English conflict. Both adversaries preyed painfully on American shipping, but President John Adams, a Federalist, took a decided anti-French (anti-Revolutionary) stance. When an American Peace Commission was snubbed by Talleyrand in an obvious extortion attempt, opposition to the French reached fever pitch. The result was passage of the Alien and Sedition Acts (1797), apparently directed against France but also used viciously to silence Adams' critics in the opposition party.

John Adams, fervent patriot and Federalist (2175)

Abigail Adams, his wife, was articulate (2176)

Adams as U.S. Ambassador to George III court (2178)

Conflict with France at Boiling Point

France's interference with American commerce resulted in open naval hostilities (2179)

Federal carriage with Washington in command threatens France (2180)

France demanding at dagger point tribute from U.S.—XYZ affair (2181)

Tempers in Congress flared up in party fights (2182)

Song "Hail Columbia" aired patriotic feeling (2183)

Th: Jefferson (2184)

THOMAS JEFFERSON, who followed Adams, had been ambassador to France at the outbreak of the Revolution. His close relations with the French (as a disciple of the *philosophes* of the Enlightenment) led him to a policy of détente loudly decried by the Federalists. But it paid off handsomely when Napoleon, hard pressed for money to support his armies, agreed to sell the Louisiana Territory for a little more than $13 million. The size of the United States more than doubled overnight.

Thomas Jefferson at eighty-two. (2185)

Jefferson arriving for his first inauguration (2186)

Francophile Jefferson satirized as foe of U.S. Constitution (2187)

Monticello, Jefferson's home, based on his designs (2188)

Understanding the French, Jefferson achieved rapprochement with Napoleon (2189)

Louisiana Purchase completed; Raising American flag (2193)

Lewis and Clark on expedition, guided by Sacajawea (2190)

Incident during Lewis and Clark Expedition, 1803-1806 (2191)

Signing of Louisiana Purchase agreement: Monroe, Livingston, Barbé-Marbois (2192)

Map showing territory acquired through Louisiana Purchase (2194)

Tripolitan pirates boarding U.S. ship to exact tribute money (2195)

Trouble with Tripoli

THE BARBARY PIRATES had long preyed upon American shipping, seizing goods and ransoming sailors for exorbitant sums. On Jefferson's initiative, the pirates were subdued and a treaty signed.

Stephen Decatur (2196) entered Tripoli, burned U.S. Frigate *Philadelphia* (2197) held captive by pirates.

James Madison (2198)

MADISON'S PRESIDENCY was marred by a rather pointless conflict with England, whose interference with American shipping (during her war with France) offended American patriots. In 1812 the United States declared war on England. But with the French conflict resolved, England turned to forceful pursuit of "Mr. Madison's War." At one point, British forces sacked and burned Washington.

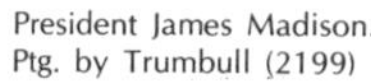

President James Madison. Ptg. by Trumbull (2199)

Impressment of seamen was one of the causes of 1812 war with England (2200)

U.S.S. *Constitution* blasts H.M.S. *Guerrière* into submission in August, 1812 (2201)

Perry at Lake Erie: "We have met the enemy and they are ours." (2202)

British have to take bitter draught of Perry's victory, Sept. 1813 (2203)

Hartford convention attacked "Mr. Madison's War" (2204)

British burned Washington, D.C. in the summer of 1814 (2205)

Dolly Madison flees White House (2206)

Francis Scott Key watches Ft. McHenry's flag (2207)

Election districts in Massachusetts rearranged in form of new animal, "gerrymander", by Gov. Elbridge Gerry (2211)

The Star-spangled banner.

O say! can you see by the dawn's early light
What so proudly we hail'd at the twilight's last gleaming,
Whose broad stripes and bright stars through the clouds of the fight,
O'er the ramparts we watch'd were so gallantly streaming?
And the rocket's red glare – the bomb bursting in air
Gave proof through the night that our flag was still there?

National anthem in the handwriting of poet F.S. Key (2208)

Battle of New Orleans was fought two weeks after peace settlement (2209)

Elbridge Gerry originated "gerrymandering" (2210)

(2212A)

DESPITE THE HUMILIATION of the War of 1812, an upsurge of patriotic pride followed the conflict. James Monroe strove to bring about a "period of good feeling." Announcing the sovereignty of both North and South America, his Doctrine closed both continents to foreign colonization, enabling republics to the south to progress in peace.

Monroe runs for "People's Rights" on Republican ticket (2212)

Inauguration of Monroe marked a new "Era of Good Feeling" (2213)

Seminole Indians in Florida punished by Andrew Jackson in 1818 (2214)

President Monroe announcing Monroe Doctrine to the members of his Cabinet, in 1823 (2215)

Simón Bolivar monument in Caracas, Venezuela (2216)

Signing of Venezuela's Declaration of Independence, July 5, 1811 (2217)

Independent Neighbors to the South

NAPOLEON'S INVASION of the Iberian peninsula precipitated a crescendo of revolt from colonial status. Brazil retained a blood relationship with Portugal through Dom Pedro I, but the Spanish colonial empire collapsed under the heroic leadership of José de San Martin and Simón Bolívar. After his miraculous march across the Andes from Argentina to cut the Spanish bonds in Chile, San Martin pushed the Spanish out of Peru. Bolívar then assumed the full mantle of liberation and broke the remaining Spanish power in Colombia, Venezuela, Ecuador and Panama. The decade of the 1820s was the greatest in Central and South American history.

Bolivar defeated Spanish at Boyaca, 1819 (2218)

San Martin liberated Chile from Spanish yoke (2219)

O'Higgins in 1818 declared Chile an independent state (2220)

John Quincy Adams. (2221)

UNABLE TO MUSTER a majority of electoral votes, John Quincy Adams (with the help of Henry Clay) was elected by the House of Representatives. Adams was a scholar at heart, idealistic and visionary; he lacked the political acumen to gain support for his programs: road systems, a national university, support for the arts and sciences. The time for elitist Presidents had passed. Western forces, seeking expansion of their interests, now knocked on the portals of government.

Congressional memorial to father and son presidents, erected in Quincy, Mass. (2222)

J. Q. Adams ridiculed in Jackson poster (2223)

Adams during old age; early photograph (2224)

Congressman Adams died in Congress (2225)

"Dat ole devil Jackson" (2226)

Cartoon predicts treatment for Jackson's foes (2228)

(2227)

THE FIRST PRESIDENT out of the West, Andrew Jackson represented the democratic aspirations of the leaner lands against the mercantile power of the East. After thirty years of rule by "first families" of Virginia and Massachusetts, the people clamored for an active voice in their government. Riding the wave of populism, Jackson replaced federal employees wholesale with his democratic followers, abolished the elitist Bank of the United States, espoused hard money and the removal of the Indians from their territories.

The champion of the common man brought down the United States Bank with the support of Attny. Genl. Roger Taney and the "raggle-taggle" Democrats (2229)

Andrew Jackson's birthplace in the Carolina backwoods (2230)

Frontier judge Jackson arrests a desperado. People exulted in his rough and ready actions (2231)

Jackson campaigns at a wayside inn. Elected twice, he was idolized as a folk hero. (2232)

Inauguration of 1829 turned into tumultuous melee (2233)

Jackson's toast to the Federal Union (2234)

Banker Nicholas Biddle, Jackson target (2235)

King Andrew, "born to command" (2236)

Martin Van Buren, Jackson's V.P. and successor (2238)

(2238A)

JACKSON'S SUCCESSOR took office at a time when a depression followed the demise of the U.S. Bank (1836). Aggravated by poor crops, excessive speculation in western lands, and an industrial crisis in England, the depression took on panic proportions, aborting Van Buren's bid for re-election.

A HARD ROAD TO HOE!

Van Buren pleaded for a U.S. Sub-Treasury so that United States could become its own banker (2239)

Jackson overtly supported spoils system: federal jobs to his supporters (2237)

Technical Progress

THE AGE OF JACKSON saw rapid growth in American technology. In the forty years after 1810, American patents grew from a yearly seventy-seven to over one thousand. The most important developments were the steamboat and the locomotive. With canals and locks, America's rivers were joined into a commercial network. Meanwhile, the first practical locomotive, the Tom Thumb, began service for the Baltimore & Ohio Railway in 1830.

The construction of the Erie Canal is considered this period's greatest technical feat (2240)

Canal opened by Clinton, 1825, who poured lake water into Atlantic. New waterway linked midwest to New York (2241)

Velocipede seen in 1827 Washington, D.C. (2242)

Locomotive "Best Friend," ran in the South (2243)

John Deere demonstrating his improved steel plow (2244)

Morse works on telegraph (2245)

Savannah, first steamship to cross the Atlantic, carried no passengers (2246)

McCormick demonstrates mechanical reaper (2247)

Spiritual Awakening

NOAH WEBSTER'S *American Dictionary of the English Language* has been called a "literary Declaration of Independence." Published in 1828, it reflected a new sense of national pride and confidence. American writers such as Washington Irving and James Fenimore Cooper now explored their country's past, its frontiers, fables and folklore.

Webster's *Dictionary* showed that America had own language (2248)

Washington Irving (2249) wrote "Rip Van Winkle" (2250) and other Hudson River tales.

William Cullen Bryant in ptg. by S.F.B. Morse (2251)

James Fenimore Cooper, romantic novelist (2252)

Cooper showed frontiersmen, Indians, as admirable, resourceful types (2253, 2254)

Edgar Allan Poe, American poet, man of letters (2255)

Illustration from Poe's "The Pit and the Pendulum" (2256)

"The Raven," his famous evocation (2257)

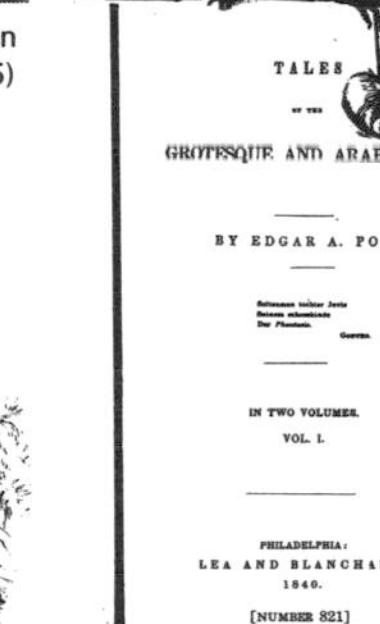
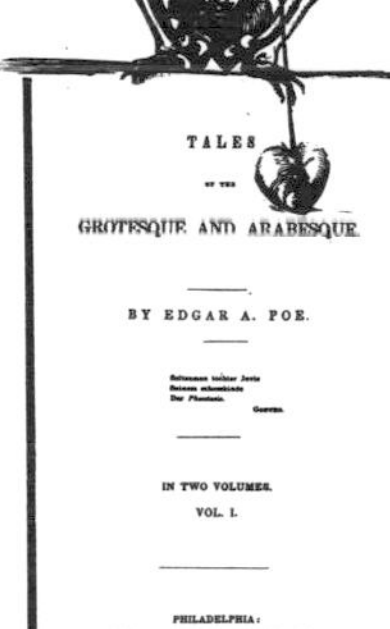
TALES OF THE GROTESQUE AND ARABESQUE.

BY EDGAR A. POE.

IN TWO VOLUMES. VOL. I.

PHILADELPHIA: LEA AND BLANCHARD. 1840.

[NUMBER 821]

(2258)

ONE IMPORTANT AMERICAN WRITER, Edgar Allan Poe, looked with disdain at the American scene, preferring somber medieval settings, ivied mansions, decaying corpses and clanking chains. A subtle practitioner of the Gothic story of terror, and father of the detective story, he had a marked influence on European literature.

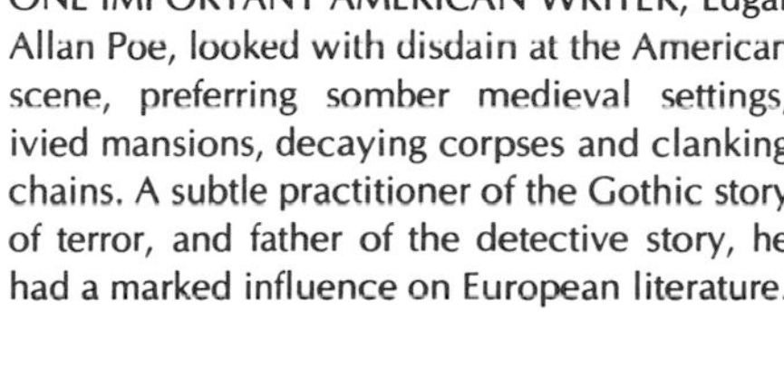
Mike Fink, the legendary Ohio keelboat man (2259)

Catlin depicted waning customs of the prairie Indians (2260)

John J. Audubon, frontiersman, pictorial biographer of American birds (2261)

Turkey—one of Audubon's priceless prints (2262)

Rev. S.F. Smith wrote the anthem "America" (2263)

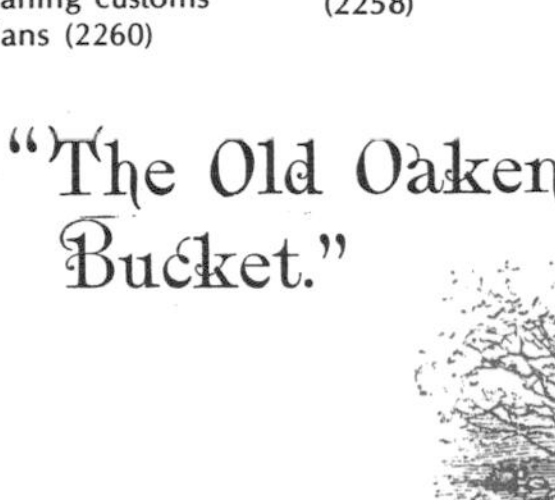

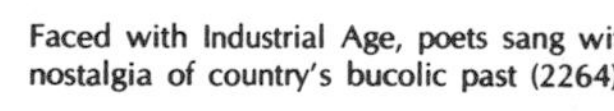
Faced with Industrial Age, poets sang with nostalgia of country's bucolic past (2264)

A
B
C
D

CHAPTER 8

Romanticism - Materialism

Nationalism

Industrialization

Capitalist Prosperity

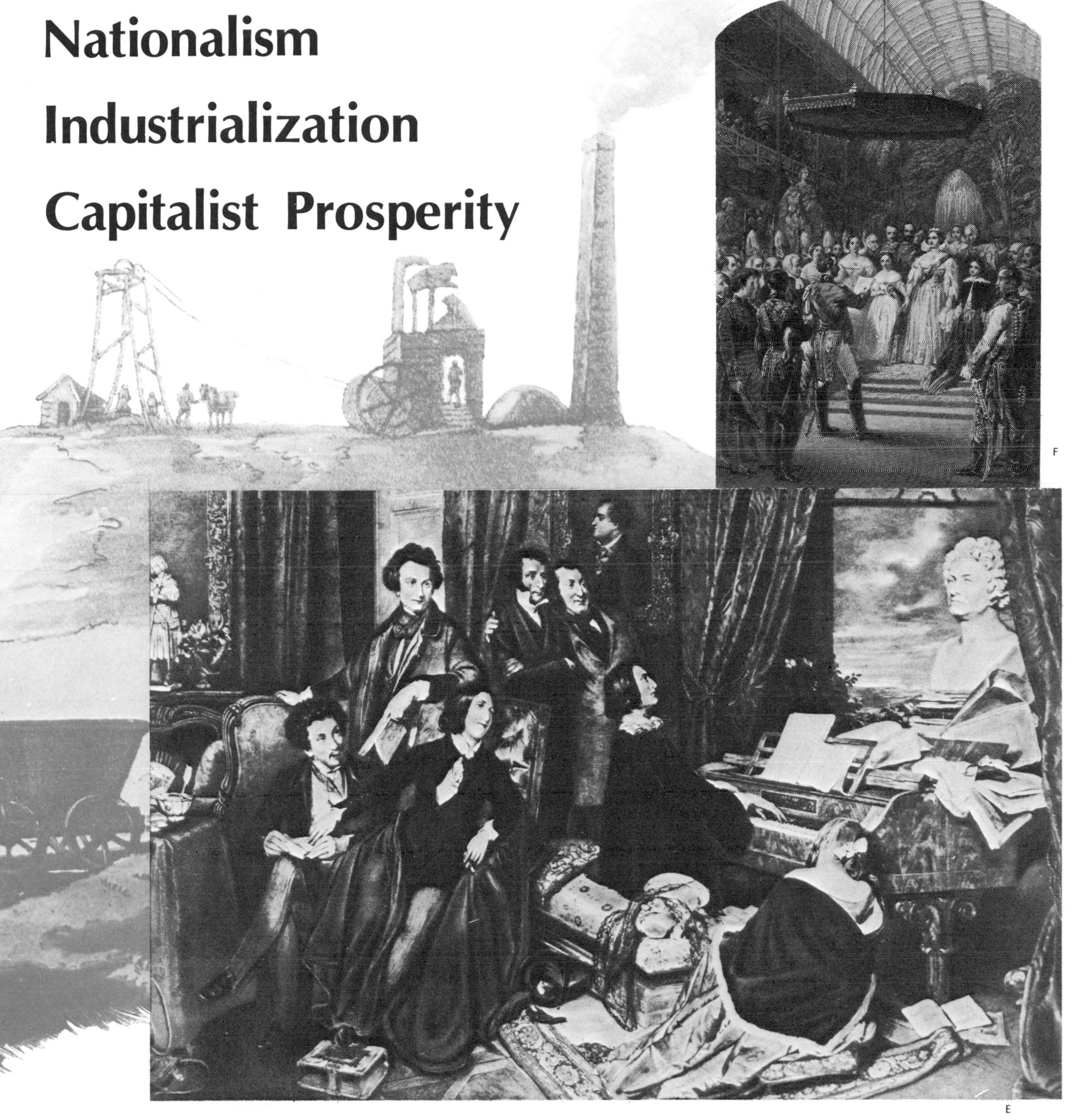

F

E

France

WITH NAPOLEON IN EXILE, the Allies restored the monarchy in France, but despite a charter providing parliamentary government, both Louis XVIII and Charles X sought to exercise absolute power. The bourgeoisie revolted in 1830; however, France ended up a monarchy again—headed by a "Citizen King," Louis Philippe. While projecting an image of bonhomie, the King was brutally oppressive and was deposed by the Revolution of 1848. Louis Napoleon, Bonaparte's nephew, was made President of the Second Republic, but he, too, seized absolute power, in 1851, and a year later France was once more an empire.

Charles X was conciliatory at first but became a dictator during reign (2265)

Paris uprising after freedom of press was suspended by Charles X (2266)

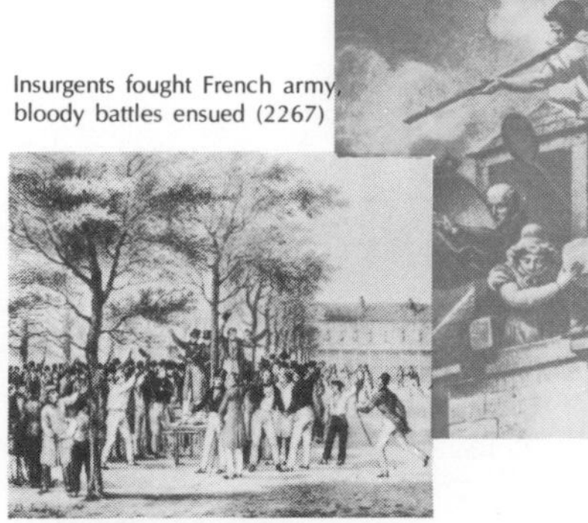
Insurgents fought French army, bloody battles ensued (2267)

Workers join revolution, man barricades at Lyon (2268)

Louis Philippe sworn in as "King of the French" (2269)

The Citizen King during a walk in Paris (2270)

He muzzled press, was hated by artists and writers (2271)

Assassination attempts against the Citizen King were frequent, but none ever succeeded (2272)

Louis Philippe escaped to England when his regime toppled in 1848 Revolution (2273)

Barricade fighters of the 1848 Revolution (2274)

Lamartine proclaims the Second Republic (2275)

Louis Napoleon's campaign for presidency of Republic (2276)

Napoleon III at the bloody Battle of Solferino (2277)

Workers storming the bastion of hated industrialists (2278)

Utopian Socialists

Saint-Simon: wealthy social planner (2279)

Louis Blanc backed state-financed industries (2280)

Socialist Proudhon axing down capitalism (2281)

Underground socialist student group during clandestine discussions (2282)

Establishing a new commune in the wilds of Texas (2283)

National workshops were attempt to solve France's unemployment problem (2284)

Fourier's *phalanstère*; land, buildings were to be owned by the commune (2285)

THE POST-NAPOLEONIC POLITICAL EXPERIMENTS were largely disastrous, inspiring the theorists to propound ways to achieve a more peaceful and productive order. Although the Utopian Socialists had little effect on practical politics, their works entered the mainstream of contemporary thought, building stones for the mighty edifice of Marx's scientific socialism.

People of Paris

LIFE FOR MOST PEOPLE, despite the political conflict of the age, was relatively tranquil, as a series of lithographs in 1830 by Carle Marlet demonstrates. The routine of daily existence seemed more important to Parisians than military or ideological battles.

Students teach each other while the teacher looks on (2286)

Public weighing station in a Paris park (2287)

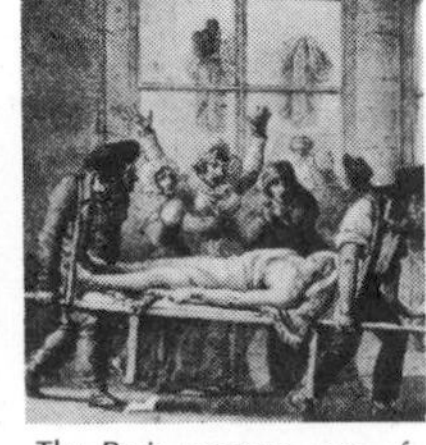
The Paris morgue: one of city's macabre sights (2288)

Moving day: a worker's family conveys its scant belongings (2289)

Parisian press was active, reading became a popular pleasure (2290)

Romantic Literature

THE NAPOLEONIC WARS left little time for the arts, except as they glorified the Emperor. But the period between the revolutions of 1830 and 1848 saw a great flowering of romantic art and literature. A new *Zeitgeist,* as Hegel called it, pervaded thought and feeling. Some writers invested the era with a haze of antique romance. Others, like Balzac, were soul-searchers.

Romanticism: dreams, yearnings, fantasies, mystic meditations (2291)

Chateaubriand: true Romanticist (2292)

Victor Hugo,leading poet and liberal leader (2293)

Hugo's *Hernani* staged: literary factions came to blows (2294)

Dumas' *Hunchback of Notre Dame* (2295)

Balzac. Sketch from a daguerreotype (2296)

Novels produced in a wholesale fashion (2297)

Balzac's *Lost Illusions* (2298)

Type from *Human Comedy* (2299)

George Sand affected male attire (2300)

Alfred de Musset as drawn by himself (2301)

Henri Stendhal's autobiographical novels expressed adventurous mood (2302, 2303)

Scribe ridiculed as literary factory. He wrote hundreds of plays (2304)

Th. Gautier proclaimed *"l'art pour l'art"* (2305)

Sainte-Beuve: literary critic and diarist (2306)

Dumas, Sr. envisions his heroes (2307)

Alexandre Dumas filled 30 vols. with romantic novels (2308)

Romantic Music

MUSIC PROVED TO BE the most congenial medium for Romanticism. As poetry took on musical qualities, music turned feverishly to the personal and poetic, and Romantic composers often burned out their lives while still young. At twenty-seven, Berlioz set Paris agog with his *Symphonie fantastique,* using a giant orchestra reflective of his own ebullience. Similarly with Chopin—suffering malaise of mind and body, he was hailed by his contemporaries as the "poet of sound."

Chopin. Daguerreotype taken in 1840s (2309)

Chopin during a recital in the palace of Prince Radziwill, his early patron (2310)

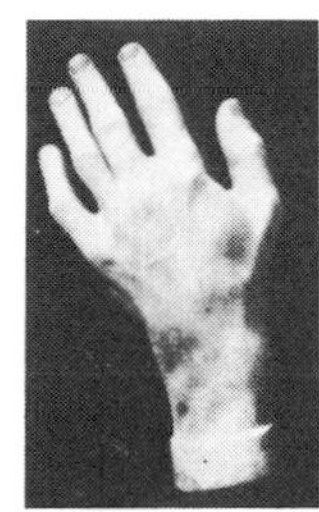
Marble replica of Chopin's hand (2311)

Berlioz, Romanticist par excellence (2312)

Young Berlioz teaching himself guitar (2313)

Berlioz lampooned as user of giant orchestras (2314)

Berlioz's wife, famed for her role as Juliet (2315)

Damnation of Faust set to music by Berlioz (2316)

Meyerbeer opera, libretto by Eugène Scribe (2317)

Meyerbeer brought grand opera to France (2318)

Jacques Halévy, noted for *La Juive* (2319)

Donizetti wrote with both hands (2319A)

Franz Liszt plays before his friends: De Musset, Hugo, George Sand, Berlioz, Rossini, Mme. D'Agoult (2320)

The Arts in Germany
Apogee of Music

THE TURBULENCE OF THE NAPOLEONIC WARS reverberated in the German music of the age: tempos accelerated, themes became broader and bolder. Ludwig van Beethoven emerged as the great Janus figure, anchored in classical form but reaching out for Romantic emotional power. At the same time, the association between poet and musician became a close one. Like Berlioz, who drew inspiration from Goethe and Byron, Franz Schubert in his *Lieder* set poems by many of the Romantic writers to music. Poets and composers alike felt the need to transcend the ugliness of the everyday world with an appeal to the spirit.

Choral theme from *Ninth Symphony* (2324)

Beethoven: his art was nourished by a new vision of man's freedom and dignity (2321)

His Vienna home with the "Hammerklavier" (2322)

Beethoven strolling in Vienna (2323)

Fidelio, the only opera Beethoven wrote (2325)

Schubert in his short life wrote 603 songs (2326)

Erlkönig, Schubert's famed song based on Goethe poem of child's fantasy (2327)

Intimate concert given by Schubert for circle of his friends. Drawing by Schwind (2328)

Song cycle by Franz Schubert: *Die Schöne Müllerin* (2329)

Mendelssohn wrote his finest compositions before he was eighteen years old (2330)

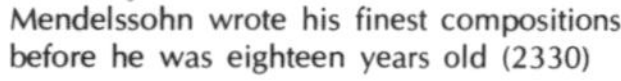

Romanticism's elfin spirit resounds in his *Midsummer Night's Dream* music (2331)

Group-singing was widely practiced in the age of Romanticism (2332)

Clara and Robert Schumann: charmed union of composer, renowned pianist (2333,2334)

Kreisleriana named for violinist (2335)

Weber's *Freischütz,* paradigm of the Romantic opera (2336)

Karl Maria von Weber conducting. His *Invitation to the Dance* is still a concert favorite (2337)

Poets, Lyricists

Paintings of Kaspar David Friedrich reflect German Romanticism (2338)

Romantic fiddler in church tower (2339)

E.T.A. Hoffmann wrote picturesque stories, the basis of Offenbach's *Tales of Hoffmann* (2340)

Novalis sought Romantic's mystic "blue flower" (2341)

Hölderlin: emotions cast in classic form (2342)

Bettina von Arnim: young charmer (2343)

Achim von Arnim wrote cycle *Des Knaben Wunderhorn* (2344)

(2345)

Sad parting—theme of Romantics (2346)

Lorelei; German fable a poem by Heine (2347)

Heinrich Heine; poet lived as exile in Paris (2348)

Resurgent German Spirit

MANY ROMANTIC WRITERS joined in the political battles of the century. In France, men like Lamartine were royalists, but most were radical liberals, like Victor Hugo, who was exiled for opposing Napoleon III. In Germany, the vision of a unified German state (there were still some thirty-eight principalities in the German Confederation) motivated the intellectual community. While men like Von Stein, Humboldt and Hardenberg undertook reform in education and finance, a spiritual awakening gained momentum—especially at the University of Berlin, with Hegel, Schleiermacher and Fichte the dominant figures.

George Frederic Hegel, philosopher historian; trenchant figure (2350)

Schleiermacher: a radiant preacher-patriot (2351)

Musicale in prosperous German Biedermeier household (2352)

Jacob Grimm lecturing to class in philology at Göttingen (2353)

The Brothers Grimm collected Germanic folklore (2354)

"The Frog Prince," typical Grimm fairy tale (2355)

Freedom! (2359)

Revolt and Reaction

A SERIES OF REVOLUTIONS spread through the German states. At the University of Berlin, students, professors and townsmen rushed to the barricades to pursue the Romantic vision of a united Germany. Successful enough to call a Parliament at Frankfurt, the revolutionaries debated a constitution while vested rulers moved to regain their power.

Wartburg Fest of 1817, when students burned emblems of reaction (2356)

Underground meeting of students demanding German unity (2357)

Manning barricades in short lived 1848 Berlin student uprising (2358)

Frederick Wilhelm IV grants watered down reform (2362)

The Frankfurt Parliament discussed unification, but to no avail (2360)

Uprising at Vienna university (2361)

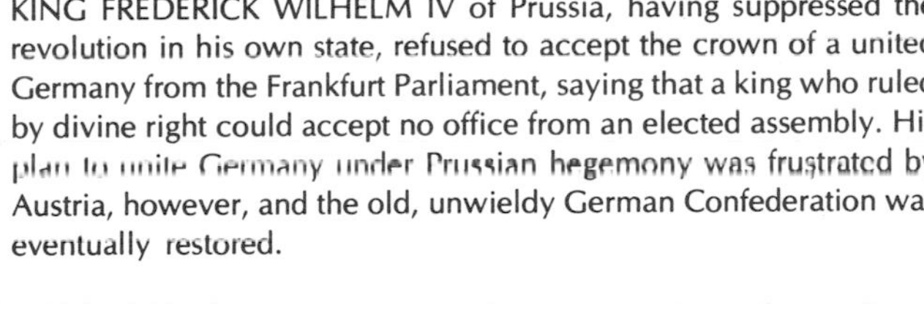

KING FREDERICK WILHELM IV of Prussia, having suppressed the revolution in his own state, refused to accept the crown of a united Germany from the Frankfurt Parliament, saying that a king who ruled by divine right could accept no office from an elected assembly. His plan to unite Germany under Prussian hegemony was frustrated by Austria, however, and the old, unwieldy German Confederation was eventually restored.

Robert Blum, German revolutionary in Vienna, put to death by firing squad (2363)

Viennese populace reads demands for ouster of the reactionary clique (2364)

Metternich resigned, fled Austria (2365)

Franz Josef weathered the storm (2366)

Refugees from Revolution

THE OPPRESSIVE ATMOSPHERE of the 1840s prompted many freedom fighters to look with longing to America. Some came, but on a short visit. Others settled here to make marked contributions to American life as entrepreneurs and political figures. Much of what is referred to as the "German element" in the U.S. population had its roots in the old "Forty-eighters"—Europe's loss and America's gain.

Kossuth, exiled Hungarian patriot, in New York (2367)

Carl Schurz, who became U.S. statesman (2368)

Friedrich Hecker, exiled, fought in Civil War (2369)

Breakthrough in Science

Chemical equipment of the mid-century (2371)

NEW INSIGHTS into the physical and chemical structure of the world, many with immediate practical results, appeared in rapid succession, marking the period as a great one for experimental science. Experiments with nitrous oxide ("laughing gas") led to the development of anesthesia, opening an era of painless surgery. Semmelweis, with a new understanding of the nature of infection, set out to eradicate childbed fever. An agricultural revolution, made possible by new fertilizers, resulted from Baron von Liebig's discoveries in organic chemistry.

Reagence glass used in experiment (2372)

Humphry Davy, famed for his safety lamp for miners (2373)

Discovery of laughing gas led to anesthesia (2374)

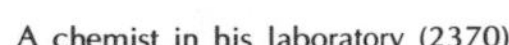

A chemist in his laboratory (2370)

Liebig linked chemistry and agriculture (2375)

Bunsen improved work in laboratories (2376)

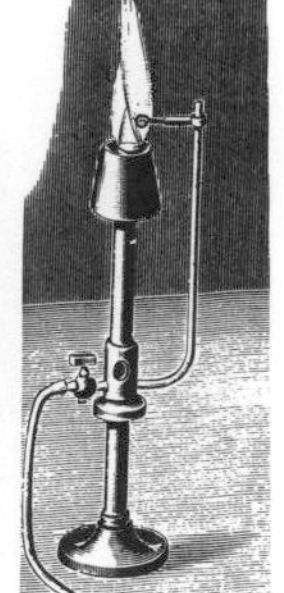

The Bunsen burner, a basic tool (2377)

Woehler synthesized aluminum (2378)

Serturner analized opium, found morphine (2379)

Berzelius, pioneered in electrochemistry (2380)

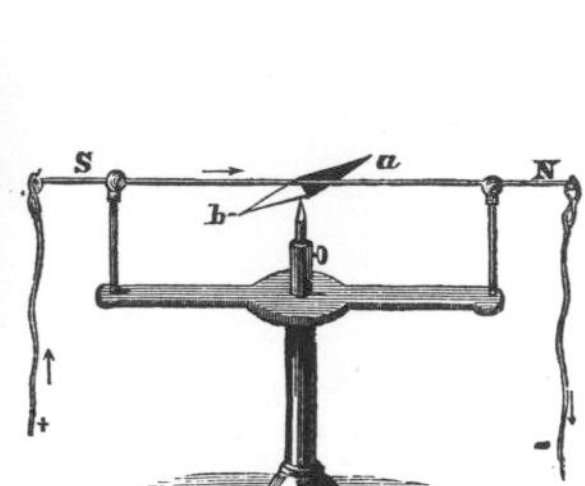

Electromagnet was basis of invention of motor (2381)

Faraday's electromagnetic induction led to rise of electricity industry (2382)

Faraday experiments in his lab at the Royal Institution (2383)

Gay Lussac in ascent to test the upper air (2384)

Gauss joined mathematics and electricity (2385)

Ohm discovered law of wire resistance (2386)

The spectroscope yielded insights into chemical structures (2387)

Arago lectures on electromagnetism (2388)

Foucault's experiment in Paris in 1851 demonstrated the earth's rotation on its axis (2389). He also invented the gyroscope.

Chemistry • Physics
Biology • Medicine

Cuvier was an influential genetic anatomist (2390)

Lyell advanced new ideas on earth's creation (2391)

Humboldt surveyed world in classic *Kosmos* (2392)

Lamarck advanced new evolution theory (2393)

Dr. Beaumont analyzed stomach's juices (2394)

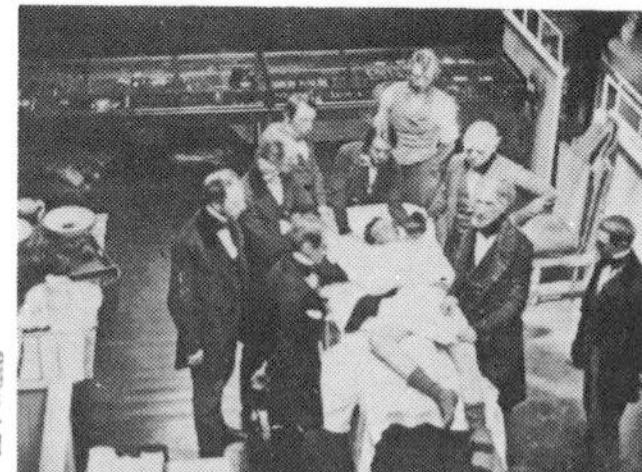

Anesthesia for surgery demonstrated in Boston General Hospital, 1846 (2395)

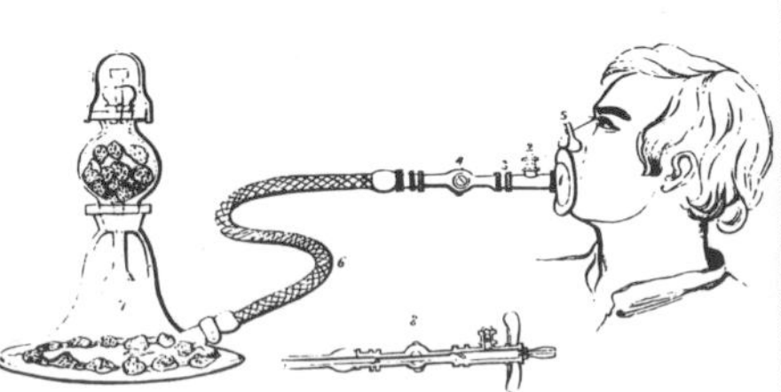

Inhaler used for administration of surgical anesthesia (2396)

Semmelweis disinfects hands to combat childbed fever (2397)

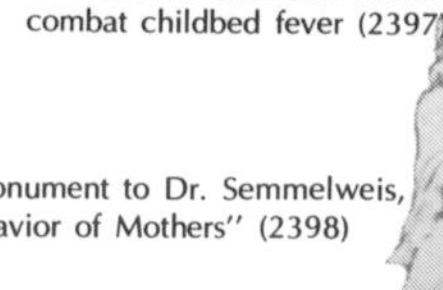

Monument to Dr. Semmelweis, "Savior of Mothers" (2398)

Inventions • Innovations

Goodyear discovered vulcanization (2399)

A model of S. Morse's first telegraph (2400)

Howe demonstrates sewing machine, revolutionizing textile field (2401)

Otis invented the first safety elevator (2402)

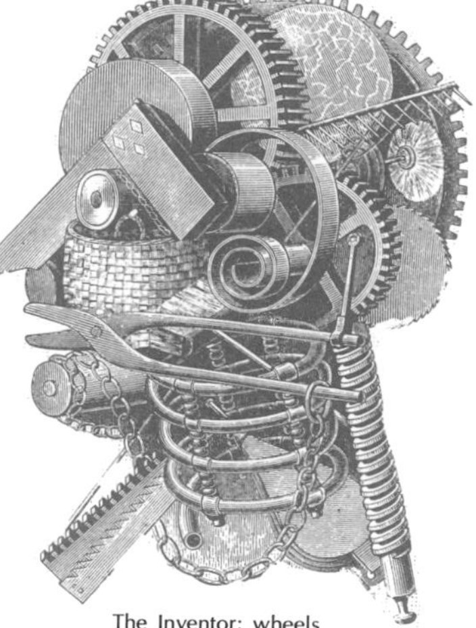
The Inventor: wheels in his head (2403)

John McAdam (2404) introduced macadamized roads using crushed stone (2405) as a base for smooth surfaces.

I.K. Brunel: railroad, ship builder (2406)

Communications Revolution

MOST INVENTIONS up to mid-century did not affect the general character of society. But now new printing methods, coupled with the telegraph, sired a cultural revolution. Before installing Koenig's rapid press, the *Times* of London printed only 250 copies per hour; the new press immediately quadrupled that output. Suddenly the latest news and comment from around the world were available to the masses, vindicating Napoleon's remark that printer's ink would do to social organization what the cannon had done to the feudal fort.

Charles Babbage (2407) spent 19 years on computer (2408), had to give up project.

Nasmyth: inventor of steam hammer (2409)

The rotating press introduced continuous flow in printing. Paper was still fed by hand (2410)

Lithography facilitated cheap production of pictures (2411)

Picture sellers brought art to the masses (2412)

Photography

EXPERIMENTS with the reaction of chemicals to light paved the way for photography, soon to become a major adjunct to the dissemination of ideas. At first a curiosity, then a medium hostile to art, photography eventually merged with printing to provide the great variety of pictorial magazines and books available today.

Daguerre's first camera (2413)

Daguerre develops the daguerreotype (2414)

Fox Talbot: instantaneous photography begins (2415)

Nadar, photographer and aeronaut (2416)

Photographer became the people's artist (2417)

Niepce co-developer of photography (2418)

Technology: Hope or Threat?

FEAR OF THE NEW TECHNOLOGY surfaced in this era. Despite many glowing predictions of the wonders society would reap from the progress of science, skeptics, including many graphic artists, focused upon their doubts and fears. Some envisioned an army of soulless behemoths and the ultimate machine that would blow up the world.

Living Made Easy: Body fanner, nutcracker, automatic wine helper (Cruikshank) (2419)

Flying by steam: Air Age prophecy (2420)

"Walking by Steam," a visionary glimpse of "auto-mobility" (2421)

Steam wagon spreads havoc in fatal explosion (2422)

Prediction of steam plow: farmer becomes leisured, cultivated gentleman (2423)

"My, how those English can work" (2424)
—Foreign observer

"England: Workshop of the World"

Blast furnace for extracting metal from raw ores (2426)

THE MOST SIGNIFICANT FACTOR in the wave of industrialization which swept England after the Napoleonic Wars was probably Bessemer's converter: by greatly reducing the price of steel, it facilitated the shift to iron machinery. The resulting "march of the iron man" changed many formerly bucolic regions into dour, industrial landscapes, dotted with "dark, satanic mills." And England's productivity soon outstripped that of every nation.

Coal deposits were explored with aid of new mining methods, steam power (2425)

First industrial use of a railroad near Newcastle coal mine (2427)

Iron mill. Steam hammer gave way to the Bessemer process (2428)

Bessemer process: blowing oxygen over molten iron to convert it into hardened steel (2429)

Sir Henry Bessemer, inventor (2430)

Rolling steel required manual labor (2431)

Metal-grinding created noxious dust (2432)

Factories were dank with bad light and ventilation (2433)

Spinning mills employed women, children exclusively (2434)

Printing on calico which first was imported from Calcutta in the 1830 s (2435)

Labor's Misery

THE RAPID, UNPLANNED EXPANSION of industry produced wretched social conditions. As masses of farm workers crowded into small manufacturing towns, families were cramped into "foul, dark warrens" without light, water or sanitation. With primitive working conditions, a laborer who drowsed at his machine might lose a limb, or even life itself. Children who were small enough to climb through narrow shafts were exploited in the mines. And so the technical miracles which brought riches to a few became a mockery in the suffering of the working class.

Factory slaves rush to their work (2436)

Spindle boy beaten by brutal foreman (2437)

Child labor abuse: hauling coal in dank mine shaft too small for men (2438)

Spitalfield weavers: family of nine and two looms in one squalid room (2439)

Destitute farm workers hope for relief, wander toward factory town (2440)

Unemployment due to industrialization was to be relieved by poorhouses (2441)

Cripple forced to work (2442)

Drinking water ladled from vile Thames River (2444)

Escape from a life of misery (2445)

Mushrooming factories turned once-bucolic countryside into devastated, polluted inferno of industry (2443)

Revolt and Reform

Bread riot in 1815 to protest against the Corn Laws which kept price of bread high (2446)

William Cobbett pleaded for parliamentary reform (2447)

Peterloo massacre of striking workers caused protest (2448)

"Iron Duke" Wellington fought reform by strong-arm methods (2449)

Demonstrations against Corn Laws led to repeal (2450)

Conservatives siding with reform movement were satirized (2451)

William IV: his half-hearted support of Reform Bill was ridiculed (2452)

WORKERS' DISCONTENT flared up in many English factory districts. The government dealt harshly with these outbursts at first, but slowly, by parliamentary give-and-take, reform movements gave the English worker more influence in government, gradually improving his lot. A modest start was made with the Reform Bill of 1832, which redistributed seats in Parliament, reflecting the importance of the swollen industrial towns. A charter of grievances was drawn up by the "Chartists"; and Cobden and Bright, leaders of the Free Trade movement, effected the repeal of the Corn Laws, thus finally lowering the price of bread.

Lord Russell, Liberal, at first reading of Reform Bill in Parliament (2453)

Chartists put up chart of reforms demanded by labor force (2454)

Manchester plant operative (2455)

Richard Cobden fought for free trade (2456)

John Bright kindled flame of parliamentary reform (2457)

Humanitarian Thrust

SO WIDESPREAD WAS AGITATION for reform during this period that England gained the reputation of a nation "obsessed with the urge for reform." Humanitarian leaders, often conscientious aristocrats, showed sympathy for the plight of industrial workers and other oppressed groups. Factory conditions were slowly improved. Even the Colonial slave found in William Wilberforce a vigorous champion.

Lord Shaftesbury (2458) backed humanitarian reforms; protected boy chimney sweeps (2459)

Distribution of clothing to the unemployed by Manchester Provident Society (2460)

Workers lived in dark rooms till 1851 window tax repeal (2461)

Elizabeth Fry, prison reformer and friend of the down-trodden (2462)

Laws against slavery were pressed by English Anti-Slavery Society (2463)

Children petition against slavery; help anti-slave movement (2464)

Cartoon of Robert Owen's New Harmony "All owing—no paying" commune (2465)

Owen: One Man Reform Party

THE MANY PROJECTS of Robert Owen earned him the above title. At his factory—a remarkable socioeconomic workshop—working hours were shortened and wages paid during layoffs. Still, he was a strict disciplinarian and called his workers "industry's living machinery."

Robert Owen's factory at New Lanark, Scotland, established in 1814, was a laboratory of social and industrial experimentation (2466)

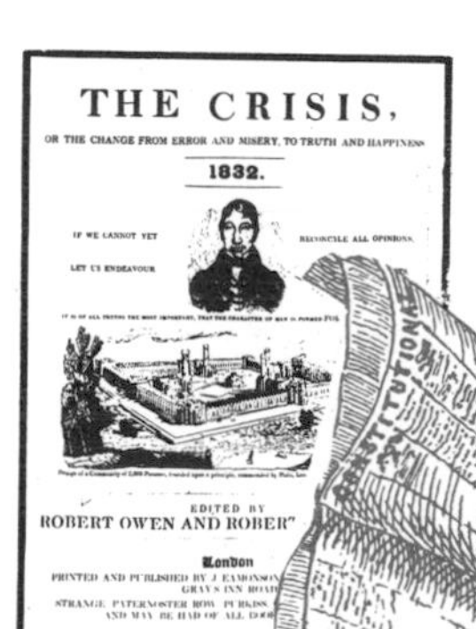
THE CRISIS,

OR THE CHANGE FROM ERROR AND MISERY, TO TRUTH AND HAPPINESS.

1832.

EDITED BY ROBERT OWEN AND ROBERT

London

One of Owen's community-oriented publications (2467)

Robert Owen in the United States (2468).

Victorian Age

Victoria crowned Queen (2469)

QUEEN VICTORIA RULED over England for sixty-four years. During her early reign, Whig and Tory ministers followed one another in quick succession. Under a regent not brilliant but dedicated to beauty, England, although the smallest of Europe's dominant powers, expanded to rule over a territory five times the size of all Europe.

Her views, at first rather liberal, became more conservative under the influence of her husband, Prince Albert. After his death in 1861, the Queen secluded herself for three years but emerged when the ministries of Gladstone and Disraeli quickened parliamentary debate, and England made giant strides in overseas expansion.

Victoria remained aloof and unperturbed by party conflict. She became the symbol of a country that took pride in industrial progress and ever-increasing prosperity.

Winterhalter portrait of young Queen (2470)

Queen Victoria and Prince Albert (2472)

Family life of Victoria and Albert set example of prim respectability (2471)

Queen opens the display of industrial might (2473)

Raising arched ribs with cranes (2474)

Crystal Palace: monument to technology had 500,000 panes of glass (2475)

Nude "Greek Slave" caused raised eyebrows (2476)

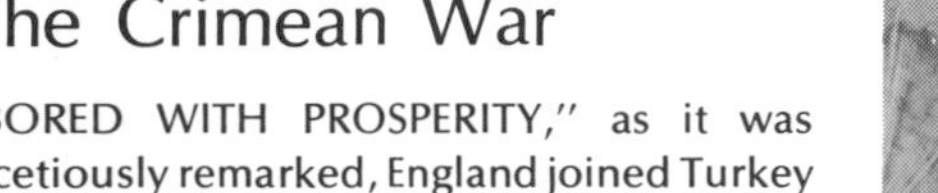

The Crimean War

"BORED WITH PROSPERITY," as it was facetiously remarked, England joined Turkey and France against Russia in the Crimean War, a badly managed campaign that produced little but incidents of personal heroism. In India, however, English complacency was disturbed by a mutiny of the Sepoys—the East India Company's native troops—against the company's oppression.

Crimean War: English soldier takes Russian rampart (2477)

Fortress artillery crew on the alert (2478)

Charge of the Light Brigade against 30 Russian guns. They were shot to pieces. Balaklava, 1854 (2479)

Florence Nightingale reformed hospital management in Crimea. Treatment of wounded was a scandal (2480)

Sepoy revolt gave Britain welcome pretext to tighten her iron grip on India (2481)

Rebels executed: tied to cannon mouths (2482)

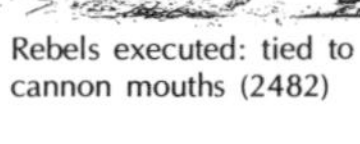

Stereoscope became television's popular predecessor (2483)

View of Life

TOUCHED BY THE MAGIC of prosperity, the middle class evolved a cozy, somewhat overstuffed way of life. They formed a society at peace with itself—the petty battles of politicians, labor and management did not seem to trouble them. With the admirable family life of their Queen as a model, Englishmen of even modest means adopted a comfortable, modest facade of bourgeois respectability.

London medicine man peddles potions (2484)

Tintype photographer develops his pictures promptly in two-wheeled darkroom (2485)

Secondhand clothing sought out in London slum (2486)

Shoeshine boys were exploited, organized in street gangs (2487)

Hansom cab, a feature of Victorian London (2488)

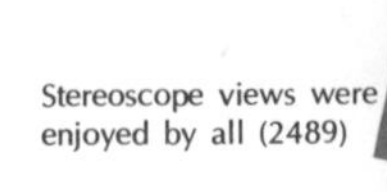

Stereoscope views were enjoyed by all (2489)

Victorian amenities: music lesson (2490)

Saturday night bath: crucial event (2491)

Victorian lads share a tricycle (2492)

Galaxy of Writers

THE IDEA THAT VICTORIAN ENGLAND lacked spirituality is not reflected in the great stream of literary works that poured from the presses. The Brontës, George Eliot, Tennyson, the Brownings, all were concerned with the delicacy of feeling which had motivated the Romantic poets. Meanwhile novelists like Dickens and Thackeray recorded the passing scene with such force that millions felt themselves caught up in their works. Daniel O'Connell, the Irish patriot, was said to be so affected by the death of Little Nell in Dickens' *Old Curiosity Shop* that he burst into sobs, exclaiming "he should not have killed her!" For the mass of middle-class readers, the novel was a vivid contemporary art form, just as the film is today.

Novelists

Charles Dickens during U.S. lecture tour (2493)

Dickens under constant pressure to write (2494)

Title page of Dickens' *Christmas Carol* showing Mrs. Fezziwig's ball (2495)

Bob Cratchit and Tiny Tim, love and hope (2496)

Mr. Pickwick: a type created by Phiz, first Dickens illustrator (2497)

Micawber lampooned false humility (2498)

"Asking for more"—famed *Oliver Twist* scene (2499)

Sidney Carton: *A Tale of Two Cities* (2500)

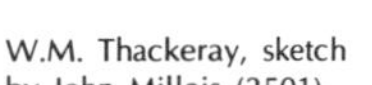

W.M. Thackeray, sketch by John Millais (2501)

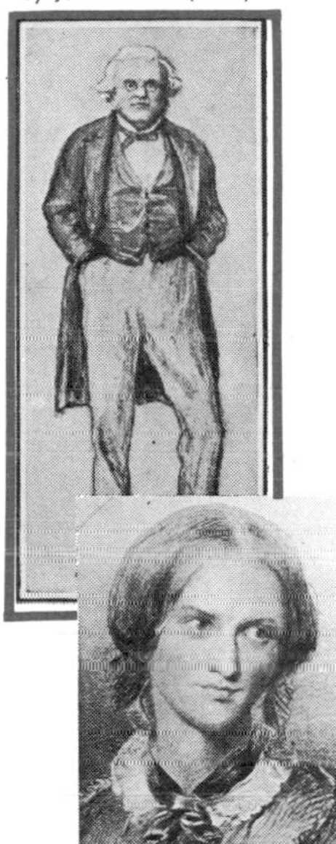

Thackeray and friends at the Garrick Club (2502)

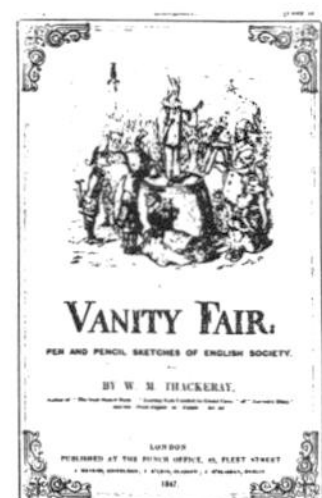

Vanity Fair, illustrated by the author (2503)

"My foot was actually uplifted to quit the shore of Albion. . . . "

Peripatetic Thackeray, self-portrait (2504)

Charlotte Brontë wrote *Jane Eyre* (2505)

George Eliot: compassion for the humble (2506)

Anthony Trollope: life in country parsonage (2507)

Poets

Alfred, Lord Tennyson (2508), poetic voice of Victorian England, was acknowledged as great poet with *Morte d'Arthur* (2509)

Readings became widespread—a Victorian passion (2514)

Robert and Elizabeth Browning, incarnation of a poetic couple in Victorian Age (2510, 2511)

The Rossettis helped found the Pre-Raphaelite school—reaction against the machine age (2512, 2513)

Historians and Essayists

Carlyle: incisive critic (2515)

Macaulay revitalized English history (2516)

John Ruskin, arbiter of good taste (2517)

Matthew Arnold, called the "kid-gloved Jeremiah" (2518)

A

B

C

D

E

CHAPTER 9

Irrepressible Conflict

Expansion and Slavery

Annals of the War

Triumph - Tragedy

F

H

G

The Vociferous Forties

IN THIS LAST DECADE, America's expansive mood expressed itself with political campaigns of unequaled gusto. To turn the tables on frontier Democrat Andrew Jackson, the Whig-Republicans staged a rambunctious campaign of image-building in 1840 to cast their candidate, aristocratic General William Henry Harrison, into the mold of a folk hero, a log-cabin primitive. But their triumph was temporary. Harrison died after thirty days in office, and John Tyler, who succeeded him, proved so troublesome to his own party that it actually expelled him.

Candidates stirred voters with slogan of America's "Manifest Destiny" (2519)

Log Cabin-Hard Cider campaign of 1840 made Harrison into a homey folk hero (2520)

Harrison occupied White House but 30 days (2521)

Raucous country rally for Wm. H. Harrison (2522)

Patriotic mood animated Whig headquarters (2523)

Clever print campaign helped Whigs win (2524)

Giant ball with slogans for "Tippecanoe and Tyler too" helped Harrison's 1840 campaign roll along to rowdy victory (2525)

John Tyler, convinced expansionist (2526)

Marcus Whitman, backed by Tyler, established Oregon mission (2527)

Fort Laramie, federal outpost, protected westward move (2528)

Oregon fever led to migration across Rockies via Oregon Trail (2529)

Santa Fe Trail: wagon trains with goods to trade in Southwest (2530)

FOUNDED IN NEW YORK in 1830, the Mormon sect of Latter-day Saints moved west hoping to find tolerance. But persecution continued—they were driven out in Ohio, then in Illinois (where mobs lynched Joseph Smith, their founder). Finally, with Brigham Young their leader, they settled in the Salt Lake Valley, a Mexican possession in what was to become Utah.

Mormon creed revealed to Joseph Smith (2531)

Enemies murder Smith outside jail (2532)

Mormons leave Nauvoo for a New Zion, move westward (2533)

Brigham Young settles colony in Utah (2534)

Seal of Rep. of Texas, adopted in 1839 (2536)

THE TEXAS QUESTION had troubled American diplomacy for nearly a quarter of a century. Mexico, when still under Spanish rule, invited the first settlers to Texas in 1821. Led by Stephen F. Austin, they grew into a prosperous community, but relations with Mexico deteriorated. In 1836 Texas declared its independence, provoking the famous attack on the Alamo. Despite petitions to Congress, the United States refused to consider outright annexation (which could mean war with Mexico) until 1845.

American settlers flocked to Texas since the 1820s, their leader Stephen F. Austin (2535)

Mexicans attacked Texas fort of Alamo in February, 1836 (2537)

Jim Bowie, Davy Crockett and all defenders died to last man (2538)

Mexico's Santa Anna defeated in battle of San Jacinto (2539)

"Remember the Alamo!" cry of revenge from all Texans (2540)

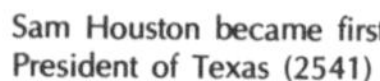

Sam Houston became first President of Texas (2541)

Frozen stream is forded by emigrant group (2542)

Steamboat used by U.S. govt. exploration expedition (2543)

Tense moment in crossing a swollen western river (2544)

Problems with Conestoga wagon as pioneers cross the plains (2545)

Westward the Course . . .

A COMPROMISE CANDIDATE, James K. Polk was virtually unknown when his name was flashed in 1844 over the newly installed Baltimore-Washington telegraph as the Democratic nominee for President. But Polk read the signs of his time acutely, adopted the concept of Manifest Destiny, by which Americans claimed the right to "overspread the continent allotted to them by Providence." Texas was annexed, and in the resulting war with Mexico, the United States won a vast bonanza—all the Southwestern territories from Texas to California.

James Polk, a dark-horse Whig candidate (2546)

Canvassing for votes in New York during 1844 Polk campaign (2547)

Polk on way to White House. He was to become one of our great Presidents (2548)

Far West border disputed by early settlers (2549)

Oregon conflict with England resolved by 1846 treaty (2550)

Cartoon against Polk, Mexican War (2551)

War with Mexico

Zachary Taylor, war hero, our ninth President (2552)

Annexation of Texas by U.S. in 1845 was one cause of Mexican War (2553)

U.S. Army stormed heights at Monterrey (2554), won at Resaca de la Palma (2555). Mexicans were brave, complete losers.

General Winfield Scott, bold strategist (2556)

Early daguerreotype shows U.S. Army detachment in a Mexican town (2557)

California Bonanza

NOMINALLY RULED BY MEXICO, California by 1841 was attracting American settlers—numerous enough to stage a revolt against Mexico in 1846, after which they set up an independent republic. Meanwhile the territory was ceded to the United States after the Mexican-American War. Just nine days before the treaty was signed, gold was discovered in California.

Greedy boy. U.S. craves Mexican territory (2558)

Frémont in Rocky Mts. seeks a route to California (2559)

In Bear Flag Revolt of 1846 (2560), California declared itself a state. U.S. took over after Mexican War. Then . . . GOLD (2561)

Sutter's Sacramento estate was overrun by forty-niners (2562)

Miner's wife tests first gold (2563) found at Sutter's Mill by James W. Marshall (2564)

Gold miner with typical paraphernalia (2565)

California miners cradling ore, always hoping to "strike it rich" (2566)

Prospector chips away at rocks looking for gold nuggets (2567)

Clipper ships advertised trips to the gold regions (2568)

Anti-Whig cartoon brands General Taylor as murderer of Mexican War soldiers (2569)

New Territories ...New Problems

AS THE NATION EXPANDED westward, the admission of each new state threatened the delicate political balance between slave-owning and "free" states. Defenders of slavery in the South were pitted against the industrial North, which opposed it for both economic and humanitarian reasons. Zachary Taylor, elected in 1849 as the general who won the Mexican War, favored the admission of both California and New Mexico as free states.

Zachary Taylor (2570), inaugurated in 1849 (2571), faced slavery problems in regions he had helped to conquer.

M. Fillmore, president after Taylor's sudden death (2572)

A Visit to the Mikado

Perry's reception in Japan. He made friendship treaty with Mikado (2573)

Japanese drawings depict Commodore Perry (2574). U.S. Marines (2575)

MILLARD FILLMORE, who succeeded Taylor, presided over the Compromise of 1850. But the slavery question was unsolved and there was only a decade of uneasy peace. More positive in its impact was Admiral Perry's visit to Japan. With the U.S. request for trade relations backed by a squadron of powerfully armed vessels, the Emperor acquiesced, breaking a two-hundred year tradition of feudal isolation.

Landways

SETTLERS PREPARING FOR THE DASH into Western territories had only one problem—getting there. Cross-country trips were hazardous, the pioneers being beset by hostile Indians, famine and disease. Clipper ships, carrying gold seekers and cargo to California, were safer, but costly and took more time. Steamboats, favored by an arterial system of connecting rivers, carried a heavy load of fortune seekers, with haste the byword, so that frequent boiler explosions made the river steamer, in Charles Dickens' words, "as safe as taking up lodging above a powder mill." Where the most intrepid steamer dared not go, flatboats and rafts carried the load.

Dauntless frontier mother and child. Statue (2576)

Angry Indians assault a pioneer wagon train (2577)

Waterways

Clipper ships carried goods West before railroad age (2580)

Family in clipper ship cabin dreams of fortune from California gold (2581)

Poster touts clipper ship express—103 days (2582)

Emigrants with households descend Ohio River on a flatboat (2583)

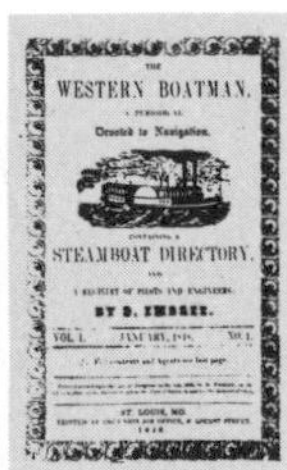

Early steamboat magazine (2584)

Disaster stalks ill-fated Donner party in 1846 High Sierras crossing (2578)

U.S. Cavalry imported camels from the Mid-East for desert packwork (2579)

Primitive raft with family in search of a new Western home (2585)

Riverboats were picturesque but unsafe. Explosions took hundreds of lives (2586)

Whaling

Critical moment: harpoonist ready for the kill (2587)

Conquered whale in the Pacific. Voyages for sperm oil at times took three years (2588)

Barreling and gauging whale oil, the principal illuminant till discovery of petroleum (2589)

IN THIS EXPANSIVE AGE, whaling dominated the maritime industries. The whaling fleet numbered 729 vessels in 1846, capable of pursuing their quarry in every clime. Centered in New Bedford, Mass., they furnished sperm-whale oil to the whole world, but nearly destroyed a magnificent species.

Lookout: "Thar she blows!" (2590)

Deadly harpoons — tools of the whaling trade (2591)

Harvard student burns the midnight oil (2592)

Expanding Intellectual Horizons

AMERICA'S NEW SENSE OF IDENTITY inspired writers to explore their cultural heritage and to fashion a new American literature. The nation's cultural reservoir was in New England, with Boston and Concord centers of literary culture. Emerson was its most articulate spokesman, celebrating "our stumps, Negroes and Indians, wraiths and rogues." While Emerson sought transcendental truths, poets and novelists explored the cultural past: Indian lore in the case of Longfellow, Puritan in the case of Hawthorne. Their works nurtured a new national consciousness.

Ralph Waldo Emerson, paragon of New England letters (2593)

Emerson in ecstasy over beauties of nature (2594)

Henry David Thoreau, environmentalist (2595)

Walden extolled solace of solitude (2596)

Thoreau's stark cabin: "Why all this bother about possessions?" (2597)

Contemplation with animal friends in the woods (2598)

Thoreau garbed for travelling (2599)

H.W. Longfellow: visionary of our poetic past (2600)

Courtship of Miles Standish became a best seller (2601)

Spreading chestnut tree: Longfellow sketch (2602)

Nathaniel Hawthorne, gothic author (2603)

Scene from *The Scarlet Letter;* the minister confesses (2604)

Locale of Hawthorne ghost story, *The House of the Seven Gables* (2605)

James Russell Lowell: polished mind (2606)

O.W. Holmes' famed essay-series. First chapter (2607)

Louisa May Alcott wrote *Little Women* (2608)

Julia Ward Howe: woman suffrage (2609)

Nearly blind, W.H. Prescott (2610) chronicled Peru and Mexico on his writing frame (2611)

Historian of the frontier, Francis Parkman (2612)

The Sea

Richard Henry Dana — sailor, author (2613)

Dana's *Two Years Before the Mast* helped end flogging at sea (2614)

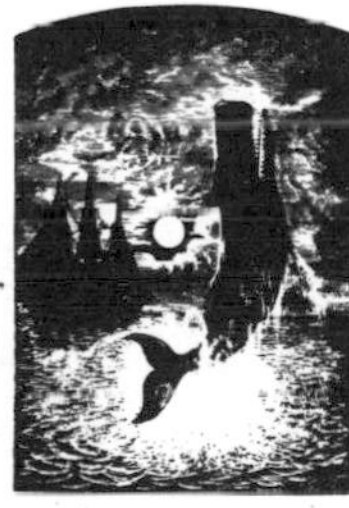

Moby Dick, Melville's symbol of doom (2615)

Herman Melville, symbolist (2616)

NEW ENGLAND'S LONG COMMERCE with whalers and China clippers also inspired its literature. Voyagers returned with both treasures and tales of adventure, among them the exotic travel books of Herman Melville. In 1851 he created the greatest sea story of them all, *Moby Dick,* which made Ahab's search for the Great White Whale a parable of man's self-destructive paranoia.

Anti-Slavery Writers

THE LITERARY CAUSE CÉLÈBRE of the era was abolition of slavery. In poems, pamphlets, manifestoes and speeches, New England writers deplored the dehumanizing effect of slavery on masters as well as slaves. Giving up all comforts to live in a dingy room beside his printing press, William Lloyd Garrison led the crusade, saying: "I am in earnest, I will be heard." But Harriet Beecher Stowe's *Uncle Tom's Cabin* became the most inflammatory work of the movement.

Harriet Beecher Stowe, abolitionist (2617)

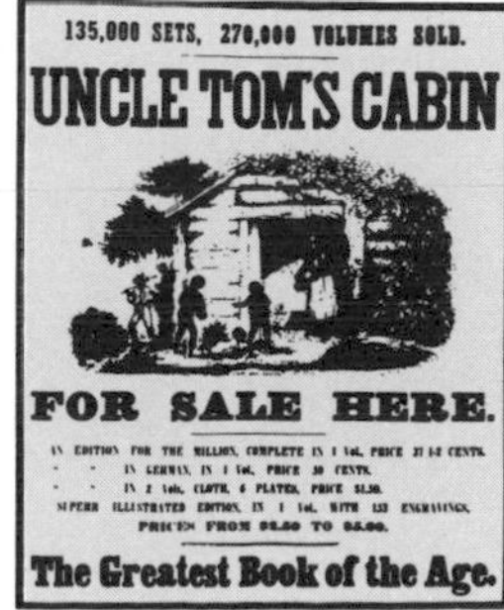

Stowe's book, said Lincoln, "started Civil War" (2618)

William Lloyd Garrison, fanatic editor (2619)

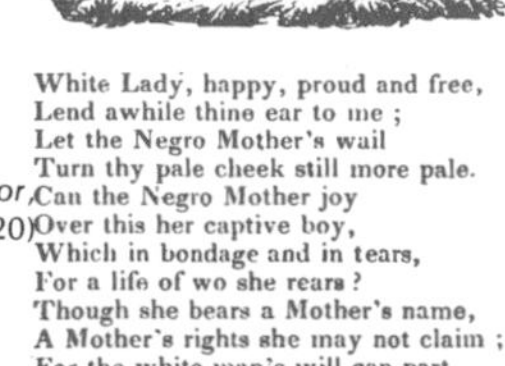

Vignette from *The Liberator,* his anti-slave journal (2620)

Southern industry: cotton and slaves. The unbalanced economy led to disaster (2621)

Slavery: the Peculiar Institution

SINCE ITS INCEPTION, America had struggled with the problem of slavery, a black blot upon the bright image of the nation's freedom. Though the Declaration of Independence advanced the belief that "all men are created equal," many of the signers went home to estates supported by slave labor. Indeed, the conviction that Southern plantation economy could not survive without slavery dulled the American conscience for decades. As the vast territories gained in the Mexican War prepared to enter the Union, the question whether they should be slave or free states generated hatred between North and South, and slavery became a burning national issue.

King Cotton rules the world with South enjoying prosperity (2622)

Slaves cramped into hold of ship. Millions died of suffocation and disease in transit (2623)

Chained slaves arrive in U.S. in sight of U.S. flag, Capitol building (2624)

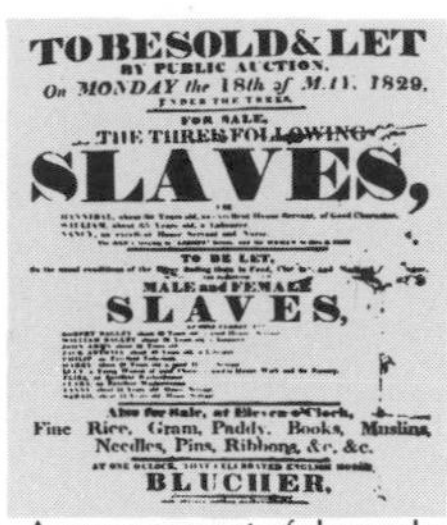

TO BE SOLD & LET
BY PUBLIC AUCTION,
On MONDAY the 18th of MAY, 1829,
FOR SALE,
THE THREE FOLLOWING
SLAVES,
TO BE LET,
MALE and FEMALE
SLAVES,
Also for Sale, at Eleven o'Clock,
Fine Rice, Gram, Paddy, Books, Muslins, Needles, Pins, Ribbons, &c. &c.
BLUCHER,

Announcement of slave sale in a Southern state (2625)

English cartoon condemns the brutality and greed of Amerian slave owners (2626)

Slaves kidnapped from their quarters to be resold by corrupt traders (2627)

Barbarity "committed on a free African"—beaten to death on the road (2628)

Cold-water treatment to punish a recalcitrant slave (2629)

Popular song honoring fugitive slaves (2630)

Shackles (2630A)

Free State versus Slave State

AS PASSIONS ROSE, Northern abolitionists fulminated against the inhumanity of slavery, while Southern apologists emphasized its benevolent aspects. Senator Henry Clay led efforts to smooth tempers with compromise. Legislation passed in 1850 admitted California as a free state, but gave free choice to the people of New Mexico and Utah when these territories should join the Union. The South was appeased by new and stringent provisions for the return of runaway slaves.

Family in front of slave cabin on a cotton plantation (2631)

Negro banjoist: "My Old Kentucky Home" (2632)

Blacks on plantation husking corn (2633)

Nocturnal spirituals sung in black quarters (2634)

Fugitive slaves arrive in Indiana station of the Underground Railroad (2635)

Fugitive emerges from box in which he has been smuggled North (2636)

Sojourner Truth escaped, helped run-aways (2637)

Clay proposes Compromise of 1850 to balance slave and free states (2638)

RATHER THAN DICTATE to new states, Stephen A. Douglas, a Democrat from Illinois (the "Little Giant" later to become famous during the Lincoln-Douglas debates), propounded "popular sovereignty": Let every new state entering the Union freely make its own decision on the slavery issue. But the laws Douglas sponsored in 1854 merely increased sectional antagonism, turning the Territory of Kansas into a battleground of warring factions.

Stephen Douglas: Let the states choose sides (2639)

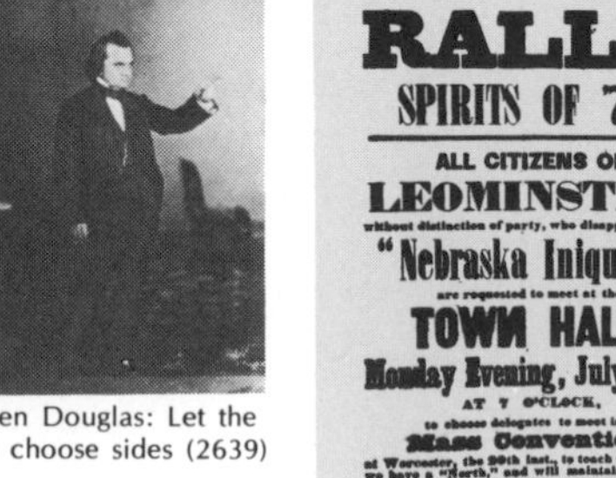

RALLY
SPIRITS OF '76!
ALL CITIZENS OF
LEOMINSTER,
without distinction of party, who disapprove of the
"Nebraska Iniquity,"
are requested to meet at the
TOWN HALL,
Monday Evening, July 10th,
AT 7 O'CLOCK,
to choose delegates to meet in a
Mass Convention,
at Worcester, the 20th inst., to teach the "South" we have a "North," and will maintain our CONSTITUTIONAL RIGHTS.
CALEB C. FIELD, LEONARD BURRAGE, MERRITT WOOD.
Leominster, July 6, 1854.

Rally to support local option on slavery (2640)

Gladiator Douglas fights inequitous foes (2641)

J.C. Calhoun, the South's brilliant advocate (2642)

Bleeding Kansas

Fight erupts in Fort Scott, Kansas, between Free-Soilers and invading slave owners from Missouri (2643)

Southern ruffians come to fight abolitionists (2644)

Kansas settlers voting on slavery issue (2645)

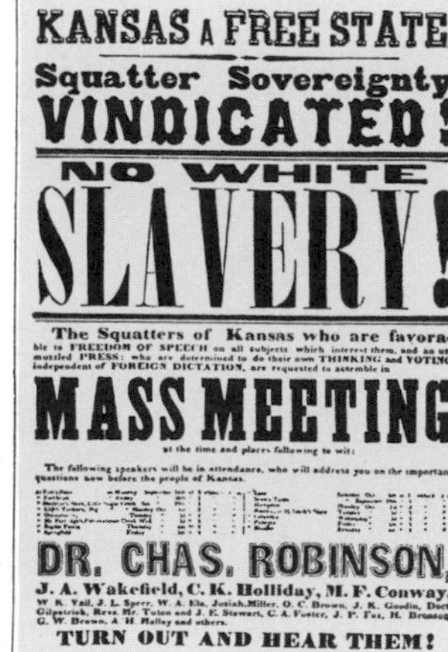

Meeting to discuss Kansas' stand in slavery controversy (2646)

Birthplace of Republican Party, 1854. It took a strong anti-slavery stance (2647)

First party meeting of Free-Soil Republicans in Pittsburgh's Lafayette Hall, 1856 (2648)

South derided "Black Republicans" (2649)

"Song of the Free-Soilers"

We cross the prairies as of old
The pilgrims crossed the sea,
To make the West, as they the East
The homestead of the free.

WITH THE CHOICE OF SLAVERY or freedom in the offing, Free-Soilers poured into Kansas to provide the majority vote needed. Outraged slave owners struck back with the "Missouri Ruffians," who staged retaliatory raids on Free Soil communities. Free-Soilers blamed the Democrats for "Bleeding Kansas," using the phrase as their battle cry, and the rest of the nation soon took sides. In 1856 the "Free Soil Republicans" nominated John C. Fremont as their first presidential candidate, but Democrat James Buchanan won. As the new President tried to straddle the issue, the Supreme Court decision in the Dred Scott case, defining black Americans as mere chattels, inflamed it further.

James Buchanan had the support of Tammany Hall. He was called "doughface"—Northerner favoring slavery (2650, 2651)

Political turmoil was aggravated by Panic of 1857. Ensuing unemployment helped Republicans (2652)

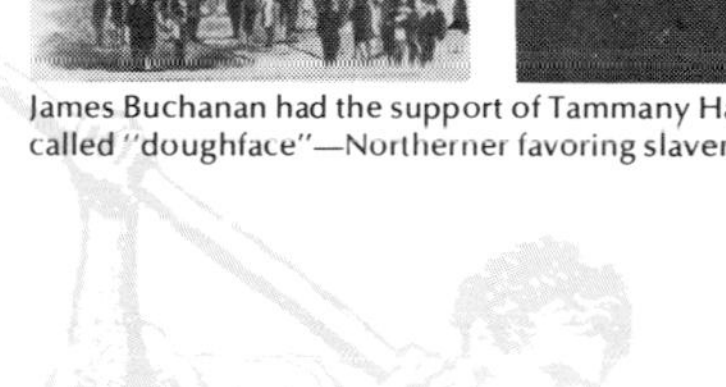

The Rise of Lincoln

ILLINOIS FREE SOIL REPUBLICANS made an astute choice in 1858: to lead their ticket they named "Honest Abe" Lincoln, a backwoods lawyer of simple virtues whose struggle for success gave him the image of a folk hero. Pitted against Stephen A. Douglas for a seat in the Senate, Lincoln gained national prominence in debates with Douglas for his eloquent defense of the anti-slavery position. He lost the Senate race, but two years later he was called upon to lead the nation.

Dred Scott, slave, sued for his rights (2653)

Courthouse (2654) where Chief Justice Taney held that slaves were not entitled to sue for freedom (2655)

Young Springfield lawyer (2657)

Lincoln the Railsplitter (2656)

Young Lincoln studying in log cabin by the light of the fireplace (2658)

Lincoln made trip to New Orleans in flatboat he had built with a friend (2659)

He was dismayed by inhumanity of slave auction he witnessed (2660)

At twenty-one, became clerk in Salem, Ill. store (2661)

Lincoln, defense attorney in murder case (2662)

Lincoln-Douglas debate, 1858. Lincoln pleaded for "slavery's ultimate extinction" (2664)

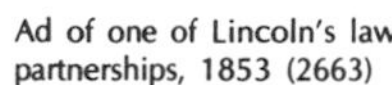

ABRAM LINCOLN, Springfield. W. H. LAMON, Danville.
Lincoln & Lamon,
ATTORNEYS AT LAW,
HAVING formed a co-partnership, will practice in the Courts of the Eighth Judicial Circuit and the Superior Court, and all business entrusted to them will be attended to with promptness and fidelity. Office on the second floor of the "Barnum Building," over Whitcomb's Store.
Danville, Nov. 10, 1852.

Ad of one of Lincoln's law partnerships, 1853 (2663)

A Nation Split Asunder

John Brown's Raid

John Brown, erratic New England abolitionist firebrand (2665)

John Brown's fort held against U.S. Army during his short-lived "invasion" (2666)

LATE IN 1859, an odd incident occurred at Harpers Ferry, Virginia, that polarized the seething temper of the nation: seeking to foment a "slave uprising," John Brown took over the government arsenal there with eighteen men, expecting a black army to join him. Cut down by U.S. Marines under Colonel Robert E. Lee, Brown was tried and hanged. While he became a hero to the abolitionists, reaction in the South was one of horror and fear.

Lincoln's election in 1860 heightened the wave of secessionist sentiment: within a week South Carolina's legislature convened to announce an end to its ties with the Union. Ten other states followed, to form the Confederate States of America, yet Lincoln was determined to preserve the Union, declaring: "No state upon its own mere action can get out of the Union." But the issue was to be tested by war.

Fire Engine House in which Brown, 13 whites and 5 blacks had holed themselves up (2667)

Capture of Brown by Union troops under Colonel Robert E. Lee (2668)

John Brown, wounded during the raid, before court in Charleston (2669)

Brown, condemned to hang, became martyr of abolitionism (2670)

Lincoln during the 1860 campaign (2671)

Lincoln tries to glue federal union (2672)

"Wide Awakes" campaigning for Abe Lincoln (2673)

Secessionists unfurl their flag in Charleston, S.C. (2676)

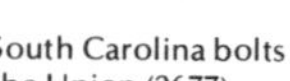

CHARLESTON MERCURY EXTRA:

UNION DISSOLVED!

South Carolina bolts the Union (2677)

Jefferson Davis becomes South's President (2678)

N.Y. cheered Lincoln at Cooper Union (2674)

Washington greets Lincoln for inauguration (2675)

"Defender of the South" Jefferson Davis (2679)

Title of the Confederate national anthem (2680)

Buckle worn by Army of Confederacy (2681)

THE WAR BEGAN on April 12, 1861, when General Beauregard fired upon a garrison of federal soldiers at Fort Sumter, S.C.. Declaring an insurrection, Lincoln called for 75,000 volunteers. Both sides began to mobilize in earnest, though neither could have foreseen that of the 2,300,000 who fought, one in four would be killed.

Union recruiting poster (2682)

Bombardment of Fort Sumter, official start of the war (2683)

New York recruiting office lists bounties for enlistment (2684)

Recruit welcomed to Ohio volunteers. Draft did not start till 1863 (2685)

Drumming up soldiers for Confederate Army (2686)

Confederate officers are fitted out (2687)

Union volunteer, 1861 (2688)

Young Confederate private (2689)

Union mottoes (2690, 2691)

Annals of the War

AT THE OUTSET, despite Northern superiority in industry and finance, the South had several advantages: better generals, a larger number of trained soldiers, a united home front and a tradition of martial spirit. But two Confederate assumptions proved wrong: that the North would not fight very long, and that England would aid the Confederacy. The grand strategy seemed simple at first: with Richmond and Washington but 110 miles apart, it was assumed (perhaps naïvely) that the conquest of either capitol would end the war. In their initial assault, and at the calamitous Battle of Bull Run, the Confederates nearly succeeded. In general, during the first two years, they seemed to hold the initiative.

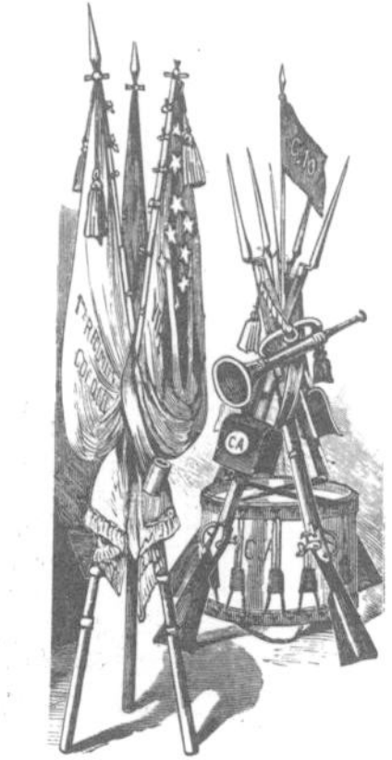

Confederate symbols (2692)

1861

First Battle of Bull Run, 30 miles from capital; Union routed (2693)

"Stonewall" Jackson was victor at Bull Run (2694)

Florida—first Confederate commerce raider, English-built, harassed Union ships (2695)

Trent Affair strained Union relations with England to breaking point (2696)

1862

Battle of ironclads, *Merrimac* and *Monitor*, March 9 (2697)

General Lee (2698) stops McClellan threatening Richmond in fierce Seven-Day Battle, Malvern Hill (2699)

Battle of Antietam: Lee's invasion strategy fails (2700)

Union black soldiers slaughter Confederate bloodhounds (2701).

The war's bloodiest battle. 25,000 soldiers died at Antietam (2702)

Lincoln met with McClellan at Antietam; dismissed him (2703)

Burnside, new Union commander (2704), met Lee at Fredericksburg, was unsuccessful in his attempt to overrun Richmond (2705)

General Hooker, new commander of Army of the Potomac (2706)

1863

Emancipation Proclamation presented to Cabinet (2707)

THE TIDE TURNED for the Union in 1863. Lincoln's Emancipation Proclamation had given the struggle the character of a moral crusade: a civil conflict now became, in the eyes of the world, a fight against human inequality, to fulfill the dream of America's Founding Fathers. Lee's last heroic attempt to encircle Union forces and march into Washington was defeated at Gettysburg.

Lincoln with black family at White House (2708)

Porter's fleet helps Grant split Confederacy at Vicksburg (2709)

Gettysburg: Lee's last attempt to invade North is foiled (2710)

Lincoln delivers Gettysburg Address on Nov. 11 (2711)

Bounties lured recruits to join new regiments (2712)

The draft: "A rich man's war, a poor man's fight" (2713)

Resentment erupted in bloody New York Draft Riots. Blacks suffered most (2714)

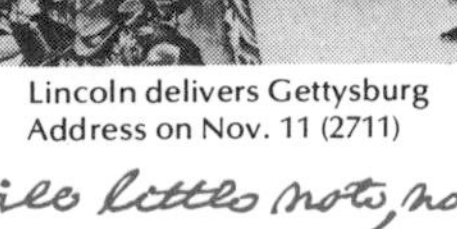

Lincoln's final draft of the Gettysburg Address (2715)

1864

Grant made the Union's military leader (2716)

Battle of Wilderness in May was bloody but indecisive (2717)

Grant: "I propose to fight it out" (2718)

Sharpshooters before Petersburg (2719)

"Great Dictator"—mortar used in siege of Petersburg, key to Richmond (2720)

Lincoln Re-elected

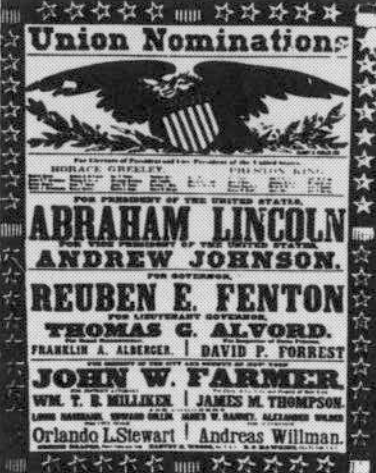

Lincoln triumphs over party strife (2721)

Copperheads, peace seekers, called Lincoln inept dictator (2722)

THE YEAR 1864 brought the Union closer to victory. Grant's determination to "fight it out on the line," despite fearful losses, made the home front apprehensive, playing into the hands of the Copperheads, the Northern Democratic peace party. Still, Lincoln was re-elected. Despite the increased fury of battle, Lincoln felt for the South, envisioning a lenient peace.

Generals of Shenandoah Army casting votes in camp (2723)

Sherman's March

General Sherman (2724) moved into Georgia, took Atlanta, destroyed industries, scorched the earth (2725)

Destruction of railway lines broke back of South (2726)

The march through Georgia became a holocaust (2727)

Sherman's campaign devastated the Southern economy (2728)

Union Navy throttles South

UNION NAVAL STRATEGY was twofold: strangle Confederate commerce by blockading the coasts, and dominate the Mississippi Valley. Union forces controlled the Mississippi early in the war, but the coastal blockade was hampered by daring and effective Confederate raiders. With Farragut's victory at Mobile Bay, however, the Confederacy lost the last hideout for its naval forces.

Kearsarge sinks *Alabama*. It had ravaged 65 Union ships (2729)

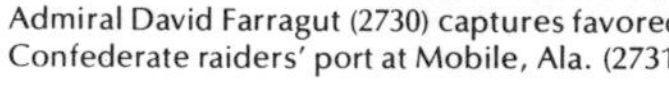
Admiral David Farragut (2730) captures favored Confederate raiders' port at Mobile, Ala. (2731)

Some Generals

Gen. Meade commanded Army of Potomac at Gettysburg (2732)

General Thomas, "Rock of Chickamauga" (2733)

H.W. Halleck, Lincoln's military advisor (2734)

Jubal Early led Southern push on Washington (2735)

Gen. Beauregard, C.S.A., "Hero of Sumter" (2736)

"Little Phil" Sheridan won the Battle of Shenandoah by famous ride (2737)

John Hunt Morgan shook Union morale by his daring Kentucky raids (2738)

THE CIVIL WAR brought to the fore a dazzling group of generals staunch of character, crafty in the wiles of strategy. As a rule, the military leaders of the South surpassed those of the North, with Lee as the paragon both as a man and as a military genius.

Cavalryman charging (2739)

Confederate cavalryman (2740)

The Union's War Machine

Heated cannonball is a delicate problem for artillerymen (2743)

(2744)

Artillery training. A gun squad of four could fire 2-3 rounds a minute (2741)

Steam-driven tankette, proposed but not accepted by Union command (2742)

Occasional use was made of armored artillery railway cars (2745)

Railroad mortar battery taking on munitions. Brady photo (2746)

THE UNION'S MILITARY SUPERIORITY was obvious from the start, but most Union generals failed to exploit it effectively. Not until 1863 did the efficient use of Union weapons bring results, and Lincoln was largely responsible for this improvement. A perennial tinkerer with a keen perception of the mechanics of war, he was fascinated with tanks, machine guns, rockets and mines, and became his own "office of research and development," introducing the breechloading rifle. Once he was almost killed while witnessing a rocket experiment.

Union Army managed U.S. Military R.R., built precarious wooden viaducts (2751)

Transportation

Headquarters baggage wagon for General Grant's gear (2747)

Mule driver working for Union Army (2748)

Moving troops by rail. Railroads gave Union logistic superiority (2749)

Army engineers laying down a corduroy road through a southern swamp (2750)

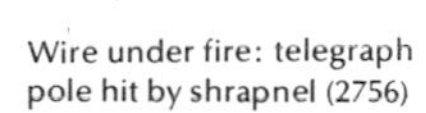

Wire under fire: telegraph pole hit by shrapnel (2756)

Communication

EFFECTIVE CONTROL OF THE NATION'S railroad system was a great strategic asset for the Union forces. At the outset, the North owned 70 percent of existing track, and this was rapidly expanding under the U.S. Military Railroad system. Meanwhile the telegraph linked most of Grant's forces, enabling him to coordinate his strategy. Telegraph reports also brought the war home to Northern readers.

Reconnaissance balloon checks blockade (2753)

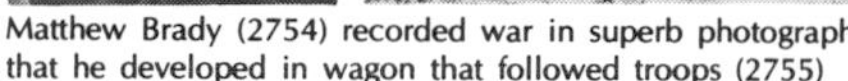

Matthew Brady (2754) recorded war in superb photographs that he developed in wagon that followed troops (2755)

Old tree made into signal tower (2752)

Medical Services

BATTLE LOSSES REACHED tragic proportions in the Civil War. Disease, rather than bullets, killed seven out of ten wounded soldiers despite a dedicated "sanitary commission." With no real knowledge of the nature of infection, surgeons operated in "pus-stained coats" with contaminated instruments that often caused death.

Union field hospital: surgeons worked without asepsis and anesthesia (2757)

Orderly compounds medication (2758)

Surgeons at work: Sanitary Corps is ready with ambulance (2759)

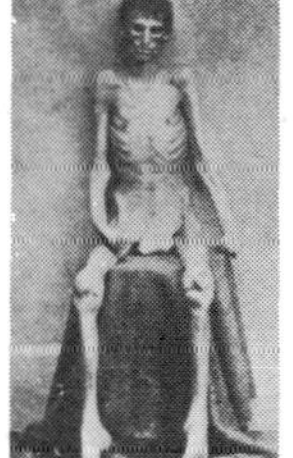

Ill-treated, starved war prisoner (2760)

Homefront Mobilized

Southern belles sew, urge the men to fight (2761)

Women bring in harvest while husbands are in army (2762)

Cartridge makers at work in Union arsenal (2763)

Military fashion for ladies (2764)

Women clerks leaving work at U.S. Treasury Dept. (2765)

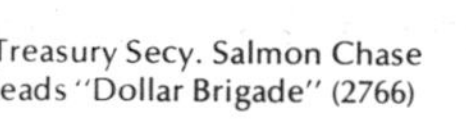

Treasury Secy. Salmon Chase leads "Dollar Brigade" (2766)

1864: Triumph...Tragedy

WITH RICHMOND as his objective, Grant moved relentlessly southward in March 1864, after his elevation to commander of all Union forces. Undaunted by his heavy losses (more than 60,000 in June—total strength of Lee's army), Grant moved on, surrounding Petersburg in order to cut off the Confederate capitol's communications. Finally, on April 2, 1865, Lee gave up Petersburg. Richmond became exposed and was evacuated. Lee moved his army westward. Encircled by Grant's pursuing forces and Sherman's army, he had to surrender. The war was over.

Patriotic book for children: a primer on the Great War (2767)

Fort Fisher stormed, Wilmington, N.C., falls: South's last gateway to outside world (2768)

Lincoln's Second Inaugural, March 4, 1865. Photograph by Matthew Brady (2769)

With malice toward none; with charity for all; with firmness in the right, as God gives us to see the right, let us strive on to finish the work we are in; to bind up the nation's wounds; to care for him who shall have borne the battle, and for his widow, and his orphans—to do all which may achieve and cherish a just and a lasting peace among ourselves, and with all nations.

President Lincoln's view of Reconstruction expressed in Second Inaugural address (2770)

Peace terms discussed on the *River Queen:* Lincoln, Sherman, Grant, Porter (2771)

Last Nast cartoon of Lincoln, City Point, March 23, (2772)

Petersburg falls, Grant congratulated (2773)

Richmond abandoned April 2 and set afire; 2,000 prisoners taken by Gen. Weitzel (2774)

Lincoln in Richmond receives joyous welcome from black populace (2775)

The End: Appomatox

Grant nears McLean house, Appomattox, for momentous meeting with Lee (2776)

Lee wore new outfit; Grant was in muddy coat (2777)

Lee and Grant amicably settle on terms (2778)

Lee: "Peace the sole object of all." Ink sketch (2779)

Lee's soldiers fed with Union rations (2780)

CHIVALRY PREVAILED when Grant and Lee conferred, on April 9, 1865, at Appomattox Courthouse to discuss surrender terms. Lee's soldiers were paroled to return home, retaining their horses, and officers their sidearms; 25,000 rations were issued to the Confederates by the Union Army.

(2781)

COURIER---EXTRA.

National Calamity!

Lincoln & Seward Assassinated!!

Ford's Theatre (2783). On April 14, Lincoln went to see actress Laura Keene perform (2784)

"Satan tempting Booth to murder Lincoln" (2785)

Black walnut rocker put in loge for Lincoln's comfort (2786)

John Wilkes Booth jumps, falls on stage (2787)

Booth apprehended by federal troops in a Virginia tobacco barn (2788)

Four Lincoln conspirators hanged in old Washington Penitentiary on July 7 (2789)

Lincoln's coffin on display in Washington streets (2790)

Lincoln's funeral train left Capitol April 21, made many stops, reached Springfield May 3 (2791)

ONLY A FEW HOURS after Lincoln assured his Cabinet he would "hang no rebels," he was assassinated at Ford's Theatre on April 14, 1865. Tragically, the crazed vengeance of actor John Wilkes Booth ended all hope of a fraternal reunion. President Andrew Johnson soon became engulfed in bitter struggles with a vindictive Congress.

"Break every yoke—Let the oppressed go free" (2792)

Freedmen's Bureau tried to find work and cushion hardships for freed slaves (2793)

Free slave goes to Texas in quest of a new life (2794)

Chair vendor—some blacks opened own business (2795)

RADICAL REPUBLICANS, in control of Congress, made reconstruction as punitive and tortuous as possible. Their leader, Thaddeus Stevens, suggested that Confederate states be treated as conquered provinces, not to be readmitted into the Union until loyalty was proven. The black vote, now guaranteed by the Fifteenth Amendment, and Negro rights, were manipulated by Northern carpetbaggers and native scalawags for their own interests. Meanwhile the Radicals conducted a hate campaign against President Johnson, who advocated clemency.

All ages went to Freedmen's Schools to learn to read and write (2796)

Union relief stations set up to help the sick and aged (2797)

Poor but proud: most whites felt bitter to see blacks free (2798)

Carpetbaggers exploited, controlled blacks (2799)

To ensure racial supremacy, Klan attacked blacks and their friends with brutal assault, arson, rape, lynchings (2800, 2801)

First vote. Often ex-slaves had to fight to vote (2802)

S.C. legislature was under dominance of blacks (2803)

Jim Crow railway car. Black ordered to the rear (2804)

JOHNSON'S IMPEACHMENT was not openly based on his policy of conciliation. To hamstring the President, Radical forces passed the Tenure of Office Act, forbidding the dismissal of Cabinet officers without approval of Congress. When Johnson asked for the resignation of Edmund Stanton, he was impeached, but acquitted in the Senate.

Tailor shop which Johnson ran in Greeneville, Tenn. (2805)

Johnson continued Lincoln's conciliatory policy (2806)

Thaddeus Stevens, bitter foe of Johnson (2807)

Johnson given summons for impeachment (2808)

Impeachment of Johnson was engineered by Radical Republicans who failed by one vote to bring in their verdict (2809, 2810)

"Mr. Seward's Icebox"

THOUGH ALASKA WAS TO PROVE enormously valuable, economically and politically, its purchase from Russia in 1867 was popularly called "Seward's Folly" (after Johnson's Secretary of State). It was only after gold was discovered in the Klondike region (1880) that attempts were made to settle Alaska.

Seward urged Alaska's purchase by U.S. (2811)

Sitka was the Russian capitol, center of culture and seat of the Russian-American Fur Company (2812)

Purchase of Alaska. U.S. paid $7 million, or less than three cents per acre (2813)

Cartoon lampooning the purchase of big lump of Russian ice for a great big bag of U.S. money (2814)

A
B
L'INTERNATIONALE
Steinlen
Piano: 3f
Pt Format: 1f
Musique de
DEGEYTER
FRD KRUPP ESSEN
BRITISH AMERICA
AFRICA
AMERICA
AUSTRALIA
C

CHAPTER 10

Rising Empires

Scramble for Colonies

Social Unrest

Science and the Arts

D

E

F

G

H

France - Second Empire

RETURNING FROM EXILE after the Revolution of 1848, Louis Napoleon (Napoleon I's nephew) was elected President of the Second Republic, largely because of his famous name. After a coup with the aid of his half brother, the Comte de Morny, he became Napoleon III (1852). He proved to be a fairly enlightened despot, stimulating industry and trade at home while seeking to restore French glory abroad.

Attempting to aid the unification of Italy, he suffered heavy losses from the Austrians at Solferino in 1859, and shamefully abandoned his Italian allies. To regain lost popularity, he tried to expand French influence by placing a puppet, Emperor Maximilian, on the Mexican throne. The United States reacted belligerently, French troops were withdrawn and the hapless Maximilian was executed. Lured into war by Bismarck, Napoleon was defeated in 1870 and deposed the following year.

Napoleon III, "Root of all evil" (2815)

A restless ruler, Napoleon III was intent to meddle in Europe's affairs, was called "fortune hunter" (2816)

President Napoleon lifted to imperial power (2817)

Napoleon III eulogized as guarantor of peace (2818)

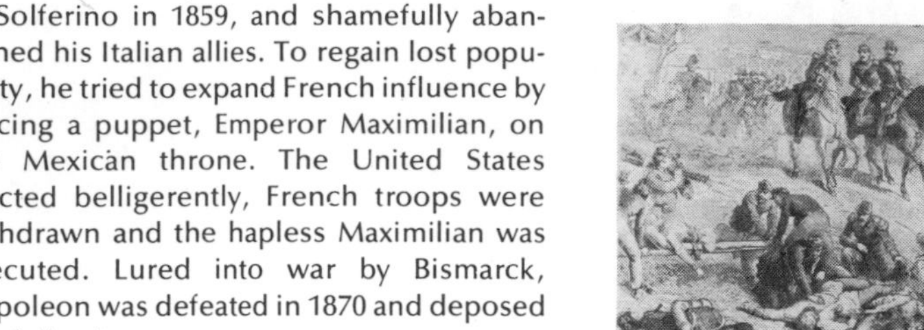

Bloody battle of Solferino led to International Red Cross (2819)

Clara Barton, inspired by Dunant, founded Amer. Red Cross (2820)

Orsini's attack: Napoleon escaped uninjured (2821)

Mexico

Carlotta and Maximilian ruled Mexico under auspices of France (2822, 2822A)

Maximilian was executed when France withdrew support (2823)

Suez

De Lesseps, mentor of the Suez Canal (2824)

Empress Eugénie at canal opening in 1869 (2825)

Completion of Suez Canal was French technical coup (2826)

French industry flourished under Napoleon III. Production of iron and coal doubled (2827)

Haussmann made Paris glamorous city (2828)

Foreign wars strained French state finances; Daumier (2829)

The court of Emperor Napoleon III and Queen Eugénie was admired for its brilliance (2830) and beauty (2831)

Parisians had fun in spite of repressive regime (2832)

Italy Unified

THE RISORGIMENTO saw its patriots divided into three groups: Mazzini's radicals; conservatives who favored papal supremacy; and moderates who looked to the House of Savoy. Thanks to the genius of Count Cavour, Prime Minister of King Victor Emmanuel, the latter group prevailed and, with Sicilian patriot Garibaldi and his "Red Shirts," achieved a united Italian State.

Mazzini: a united Italy his ardent hope (2833)

Cavour's political acumen forged Italian unity (2834)

Garibaldi: grass roots freedom fighter (2835)

Italy's boot stuffed with foreign invaders, France, Russia, Austria (2839)

Carbonari, aristocratic anti-foreign revolutionaries in Modena (2836)

Garibaldi leading Sicilian freedom fighters (2837)

Victor Emmanuel meets Garibaldi, who submits to the new king (2838)

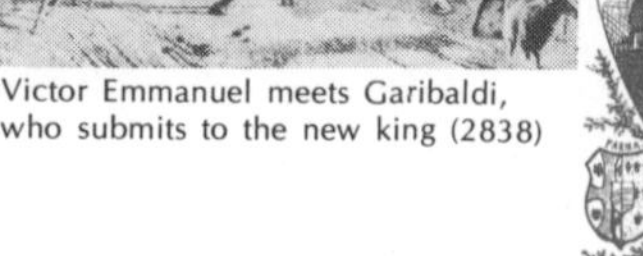

Glory of a united Italy. Nast woodcut (2840). Napoleon III first sponsored Italian unity, betrayed it, lost influence on the peninsula.

Germany - Age of Bismarck

COUNT OTTO VON BISMARCK, Prime Minister of Prussia, had a low opinion of idealistic revolutions. "Freedom and Unity" was the motto on the flag of German barricade fighters in 1848, but he believed that only "Blood and Iron" would unify Germany. To weld the loosely organized North German Confederation into a formidable European power, Bismarck first challenged the traditional hegemony of Austria, defeating her in the Austro-Prussian War of 1866. Then, to demonstrate beyond a doubt Prussia's primacy among German states, he precipitated war with France. The Ems dispatch by King William of Prussia covering a minor diplomatic problem was made public in a shrewdly edited version so insulting to France that Napoleon III was forced to declare war. Bismarck easily defeated the French, capturing the emperor at Sedan.

Moltke: made General Staff supreme (2842)

Prussian soldier (2843)

Imperial council of war discusses final Prussian strategy against France (2844)

Spike helmet, a symbol of German militarism (2845)

Meeting of the Prussian General Staff, charged with supervision of Germany's military might (2846)

Prussia, after victory in Danish war, turned against ally Austria to end the latter's dominance (2847)

Otto von Bismarck, the Iron Chancellor (2841)

Franco-Prussian War

Bismarck called "ablest European statesman" (2848)

Ems telegram tricked France into war (2849)

Franco-Prussian War: France defeated in 3 months (2850)

Surrender at Sedan, Sept. 1870, ended the Second Empire (2851)

Napoleon III, prisoner, meets Bismarck after battle (2852)

William I of Prussia, proclaimed Emperor of German Reich, Versailles, 1871 (2853)

Bismarck forged a unified Germany in 1871 (2854)

War continued after surrender of Sedan; German siege guns before Paris (2855)

Gambetta escaped from Paris by balloon, resisted Germans (2856)

He formed government in Tours, received microfilm reports (2857)

Holocaust in Paris

FOR FRANCE, the war had a bloody aftermath. Irked by the presence of German troops and enraged by the humiliating peace terms (loss of Alsace-Lorraine plus a five-billion-franc indemnity), the Paris Communards staged a revolt against the ruling National Assembly. The government under Thiers suppressed the Communards by executing no fewer than 20,000 suspects.

1871 Frankfurt Peace: France cedes Alsace-Lorraine to Germany (2858)

Victorious armies goose-step in Berlin. Germany supreme power (2859)

Bismarck cuts up the map of Europe, helps himself to Alsace-Lorraine (2860)

RÉPUBLIQUE FRANÇAISE

Nº 388 LIBERTÉ — ÉGALITÉ — FRATERNITÉ Nº 388

COMMUNE DE PARIS

COMITÉ
DE SALUT PUBLIC

Que tous les bons citoyens se lèvent!
Aux barricades! L'ennemi est dans nos murs!
Pas d'hésitation!
En avant pour la République, pour la Commune et pour la Liberté!

AUX ARMES!

Paris, le 22 mai 1871.

Le Comité de Salut public,
ANT. ARNAUD, BILLIORAY, E. EUDES,
F. GAMBON, G. RANVIER.

Poster urges resistance to Third Republic (2861)

Blasting Napoleon column in Place Vendôme (2862)

Brutal mass execution crushed leftist Paris uprising (2864)

City Hall and Tuileries of Paris set afire in uprising of Communards, May 1871 (2865)

Women fought valiantly during Commune (2863)

New Reich Ruled with Iron Hand

"Blood and iron will decide the questions of the day" (2867)

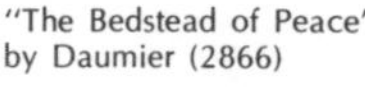

"The Bedstead of Peace" by Daumier (2866)

Keeping down jack-in-the box: Socialism (2868)

Kulturkampf: Bismarck had fear of papacy (2869)

Germany passed England in steel production thanks to iron and coal mines of Alsace-Lorraine (2870)

"IRON CHANCELLOR" Bismarck ruled Germany for twenty years, manipulating the Reichstag to acquiesce to his aims. His first campaign, the *Kulturkampf,* suppressed the Catholic Church, but Bismarck soon found the socialists more dangerous than the Catholics. The Anti-Socialist Laws of 1876 forced them underground. To undercut socialist leaders, Bismarck adopted a far-sighted welfare program, providing workmen's insurance for sickness, accidents and old age half a century before it appeared elsewhere. His diplomacy isolated France and established German leadership in Europe.

Arms manufacture became German monopoly (2871)

Krupp works of Essen built Europe's most powerful guns, supplied them all over the world (2872, 2873)

Bismarck at Berlin Congress of 1878. To isolate France he cultivated friendship of Russia, Austria, England (2874)

Emperors of Germany, Austria, Russia. Their alliance was short-lived (2875)

Triple Alliance of Austria, Germany, Italy, became one of power blocs that divided Europe into two camps in pre-World War I days (2876)

Emperor William I at a reception (2877)

Frederick III reigned only 88 days (2878)

William II (2879), eager to make Germany world power, "dropped the pilot" (2880)

WHILE EUROPEAN IMPERIALISTS, with England in the lead, scrambled for colonies, Germany under Bismarck remained aloof, declaring herself "satiated" with territory while she pursued industrial expansion at home. This policy enabled Bismarck to become the leading power broker in Europe. But it did not suit young William II. Convinced that Germany had a divine world mission, William demanded that Germany enter the race for colonies, and after a battle for power the aging chancellor was dismissed in 1890.

France: Third Republic

FRANCE MADE A REMARKABLE recovery from defeat in the Franco-Prussian War, paying enormous reparations within three years, progressing industrially and acquiring more colonies than any other nation except Britain. But the equilibrium of the Third Republic remained fragile: monarchists tried (unsuccessfully) to restore absolute rule, while the Dreyfus case revealed the dominance of a corrupt military clique.

Vengeance: France's hope after defeat (2881)

Thiers in delicate balance between royalists, republicans (2882)

French President MacMahon favored royalists (2883)

Boulanger, a threat to Third Republic (2884)

Strong anti-clerical bias in popular journal (2885)

The Dreyfus trial aroused world opinion by showing the presence of a powerful military clique and rampant anti-Semitism (2886)

Captain Dreyfus expelled from French army (2887)

Convicted of treason, Dreyfus was imprisoned on Devil's Island (2888)

Zola proved forgeries were used against Dreyfus (2889)

Eiffel Tower, erected in 1889, symbolized Third Republic's resurgent spirit. France prospered, acquired a colonial empire second only to Britain's (2890)

Labor and Socialism

THE REFORM MOVEMENTS of the 1840s sought to lighten labor's burden in the new industrial economy, but met with modest success. The appearance of Karl Marx's *Das Kapital* (1867) proved a forceful stimulus to socialist groups, providing both an ideology and a program of action. Believing that the free-enterprise system, chaotic and unjust in its control of production, was on the verge of collapse, Marxism endorsed a class struggle to topple it. Some, like the German Workingman's Party, sought to achieve this aim by parliamentary means; others, like the Russians, turned to revolution.

The Yoke of Labor: factory workers march sullenly to work. Steinlen lithograph (2891)

Labor unchained storms the bastions of hated capitalistic overlords (2892)

Portents of labor unrest: strikers band together in European factory (2893)

Labor subject of art: "The Man with the Hoe." Millet (2894)

Capitalists viewed labor as cogwheel in the machinery of industry (2895)

Manifest

der

Kommunistischen Partei.

Marx declaring capitalist system corrupt, predicted proletariat's world control of production (2896, 2897)

Engels, Marx's life-long associate (2898)

International Working Men's Association

CARD OF MEMBERSHIP

This is to Certify that Cit. H. Jung was admitted a Member of the above Association in September 1864 and paid as his Annual Subscription for the year 1869 0. 2. 0.

R. Shaw Corresponding Secretary for America

Cor Sec for Belgium | Jules Johannard Italy

Eugène Dupont France | Anthony Zabicki Poland

Karl Marx Germany | H. Jung Switzerland

Treasurer | J. George Eccarius Sec. to Gen. Council

To promote socialist revolt, labor formed global association (2899)

Song of the labor movement (2900)

Congress of moderate-wing German socialists (2901)

Liebknecht (2902) and Bebel (2903): Socialism to be realized by parliamentary means.

Russian Radicals

Herzen, Romantic rebel (2904)

Bakunin, anarchism's theorist (2905)

Kropotkin turned against Marx (2906)

Nast warned labor of siren call of Communism (2907)

Lenin elaborated Marxist theory during his exile in Switzerland (2908)

English Moderates

FABIANISM, the English version of socialism, was named for the Roman General Fabius Maximus, who defeated stronger forces by elusive harassment. Founded by George Bernard Shaw, among others, the Fabian society attracted middle-class intellectuals who sought reform by forcing Parliament to recognize abuses. Later, James Keir Hardie helped found the Independent Labor Party.

Anarchist. Most tried to spread radicalism in America (2909)

Bloody Sunday. Protest in London, 1887 (2910)

Fabians wished to establish socialism gradually. Shaw and the Webbs were first members (2911)

Hyde Park soapbox orator in pleas for social justice (2912)

Orator calls for action by Workingman's Party (2913)

Beatrice and Sidney Webb: social justice within the framework of government (2914)

The new "Member of the Board." Labor begins to demand its share in industrial management (2915)

Giant to the East

VAST, MONOLITHIC, AUTOCRATIC—Russia was barely touched by the storms of change sweeping across Europe. Still, a feeling of guilt pervaded the ruling class when it faced the peasants, whose miserable feudal servitude weakened the economic base of the country. Saying "it is better to abolish serfdom from above than to wait until it is abolished from below," Czar Alexander II freed the peasants from their feudal overlords in 1861. Their bondage continued, however—the peasants were required to pay (over forty-nine years) for the land "given" them.

Though Alexander II was aware of the need for change, his policies angered both autocratic conservatives and intellectual liberals. Ironically, the intellectuals, seeking to speed reforms, assassinated Alexander II in 1881. Under his successor, Alexander III, things became worse. He was a rigid autocrat whose policy of "Russification" drove intellectuals underground and led to pogroms against the Jews (who staged a mass exodus from Russia in the 1880s).

Coat of arms of the Romanovs (2916)

Czar's elite troops protect palace, St. Petersburg (2917)

Circassian Cossacks were czar's permanent escorts (2918)

Nicholas I calming peasant populace during outbreak of the plague in 1831 (2919)

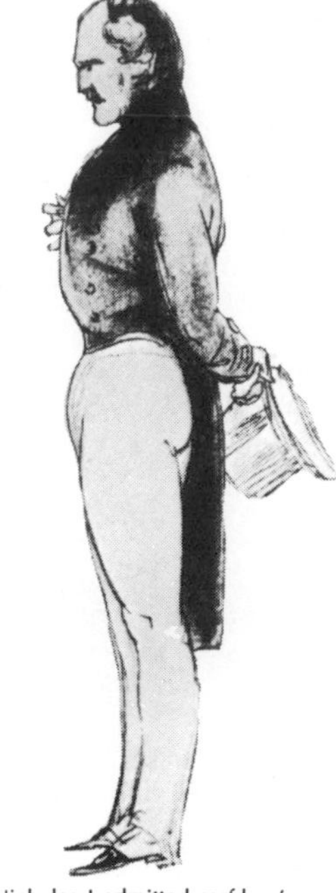
Nicholas I admitted serfdom's misery but acquiesced (2920)

Alexander II, called the Czar Liberator. Reforms profited landowners (2921)

Serfs emancipated. They had to pay for land they were "given" (2922)

Czar Alexander II assassinated on day he had signed new reform act (2923)

Terror against nihilists erupted after Czar's death. Reforms ceased (2924)

Alexander III returned to despotic rule of most conservative type (2925)

Attempts to exterminate underground press and to stem tide of nihilism (2926)

Jews persecuted as minority trying to resist "Russification" (2927)

Political suspects by the thousands exiled to prisons in Siberia (2928)

Peasant Life

Government inspectors were known for abuse of Russian peasants (2929)

Farmers worked without benefit of modern technological aid (2930)

Villages, self-contained economic units, ran workshops for daily needs (2931)

Boy hardware vendor (2932)

Writers

RUSSIA'S PERIOD OF DISILLUSIONMENT and searching self-doubt brought forth a galaxy of great writers. Their novels reflected the jarring gulf between landowners and serfs, and the anxieties created by the atmosphere of revolt and supression. Tolstoy transcended these issues in *War and Peace,* a towering work of world literature.

Dostoyevsky: crime and punishment (2933)

Turgeniev describes Russia's changing social scene (2934)

Tolstoy visits Chekhov, dramatist and short-story writer (2935)

In his last year Tolstoy forsook wealth, joined the humble (2936)

England...

DOMINATED BY THE PERSONALITIES of William Gladstone and Benjamin Disraeli, Liberal and Conservative parties alternated in power during the late Victorian era. Gladstone, the Liberal leader, was deeply religious and took a high moral tone, advocating free trade and opposing imperialism. The Conservative Disraeli, a popular novelist and witty, urbane orator, favored territorial expansion and a revival of the feudal alliance (based on mutual recognition of rights and responsibilities) between workers and the aristocracy. His adroit maneuvering passed the Second Reform Bill of 1867, adding two million workers to the electorate and "dishing the Whigs." Favored by Victoria, Disraeli ensured England's route to India by buying (unknown to Parliament) a controlling interest in the Suez Canal.

Gladstone—"the People's Bill"—backed the masses against the classes (2937)

Disraeli's first speech (2938)

Gladstone attacking Disraeli's first budget in House of Commons debate, 1852 (2939)

Gladstone: mesmeric public speaker (2940)

Disraeli: a conservative with liberal reform ideas (2941)

Disraeli secretly bought Suez shares (2942)

Royal Durbar declares Victoria Queen of India (2943)

Disraeli receives Order of the Garter (2944)

Congress of Berlin in 1878: Disraeli in discussion (2945)

Gladstone with Queen, who disliked him (2946)

John Bull extends vote to England's workers (2947)

Ireland: Struggle for Home Rule

GLADSTONE EARNED THE NICKNAME "the People's Bill" for his concern with social legislation. But his attempts to solve the persistent problem of Anglo-Irish relations were less successful. Though he passed laws protecting Irish tenant farmers from harsh treatment by absentee landlords, the Irish clamored for Home Rule. Gladstone's effort to give it to them split his own party. When the House of Lords defeated his second attempt to pass the bill, he retired (1894).

Captain Boycott "boycotted," expelled by the Irish Land League (2948)

A costly potato crop: soldiers ensure orderly harvest (2949)

Daniel O'Connell, "Liberator," pressed freedom claims (2950)

Charles Stewart Parnell expelled from the House of Commons (2951)

Protest meeting in Belfast against British absentee landlords (2952)

Gladstone introduced First Home Rule Bill in 1886. It was defeated and his Cabinet resigned (2953)

Misery in Ireland: children, victims of famine, carted to burial ground (2954)

Eviction: Irish tenant farmers unable to pay rent, expelled, left to starve (2955)

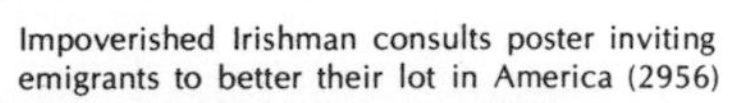

Impoverished Irishman consults poster inviting emigrants to better their lot in America (2956)

Shaping the British Empire

AS IMPERIALIST COMPETITION sent European powers scrambling around the world, England's leadership in the race was seldom questioned; one third of the British Empire was acquired between 1870 and 1890. Apologists justified this craze for conquest by seeing in it a divine mission: to bring culture to the barbarians. Today we are more aware of the dehumanization of native societies which resulted.

The most tragic victim of this cruel game was Africa. At the Berlin-Africa Conference of 1885, sixteen participants sliced up the continent. Eventually only two African states remained independent: Liberia and Ethiopia.

Irish emigrants at Cork about to embark for colonies (2958)

Symbol of the Empire (2957)

Fathers of the Canadian Federation. Canada, a dominion, in 1867 became sovereign (2959)

John Bull, master of the world (2960)

Gold mining in pioneer Australia, 1840 (2961)

Australian colony established self-government in 1850 (2962)

Colonies, growing up, have to be "refitted" (2963)

Lure of Africa

"Dr. Livingstone, I presume?" Stanley's greeting at finding the missionary (2964)

A slave's yoke is cut by Livingstone (2965)

The Mahdi occupied Sudan, Egypt (2966)

Death of General Gordon at Khartoum, Sudan (2967)

British lion ready to swallow Egypt (2968)

Battle of Omdurman ended Mahdi rule in Sudan (2969)

Zulus defeated; Zululand became colony (2970)

Leopold I of Belgium "owned" Congo (2971)

Cecil Rhodes, British capitalist (2972), established expanded South African diamond empire (2973)

Rhodes ridiculed as the African Napoleon (2974)

British military observer in Sudan campaign (2975)

Boer War

ENGLAND AT FIRST gave its Dutch settlers in South Africa (the Boers) a measure of independence. But when gold was discovered in the Transvaal, English fortune seekers poured in. Since the Boers (now quite hostile) stood in the way of Cecil Rhodes and imperialist expansion, war was declared. It took three cruel years to crush the Boers.

Dr. Jameson during his famous raid (2976)

Boers' "Great Trek" to Natal (2977)

Boers move to repel British forces (2978)

Kruger fought British in Boer War, which lasted for three inglorious years (2979, 2980)

Imperialism

Africa is being blessed with British products (2981)

Kitchener and Kipling, the sword and the pen, pillars of Empire (2982)

"White man's burden"—Kipling phrase (2983)

J. Chamberlain: colonial super-salesman (2984)

What imperialism is all about: how England colonizes Africa. A German view (2985)

Apogee of Victoria's Reign

QUEEN VICTORIA'S DIAMOND JUBILEE occurred at the zenith of British imperialism. Sovereign of the richest nation on earth, she was also "Grandmother of Europe," for many of her 15 children and grandchildren ruled (or had married those who ruled) in Russia, Germany, Scandinavia, Greece and Spain. To the millions who cheered as she made a grand progress through London in 1897, Victoria, in the sixtieth year of her reign, symbolized British hegemony over the world.

The London through which she rode reflected her image. Prosperous, cosmopolitan, spangled with beautiful parks, theaters and music halls, it projected an atmosphere of well-being.

Victoria, son, grandson, great-grandson (2986)

Queen's Diamond Jubilee, 1897. The diplomatic reception (2987)

Future Edward VII pays visit to mother (2988)

Lively London

House of Parliament (3010). The Thames from Westminster to the Tower (3010A)

- **A** Flower sellers, Trafalgar Square (2989)
- **B** Boy employed as street cleaner (2990)
- **C** London bus plastered with ads (2991)
- **D** Boy on tricycle in public park (2992)
- **E** Lord Kitchener during parade (2993)
- **F** Day at the beach of Brighton (2994)
- **G** Victorian lady on golf course (2995)
- **H** Tense moment in bicycle race (2996)
- **I** Champions of the cricket field (2997)
- **J** Arthur Sullivan, operetta's king (2998)
- **K** Mrs. Patrick Campbell (Ophelia) (2999)
- **L** Ellen Terry, friend of G.B.S. (3000)
- **M** Programme-poster for "Iolanthe" (3001)
- **N** Fan shows the Mikado influence (3002)
- **O** Katisha, the formidable fiance (3003)
- **P** London scare: Jack the Ripper (3004)

Thomas Hardy poetising. Beerbohm cartoon (3005)

R. L. Stevenson: travel, adventure stories (3006)

Oscar Wilde: sardonic social comedies (3007)

Swinburne: great lyric poet (3008)

Lewis Carroll: classics for children (3009)

Men of Letters

VICTORIAN SELF-SATISFACTION inevitably brought forth odd behavior or manners that challenged the stuffiness and moral confinement of the age. But the ugly end of Oscar Wilde whose wit failed to protect him from imprisonment on morals charges, demonstrated the power of the establishment.

New Scientific Concepts

▲ The phenomenon of sound (3011)

AS MATERIALISM REPLACED Romanticism in the second half of the nineteenth century, physics dethroned metaphysics in a scientific "coup d'état." Observable "fact" now dominated thought, in both the worldly realities of commerce and the esoteric processes of the laboratory. As Dickens' character Mr. Gradgrind put it: "In this life we want facts, sir, we are never to fancy." New facts, however, proved less important than bold generalizations. For example, exploring the relation between motion and heat (as in the steam engine), thermodynamics produced a theory of heat energy based upon the excitation of molecules.

Count Rumford measured heat by drilling a cannon bore, formulated work-heat relationship (3012)

Carnot: law of thermodynamics (3013)

Joule found laws of heat-electricity (3014)

Maxwell: heat and electricity (3015)

Berthelot: foremost thermochemist (3016)

Kelvin devised scale of temperature (3017)

Evolution

AS PHYSICISTS REVISED the concept of matter, Charles Darwin brought forth a new explanation of the origin of species, challenging the account given in Genesis. His theory that species developed through "survival of the fittest" was not wholly original, but his careful documentation and rigorous argument compelled acceptance. While Darwin's work revolutionized the life sciences—zoology, genetics, anthropology—it also had profound practical implications. "Social Darwinists" could justify the most reckless capitalistic competition on the grounds that "survival of the fittest" was the law of nature and thus the law of God.

Darwin's theory ridiculed in *Punch* cartoon (3028) ▼

Pigeons in Darwin's early work (3029)

Charles Darwin: naturalist and evolutionist (3030)

Darwin tests speed of giant tortoise during Galápagos exploration (3032)

ON

THE ORIGIN OF SPECIES

BY MEANS OF NATURAL SELECTION,

OR THE

PRESERVATION OF FAVOURED RACES IN THE STRUGGLE FOR LIFE.

BY CHARLES DARWIN, M.A.,

FELLOW OF THE ROYAL, GEOLOGICAL, LINNÆAN, ETC., SOCIETIES; AUTHOR OF 'JOURNAL OF RESEARCHES DURING H. M. S. BEAGLE'S VOYAGE ROUND THE WORLD.'

LONDON:
JOHN MURRAY, ALBEMARLE STREET.
1859.

The right of Translation is reserved.

Origin of Species, 1859: species not stationary. They evolve, modify during descent (3031)

Toward Atomic Energy

Mendeleev arrayed elements in "Periodic Table" (3018)

Hertz confirmed Maxwell's theory of light (3019)

Vacuum tube emissions traced by Crookes (3020)

Röntgen, discoverer of X-rays (3021)

CRUCIAL, TOO, WAS Hertz's discovery of "photo-electricity" (in which certain substances produce a negative charge when stimulated by light) plus observations of the mysterious light given off by radioactive metals. These insights challenged the concept of the atom as the final, irreducible building block of the universe. The atom itself was proved to consist of smaller charged particles: protons, neutrons, electrons.

▲ Orbital representation of atomic structure (3022)

Becquerel: a creator of electrochemistry (3023)

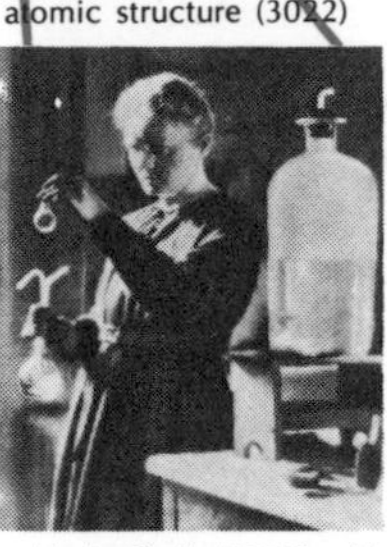

Marie Curie (3024) with her husband Pierre (3025) investigated uranium, discovered polonium, radium.

J. J. Thomson showed cathode rays to be subatomic, electrically charged electrons (3026)

Ramsay discovered radium emanates helium (3027)

Genetics

Th. H. Huxley—Darwin's ardent defender (3033)

Weismann: inherent traits only are inherited (3034)

Francis Galton founded the science of eugenics (3035)

Mendel formulated plant-heredity laws (3036)

De Vries: mutations affect heredity (3037)

Luther Burbank, plant geneticist (3038)

Medicine's Golden Age

ACCEPTANCE OF THE GERM THEORY at this time made "safe surgery" possible and established preventive medicine. For these advances, humanity was indebted to a French chemist, Louis Pasteur, who proved that many diseases are caused by bacteria. He tracked them down and found the way to combat them by applying "antitoxins." In the field of surgery, Joseph Lister similarly came to the conclusion that postoperative blood poisoning (a plague of old-time surgery) resulted from germs invading the wound. He introduced heat sterilization of instruments and a carbolic-acid spray, which dramatically reduced the risk of infection.

Claude Bernard, founder of experimental medicine, famed for research on liver, diabetes (3039)

"To us in the medical profession . . . the great boon of this wonderful century . . . is the fact that the leaves of the tree of Science have been for the healing of the nations. This is the Promethean gift of the century to man."

—Sir William Osler

Vaccination against rabies in Pasteur's laboratory (3040)

"Children inspired his loving solicitude" (3041)

Pasteur developed germ theory of disease, opened era of preventative medicine (3042)

Metchnikoff used animals to study digestion (3043)

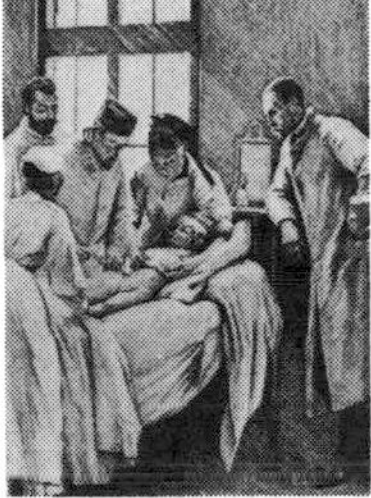

Roux saves children, uses diptheria vaccine (3044)

Robert Koch discovered tubercle bacillus (3045)

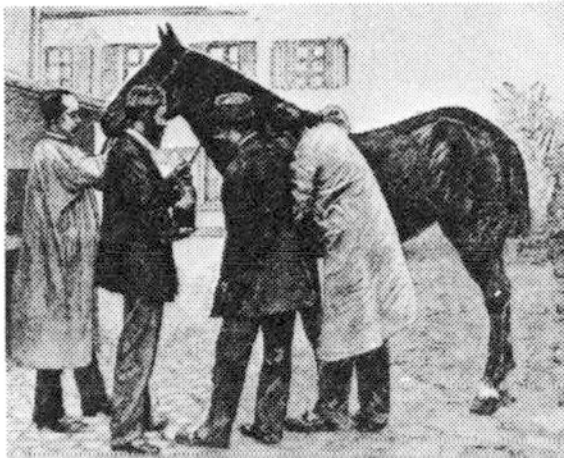

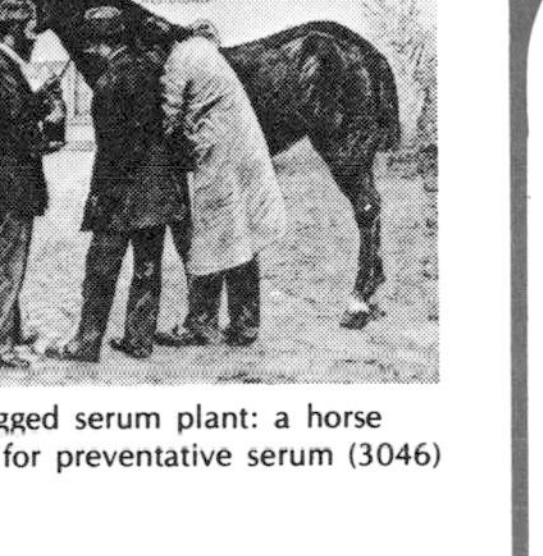

Four-legged serum plant: a horse tapped for preventative serum (3046)

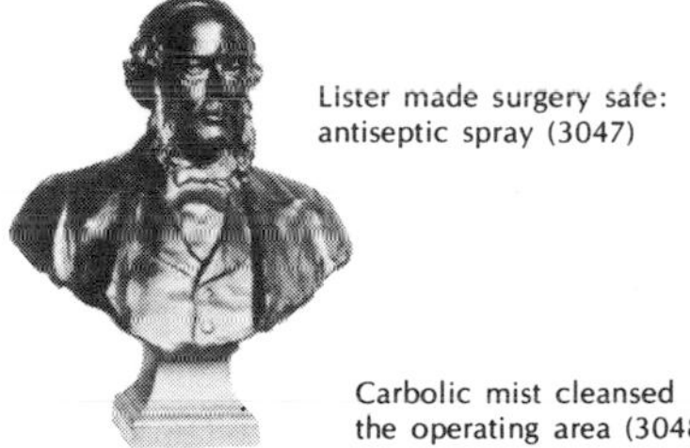

Lister made surgery safe: antiseptic spray (3047)

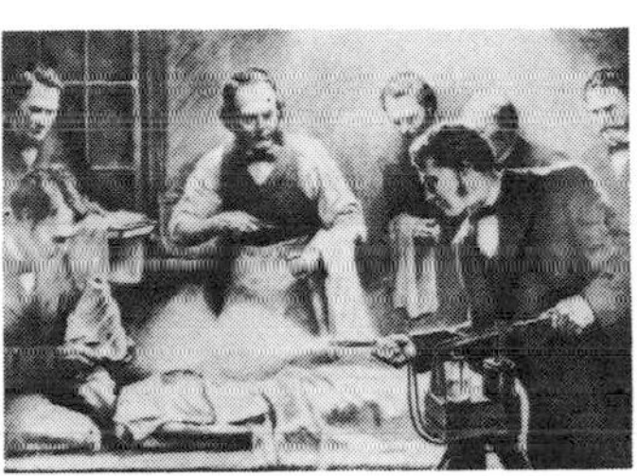

Carbolic mist cleansed the operating area (3048)

CELL THEORY

Schleiden discovered the nucleus of the cell (3049)

Cancer cells from Virchow's *Cellular Pathology* (3051) ▶

Virchow: "cells on rampage cause of body's ills" (3050)

RUDOLPH VIRCHOW, the founder of cellular pathology, typifies an age in which scientists reached for broad new concepts. His description of the body as a humming "cell state" and disease as "simply a civil war" between the cells remains uncontested.

The Freudian Revolution

ALTHOUGH FREUD BEGAN his career as a medical researcher, he decided to open his own practice in anticipation of marriage. Specializing in the mentally disturbed patient, he investigated psychic phenomena previously thought beyond classification. He proved that dreams, fantasies and neuroses have identifiable causes. In tracing these causes, he introduced the idea that the psyche functions on two levels, the second being subconscious yet a determining factor in mental disturbances. His theories had a profound influence on modern society.

Hypnotized woman (3057)

Cocteau interprets Freud (3058)

Charcot's clinic where Freud studied hysteria (3052)

Breuer joined Freud in psychic studies (3053)

Jung: theory of complexes; intro-, extroversion (3054)

Adler: psychopathology of everyday life (3055)

Havelock Ellis: interplay of sex and psyche (3056)

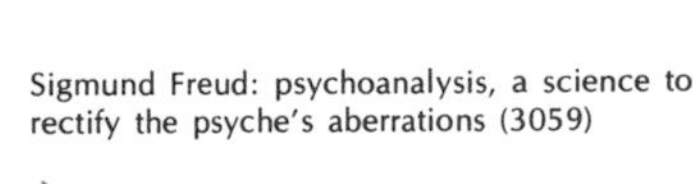

Sigmund Freud: psychoanalysis, a science to rectify the psyche's aberrations (3059)

...an age packed with material accomplishments ...radiant works in the realm of the Spirit.

AS IN OTHER FIELDS, there was a move away from Romanticism in literature, philosophy and history at this time. The scientific observation of man's individual or social behavior was now likely to take precedence over idealistic theory. Historical romancing was giving way to historical research based on facts.

But counterforces were also at work, lending a rich ambiguity to the spirit of the age. The cold positivism of Comte (who initiated the term "sociology" and the concept of "mass man") was balanced against the existential yearnings of Schopenhauer, Kierkegaard and Nietzsche. And the ethereal voice of music was still heard, reminding "mass man" of his individual soul.

Philosophy

Schopenhauer: Will, Idea in tragic struggle (3060)

Kierkegaard: agony at man's limitations (3061)

Nietzsche: salvation of man is superman (3062)

Sociology

Spencer: happiness goal of society (3068)

J.S. Mill: proposed a free-swinging economy (3069)

Durkheim: scientific study of social order (3070)

Comte: facts are the core of science (3063)

Psychology

Binet: intelligence is measurable (3064)

Wundt: experimental psychology (3065)

Wm. James propounded pragmatism (3066)

Runner's blood pressure measured (3067)

History

Ranke: "to retell how it really was" (3071)

Mommsen: new stress on documentary study (3072)

Burckhardt: historian of the Renaissance (3073)

Renan interpreted divine deeds rationally (3074)

Taine stressed facts and observation (3075)

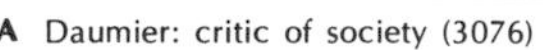

Artists

Writers

A Daumier: critic of society (3076)
B Corot: early Impressionist (3077)
C Monet: shimmering lights (3078)
D Cezanne: beyond realism (3079)
E Manet: reality's lucidity (3080)
F Van Gogh: dazzle of color (3081)
G Gauguin: lure of the exotic (3082)
H Rodin: ideas in marble (3083)
I Whistler: enfant terrible (3084)
J Zola: mirrors life (3085)
K Flaubert: reality observed (3086)
L Maupassant: short-stories (3087)
M Baudelaire: aesthete (3088)
N Mallarmé: symbolist (3089)
O Zola title page (3090)

The Musical Arts

ALTHOUGH JOHANNES BRAHMS filled his music with romantic themes, he used classical forms, providing a tonal image nostalgically at odds with the world around him. Yet, as the last of music's "Great B's" (with Bach and Beethoven), he was a giant.

THE NEED FOR LIGHTER MUSIC, to please the new paunchy capitalist, was met in France by Jacques Offenbach. Overtly frivolous, his breezy operettas made Parisians happy and Offenbach rich. Meanwhile the Viennese danced to the waltzes of Johann Strauss that spilled over into *Die Fledermaus*.

Brahms: classic form, romantic spirit (3091)

Bruckner: monumental symphonist (3092)

César Franck: French master of symphonic improvisations (3093)

Johann Strauss: glittering Vienna danced to his lilting waltz tunes (3094)

Manuscript of world's greatest waltz, *An der schönen blauen Donau* (3095)

Rage of Vienna—Herr Strauss (3096)

Offenbach, creator of light opera (3097)

Verdi conducting *Aida* at Paris Opera (3098)

Verdi's *La Traviata*. Title cover: Violetta (3099)

Wagner: nationalistic supermusician (3100)

Valkyrie: Germanic myth figure (3101)

Wagner assaults the musical ear (3102)

GIUSEPPE VERDI'S EARLY MUSIC was tied to Italy's desperate and tragic history. His later works remain universal favorites: exuberant, melodic and lavish in showmanship.

LIKE BISMARCK UNIFYING EUROPE, Wagner set out to unify the arts, fusing literature, drama and music into one gigantic spectacle. His major work, the four-part *Ring of the Nibelung*, translates German imperialism into the language of aesthetics: full-throated gods and heroes—the colossi of Germanic legend—sing of their unchained tempers, revealing (perhaps unintentionally) their meanness, guile and lust for power. Wagner's music, bewitching in itself, is fanatic Aryanism.

Wagner's orchestral gigantism lampooned (3103, 3104, 3105)

DEBUSSY ABANDONED familiar concepts of melody, tonality and form. His shimmering tone poems, which were influenced by symbolism and by Javanese orchestras, hit Paris like a whirlwind and marked a turning point in music.

RUSSIAN COMPOSERS borrowed much from folklore. The color, pomp and intoxication of the Slavic fairy world appear in Rimsky-Korsakov. Tchaikovsky, though he clung to classical forms, filled them with melancholy Slavic sentiment.

Debussy's *Afternoon of a Faun:* music reflecting impressionism's airy glitter (3106, 3107)

Puccini's *Tosca:* tale of murder (3108)

Moussorgsky echoed folk tunes (3109)

Tchaikovsky: Russia's classical master (3110)

Swan Lake (3111) and *Nutcracker Suite* reflected Tchaikovsky's passion for the dance.

Rimsky-Korsakov combined exotic and Russian elements (3112)

Glamour of Paris Opera opening (3113)

Nutcracker Suite figure (3114)

A

B

C

CHAPTER 11

U.S.: Industrial Giant

Enterprise - Invention

Waning Frontier

Rise of Cities

F

D

E

Post Civil War America

IF THE CIVIL WAR split America apart, the railroads bound her together again. Railroads—"the quickest centralizing force of modern times" (Garfield)—supplied all parts of the nation with goods, thanks to the rapid development of mass production, much of it originally designed to equip the Union Army. Raw materials from the South and West—copper, lead, silver, lumber, as well as livestock and produce—poured into urban manufacturing centers over the railroads. In the decade after Appomattox, the Northeast burst into the Industrial Age with the force of a volcanic eruption.

Railroads brought goods and people West, created boom in Eastern industry (3119 A)

Railroads

Blasting a mountain range for tracks of Transcontinental Railroad (3115)

Chinese coolies joined Irishmen in epic construction job (3116)

Each mile of track laid was government-financed (3117)

Rails reach summit of Rocky Mountains (3118)

Promontory, Utah, May 10, 1869—joining of rails with golden spike (3119)

THE TRANSCONTINENTAL RAILROAD, completed in 1869, was the most important factor in the new network of national trade. A virtual army of more than 20,000 Civil War veterans, Irish immigrants and Chinese coolies labored to build it in just three years. The new link between East and West proved a bonanza for its builders, who were given 23 million acres of free federal land, easy loans and a decisive voice in the settlement of the West.

Studebaker carriage factory in South Bend, Indiana, tied up with railroad to facilitate product shipment (3123)

Industry

Dazzling molten metal is poured during Bessemer steel process (3120)

Kelly converter produced steel at greatly reduced price (3121)

Assembly line in early steel foundry (3122)

Georgia melons are shipped from Atlanta by rail to eager northern markets (3124)

Chicago meat-packing plants pioneered in use of continuous production lines, mechanization (3125)

Montgomery Ward, mail marketer of mass-produced goods (3126)

Cornucopia of goods. Symbol from Sears, Roebuck catalogue (3127)

Oil: New Power Portent

John D. Rockefeller, oil tycoon (3131)

CRUDE OIL, THE "BLACK GOLD" that soon was to power the new economy, seemed a mere curiosity to farmers who gathered it from a "polluted" creek near Titusville, Pennsylvania. But when a Yale chemist (Benjamin Silliman) developed an inexpensive refining process to produce kerosene, there was a mad rush for the Pennsylvania oil fields. Cheaper as a lamp fuel than whale oil, kerosene seemed to have a great future. Nobody saw it more clearly than John D. Rockefeller, a commission dealer in Cleveland. With an initial capital of $4,000, he began to buy up oil refineries. By 1879 he had cornered 79 percent of the refining capacity of the U.S. and most of the world market for oil.

First U.S. oil well drilled in Titusville, Pa., 1859 (3128)

Oil refinery poster. Rockefeller monopolized this field (3129)

Uncle Sam, supplier of oil to light up the world. Trade card (3130)

Big Operators

The Bulls and the Bears (3132)

BUSINESS ETHICS TOOK A BEATING at the hands of the big operators who now led America's effulgent economy. Greedily they exploited the nation's virgin resources, seeking—through shady methods of corporate financing—to build fortunes overnight. All of the new tycoons—among them Fisk, Gould, Carnegie and Rockefeller—as a rule unscrupulous in their dealings, shared an uncanny vision of the future, as well as a dashing style.

Capitalist moneygrubber besieged by poor (3133)

Daniel Drew speculated in Erie R.R. stock; with Gould, won control from Vanderbilt (3134)

Speculative frenzy made broker "A slave of the tape" (3135)

Jay Gould (3136), Jim Fisk (3137), speculators, ruined Erie R.R., cornered the gold market.

Commodore Vanderbilt, railroad mogul (3138)

Wall Street magnate: "King of the Curb" (3139)

Syndicate of bankers discussing bond issue with August Belmont (center) presiding (3140)

Black Friday, Sept. 24, 1869. Credits crisis due to gold shortage, speculation (3141)

"Vanderbilt nightmare" has public suffering (3142)

Railroad directors milking stockholders, public (3143)

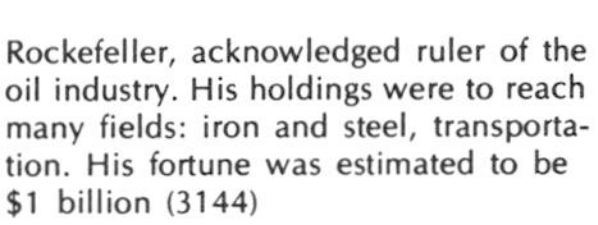

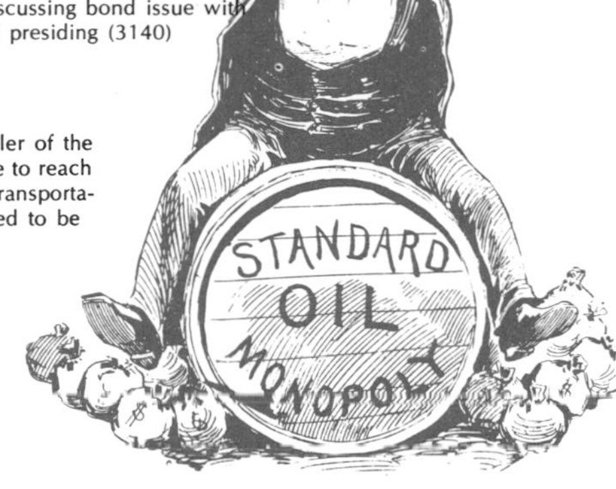

Rockefeller, acknowledged ruler of the oil industry. His holdings were to reach many fields: iron and steel, transportation. His fortune was estimated to be $1 billion (3144)

Grant Administration

GENERAL ULYSSES S. GRANT, a superb military man, hated politics and voted only once in his life. He was a poor choice as President during a period of ruthless business competition. Unfamiliar with the ways of government, he tolerated the corruption of high officers in his Administration. This became so blatant that the liberal wing of his own party bolted, backing Horace Greeley in 1872. But the monied interests, waging a vicious campaign against Greeley, saw to it that Grant was re-elected. Even in his second term, the General-President remained infected with the corruptive virus of the time: the belief that a rich man was automatically a good man. Involved in financial scandals throughout his Administration, Grant himself died poor, though his memoirs earned nearly half a million dollars for his heirs.

Grant in Galena, Ill. Depot, 1869, departing for Washington (3145)

Election speech: "He made a bow and that was all he said" (3146)

Accused of military carpet-baggery (3147)

Honest Grant duped by crooked friends (3148)

Whiskey Ring scandal rocked Grant Administration (3149)

Greeley ran against Grant in 1872 election (3150)

He went down in smashing defeat and died a month after Grant was elected (3151)

Jay Cooke (3152). Crash of his banking house in 1873 precipitated five-year-long U.S. depression (3153)

Grant dismisses Belknap (3154)

Grant and family at summer home in Mt. Gregor, N.Y. (3156)

During his last sickness, writing his famed memoirs (3157)

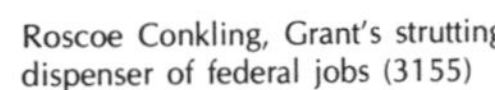

Roscoe Conkling, Grant's strutting dispenser of federal jobs (3155)

Proud Centennial

RUSHING BUOYANTLY into industrialization, America paused in 1876 to survey its accomplishments at the Philadelphia Centennial Exposition. There was much to be proud of, especially the evidence of the nation's inventive genius. Its symbol was the giant Corliss engine—40 feet high, and generating 1,500 horsepower—billed as the "Eighth Wonder of the World." Less gigantic but more important was Alexander Graham Bell's telephone, which made its first public appearance here.

Triumphant Uncle Sam bestriding his century of progress (3158)

Souvenir of the Philadelphia Centennial Exposition. All America focused on its wondrous displays (3159)

Corliss engine: miracle of horsepower (3160)

Wheelchair visitor (3161)

Model: torch of Liberty (3162)

Innovation: hot-dog seller (3163)

Bell demonstrates telephone to Emperor Dom Pedro (3164)

Telephone: the Exposition's most salient novelty (3165)

Upsurge of Invention

THE PRODUCTS OF YANKEE INGENUITY, surveyed by ten million visitors at the Centennial, were more than mere curiosities—they were prototypes of devices which, once mass-produced, would alter the life style of the entire Western world. The Age of Technology, with both blessings and curses, received a mighty impetus at the Philadelphia Exposition.

Patent Office files bulged with new schemes and inventions (3166)

Transcontinental "palace car", 1878, a refinement of first Pullman sleeping car design (3167)

Pullman explains his quiet wheel (3168)

Westinghouse air brake brought about safety of trains, rail crossings (3169)

C.L. Sholes perfected the typewriter (3170)

Mergenthaler mechanized setting of type (3171)

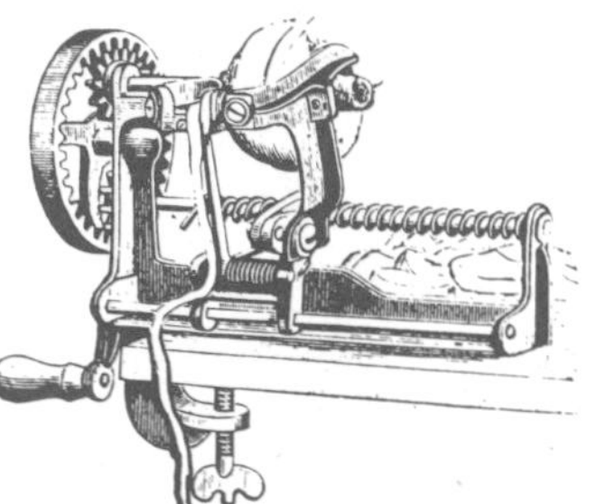

Patented gadget to pare apples (3172)

Chair with cooling mechanism (3173)

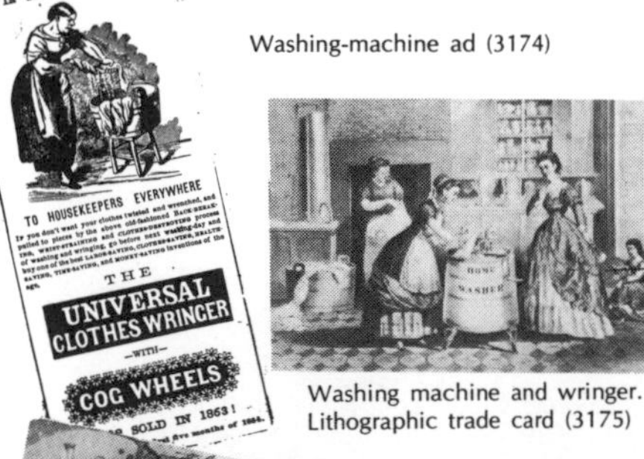

Washing-machine ad (3174)

Washing machine and wringer. Lithographic trade card (3175)

Old-time needle-working (3176)

New-time machine-sewing (3177)

Decoy for use by streetcar to avoid frightening nervous horses (3178)

Unicycle patented in 1869 was made entirely of steel (3179)

Hand truck—to help convey heavy factory loads (3180)

Problem of old-time coal-heating (3181)

Comfort of new circulating-hot-water radiator (3182)

The Monumental

When Brooklyn Bridge opened, 1883, it was longest in the world (3183)

Statue of Liberty, dedicated in 1886: Franco-American amity (3184)

Edison . . .

AMERICA'S MOST PROLIFIC INVENTOR was Thomas Alva Edison, whose laboratory at Menlo Park became the model for American industrial · research—an "invention factory." Not primarily interested in marketing his inventions, Edison (who held more than a thousand patents) usually sold his developed products for exploitation by others. Yet his inventions changed the shape of daily life.

His greatest achievement was the electric light. Edison developed not only the lamp itself, but a whole distribution system that made electricity a new power in the world.

Thomas A. Edison in his library with statue of Electricity (3188)

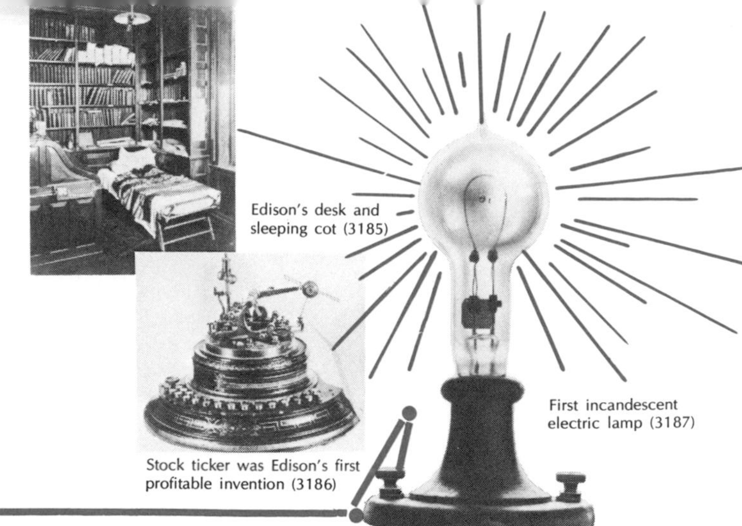

Edison's desk and sleeping cot (3185)

Stock ticker was Edison's first profitable invention (3186)

First incandescent electric lamp (3187)

Edison with phonograph. Its musical potential evolved later (3189)

Uncle Sam salutes the new phonograph (3190)

A novelty: "Talking Doll"; its inner workings (3191)

Edison lights electric lamp. It burned for 40 years (3192)

Edison's "highwaisted" electric generator (3193)

Edison experimented briefly with electric trains (3194)

Kinetoscope, ancestor of today's cinema (3195)

Edison demonstrating his new motion picture projector (3196)

Inside his first studio, Orange, N.J. (3197)

Early movie poster (3198)

Living Electrically

Primitive electrical generator, hand-cranked by two men (3202)

Electricity revolutionized metalworking: welding by means of voltaic arc (3199)

Early computer powered by storage battery (3200)

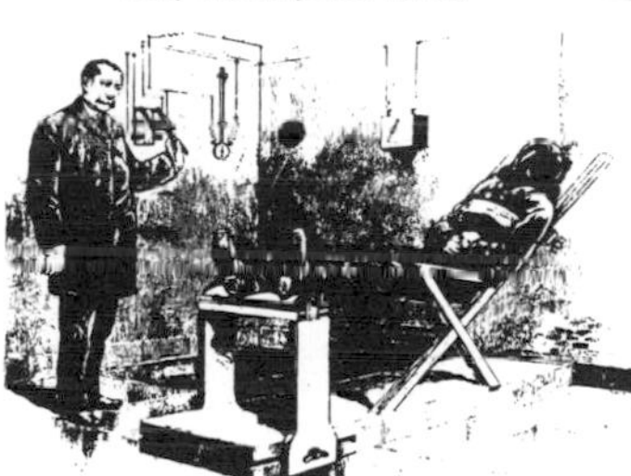

Dying electrically: electric chair was first used in 1889 (3201)

Edison's first power station opened at Pearl Street, New York (3203)

Electric dental drill replaced foot-operated device (3204)

Electro-therapeutic bath to cure rheumatism and other ills (3205)

Electric iron relieved pressing chores (3206)

Madison Square, N.Y., with electric street light (3207)

Wires emerge from power station (3208)

Westinghouse develops alternate current, which was opposed by Edison (3209)

Nikola Tesla, ingenious electric inventor (3210)

Charles Steinmetz, long-time Edison associate (3211)

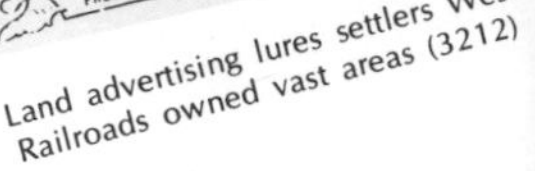
Land advertising lures settlers West. Railroads owned vast areas (3212)

Opening of the West

PARALLEL PERFORMANCES occupied the American stage in the 1870s: the triumph of industrialization in the East, the saga of the pioneers in the West. Lured by the prospect of riches, settlers poured into the Western plains to claim free landholdings under the Homestead Act of 1862, but the dangers often overwhelmed them: hostile Indians, the ferocity of nature, poverty and anxiety. Without money to buy plows, many settlers could not cultivate the heavily matted sod of the prairie, while water for irrigation was always a problem. Nevertheless, on balance they accomplished wonders. Within a decade their wheat production fed the cities of America; within half a century it would feed the world.

Proposed prairie wind wagon (3213)

Pilgrims of the plains going West. 1871 woodcut by A.R. Waud (3214)

Settlers

Homesteader's cabin and clearing amid towering giants of the forest (3215)

Woman collecting buffalo chips to serve as winter fuel (3216)

Sod house, in which families had to weather brutal winter (3217)

Minnesota couple sporting their Sunday best (3218)

Towns: Boom and Bust

WESTERN TOWNS SPROUTED at river crossings or railheads, the location of the latter dictated by railroad bosses, who owned all the land, thanks to federal largess. In the Far West, "ghost towns" were the remains of gold strikes that had failed, buildings abandoned to gather dust when the bonanza was over.

Kansas land office ready to do business (3219)

Pioneer legislature decides on the location of new capital (3220)

Settlement in Moro, Oregon, near railroad that ensures access to markets (3221)

Main Street in Rufus, Oregon. Farm wagons leave deep tracks in muddy dirt road (3222)

Storefronts proudly pictured in young Nebraska frontier settlement (3223)

Main Street, Denver, Col. Silver bonanza in '70s made it a bustling boom town (3224)

Hannibal, Mo.—its lovely riverfront immortalized by Mark Twain (3225)

Trail of the Cowboy

The long drive from Texas over free grass lands to the Kansas cow towns (3226)

Southwestern town; street life (3227)

Trail weary cow hands relax outside the saloon (3228)

Prairie was spotted with ghost towns. Settlers, miners had moved on (3229)

THE LEGENDARY COWBOYS, serving the interest of ranchers who wished to take advantage of a free grass corridor stretching from Texas to the East, drove their herds hundreds of miles, developing a system of trails—the Western, the Chisholm, the Shawnee—to railheads or slaughterhouses at Dodge City, Abilene or Kansas City. At the end of the road, fabulous profits awaited them. Meanwhile the ranchers freely appropriated vast domains in the Southwest as breeding grounds.

Remington drawing of typical cowboy (3232)

Ranch cattle and mavericks found were branded by cowboys in far-ranging yearly roundup (3230)

Changing the guard: waking the relief watch, to ride herd at night (3231)

"Cowboy hieroglyphics"—brand marks to identify cattle of rancher (3233)

Stampede—the dread of the drive (3234)

(3235)

Barbed Wire Changes Western Life

BARBED WIRE, invented by J. F. Glidden in 1874, ended the free-roaming drives of the cattlemen and changed the whole topography of the West. Cheap enough to fence in vast acreage, barbed wire protected the prairie farmer himself from grazing herds. Farms expanded, and railroads gradually replaced the arduous overland cattle drives.

Barbed wire fences enabled prairie farmers to counter encroachment of cowboys (3236)

Cattle ranchers used wire fences for protection against the onrush of roaming herds (3237)

PATENT STEEL BARB FENCING

Invention of barbed wire by Glidden initiated new era in farming (3238)

Prairie homesteader stakes out his domain with wire fencing. Painting by John Steuart Curry (3239)

Thirty horses pull combine in Oregon wheat field (3240)

Agri-technology advances: steam-threshing on an Oregon farm (3241)

Huge Western bonanza farms absorbed the land of derelict settlers (3242)

"The End of the Trail." Sculpture by J. E. Fraser. Indians were chased from their land (3245)

THE PLAINS INDIANS presented an unwelcome obstacle to most settlers. Homesteaders and mining operators coveted Indian lands, while hunters and trappers slaughtered the buffalo for their hides, robbing the Indians of essential food and clothing. The government promoted the cause of the settlers, allowing whole tribes to be destroyed through warfare, harassment or removal to reservations where they could not survive.

U.S. soldier scalps Indian (3243)

Gen. George Custer. Brady photo (3244)

Custer's last stand, June 1876. Sioux killed all 260 men of his group (3246)

Comanche, Custer's horse, sole survivor of the Little Big Horn massacre (3247)

Carnage at Wounded Knee: 200 Indians slaughtered by the U.S. military (3248)

Indian hunts for food and an occasional hide (3249)

Wholesale slaughter of buffaloes from Kansas-Pacific Railroad train (3250)

Hunter flaunts newly skinned hide (3251)

Buffalo hunters with prey. Fur caps and coats became Eastern fashion (3252)

Families expelled after Battle of Bad Axe (3253)

A Proud Race Vanquished

Indian reservation: officials issue government food, clothing (3254)

Geronimo, Apache chief, wrote autobiography (3255)

Sitting Bull, leader at Little Big Horn (3256)

Chief Joseph led the Nez Percé tribe (3257)

Sharp Nose, heroic chief of the Arapaho tribe (3258)

The Turbulent West

DESPITE THE CIVILIZING EFFECT of the transcontinental railroad, the West remained a rough country through the 1870s and '80s. In the plains, government troops fought back the Indians, but many regions lacked even scanty military protection and were easy prey for desperadoes. Many of these, like Jesse James, who had discovered the profitability of train robbery, were graduates of the border banditry nurtured during the Civil War. They aroused both fear and admiration, stimulating the peculiar American fascination with badmen and their derring-do exploits.

The mail robbery in Port Neuf Canon (3259)

Shoot-out in a Western town. "Been looking for you." Drawing (3260)

Greeley goes through the roof on trip west (3261)

Train holdups succeeded because of no federal protection (3262)

"Unwelcome visitor." Robber terrorizes woman (3263)

Train conductors counterattack invading train robbers (3264)

Masked robbers go shopping, "gut" a Montana store (3265)

Billy the Kid; early daguerreotype (3266)

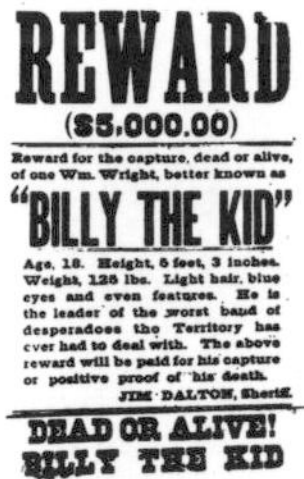
REWARD
($5,000.00)
Reward for the capture, dead or alive, of one Wm. Wright, better known as
"BILLY THE KID"
Age, 18. Height, 5 feet, 3 inches. Weight, 125 lbs. Light hair, blue eyes and even features. He is the leader of the worst band of desperadoes the Territory has ever had to deal with. The above reward will be paid for his capture or positive proof of his death.
JIM DALTON, Sheriff.
DEAD OR ALIVE!
BILLY THE KID

Reward poster: get Billy the Kid (3267)

Billy the Kid killed by Sheriff Pat Garrett at Fort Sumner. The fabled desperado was twenty-two years old (3268)

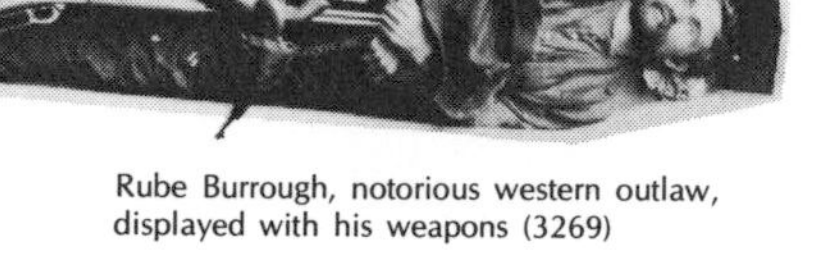
Rube Burrough, notorious western outlaw, displayed with his weapons (3269)

Good Guys and Bad Guys

Black Bart, dapper outlaw (3270)

Jesse James: only known photo (3271)

Calamity Jane, South Dakota outlaw (3272)

Bob Younger, bank holdup man (3273)

Vasquez, bad hombre, stage robber (3274)

Sheriff and posse who captured the Canon Diablo train robbers (3275)

Wyatt Earp, Dodge City lawman (3276)

Last Land Grab

THE LAST OF THE FEDERAL LANDS opened to settlers was a two-million acre parcel near the center of the Oklahoma Territory. At noon, April 22, 1889, in a wild stampede, 50,000 "boomers" rushed in to claim it.

The Oklahoma Land Rush on April 22, 1889, that led "boomers" to grab last "unassigned U.S. lands" (3277)

After the Oklahoma rush, no more frontier (3278)

Showmen Perpetuate Western Legend

AS RAILROADS EXPANDED and farmers domesticated the frontier, the role of the American cowboy diminished. In urban America, however, his legendary skill, daring and self-reliance were idealized, providing an eager audience for the Wild West shows of Buffalo Bill. Theatrical Indian raids, feats of marksmanship and trick riding established a mythical heroism which served to hide much that was inglorious about the conquest of the West.

Poster for one of Buffalo Bill's acclaimed shows (3279)

I AM COMING

Cody took his show to Europe, met Queen Victoria (3280)

Sharpshooter Annie Oakley, popular performer (3281)

Literature and the Waning Frontier

THE MISSISSIPPI RIVER, once America's greatest artery of commerce, declined in importance as railroads expanded: trade now rattled into Chicago or St. Louis rather than floating down to New Orleans. But the romance of the riverboat lived on in the tales of Mark Twain, which brought the bustling life of the Mississippi's great days again before the national mind. Twain's works reflected the growing pains and also the humor of an expanding America: frontier life in the Nevada hills (*Roughing It*), the spurious habits of the money grubbers (*The Gilded Age*), America's defiance of European arrogance (*Innocents Abroad*).

Group of boys watching boat, from *Life on the Mississippi* (3282)

Mark Twain as a young pilot on the Mississippi (3283)

Middle-aged Mark Twain recalls his life (3284)

Author writing his autobiography (3285)

"Jumping Frog" story made Mark Twain a literary celebrity overnight (3286)

Huck Finn lived by his wits (3287)

Incident in Twain's *Tom Sawyer* (3288)

Roughing It: frontier impressions (3289)

In his old age, Mark Twain did most of his writing lying in bed (3290)

Western Writers

James Whitcomb Riley, Hoosier rhymester (3291)

Bret Harte: short-story writer (3292)

Mine camp: locale for many Harte tales (3293)

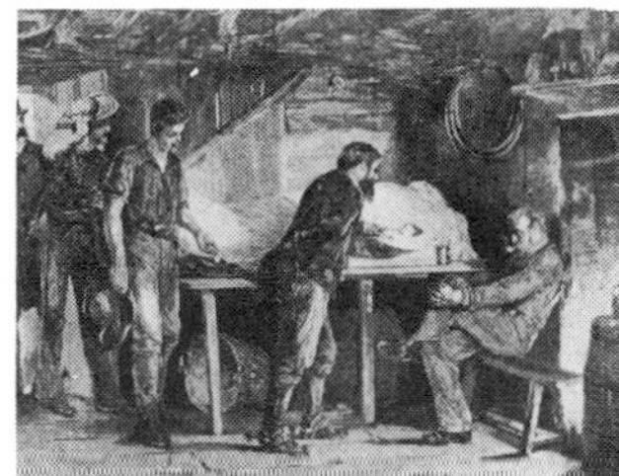

Harte's "The Luck of Roaring Camp"-famous local-color fiction (3294)

Wister's *The Virginian*, frontier classic (3295)

Middle West towns were dull, dry, monotonous (3296). Many young writers, discouraged, flocked to the city.

Small-town nostalgia: the old swimming hole (3297)

Frederic Remington's statue "The Bronco Buster" (3298)

Typical dime-novel illustration (3299)

Lurid tales attracted young readers (3300)

Titles showed prophetic technical schemes (3301)

Horatio Alger: boys' inspiration (3302)

Alger gospel: Be good and diligent; you will be handsomely rewarded (3303, 3303A)

Alger promulgated rags-to-riches philosophy (3304)

DIME NOVELS SATISFIED the craving, particularly of the young, to read about Indians, outlaws and life in the West. After the 1880s, the popular topics changed to train robbers and detectives, and later to flying machines and aerial battles—stories which were said to have inspired the Wright brothers to embark on their first flying experiments.

A Twenty Year Tug of War 1876-1896

Democratic Donkey. Woodcut by Thos. Nast (3305)

IN A DECADE CHARGED with high political voltage, presidential campaigns became acrimonious. Though Samuel Tilden won the popular vote in 1876, a contrived dispute in the Electoral Commission gave the election to Republican Rutherford Hayes. Angry Democrats acquiesced only after Hayes promised to remove federal troops from the South, where they served to enforce Reconstruction policies. As the "solid (Democratic)" South" rose again, whites regained power, and blacks lost the semblance of equal rights provided by military protection during the Reconstruction Era.

Republican Elephant. Woodcut by Thos. Nast (3306)

WE'LL GO FOR HAYES!

Hayes' campaign led to corrupt election as he became known as President "Rutherfraud" (3307)

Tilden was robbed of a clear-cut victory (3309)

Electoral Commission investigated returns, declared Hayes victor by straight partisan vote (3310)

Rutherford B. Hayes, 19th President (3308)

Hayes receives report on electoral vote (3311)

Hayes as friend of the black race (3312)

First Family life was exemplary, helped restore respect to the Presidency (3313)

Political Sisyphus—task of Civil Service reform (3314)

Garfield

PRESIDENT GARFIELD, assassinated in 1881 by a frustrated office-seeker, was a victim of the struggle for Civil Service reform. Under the spoils system, hordes of office-seekers had been descending on Washington each Inauguration Day, demanding that offices be vacated to give them jobs. Garfield, like Hayes before him, sought to end this practice.

Garfield assassinated by Charles Guiteau, vexed office-seeker (3315)

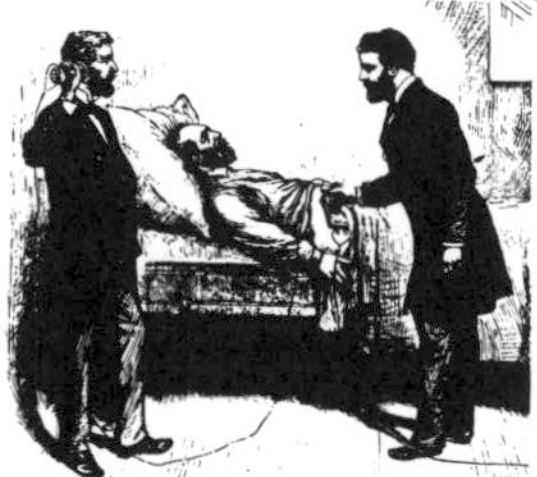

Dr. Graham Bell tries to locate bullet by electrical device (3316)

Chester Arthur (3317), sworn in after Garfield's death (3318), was unexpected champion of Civil Service.

Civil Service exams were ordered by Pendleton Act of 1883 (3319)

Farmers Grow Restive

DISCONTENT AMONG WESTERN FARMERS, dismayed by drought, inflation, declining farm prices and rising railroad rates, led to the formation of the Populist Party in 1892. Tall, magnetic Mary Lease, "the Patrick Henry in petticoats," was one of the leaders, admonishing farmers to "raise less corn and more hell." Stirred by the business panic of 1893, the Populist movement grew into a "swirling tornado" of middle American determination.

I FEED YOU ALL!

Farmers clamored for voice in running society they fed, criticized corruption of bankers and merchants (3320)

Railroads eating up farm profits galled Western farmers (3321)

Money: Silverites and Greenbackers

Uncle Sam blinded by silver mania (3322)

Against unrestricted money coinage (3323)

AS SILVER DECLINED in value, Western miners clamored for its use in coinage, which would prop up the price. Farmers, caught in a money pinch through the scarcity of gold, backed the mining interests. A limited purchase of silver under the Bland-Allison Act failed to satisfy either miners or farmers. Both groups continued to holler for cheaper money.

Silverites scoff at the issue of flood of paper money (3324)

Anti-Greenbacker: "Glad to see you, Specie!" (3325)

U.S. silver dollar (3326, 3327)

Grover Cleveland, weighty reform President (3328)

Cleveland—1885-1889

CAMPAIGN CHICANERY reached a new low in 1884 when Grover Cleveland, a "clean government" candidate, was attacked for fathering an illegitimate child. While Republicans (for Blaine) sang "Ma, where is my Pa?," the Democrats answered "Gone to the White House, ha, ha, ha." But when bigot Samuel Burchard attacked the Democrats, Catholic backlash swung New York State to Cleveland.

"I Want My Pa"—Cleveland admitted he had an illegitimate child (3329)

Campaign of 1884: rancor, wild mudslinging (3330)

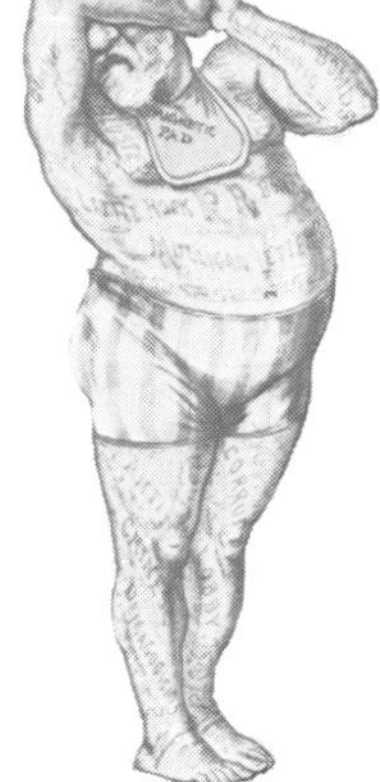

Republican Blaine as Phryne, bares crooked deals (3331)

Mugwumps: Republicans backing reform-Democrat Cleveland (3332)

Rev. Burchard calling Democrats "party of rum, Romanism and rebellion" (3333) made Cleveland winner (3334)

Tariff reform: Cleveland's prime program (3335)

Civil Service: "A public office is a civic trust" (3336)

President resisted veterans' demand for a bonus (3337)

Harrison

BENJAMIN HARRISON, elected in 1888, favored big business, equating protectionism (high tariffs) with Americanism. In 1890, the McKinley Tariff Act fixed protective rates at their highest level ever. Also, mining interests won passage of the Sherman Silver Purchase Act, producing a financial crisis which was to plague Cleveland's second term.

Benj. Harrison, a pawn of monied monopolists (3338)

Growing outcry against abuses and power of monopolies (3339) led Sen. John Sherman to formulate 1890 Anti-Trust Law (3340)

Cleveland - Second Term

CLEVELAND HAD TO FACE growing economic panic and unemployment. A Populist march on Washington (under Coxey) dramatized the crisis, aggravated by Cleveland's use of federal troops to suppress the Pullman strike.

Election plate showing Cleveland with V.P. Adlai Stevenson (3341)

Election badge has Harrison weighing in against incumbent Cleveland (3342)

Tom Reed, "Tsar" of House of Representatives (3343)

Panic of 1895 darkened second term (3344)

Coxey's Army clamored for bonus, relief (3345)

Cleveland had strong popular support (3346)

The New South

ITS PLANTATION ECONOMY destroyed, the South lay prostrate during the Reconstruction era, racked by party strife and racial tension. But recovery began in the 1880s. Northern capitalists now backed the exploitation of coal, iron, lumber and phosphate resources. Buoyed by a new self-confidence, the South began to establish its own industrial economy.

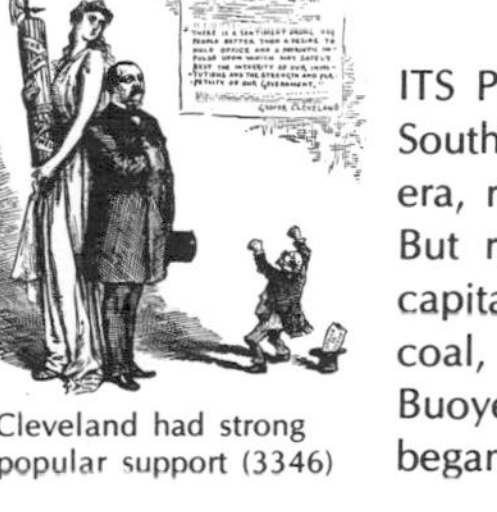

The South competes with New England mills (3349)

L.Q.C. Lamar, Southern statesman, patriot (3347)

H.W. Grady coined phrase "The New South" (3348)

Cigarette industry created new jobs for vast number of Southern girls (3350)

New Orleans: its humming wharves a symbol of the resurgent South (3351)

Black workers employed in Charleston, South Carolina, phosphate plant (3352)

Broadway, 1869: people feared crossing the tumultuous thoroughfares (3353)

Lure of the City

POSTWAR INDUSTRIALIZATION turned the United States into a nation of city dwellers as an ever increasing contingent of the labor force migrated to workshops and factories, freight and transportation centers. Those who hoped to "get rich quick" instinctively felt that the city was the place to try, and joined the influx.

Summer night in slums: "families huddled together, panting, praying for air" (3354)

Immigration

BUT THE PHYSICAL STRUCTURE of the cities was inadequate to absorb the rural newcomers, let alone the millions of foreign immigrants. Herded into sweatshops to work dismally long hours for starvation wages, many succumbed to disease and despair. Newcomers to tightly packed slums were "crowded to suffocation."

The city: a lure for restless youth (3355)

Apprehensive parents bid farm boy farewell (3356)

Immigrants pass Statue of Liberty. In 1880s, millions came (3357)

Italian family at Ellis Island, N.Y. (3358)

Processing of immigrants, Castle Garden, N.Y. (3359)

Melting pot for quick assimilation (3360)

Newcomers seek a way in the new land (3361)

Irish Aid Society looked after indigent compatriots (3362)

Squalor of tenement living revealed by Jacob Riis photograph (3363)

Despair prevailed in N.Y.'s sweatshops: working through the night merely to subsist (3364)

Piece goods delivered to finisher by woman for pennies a day (3365)

Sweatshop owner browbeats servile seamstress who gets 5c/hr. (3366)

Ethnic Enclave

Immigrant enterprise: Italian peddler sells snack to young mother (3367)

Barrel organ beggar plays old tunes (3368)

Shoeshine boy with friendly cop (3369)

Children flock around Lower East Side public water fountain (3370)

The City's Ills

THE CITIES' FACTORY FUNNELS brought pollution and filth. Ill-smelling stables and layers of horse manure further contributed to the stifling atmosphere. Municipal facilities were at times so strained that garbage piled along the sidewalks made some streets impassable on foot. Foreign visitors pronounced the New York of the 1880s a "nasal disaster."

A Garbage obstructs New York street (3371)
B Grafter helps himself to city funds (3372)
C Pittsburgh fouled by factory fumes (3373)
D Tweed, mastermind of corruption (3374)
E Policeman loses in street shoot-out (3375)

Labor Breaks its Shackles

MORE THAN FOUR THOUSAND millionaires were counted in 1892 by the New York *Tribune*. But while Marshall Field's income was calculated at $600 an hour, he paid his shopgirls $3 a week. Industrialists saw human labor as a raw material, like iron ore, to be stripped of its vitality and flushed away.

In 1877, with prices rising, the wages of railroad men in Chicago were cut 10 percent. The distressed workers resorted to violence, but with little success. The wildly vituperative uprising, put down by the Army, was pictured by the press as an "anarchist rebellion."

For fear of being locked out, less than 10 percent of the labor force was unionized prior to 1900.

Corporate octopus deprives workers of jobs, security, sustenance (3377)

Labor chained to treadmill of technology (3376)

Workers demonstrate, show strength (3379)

Iron casting forces laborer to work in a backbreaking stance (3380)

Steady work . . . "nothing steady but worry and misery." Lith., *Puck* mag. (3381)

Amputee railroad man goes to work (3382)

The symbol of labor (3378)

Gompers forged powerful labor federation (3383)

U.M.W.A. was founded in 1890, gained management acceptance (3384)

Pullman strike, 1894. Infantry "giving the butt" to striking workers (3385)

Riddle of Haymarket bomb explosion was never solved (3386)—but "anarchists" were hanged on circumstantial evidence (3387)

Child Labor

STRUGGLING FOR SUBSISTENCE, many immigrant families were forced to rely on their children for added income, sending them to work in cotton mills and mines "as soon as they could stand up." These oppressed youngsters, at times bringing home as little as a dollar and a half a week, were poisoned by dust and fumes, maimed by accidents, often warped for life in body and soul.

A mine "tipple boy." Hine photo (3389)

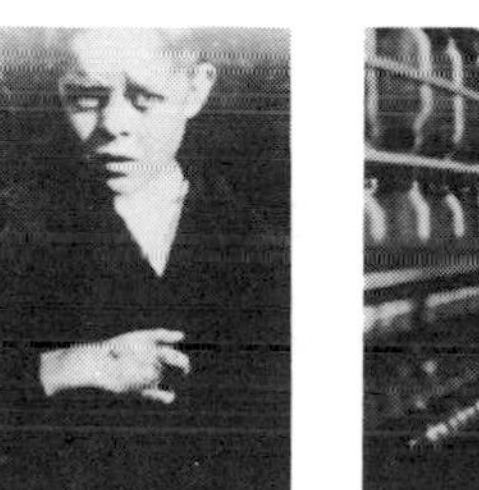

Barefoot spindle boy imperiled by twirling machine (3390). Many children were killed or maimed for life (3391)

Factory girl—a poignant plea by photographer Hine (3392)

Women are PEOPLE!

WORKING WOMEN, usually paid half what men earned, were among the staunchest supporters of labor unions, champions of "equal pay for equal work." Between 1880 and 1890, the number of women breadwinners rose from two to four million. Still, the suffrage movement faced a thirty-year battle for the ballot.

Arresting perky pickets (3393)

Victoria Woodhull (3394), stock broker and friend of Vanderbilt, battled for equal political rights for women (3395)

Wyoming women, first to gain vote (3396)

Temperance crusade was proving ground for womens' rights (3400)

Susan B. Anthony, led suffragettes (3397)

Women's Rights Convention in 1880 lobbied for political equality (3398)

Carrie Nation, vociferous teetotaler, axe-carrying crusader (3399)

Belva Lockwood ran twice for U.S. presidency (3402)

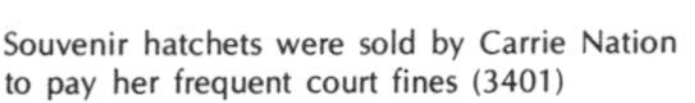

Souvenir hatchets were sold by Carrie Nation to pay her frequent court fines (3401)

How America Lived

HIGH SOCIETY IN THE GILDED AGE found pleasure in the display of wealth. Extravagance and even flagrant waste prevailed: elaborate dress, fabulous cuisine and dollar bills provided to light the gentlemen's cigars! There were hunting parties, fancy balls, boxes at the opera. Transatlantic crossings filled the social schedules, while the press lavished a fawning attention upon every occasion, such as Mrs. Vanderbilt's $250,000 banquet, or Mrs. Astor's "little" dinner party with but twelve courses instead of the usual twenty.

An evening gala in Newport, R.I., among "The Four Hundred" (3404)

Private dinner party at Delmonico's, New York's swankiest hotel (3405)

Mrs. Clapp, society belle (3406)

High Society

Society couples scanning the house from the loge at the opera (3407)

A guest at Bradley Martin's Masquerade Ball (3408)

A society quail hunt on Long Island (3409)

A yacht: J.P. Morgan said if you ask the cost you can't afford one (3410)

The winner's circle at New York Horse Show (3411)

Ward McAllister: "The Four Hundred" (3412)

Rockefeller and wife return from a trip (3413)

Millionaire Diamond Jim Brady (3414)

Andrew Carnegie. Photo, 1902 (3415)

Vanderbilt family younger set (3416)

Mr. and Mrs. Frick, Fifth Avenue (3417)

Vanderbilt daughter Consuelo (3418)

Mrs. Stuyvesant Fish, N.Y. society leader (3419)

Lorgnette (3403)

Home Sweet Home

"The Breakers," Vanderbilt cottage, in Newport, Rhode Island (3420)

Potter Palmer House, Chicago; landmark of gilded age (3421)

Schwab château on Riverside Drive, New York (3422)

Viscaya, Deering palazzo on Biscayne Bay, Florida (3423)

The Middle Class

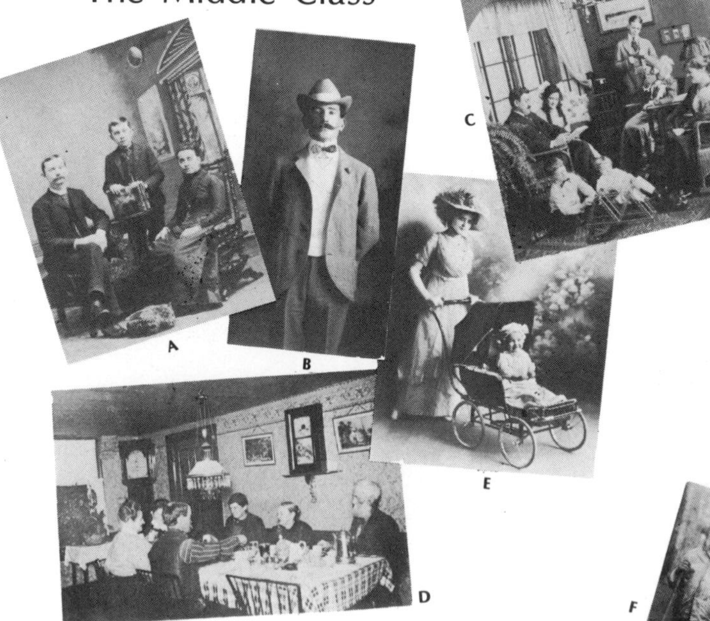

A Small-town family group (3424)
B An Oregon gentleman (3425)
C Life in Victorian home (3426)
D Dinner in U.S. farmhouse (3427)
E Taking baby for an outing (3428)
F Street cleaner and police (3429)
G Two high school graduates (3430)
H Formal Victorian musicale (3431)
I The Remington "typewriter" (3432)
J The doctor in Chicago (3433)
K A village barber shop (3434)
L Grocery store and family (3435)
M Wooden cigar store Indian (3436)

Rise of Leisure

(3437)

AS PROSPERITY BROUGHT LEISURE to more upper-class Americans, the problem of "what to do with it" arose. After pursuing success obsessively, Americans had to learn how to play. Foreign visitors observed that even American games were hurried, "reflecting the frenetic pace of the entrepreneur." Aided by new means of transportation, people planned picnics in the park, camping trips or Sundays at the beach. Vacations, unknown earlier in the century, loomed as a prospect for the workingman. The well-to-do were restlessly spending their summers at resorts, spas or in Europe.

New York beer garden. Leisure hours exuding German *Gemütlichkeit* (3439)

Prepared for hike and camp (3440)

Ready to take a dip (3438)

Old fisherman in Maine lake (3441)

Amateur photographer snaps friends on a bench in Central Park (3442)

Ferris wheel: built for 1893 Exposition (3443)

Summer romance: vacation trips and resorts became features of upper-class life (3444)

Coney Island, New York's glittering mecca (3445)

Family frolics in the surf at a resort on the New Jersey shore (3446 A)

New England summer resort; ladies on a donkey ride (3446)

Cook agent booking European trip (3447)

Vacation coach: city dwellers bound for the Catskill Mountains (3448)

Sports: Athletes and Spectators

COMPENSATING BY WAY OF SPORTS for loss of the outdoor life, many city dwellers joined in the cult of physical exercise. But for those who preferred to watch, promoters were eager to stage games, and many players, anxious to give the public a good show, played ruthlessly. Objecting to college teams involved in such mayhem, Cornell's President Andrew D. White declared, "I will not permit 30 men to travel 400 miles to agitate a bag of wind."

Baseball became national sport in 1876 with founding of National League (3450)

Costly trips in the summer sun (3449)

First National Lawn Tennis Tournament in 1872 on Staten Island, N.Y. (3451)

College football often deteriorated into fierce slugging competitions (3452)

Dr. J. Nasmith used peach basket for new game: basketball (3453)

Bowler (3454)

Writers and Readers

Magazines appealed to all ages and family members (3455)

A WIDER INTEREST in the arts was another result of increased leisure time. Despite the materialism of the age, opera, theater and literature attracted thousands of new patrons. Authors explored American themes: the culture shock of travelers exposed to European decadence (Henry James); the moral hazards of the successful businessman (William Dean Howells).

A Emily Dickinson, cryptic lyricist (3456)
B Walt Whitman exults in America (3457)
C Stephen Crane: gripping novels (3458)
D Henry Adams, historian, critic (3459)
E Henry James, prolific novelist (3460)

A B C D E

Poster (3461)

Magazine cover (3462)

OCEAN STEAMSHIPS.

CUNARD

EUROPE VIA LIVERPOOL

LUSITANIA

Fastest and Largest Steamer
now in Atlantic Service Sails
SATURDAY, MAY 1, 10 A. M.
Transylvania, Fri., May 7, 5 P.M.
Orduna, - - Tues., May 18, 10 A.M.
Tuscania, - - Fri., May 21, 5 P.M.
LUSITANIA, Sat., May 29, 10 A.M.
Transylvania, Fri., June 4, 5 P.M.

Gibraltar–Genoa–Naples–Piraeus
S.S. Carpathia, Thur., May 13, Noon

ROUND THE WORLD TOURS
Through bookings to all principal Ports of the World.
Company's Office, 21-24 State St., N. Y.

NOTICE!

TRAVELLERS intending to embark on the Atlantic voyage are reminded that a state of war exists between Germany and her allies and Great Britain and her allies; that the zone of war includes the waters adjacent to the British Isles; that, in accordance with formal notice given by the Imperial German Government, vessels flying the flag of Great Britain, or of any of her allies, are liable to destruction in those waters and that travellers sailing in the war zone on ships of Great Britain or her allies do so at their own risk.

IMPERIAL GERMAN EMBASSY

WASHINGTON, D. C., APRIL 22, 1915.

A

B

C

D

E

CHAPTER 12

Progress and World Conflict

American Empire
Art and Artists
Global Realignment

U.S. Assumes World Role

Uncle Sam, aloof from world politics, watches Europe from his comfortable pedestal (3463)

AS THE FRONTIER VANISHED, U.S. wealth increased—tenfold between 1850 and 1900—productive capacity swelled enormously —U.S. steel production outstripped that of France and England combined—and industrialists began to look for new worlds to conquer. "There are more workers than there is work," said Senator Beveridge, "and more capital than there is investment. . . . we must find new markets." Proponents of a new imperialism hid their lust for expansion behind pious oratory, chanting that America was "chosen by God to lead the regeneration of the world." But before they could get their way, they faced a serious challenge from the hard pressed, over-burdened farm belt.

Expansionist rooster crows noisily—new credo of U.S. imperialism (3464)

Western Farmers vs. Moneyed East

"The Commoner" Wm. Jennings Bryan (3465)

Populist strategy meeting during the 1896 Democratic convention in Chicago (3466)

Mary Lease, Kansas Populist leader (3467)

Souvenir plate, McKinley–Roosevelt campaign (3468)

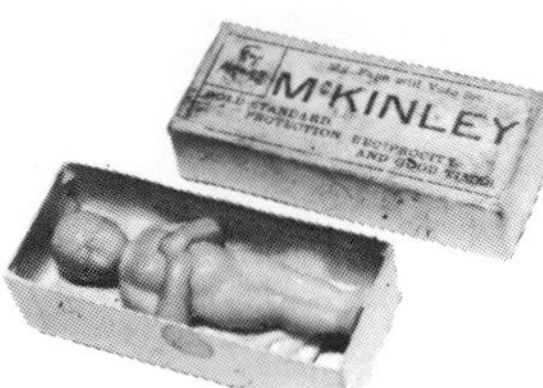

Soap doll appeals to family for McKinley support (3469)

Bryan's "Cross of Gold" speech lampooned (3470)

Cartoon laments anti-silver crusade (3471)

BACKED BY A HOST of disgruntled farmers and Free-Silverites, William Jennings Bryan won the Democratic presidential nomination in 1896. In his "Cross of Gold" speech Bryan, a great orator, scorched the "Gold Bugs" (advocates of hard currency and protection for industry), pleading for silver certificates and easier money to help debt-ridden farmers and exploited workers.

Mark Hanna - McKinley's mentor, supporter (3472)

Industrial monopolists corner a servile Uncle Sam (3473)

Ten Weeks to Win an Empire

Imperialist Uncle Sam waits for Cuba's fall into his waiting basket (3474)

McKINLEY'S ELECTION in 1896 brought the imperialists to power. Soon the barons of the "yellow press," Pulitzer and Hearst, whipped up a wave of interventionist sentiment, capped by a never-to-be-explained explosion which sank the battleship *Maine* in Havana harbor on February 15, 1898. This forced the United States into the Spanish-American War, and after a short triumphant conflict, there was a new overseas empire which included Cuba, Puerto Rico, Guam and the Philippines

Cuban freedom fighters bound and murdered by Spanish troops of General Weyler (3475)

Mysterious explosion of *U.S.S. Maine* triggered the war with Spain (3476)

U.S. cartoon reviles Spain's bestial brutalities (3477)

Cuba as the victim of U.S.–Spanish antagonism (3478)

Recruiting rally in New York City (3479)

Admiral Dewey at Manila Bay (3480)

American soldier in field outfit (3481)

Col. Theodore Roosevelt (3482) recruited "Rough Riders," led them in daring charge up San Juan Hill (3483)

Hawaiians cheer U.S. annexation (3484)

Admiral Mahan urged expansion of Navy to safeguard U.S. influence, power (3485)

Hearst beat war drum to up his papers' circulation. "War cost me three million dollars," he blatantly confessed (3486)

Joseph Pulitzer sensationalized atrocities, helped push U.S. into the war (3487)

Philippine Insurrection

THOUGH AMERICA PROMISED self-government to her new possessions, an expansion-minded Congress wanted to keep full control of the Philippines, hoping to annex them. The suspicious Filipinos, led by Aguinaldo, staged an insurrection that took three years and 56,000 troops to quell.

Col. Duboce's California volunteers drive the Filipinos out of a rebel stronghold (3488)

Aguinaldo is crushed by American might (3489)

Sen. Foraker backed McKinley's imperialist policies (3490)

Yellow Fever Conquered

ENEMY BULLETS took few lives in the Spanish-American war, but yellow fever claimed thousands. When Dr. Walter Reed in 1900 identified a mosquito as the disease carrier, a campaign began to exterminate it. Guided by Dr. William Gorgas, the U.S. Medical Corps succeeded in stamping out yellow fever in the Panama Canal Zone.

Yellow jack mosquito (3491), first named by Dr. Carlos Finlay (3492)

Fever regions set afire to stamp out disease (3493)

Dr. Walter Reed and aides tracked down the disease vector (3494)

McKinley Reelected

McKinley in 1900: eager internationalist (3495)

Roosevelt campaigned vigorously (3496)

Full dinner pail: McKinley prosperity symbol (3497)

Bryan poster. He was anti–imperialist (3498)

McKinley, assassinated in 1901 by anarchist Czolgosz (3499)

Roosevelt: Enlightened Imperialist

TEDDY ROOSEVELT, the youngest and most ebullient leader of the era, was disliked by the Republican Party's "Old Guard." They planned to "kick him upstairs" in 1900, after a term as New York's reform governor, by tacking him onto the ticket as Vice President. Ironically, Roosevelt became President.

Roosevelt's foreign policy was characterized by the "Big Stick." Expanding the Monroe Doctrine to assert American rights to intervention in the affairs of island neighbors, Roosevelt needed the Panama Canal to give the Navy access to both oceans. When Colombia refused to grant a right of way across the isthmus, Roosevelt recognized the Colombian province of Panama as an independent republic in order to get the desired lease of land.

New York City's Board of Health included Police Commissioner Roosevelt (3500)

Assistant Secretary of the Navy (3501)

Rough Rider button (3502)

Roosevelt swung big stick to make Caribbean an American lake (3503)

Monroe Doctrine applied to South America (3504)

Roosevelt operates Canal steam shovel (3505)

Dr. Gorgas, sanitarian of Canal region (3506)

Panama Canal took ten years to build; cost was over 365 million (3507)

Turn of the Century Events

Klondike gold rush, 1898. Few found wealth (3508)

The first Hague Peace Conference failed at arms limitation (3509)

Settlement of anthracite strike, 1902, set precedent for industrial disputes (3510)

Earthquake destroyed most of San Francisco (3511)

When Taft, who weighed 354 pounds, was High Commissioner of the Philippines, he fell ill. Sec. of War Elihu Root cabled to ask how he was. Taft replied he was fine, had just ridden 25 miles on horseback. Root cabled back: "How is the horse?"

William Howard Taft, equestrian (3512)

President Roosevelt shields the Common Weal (3513)

T.R.—Dynamic Innovator

ROOSEVELT'S DOMESTIC PROGRAM aimed to protect the consumer from grasping trusts and to preserve America's natural resources. A charismatic, restless President, he plunged into reform legislation enthusiastically, coining catchy phrases like "Square Deal" and "malefactors of great wealth." Though he warned against the "muckrakers," as he called America's social critics, he was allied with them in promoting the Pure Food and Drug Act of 1906, government actions against beef and sugar trusts, and the creation of national forests, which protected 148 million acres of virgin timber from the lumbermen. He also promoted measures to regulate interstate commerce, particularly railroad rates.

Teddy the trustbuster was loud but acted with restraint (3514)

He fought to ensure equality for oppressed black race (3515)

Booker T. Washington, black educator (3516)

G. W. Carver, brilliant agro-chemist (3517)

W.E.B. DuBois demanded schools for blacks (3518)

Roosevelt and naturalist John Muir at Yosemite Park (3519)

Roosevelt loudly endorsed conservation (3520), clashed with chief forester Pinchot (3521)

The Muckrakers

Meat-packing industry abuses prompted Roosevelt "to rake up the muck" (3522)

Upton Sinclair's *The Jungle* led to meat scandal (3523)

L. Steffens: *Shame of the Cities* (3524)

Ida Tarbell exposed Std. Oil Co. (3525)

Food laboratory headed by Dr. Harvey Wiley enforced 1906 Pure Food and Drug Act (3526)

A Bully Life

Roosevelt in early Wright plane. He was first President fo fly (3527)

The Roosevelt family on their estate in Oyster Bay, Long Island, N.Y. (3528)

Teddy Bear implied endearment (3529)

Headstrong, lovable daughter Alice (3530)

"I feel fit like a Bull Moose" (3531)

With rhino during his African safari (3532)

Taft election poster (3533)

Taft vs. the Progressives

WILLIAM HOWARD TAFT, Roosevelt's hand-picked successor, prosecuted twice as many anti-trust cases as Roosevelt. He also created new government departments for Labor and Commerce. But Roosevelt was displeased, calling Taft a "standpatter." Teddy bolted the Republican Party in 1912 to run for President on the progressive "Bull Moose" ticket. The split sent Democrat Woodrow Wilson to the White House.

Payne-Aldrich tariff reductions were disappointing to liberals (3534)

Taft signs 1912 Arizona-New Mexico Statehood Bill (3535)

PROGRESSIVE PARTY
"PASS PROSPERITY AROUND"

Progressive party nominated Roosevelt in 1912, but Wilson won (3536)

WE WANT OUR TEDDY BACK!

Electorate ignored pleas to return Teddy (3537)

Senator Robert La Follette, popular progressive (3538)

Roosevelt fights for his old chair (3539)

Roosevelt's Bull Moose campaign clashed with conservative party regulars (3540)

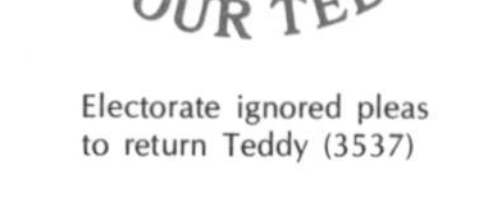

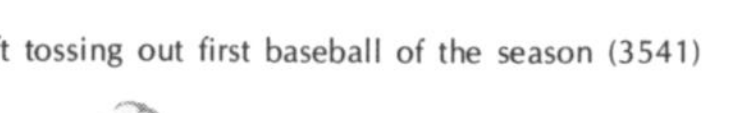
Taft tossing out first baseball of the season (3541)

(3542)

America Speeds into the Automotive Age

ORIGINALLY A PLAYTHING of the rich, the automobile soon became a dominant social and industrial force. The first workable model in America wasn't built until 1896, but by 1912 there were ninety-three automakers. The glass, rubber, steel and lacquer industries were greatly stimulated, and road-building programs, eventually costing billions, were begun. Altogether the motorcar had a powerful impact on America's life pattern.

Happy motorists have no time for toll house stop as they burn up the road on a Sunday outing (3543)

Decked out in a duster (3544)

Automobile air-pollution defense (3550)

Ford with first Detroit-built automobile (3545)

Original stock of Ford Motor Co. in 1903. Ford owned 225 shares (3546)

Final assembly line at Ford Motor Co.'s Highland Park plant (3547)

Oldsmobile in early hill climb drive test (3548)

Atrocious roads hampered cross-country drives (3549)

First Standard Oil gas station opened in 1912 in Columbus, Ohio (3551)

Emergency gas can fills the tank of a dry auto (3552)

W.K. Vanderbilt, rich race-sponsor, fixes tire of 1901 "Red Devil" (3553)

Barney Oldfield, king of the racing drivers (3554)

Indianapolis race course; early poster (3555)

1909 Pierce Arrow was the classiest car (3556)

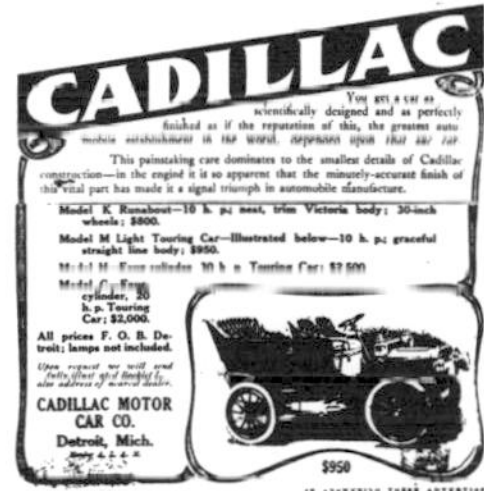

Low-priced Cadillac in 1907 retailed for but $800 (3557)

Duryea bros. were famed auto makers (3558)

Solar lamps for safe night driving (3559)

Motored unicycle was gyro-balanced (3560)

French couple takes outing in motor tricycle (3561)

Man Takes to the Air

THE FIRST FLIGHT of a heavier-than-air craft took place in 1903, launched by the Wright brothers at Kitty Hawk, North Carolina. But air travel long remained a curiosity, lacking the concerted industrial push given to the automobile. Flying became a spine-tingling sport, the province of an international group of daredevils who seemed primarily intent on breaking records (or their necks).

Orville and Wilbur Wright initiated air age (3562)

First powered flight. Orville Wright flew 852 feet, was aloft 59 seconds (3563)

Glenn Curtiss turned from bicycle mechanic to avid aviator (3564)

First flight from deck of battleship *Birmingham,* 1910. A Curtiss biplane was used (3565)

Many contraptions were rigged up but never left the ground (3566)

Otto Lilienthal tested gliders from man-made hill (3567)

Blériot flies English Channel (3568)

Simulated bird planes never worked (3569)

Chanute designed multi-winged gliders (3570)

Imperialism and the Far East

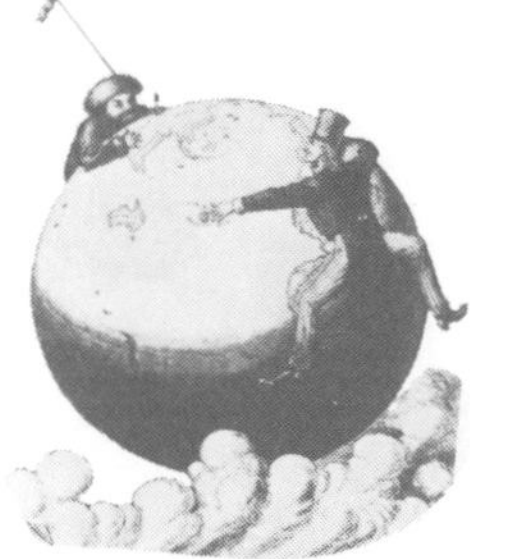

Two young giants, Russia, U.S., reach for Pacific isles (3571)

SEEING THE ORIENT as a natural target for commercial expansion, European powers had wrangled trade concessions from China as early as 1860. But the Europeans had not counted on Japan: transforming her culture from a backward feudal order into modern industrialism within three decades, Japan was now ready to compete with Europe, winning a coveted entrance into Manchuria in the Sino-Japanese War of 1894. England and the United States tried to establish free trade in Chinese ports, declaring an "Open Door" policy (1900). Still, Japan asserted its dominance when it collided with Russia in the Russo-Japanese War of 1904-1905. To the world's amazement, the tiny island nation soundly trounced the powerful and overconfident Russian giant.

Treaty of Tientsin, 1858, opened China to Western traders, missionaries (3572)

Peking assaulted by combined French and English forces (3573)

Formosa is ceded to Japan after the Sino-Japanese War (3574)

Germany occupies Chinese Kiaochow, 1898 (3575)

Empress Tz'u Hsi, hated "foreign devils" (3576)

John Hay, U.S. Secy. of State (3577). His Open Door policy freed Chinese ports to all (3578)

Boxer Rebellion: daring U.S. Marines on Peking Wall force open gate (3579)

Japan . . . Expanding Power

Japan within decade became dominant Asian power (3580)

Emperor Meiji made Japan modern state; its constitution mirrored Prussia's (3581)

Japan dares Russian bear before 1904 war (3582)

Japan bombards Port Arthur, gives Russia decisive beating (3583)

Roosevelt umpired the Russo-Japanese peace treaty (3584)

Russia. . .Growing Unrest

DEFEATED BY JAPAN, Russia faced emboldened revolutionary forces at home. When nervous troops opened fire upon a peaceful demonstration in St. Petersburg in 1905, open revolt broke out. Other uprisings soon threatened the czarist regime, but Prime Minister Stolypin managed to restore "order," and the revolutionaries suffered a serious setback.

Czar Nicholas II dons doomed crown (3585)

Czar and Czarina upheld the old autocracy (3586)

Street barricade during 1905 Revolution. Nicholas made scant concessions (3587)

People hoped Romanoffs would blow away (3588)

Sword-rattling Kaiser

GERMANY, TOO, was on a collision course. After Bismarck's resignation in 1890, Kaiser Wilhelm claimed a "divinely ordained" mission, and managed to alienate most of Europe by his arrogance. With his traditional ally, Austria, Wilhelm joined with Italy to form the Triple Alliance. It proved a weak combine when measured against the Triple Entente of England, France and Russia.

Enfant terrible William II upsets fellow dynasts by rocking boat of Europe (3589)

Pompous portrait dubbed "a declaration of war" (3590)

The Kaiser hunts wild game to relax from stalking other countries (3592)

William visits Jerusalem to be Arab lord protector (3593)

Morocco crisis: William II provoked tension (3594)

Imperialist William II, backed by army, envisioned self as global ruler (3591)

Major European powers try to hold lid on seething Balkan problems (3595)

Edwardian England

LONG RESTRAINED by the "widow's cap," England enjoyed the new mood set by Edward VII when he ascended the throne at last, in 1901. Sweeping away the dour, stuffy attitudes of Victoria's era, Edward set up a glittering court, and surrounded himself with a galaxy of glamorous women. His days taken up with races, regattas and foreign travels, Edward still took a strong hand in the diplomacy of shaping England's foreign affairs.

"There is an avuncular benevolence about the King" (3596)

King Edward VII is crowned in 1901. He was to reign but nine years (3597)

Edwardian London took on a more cosmopolitan air as Victorian restraints were slowly lifted (3598)

Mark Twain greeted by King and Queen (3599)

Edward surrounded by bevy of beauties (3600)

Germany and England in naval race (3601)

Edw. VII, son (Geo. V) and grandson (Edw. VIII) (3602)

Future King George V, Queen Mary visit London before their coronations (3603)

THE TRIPLE ENTENTE

EDWARD VII DETESTED his nephew, William II of Germany, and admired the French. Joining France's Foreign Minister Delcassé, he patched up the old rivalry between England and France to oppose the threat of German expansion. Russia joined this alliance to form the Triple Entente, which made Germany's encirclement complete.

France, England defy Germany (3607)

Viscount Grey (3608) formed the Triple Alliance. Germany was surprised (3609)

LIBERAL THRUST: Parliament pursued reform during Edward VII's reign. The conservative House of Lords lost its age-old veto power with the Parliamentary Act of 1911—high point of this movement.

H.H. Asquith, Liberal Prime Minister (3604)

Lloyd George, Churchill—Liberal allies (3605)

Attack on the Lords' veto power (3606)

Writers

EDWARDIAN AUTHORS, though they formed no literary school, were a lively group. Arnold Bennett's fast-paced narratives brought new life to the novel, while Shaw's wit and reformist zeal enlivened the theater. A popular fascination with science inspired the fiction of H. G. Wells, and William Butler Yeats brought about an Irish literary renaissance.

Arnold Bennett wrote fast-paced stories, novels about Staffordshire region (3611)

Suffragettes

WHEN JOHN STUART MILL presented a bill in Parliament in 1865, aimed at giving women equal rights, it did not pass. But after 1900 the suffragettes renewed the fight with vigor. Despite popular outrage at some of their methods, Englishwomen thirty years of age and over gained the right to vote in 1918.

Resolute placard bearer (3620)

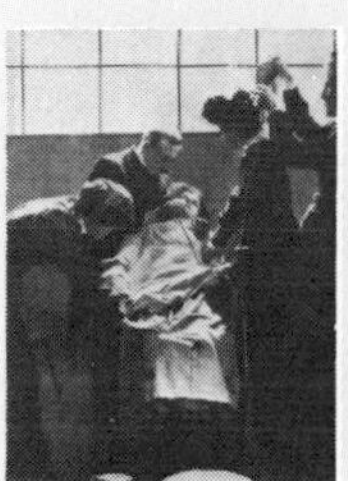
"Dangerous" suffragist fed in jail (3621)

Shop window smashed by suffragists (3622)

Demonstrator arrested by burly bobby (3623)

Joseph Conrad: men stand against the sea (3612)

Shaw attacked Victorian ways (3613), proposed a mild socialism (3614)

W.B. Yeats, Irish poet and dramatist (3615)

H. G. Wells excelled in science fiction (3616)

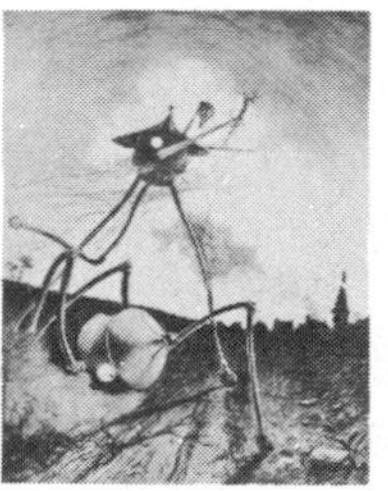
Invasion from Mars, Wells fantasy (3617)

Conan Doyle: tales of Sherlock Holmes (3618)

Max Beerbohm, cartoonist and urbane wit (3619)

Quantum Jump of Science

THE WAVE THEORY in the nineteenth century had established the relationship between light and electromagnetism. Still, many phenomena remained unexplained. Max Planck resolved some of the paradoxes in his quantum theory, which held that energy was emitted in "quantas"—bundles—rather than in waves. It led to a new assessment of the nature of matter. Developing these concepts further, Einstein reformulated the relationships between light, energy, mass, and velocity. With this theory of relativity and the quantum theory of Niels Bohr, the atomic age came into its own.

E. Rutherford founded nuclear physics (3625)

Max Planck formulated quantum theory (3626)

A. A. Michelson, U.S. physicist, made studies on the velocity of light (3627)

(3624)

ENTWURF EINER VERALLGEMEINERTEN RELATIVITÄTSTHEORIE UND EINER THEORIE DER GRAVITATION

I. PHYSIKALISCHER TEIL VON ALBERT EINSTEIN

II. MATHEMATISCHER TEIL VON MARCEL GROSSMANN

LEIPZIG UND BERLIN
DRUCK UND VERLAG VON B. G. TEUBNER
1913

Albert Einstein revolutionized physics with his theory of relativity in 1905 (3628, 3629)

Victor Hess explored cosmic radiation (3630)

Nernst expanded the frontiers of thermodynamics (3631)

Emil Fischer synthesized sugars, caffein (3632)

Niels Bohr: new concept of atom, quantum theory (3633)

Epochal Inventions

THE CLOSE CONNECTION between research and technology was demonstrated by the appearance of new inventions in communications, heat engineering and automotive design. Research in thermodynamics led to Diesel's engine, while new insights into the nature of sound and light produced Lee De Forest's cathode ray tube.

Arthur Korn, pioneer in electric transmission of pictures (3634)

De Forest: 300 patents in radio, films (3635)

Ch. Kettering invented the self-starter (3636)

Diesel developed principle of autoignition (3637)

Diesel's first engine (3638)

Medicine

TECHNOLOGICAL INVENTIONS also affected medicine. From the string galvanometer, which measures very small currents, Willem Einthoven developed the cardiograph, a basic diagnostic tool which records the pattern of heartbeats. Dr. Paul Erlich, seeking a substitute for vaccines cultured in animals, produced the synthetic drug Salvarsan, a first in chemotherapy. Early in the new century, the conditioned-reflex experiments of Pavlov established a basis for the new behavioral sciences.

Pavlov dog demonstrates conditioned reflex (3639)

New Concepts

Electrocardiograph was developed by physiologist Einthoven (3640)

Laboratory where Pavlov studied animal reaction to stimuli (3641)

Pirquet advanced concept of allergic disease (3642)

F.G. Hopkins studied vitamins in diet (3643)

Eijkman: beri-beri is a deficiency disease (3644)

New Procedures

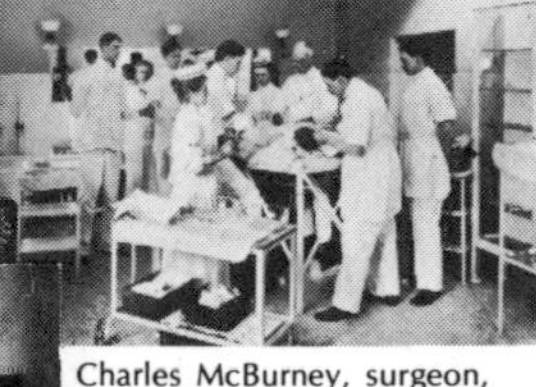

Charles McBurney, surgeon, appendectomy specialist (3645)

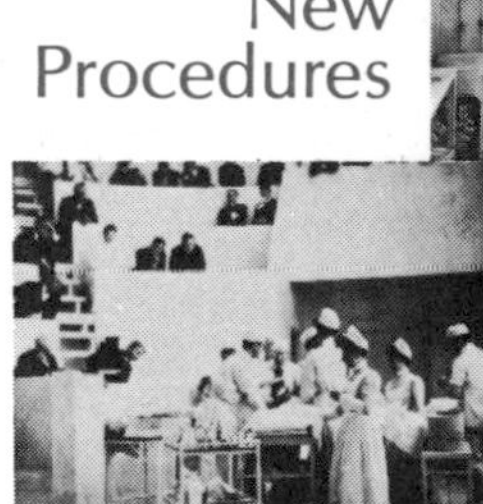

Halsted: rubber gloves; new surgical techniques (3646)

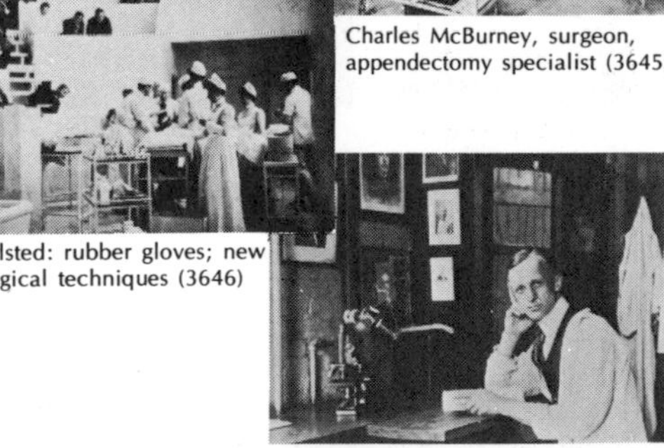

Harvey Cushing, leading exponent in field of brain surgery (3647)

Chemotherapy & Diagnosis

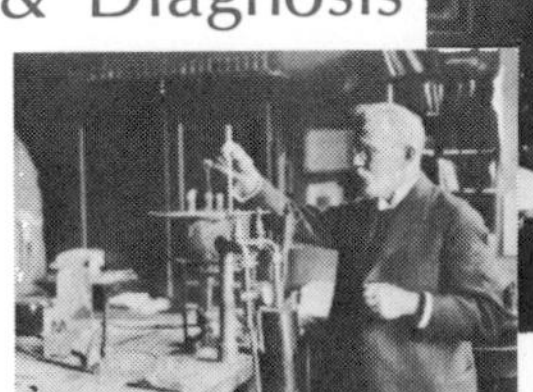

Paul Ehrlich, chemotherapist, discovered Salvarsan (3648)

Wassermann found simple test for syphilis (3649)

Bela Schick introduced diphtheria test (3650)

Riva-Rocci blood-pressure gauge, was invented in 1903 (3651)

The Arts Become Cosmopolitan

Music

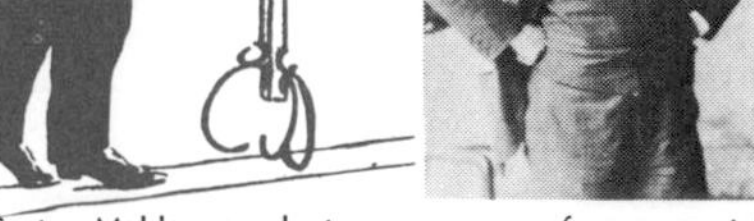

Gustav Mahler, conductor, composer of monumental symphonies, song cycles of lyric poetry (3652, 3653)

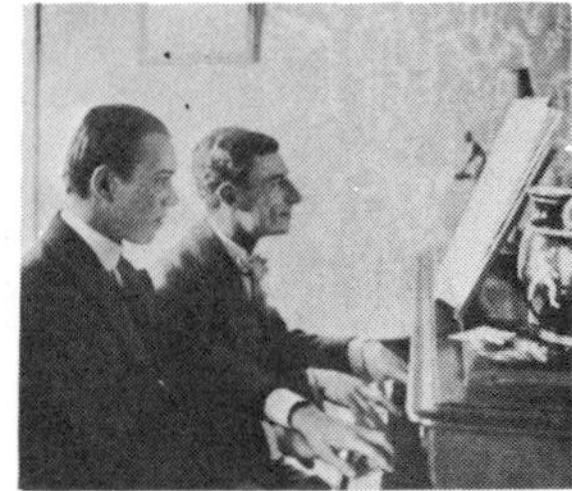

Maurice Ravel in piano duet with dancer Waslaw Nijinsky (3654)

Der Rosenkavalier, by Strauss (3655)

Strauss with librettist Hofmannsthal (3656)

Mary Garden in Strauss' opera *Salomé* (3657)

Richard Strauss as "Neurosenkavalier" (3658)

International Stars

Puccini (3659) wrote operas rich in melodic and romantic effects: *Tosca*, a story of murder (3660)

Schumann-Heink: diva, lieder specialist (3668)

Metropolitan Opera, New York (3669)

Caruso, greatest of opera tenors (3670)

Nellie Melba, prima donna (3671)

Program of N.Y.'s famed "Met" (3672)

Impressario Gatti-Casazza (3673)

Joseph Hoffmann as a child prodigy (3674)

Paderewski: pianist, statesman (3675)

WHILE POLITICAL LEADERS in an age of national rivalries were obsessed with the aggrandizement of their own domains, the arts acquired an international glamour rarely achieved before or since. Artists might express their national idiom, but their art, it was felt, belonged to the world. Even restrictive national states took pride in their international stars. Chaliapin was as enthusiastically applauded in New York as in St. Petersburg. Caruso, Melba, Schumann-Heink, all became world figures.

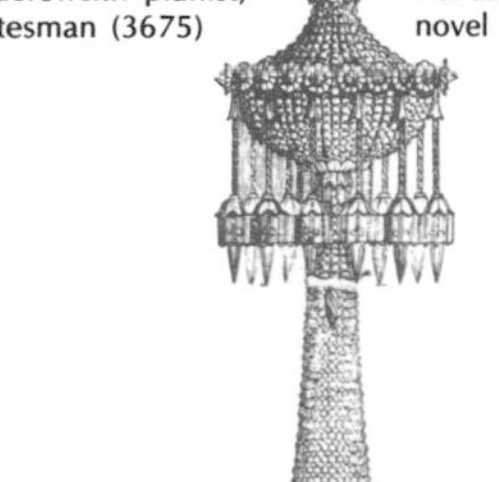

(3685)

Ballet

Stravinsky with Nijinsky (3661)

Diaghilev, creator of Ballet Russe. pivotal to modern music (3662)

Diaghilev's "Firebird," with music by Stravinsky (3663)

Nijinsky in "Afternoon of a Faun" ballet (3664)

Vera, Michael Fokine: "Scheherazade" (3665)

Manuel de Falla and balletist Massine in Alhambra (3666)

Pavlova in "Death of the Swan" (3667)

Dramatists and Writers

Ibsen: period's greatest dramatic playwright (3676)

Strindberg: dramas of marital conflict (3677)

Maeterlinck: symbolist plays, poems (3678)

Schnitzler: erotic comedies (3679)

Anatole France, a master stylist (3680)

Rolland: ten-vol. novel (3681)

Proust: *À la Recherche du Temps Perdu* (3682)

Colette: her forte was the short story (3683)

Rainer Rilke: lyric poems, tales (3684)

BALLET EMERGED as the most exciting of art forms in this period. As dancers of unequaled talent and training appeared, composers like Ravel and Stravinsky provided sensational new musical scores. The presiding genius of this upsurge in the dance was Diaghilev, the Russian impresario whose Ballet Russe took Paris by storm in 1909. His brilliant showmanship encouraged the new musical idiom of atonality, so germane to balletic expression.

The Arts: continued

Theater marquee (3686)

Anna Held, diminutive vaudevillian (3687)

George M. Cohan as a youth (3688)

The Red Mill, by Victor Herbert, Irish-American operetta composer (3689)

Typical Cohan Bway. show poster (3690)

Strongman Sandow in vaudeville (3691)

George Jessel begins his show-biz career (3692)

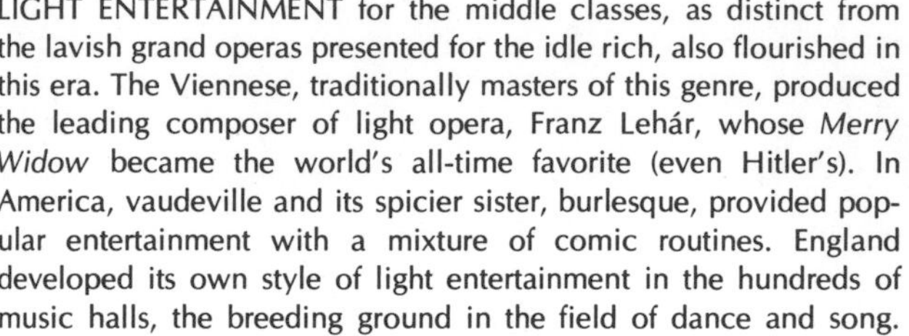

LIGHT ENTERTAINMENT for the middle classes, as distinct from the lavish grand operas presented for the idle rich, also flourished in this era. The Viennese, traditionally masters of this genre, produced the leading composer of light opera, Franz Lehár, whose *Merry Widow* became the world's all-time favorite (even Hitler's). In America, vaudeville and its spicier sister, burlesque, provided popular entertainment with a mixture of comic routines. England developed its own style of light entertainment in the hundreds of music halls, the breeding ground in the field of dance and song.

Lehár's *Merry Widow*, first produced in 1905 (3693)

W. C. Fields started as stage juggler (3694)

Sheridan and Mack, vaudevillians (3695)

Oscar Hammerstein built theaters (3696)

Early Movies

(3697)

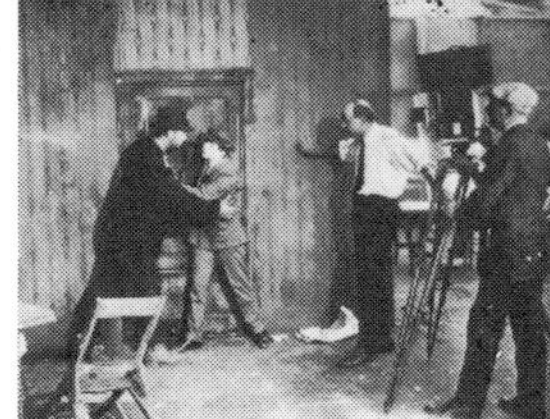

Production of motion picture in nickelodeon era (3698)

Great Train Robbery, Edison's classic; screen's first true story-picture (3699)

Judith of Bethulia, early religious epic with actress Blanche Sweet (3700)

D. W. Griffith, pioneer producer-director (3701)

Mary Pickford acted from age five, was "America's Sweetheart" (3702)

William S. Hart: stage to Western film hero (3703)

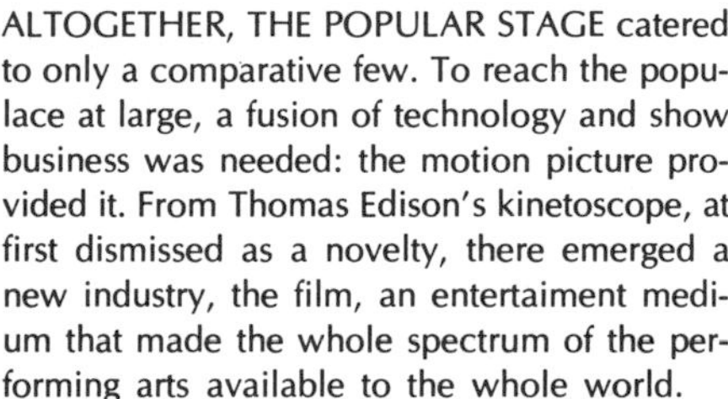

ALTOGETHER, THE POPULAR STAGE catered to only a comparative few. To reach the populace at large, a fusion of technology and show business was needed: the motion picture provided it. From Thomas Edison's kinetoscope, at first dismissed as a novelty, there emerged a new industry, the film, an entertaiment medium that made the whole spectrum of the performing arts available to the whole world.

Slapstick comedy by Mack Sennett (3704)

Intermission sign used in early motion picture theater (3705)

The City in Literature

THE MASS MIGRATION from farm to city now changed the focus of American literature. Abandoning the romantic communion with nature, writers turned to the mixture of marvels and horrors to be found in the metropolis. As O. Henry discovered the romance of the low and lonely, Dreiser described with epic force the city's "blundering, inept cruelty."

Edith Wharton (3706) depicted New York's rich, their foibles, entanglements (3707)

O. Henry (3708) excelled in surprise endings, wrote of N.Y. "city of mysterious strangers" (3709)

Newspaper office on N.Y.'s Lower East Side, vortex of literary talent (3710)

Theodore Dreiser described agonies of humans trapped by society (3711)

◀ Finley Peter Dunn (3712): dialect sketches with Mr. Dooley, an urban sage (3713)

Flatiron Building, New York, in 1902 the world's tallest building (3714)

Woodrow Wilson

Wilson: academician to progressive N.J. governor, U.S. president (3715, 3716)

MANY OLD .PROS SNEERED when the Democrats nominated Woodrow Wilson for President in 1912. A professor-historian in the rough-and-tumble of politics? But Wilson, an inspired writer on American history, had moved on from being president of Princeton University to governor of New Jersey in 1910. With Republicans split between Taft and Roosevelt, Wilson won the election, becoming the nation's most atypical President, yet one of its greatest. He led a powerful program of internal reform, lowering protective tariffs, curbing monopolies, improving working conditions. All this, he accomplished in his first term.

The Democratic donkey revitalized, Woodrow Wilson its new rider (3717)

Domestic Reforms

Governor Wilson receives news of 1912 Democratic candidacy (3718)

Exhibit demonstrates Wilson's bold anti–high-tariff crusade (3719)

Panic waits at door of new Fed. Reserve (3720)

Giving biting lecture to greedy money trusts (3721)

Wilson signing bill that restricts child labor (3722)

South of the Border

V. Huerta, controversial Mexican dictator (3723)

Pershing during campaign to apprehend Pancho Villa (3724)

Pancho Villa, legendary bandit, revolutionary leader (3725)

In 1914, Victoriano Huerta usurped power in Mexico, defying Wilson's demand for a legitimate election. Wilson showed his displeasure by sending troops to Veracruz, and backed Caranza as the new president. In the ensuing turmoil, Pancho Villa, a bandit general, staged a raid on Columbus, New Mexico. General John J. Pershing with 6,000 troops crossed into Mexico, but failed to catch him. Villa became a folk hero, admired in his own country and in the United States.

June 28, 1914: The Powder Keg Explodes

HEIR TO AUSTRIA'S THRONE IS SLAIN WITH HIS WIFE BY A BOSNIAN YOUTH TO AVENGE SEIZURE OF HIS COUNTRY

New York Times headline (3726)

Archduke Franz Ferdinand and wife one hour before attack (3727)

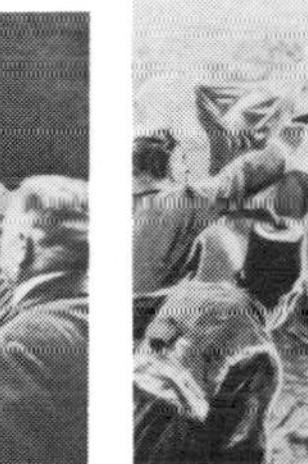
Assassination on June 28 precipitated war (3728)

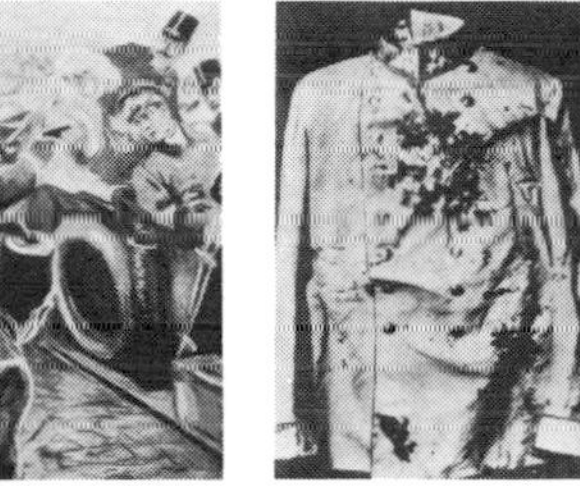
Archduke's bloody uniform (3729)

Serbia enjoys prospect of a Balkan War (3730)

Germany Moves

Berlin, Aug. 1914: news of mobilization (3731)

German soldiers depart for war cheered by their families (3732)

English poster asks for volunteers (3733)

Schlieffen plan: attack through Belgium (3734)

First Marne battle lost; Moltke dismissed (3735)

Rape of Belgium outraged democratic world (3736)

Hindenburg with the General Staff. He defeated Russians at Tannenberg (3737)

Russian retreat. 125,000 prisoners taken (3738)

TRIGGERED BY ETHNIC QUARRELS between Austria and Serbia, World War I broke out on August 1, 1914, eventually involving twenty-seven nations and causing 15 million casualties.

When a Serbian provocateur assassinated the Austrian heir at Sarajevo, Austria retaliated by invading Serbia. This threatened Russia in her Balkan hegemony, and she declared war on Austria. France was forced to aid Russia, and England rushed to the side of France. Germany, on Austria's side, moving with lightning speed against France, scored remarkable victories at first, advancing to within twenty-five miles of Paris. On the Eastern Front, although Von Hindenburg trapped the Russians, the vaunted breakthrough was not achieved.

The 42-cm. gun used by advancing Germans to pulverize French fortifications (3739)

World War I

STALLED IN 1915 AT THE BATTLE of the Marne by combined French and British forces, the German steam roller gave way to the grinding attrition of trench warfare. Seesaw battles along this front seldom gained more than a few miles, at a staggering cost. At the Battle of Verdun in 1916, 700,000 were killed or wounded, and the French countryside became a "no man's land."

German machine gunners near Rheims (3740)

British, Belgian soldiers in painful retreat (3741)

Victim of Sept. 1915 Marne battle (3742)

Stalemate in the West

Gen. Falkenhayn lost at Verdun (3743)

Defenders of Verdun: "They shall not pass" (3744)

Pétain masterminded Verdun defense (3745)

Civilian taxis, trucks en route to reinforce besieged Verdun (3746)

Tanks first used in 1916 Battle of Somme; strategic importance slowly recognized (3747)

Turkish Threat Blunted

THE TURKS, ALLIED WITH GERMANY, threatened English supply lines to India and to Russia. This prompted Winston Churchill, then First Lord of the Admiralty, to suggest a landing at Gallipoli. It failed miserably, but in 1917 a land force under General Allenby chased the Turks from Palestine, freeing the Near East.

Churchill plans Gallipoli assault (3748) to wrest Dardanelles from Turks, open road to hard-pressed Russia via Black Sea (3749)

Gen. Edmund Allenby (3750) took Jerusalem, elimated Turkish Near East threat (3751)

Aerial Heroics

EXCEPT FOR RECONNAISSANCE, aircraft were of minor importance in World War I, yet German flying aces like Von Richthofen (the "Red Baron") gained a world-wide cultish admiration. Unlike the massive, faceless armies, the fliers maintained the dash of an earlier chivalric warfare and derring-do.

Fokker's tri-plane, sensational German combat aircraft (3752)

British Sopwith "Camel" took on German Luftwaffe (3753)

Von Richthofen, W.W.I. famed Red Baron (3754)

Von Richthofen squadron ready for combat (3755)

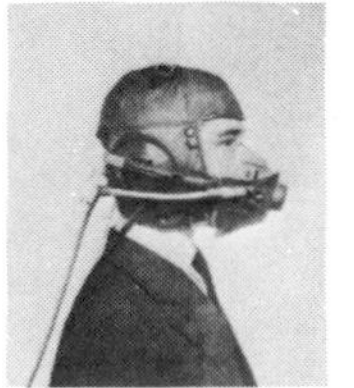

Flier with high-altitude breathing mask (3756)

German Rumpler Taube with birdlike wings (3757)

Zeppelin attack warning (3758)

World War I anti-aircraft gun on wooden stand (3759)

U-Boats Strike

THE GERMAN FLEET remained bottled up through most of the war, except for the indecisive battle of Jutland. But German submarines, unleashed to destroy merchant vessels and troop transports, posed a constant threat. In February, 1917 the Kaiser ordered unrestricted submarine warfare.

CUNARD

EUROPE VIA LIVERPOOL
LUSITANIA
Fastest and Largest Steamer now in Atlantic Service Sails SATURDAY, MAY 1, 10 A. M.
Transylvania, Fri., May 7, 5 P.M.
Orduna, - - Tues., May 18, 10 A.M.
Tuscania, - - Fri., May 21, 5 P.M.
LUSITANIA, Sat., May 29, 10 A.M.
Transylvania, Fri., June 4, 5 P.M.

Gibraltar–Genoa–Naples–Piraeus
S.S. Carpathia, Thur., May 13, Noon

ROUND THE WORLD TOURS

NOTICE!

TRAVELLERS intending to embark on the Atlantic voyage are reminded that a state of war exists between Germany and her allies and Great Britain and her allies; that the zone of war includes the waters adjacent to the British Isles; that, in accordance with formal notice given by the Imperial German Government, vessels flying the flag of Great Britain, or of any of her allies, are liable to destruction in those waters and that travellers sailing in the war zone on ships of Great Britain or her allies do so at their own risk.

IMPERIAL GERMAN EMBASSY

Ad warns travelers of U-boat threat (3760)

Lusitania sinking on May 7, 1915, pushed U.S. closer to war on Allies' side (3761)

German U-boats ruthlessly attacked neutral and Allied shipping in the Atlantic (3762)

Jutland, May 31, 1916, major W.W.I sea battle, was indecisive (3763)

Torpedoed British merchantman about to sink to the bottom (3764)

THE HONOR OF THE NATION

Wilson pronounced tenet of honorable nation "too proud to fight" (3765)

U.S. Forced into Conflict

ADHERING TO NEUTRALITY at the war's onset, Wilson reflected the majority sentiment, which felt American could "legislate itself out of the conflict." Yet the country leaned heavily toward the Allies, contributing billions in loans. Despite Wilson's second-term campaign slogan, "He kept us out of war," shipping losses to German submarines forced Wilson's hand, and he finally asked Congress to declare war on Germany (April 6, 1917).

Women organized, demonstrated to keep U.S. out of world conflict (3766)

Wilson campaign truck of 1916 lists his many domestic reforms and accomplishments (3767)

Wilson's promise of peace remained unfulfilled (3768)

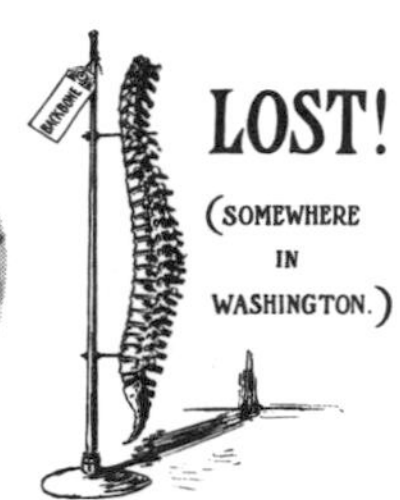

Wilson's pacifism scored as lack of courage (3769)

Uncle Sam accused of preaching peace, pursuing war by weapons sales (3770)

War declared on Germany on April 6, 1917 (3771)

May 1917, Wilson starts Selective Service (3772)

Doughboys being trained in bayonet attack (3773)

Enemy alien fingerprinted. Anti-German feeling high (3774)

Chaplin exhorts Liberty Bond drive (3775)

War poster entreats U.S. citizens save food (3776)

HOMEFRONT MOBILIZED

THE HOME FRONT, with women doing more than their share, backed the fighting men with a surge of patriotism. Sauerkraut became "liberty cabbage." Voluntary rationing and victory gardens were part of the "Hooverizing" program of the national Food Administrator that included heatless Mondays, meatless Tuesdays, porkless Saturdays and gasless Sundays.

Female workers employed in American makeshift munitions factory (3777)

U.S. soldier takes his leave (3781)

UNPREPARED TO FIGHT, with a standing army of only 121,000 men, America mobilized with astounding efficiency. An army was conscripted and a War Production Board was created to arm it and supply it. Only 14,500 troops were initially in General Pershing's American Expeditionary Force. More than two million civilian soldiers had gone "over there" by the war's end.

Women Volunteer Corps member works on automobile (3778)

Girl Scouts collect peach pits used to extract medicinal oil (3779)

Montgomery Flagg with famed war posters (3780)

The Yanks are Coming

THE U.S. HAD CREATED the largest, best-equipped army up to that time but many of the inexperienced "doughboys" required extensive training in France. Aside from their military adventures, however, there were recreational interludes at Red Cross canteens and gustatory treats handed out by Salvation Army lasses. The war proved for many a robust, exciting cultural experience. "How ya gonna keep 'em down on the farm," went the popular song, "after they've seen Paree?"

Departing troops were high-spirited, foresaw an early end to the war (3782)

Pershing in France, June, 1917 (3783)

First American troops in France (3784)

Classic George M. Cohan World War I song (3785)

Eddie Rickenbacker, credited with twenty-six air victories (3786)

Gen. Mitchell headed U.S. air forces in France (3787)

Handmade airplane wings in a 1918 woodworking shop (3788)

Loading bombs. Strategy was not very effective (3789)

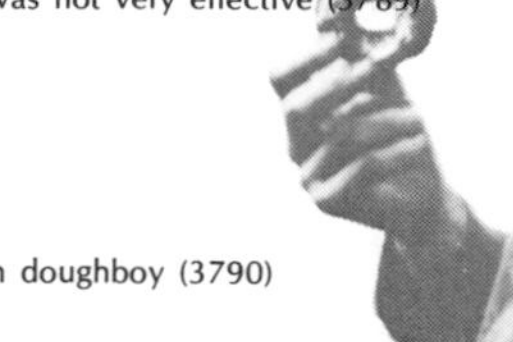

The American doughboy (3790)

Russian Revolution

A WEAK PARTNER from the beginning, Russia had served the Allies by diverting German forces to a second front. But Czar Nicholas II's regime, faced with famine and despair, collapsed in 1917 under a mounting wave of social and political discontent. Germany, secretly encouraging the radical Bolsheviks, helped to bring Nicolai Lenin back to Russia. Assuming power on November 6, 1917, Lenin soon concluded a separate peace with Germany in order to free his hands to further the revolution. In turn, Germany could now throw her combined forces onto the Western Front.

(3791)

Kerensky, head of the moderate provisional government, pledged to stay in war (3792)

Radicals gained upper hand in factories of Petrograd (3793)

Lenin crosses Gulf of Finland on way to Russia. Germans planted this "plague bacillus"* (3794)

* Churchill

Bolsheviks urged Russian soldiers to quit the war, surrender (3795)

Poster: the October Revolution (3796)

Russian soldiers and sailors joining ranks of the revolutionaries (3797)

Lenin harangues crowd (3798)

Nicholas II prisoner in Siberia (3799)

Leon Trotsky, loyal to Lenin (3800)

Starvation in post-war Russia (3801)

1918: Allied Victory

ATTACKING WITH REDOUBLED FORCE in its March Offensive of 1918, the German army drove a dangerous bulge into Allied lines. But in midsummer fresh American troops managed to prevent a German breakthrough. When a mutiny began to spread through Germany in November 1918, William II was forced to abdicate, and the country had to surrender.

Poised for 1918 German spring offensive (3802)

Foch, Pershing agree to join French, Yanks (3803)

U.S. patrol in "no man's land," March 1918 (3804)

American troops going "over the top" hit by German gas attack (3805)

At Château-Thierry, Americans kept Germans from crossing Marne, threatening Paris (3806)

Yanks in French Renault tanks advance in Marne region (3807)

Sgt. York captured 132 prisoners (3808)

Last gunshot of the war fired on Nov. 11, 1918 (3809). Yanks rejoice at news of German surrender (3810)

Germany Surrenders

Armed political revolt in Germany precipitated armistice (3811)

Armistice signed in Foch's railroad car in forest near Compiègne (3812)

Kaiser abdicated, fled to Doorn, Holland (3813)

German weapons and materiel destroyed after armistice (3814)

American sentry guards the Rhine frontier (3815)

Doughboys Go Home

THE YANKS IN UNIFORM, soldiers and sailors alike, pressed to get home at war's end, shouting "Heaven, Hell or Hoboken by Christmas." Yet when they returned, many veterans, inspired by the excitement of continental life, felt let down by a selfish, parochial America bound for normalcy. The bonus they demanded soon became a political football.

Yanks embark for home (3816)

U.S. soldiers returned with new sophistication (3817)

Tumultuous tickertape parade, N.Y. (3818)

Returned veterans needed jobs (3819)

Imprisoned dissenters seek amnesty (3820)

Versailles: Uneasy Peace

THE TREATY OF VERSAILLES, signed on June 28, 1919 in the Hall of Mirrors in Louis XIV's opulent palace, imposed heavy penalties upon Germany: the restoration of Alsace-Lorraine to France, enormous reparations payments, occupation of the Saar and Rhineland by the Allies, and permanent restrictions on German military and industrial power. Woodrow Wilson's main objectives, to enforce the principle of self-determination for disputed territories, and to create the League of Nations, were reflected in the covenant. Unfortunately, the U.S. Senate and its isolationist leaders failed to ratify the treaty. Wilson's inability to convince the American people of the merit of his international program left him a broken man—and the League but a fading vision.

President Wilson en route to the Versailles Peace Conference (3821)

Triumphant reception by Paris populace, Dec. 1918 (3822)

Lloyd George, Clemenceau, Wilson tour Paris (3823)

Terms of peace treaty submitted to German delegation, May 1919 (3824)

Treaty signed, Versailles Hall of Mirrors (3825)

Lansing, Secy. of State, critical of Wilson (3826)

Colonel House, Wilson's trusted counsel (3827)

Signatories to the Treaty of Versailles (3831)

Paderewski, Polish envoy to peace conference (3828)

Dr. Masaryk represented Czechoslovakia (3829)

Keynes declared peace terms untenable (3830)

Failure of the League

AMERICA'S REFUSAL to join the League of Nations and the indifference of the Great Powers undermined its effectiveness and prestige. Finally, the League collapsed when England and France chose to appease Hitler's demands at Munich in 1938. The permanent peace Wilson had envisioned turned out to be but an uneasy twenty-year armistice between two wars.

League proves too heavy for Dove of Peace (3832)

Cabot Lodge, foe of Treaty, League (3833)

Wilson caught in League of Nations rapids (3834)

Humanity condemns Senate for killing peace treaty (3835)

Wilson fights for League among the people (3836)

THE WEIMAR REPUBLIC, formed after William II's abdication, was burdened by the payment of war reparations, draining the country's economy to the breaking point. To secure stability, the ruling Social Democrats allied themselves with the military. This gave the Weimar Republic a semblance of order, but also paved the way for a new militant upsurge under Hitler.

Ebert, first President of the Weimar Republic (3837)

Spartacus revolt threatens German recovery (3838)

Poverty and despair grip people (3839)

Foreign Min. Rathenau was assassinated, 1922 (3840)

A LA MEMOIRE DE
WOODROW WILSON
PRESIDENT DES ETATS-VNIS
FONDATEVR DE LA SOCIÉTÉ DES NATIONS
LA VILLE DE GENEVE

Wilson Memorial, League of Nations Palace, Geneva (3841)

WARNER BROS.
Supreme Triumph
AL JOLSON IN
THE JAZZ SINGER
WITH VITAPHONE
2.30 TWICE DAILY 8.45
Sunday Matinees 3.P.M.
APPLES
5

A B C D F G

CHAPTER 13

Normalcy to Holocaust

The "Roaring Twenties"
Depression . . . Dictatorship
Global Conflict

E

J

H

I

Democrats backed the League of Nations (3844)

Harding had an ambitious wife. He was a lady's man (3845)

...ntial ...20 (3843)

(3842)

...ed companionship ... partners (3846)

Harding photographed in White House garden. He cultivated "the presidential look" (3847)

Teapot Dome scandal exposed nasty political graft (3848)

Teapot Dome Scandal

AFTER HARDING'S sudden death in 1923, two of his appointees were convicted of turning over federal oil fields at Teapot Dome, Wyoming, to oil magnate Harry Sinclair in return for secret "loans."

Coolidge sworn in at news of Harding's sudden death (3852)

Coolidge presides over an "Academy of Silence" (3853)

Doheny (3849) accused of bribing Interior Sec. Fall (3850) to get U.S. oil leases.

Harry M. Sinclair, Teapot Dome mastermind (3851)

Image of homey Vermont farmer made Coolidge popular (3857)

A smiling President opens 1924 baseball season (3858)

Buttons helped "Cool Cal" in 1924 (3854, 3855, 3856)

The Coolidge Administration

AS VICE PRESIDENT, Calvin Coolidge, it was said, expected to do nothing, and as President he did not change his mind. An administrator rather than a leader, Coolidge declared: "The only business of government is business." He was a popular president (although somewhat taciturn) during a period of great prosperity and believed firmly in laissez-faire toward business. His Administration rejected participation in both the League of Nations and the World Court, so America pursued her own course, shirking a leadership role in world affairs.

Disarmament Eases Tensions

Disarmament: victims of a war-torn Europe look to America to shape a more peaceful world (3863)

Washington Naval Conference of 1921, convoked by Charles E. Hughes, tackled arms race (3859)

Goddess of disarmament enlightens world (3860)

Briand pursued peaceful European concord (3861)

Charles Dawes proposed fairer reparations (3862)

SOLVING THE PROBLEMS of disarmament was essential to a stable peace after World War I. The Washington Disarmament Conference was inconclusive, but the U.S.-sponsored Dawes Plan did help to avoid global problems threatened by collapse of the German economy. With its burden of reparations payments eased by a more realistic schedule, Germany was able to recover.

Stresemann & Chamberlain at Locarno (3864)

Kellogg-Briand anti-aggression pact signed by Coolidge (3865)

Coolidge beams as champion of peace in gold rich U.S. (3866)

Prohibition

AMERICA ENTERED the giddiest episode of its history in 1919 when temperance forces won ratification of the Eighteenth Amendment, outlawing intoxicating beverages. The Prohibition Bureau's 3,000 agents could not possibly suppress the drinking habits of a populace intent on fun and "wonderful nonsense." Bootlegging soon became a basic industry, and speakeasies a part of American life. Mass evasion of the law bred graft, corruption and big gangsters of the Al Capone ilk.

Sign uses logic to stress folly of drinking (3870)

LIQUOR means ALCOHOL
ALCOHOL means POISON
Why drink POISON?

Last gulps of beer ceremoniously toasted before onset of 1920 Prohibition (3867)

Temperance poster shows devilish drinker (3868)

Vollstead Act passed over the President's veto (3869)

Anti-Prohibitionists quote Bible; defend moderate drinking (3871)

U.S. Treasury agents pour seized liquor into the gutter (3872)

Prosthetic leg used to smuggle alcohol (3873)

Captured cache of liquor in coal steamer (3874)

Undercover revenue agents Izzy Einstein and "Moe" Smith, nabbed many violators (3875)

Crime

Caustic cartoon on ease of buying Tommy Gun (3879)

Illegal liquor still discovered. Prohibition bureau was inadequately manned (3876)

Knocking at door of N.Y. speakeasy (3877)

Relaxed citizens guzzle speakeasy booze (3878)

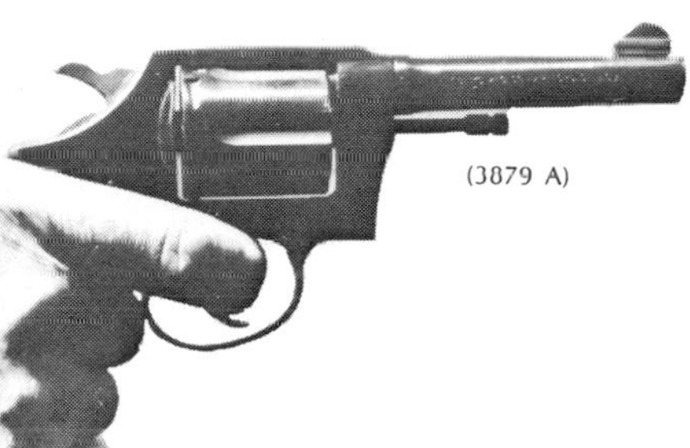

(3879 A)

Al Capone, notorious gangster, controlled liquor, prostitution, gambling (3880)

John Torio, Capone buddy, headed Chicago ring (3881)

St. Valentine's Day massacre, 1929, bloody climax of Chicago's gang warfare (3882)

Causes Célèbres

SUSPICION OF FOREIGNERS (particularly those with Communist sympathies) was endemic in this period of isolationism. When two Italian radicals, Sacco and Vanzetti, were convicted of murder on flimsy evidence, their case became a *cause célèbre* among liberals. In the same period, the Tennessee Scopes trial exposed the region's bigotry and backwardness.

Leopold and Loeb, murderers. Darrow defended them (3883)

Sacco and Vanzetti (3884), anarchists, were convicted of robbery and murder. Evidence was discredited, world-wide protest aroused (3885), they died martyrs.

Sam Insull, utility magnate suspected embezzler (3886)

Monopolist Ivar Kreuger committed suicide (3887)

John Scopes dared to teach Darwinian evolution (3888)

Clarence Darrow at Scopes trial. He clashed with William J. Bryan (3889)

Billy Mitchell argued for strong air power; was court-martialled (3890)

Flapper: symbol of new "come hither" sex (3892)

The Jazz Age

ALTHOUGH THE NOISE CAME from a small number of people during the "Roaring Twenties," the image of the era is one of gaiety and excitement. The search for "kicks" seemed to dominate the public imagination: dance marathons, acrobatics on the wing of a plane, cheap hootch—anything to "make whoopee." The syncopated beat of the jazz band and the bold defiance of the "flapper," whose short skirts and silk stockings put "sex appeal" on the map, were characteristic of the age. So were eccentric heroes and heroines, like New York's flamboyant mayor Jimmy Walker and Hollywood evangelist Aimee Semple McPherson.

"Bright new things" enliven Jazz Age party (3893)

Frenetic dance style was the rage (3895)

Musical fun with woman flutist; jazz combo sets pace of dance-floor excitement (3894)

King Oliver's Jazz Band featured young Louis Armstrong on the trumpet (3896)

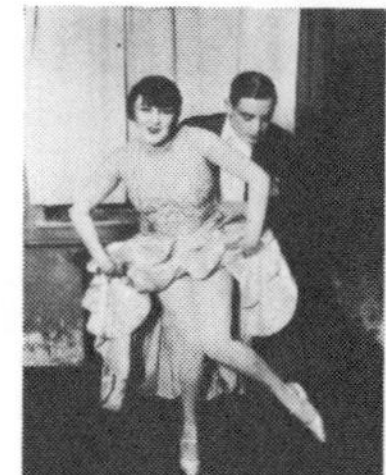

Nifty dancers demonstrate the Charleston (3897)

Jazz Age party: wild antics, music, hilarity, plenty of hootch (3898)

Dance marathon: one was 3,327 hours (3899)

Rudy Vallee, orchestra leader, crooner and life-long collegian (3900)

Duke Ellington: innovator in piano, orchestral jazz (3901)

Paul Whiteman's band debuted "Rhapsody in Blue" (3902)

Ted Lewis: "Is every body happy?" (3903)

Josephine Baker, night club dynamite (3904)

George Gershwin (3905) blended classical forms jazz. Also gifted painter. Self-portrait (3906)

Personalities

Jimmy Walker: shady, slick New York City mayor (3907)

Aimee Semple McPherson, tainted revivalist (3908)

Texas Guinan, of "Hello, Sucker" fame (3909)

Night club shenanigans with young Jimmy Durante (3910)

Cars for All People

THE STATUS SYMBOL of the Jazz Age was the automobile: slick, handcrafted cars of sybaritic luxury encased the very rich. On a popular plane, Ford's Tin Lizzie dominated the market. Still, the common man longed for luxury, and General Motors (once close to bankruptcy) sought to exploit this yearning with a sportier, more colorful car—the Chevrolet. It seriously challenged the drab repetitive Model-T, which, according to Henry Ford, was available in "any color as long as it's black."

Rolls-Royce became status symbol (3911)

Duesenberg, a mogul's car (3912)

Lady driver cranks her Model-T (3917)

Model-T Runabout, for two (3919)

Cadillac meant Hollywood success (3913)

Packard Phaeton—tops for sports (3914)

The Lincoln was Ford's luxury model (3915)

"Word magic" of Jordan's ad characterized the age (3916)

Sporty roadster, raccoon coats (3918)

Walter P. Chrysler challenged Ford with new Plymouth car (3920)

Yearly model changes created many auto graveyards (3921)

Hollywood's Glamour Years

WITH FUN AND ENTERTAINMENT on America's collective mind, the motion picture industry of the 1920s skyrocketed. Theaters appeared even in the smallest towns, and more than 35 million people, it was estimated, went to the movies every week. No other medium had ever shaped as markedly American attitudes, ideals and mores. The "come hither" look of Clara Bow, the Charleston antics of young Joan Crawford, Garbo's slouch, the kissing technique of Valentino, all were admired and slavishly imitated. Film personalities were idolized, not only for their screen performances but for their purportedly glamorous private lives, unequaled in dash and picaresque adventures.

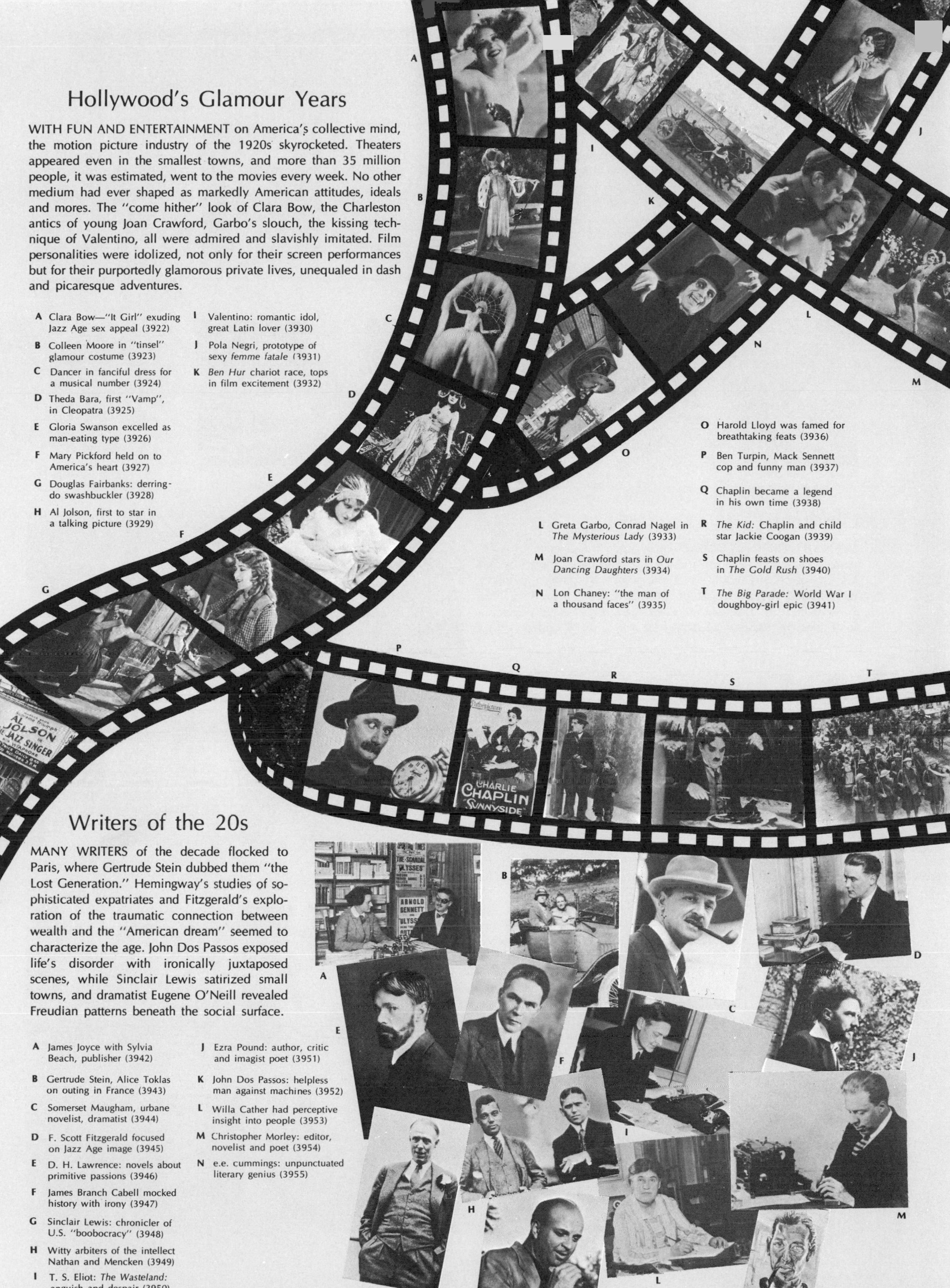

A Clara Bow—"It Girl" exuding Jazz Age sex appeal (3922)

B Colleen Moore in "tinsel" glamour costume (3923)

C Dancer in fanciful dress for a musical number (3924)

D Theda Bara, first "Vamp", in Cleopatra (3925)

E Gloria Swanson excelled as man-eating type (3926)

F Mary Pickford held on to America's heart (3927)

G Douglas Fairbanks: derring-do swashbuckler (3928)

H Al Jolson, first to star in a talking picture (3929)

I Valentino: romantic idol, great Latin lover (3930)

J Pola Negri, prototype of sexy *femme fatale* (3931)

K *Ben Hur* chariot race, tops in film excitement (3932)

L Greta Garbo, Conrad Nagel in *The Mysterious Lady* (3933)

M Joan Crawford stars in *Our Dancing Daughters* (3934)

N Lon Chaney: "the man of a thousand faces" (3935)

O Harold Lloyd was famed for breathtaking feats (3936)

P Ben Turpin, Mack Sennett cop and funny man (3937)

Q Chaplin became a legend in his own time (3938)

R *The Kid:* Chaplin and child star Jackie Coogan (3939)

S Chaplin feasts on shoes in *The Gold Rush* (3940)

T *The Big Parade:* World War I doughboy-girl epic (3941)

Writers of the 20s

MANY WRITERS of the decade flocked to Paris, where Gertrude Stein dubbed them "the Lost Generation." Hemingway's studies of sophisticated expatriates and Fitzgerald's exploration of the traumatic connection between wealth and the "American dream" seemed to characterize the age. John Dos Passos exposed life's disorder with ironically juxtaposed scenes, while Sinclair Lewis satirized small towns, and dramatist Eugene O'Neill revealed Freudian patterns beneath the social surface.

A James Joyce with Sylvia Beach, publisher (3942)

B Gertrude Stein, Alice Toklas on outing in France (3943)

C Somerset Maugham, urbane novelist, dramatist (3944)

D F. Scott Fitzgerald focused on Jazz Age image (3945)

E D. H. Lawrence: novels about primitive passions (3946)

F James Branch Cabell mocked history with irony (3947)

G Sinclair Lewis: chronicler of U.S. "boobocracy" (3948)

H Witty arbiters of the intellect Nathan and Mencken (3949)

I T. S. Eliot: *The Wasteland:* anguish and despair (3950)

J Ezra Pound: author, critic and imagist poet (3951)

K John Dos Passos: helpless man against machines (3952)

L Willa Cather had perceptive insight into people (3953)

M Christopher Morley: editor, novelist and poet (3954)

N e.e. cummings: unpunctuated literary genius (3955)

Europe: Seeds of Trouble

England

DURING THE POSTWAR YEARS, a growing demand for self-government by Britain's colonies resulted in the gradual transformation of the old empire into a looser alliance of self-governing nations. In these years, India took a giant step toward independence, led by Mahatma Gandhi and inspired by his credo of peaceful resistance and civil disobedience. Closer to home, an Irish Free State was established in 1921. But the resulting partition of Ireland was bitterly opposed by the left-wing Sinn Fein Party. This led to a period of civil war and a trauma that would not heal for decades to come.

Ramsay MacDonald headed first Labor cabinet (3956)

Eamon de Valera led Irish Free State movement (3957)

British troops in Dublin to quell Sinn Fein uprising (3961)

Gandhi: non-cooperation to gain independence (3958)

Indian riot: passive resistance and civil disobedience (3959)

Gandhi was released from prison to attend 1931 London Round Table Conference on India's status (3960)

Germany

GERMANY, DRAINED OF CAPITAL by reparation payments, tried to sustain its economy in the postwar era with paper money which became practically worthless (at one point a basketful of currency was needed to buy a loaf of bread). Monetary expert Hjalmar Schacht in 1923 stabilized the Reichsmark and restored prosperity for a time, but worldwide depression was soon to undercut it.

Unemployment, hunger, disillusionment plagued Weimar Republic in the early twenties (3962)

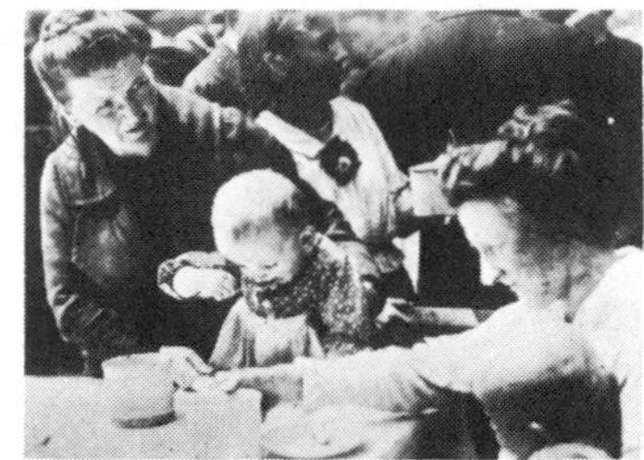

Soup kitchen run by U.S. Quakers helped starving populace (3963)

Inflation: 100,000 marks for one U.S. dollar (3964)

Fifty Million Reichsmark was worthless (3965)

Carrying money to the bank in wicker laundry baskets (3966)

Schacht stabilized the currency (3967)

Promises of prosperity kindled hopes (3968)

Threepenny Opera, by Brecht-Weill, voiced cynicism of postwar Germany (3969)

Birth of Fascism

THE THREAT OF COMMUNISM brought turbulence to postwar Italy, allowing Mussolini, a journalist turned right-wing agitator, to fill the power vacuum with his activist *squadristi.* In 1922, he marched on Rome, where King Victor Emmanuel II agreed to have him form a new cabinet. Suppressing all opposition, "Il Duce" (supported by his blackshirts) soon exercized dictatorial powers.

During the same period Hitler, imprisoned after an abortive putsch in Bavaria, wrote out his battle plan, *Mein Kampf.* Released after nine months, he renewed his attacks on the Weimar Republic, and in 1933 rose to power aided by a rising tide of public discontent.

Hitler imprisoned for Munich Putsch (3970)

After prison stay of nine months, Hitler pushed expansion of Nazi party (3971)

March on Rome in 1922, to forestall purported Communist takeover (3973)

Mussolini became dictator, crushed opposition (3974)

Mural spells out demand for subordination (3975)

Mussolini signs concordat with papacy to quell Church opposition to his one-man regime (3976)

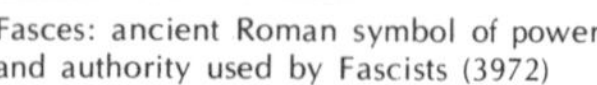

Fasces: ancient Roman symbol of power and authority used by Fascists (3972)

Lindbergh Launches a New Era

LINDBERGH DOES IT! TO PARIS IN 33½ HOURS; FLIES 1,000 MILES THROUGH SNOW AND SLEET; CHEERING FRENCH CARRY HIM OFF FIELD

(3977)

Lindbergh aimed for $25,000 Ortieg prize for first non-stop New York-Paris flight (3978)

FEW EVENTS HAVE STIRRED the world's imagination as Lindbergh's flight across the Atlantic in 1927. Alone in his silver monoplane for 33½ hours, the twenty-five-year-old aviator personified a new heroism. More newspaper space was devoted to his exploit than to the outbreak of World War I. His reception at Le Bourget airport in Paris was tumultuous. President Coolidge sent a battleship to bring him home, and his arrival in New York prompted frenetic crowds to toss 180 tons of confetti on his motorcade. A new age of aerial exploits had begun.

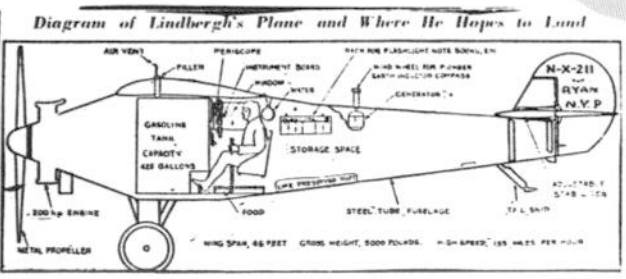

Diagram of Lindbergh plane. Ample fuel supply was the prime concern (3979)

Lindy received French Legion of Honor Medal, plaudits from Parisians (3980)

Tumultous ticker tape parade, greatest ever, poured down New York canyon (3981)

Pilot Bert Acosta set new endurance record (3982)

Amelia Earhart: first woman to fly the Atlantic (3983)

U.S. Air Mail Service started in 1927 (3984)

The Golden Age of Sports

Babe Ruth in typical batting stance (3985)

Ty Cobb: baseball legend (3986)

Knute Rockne; greatest football coach (3987)

Tunney defeats Dempsey; controversial "long count" in 1927 fight (3988)

Johnny Weissmuller at 17 breaks 440-yard swimming record (3989)

Trudy Ederle swam English Channel in record 14 hours 30 minutes (3990)

Bobby Jones, "Grand Slam" champ (3991)

THE YEARS AFTER WORLD WAR I saw a phenomenal rise of spectator sports and the adulation of its heroes. Whatever the reason, this decade brought to the fore a line-up of champions never to be matched. Proudly, people began to memorize batting averages rather than Biblical quotations, and a star like Babe Ruth wielded more power over the public imagination than Calvin Coolidge.

Bill Tilden, monarch of the courts (3992)

Helen Wills won eight Wimbleton titles (3993)

(3994)

Radio—A New World Power

RADIO GREW in this decade from a mere curiosity into a worldwide medium of communication and entertainment. (Station KDKA in Pittsburgh broadcast the first scheduled program in 1920—the Harding-Cox election returns.) By 1929 every third house in the nation was tuned in to national network broadcasts, and shortwave transmissions spanned the globe. Listeners became participants in history.

Radio ham operator in his home workshop (3995)

Radio broadcast with sound effects simulated by station crew (3996)

Miracle of loudspeaker explained in ad (4001)

Snowed-in farmer goes to church with radio headphones (3997)

Umbrella frame makes radio antenna (3998)

Irving Berlin, song writer, in early song broadcast (3999)

Alex Woollcott was called "Town Crier of Air" (4000)

Major Edwin Armstrong, inventor of radio frequency modulation (4002)

Hoover and the Crash

AMERICA SEEMED A LAND teeming with prosperity when Herbert Hoover was elected President in 1928, yet within a year her economy collapsed in the face of the Great Depression. Easy credit had grossly overstimulated speculation in stocks. Hoover, unable to stem the tide, did little or nothing to stop the debacle. Black Thursday, October 24, 1929, hit the stock market with a $40 billion loss that proved to be only the beginning of America's economic fall. Thirty thousand businesses failed in the following year. Shock waves from the U.S. disaster triggered money crises all over the world.

Herbert Hoover, WW I relief director (4003)

Commerce Sec. Hoover gives radio address during 1928 campaign (4004)

Al Smith was first Catholic to run for President (4005)

Hoover escorted to inauguration. In his address he pictured America "bright with hope" (4006)

Boom-age speculator in telephone tangle (4007)

Signaling orders from Wall Street curb (4008)

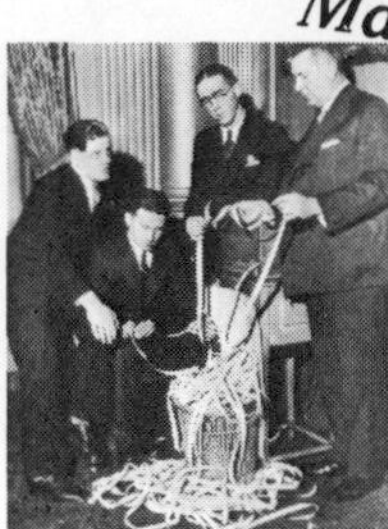

Anxious brokers study the ticker-tape (4009)

Bear flees Wall Street; market tumbles (4010)

Market in Panic as Stocks ...e Dumped in 12,894,600 ...nkers Halt It

New York *World* headline (4011)

Depression

Hiring hall sign (4012)

Employment opportunities were mostly menial, scarce (4013)

STATISTICS CANNOT CONVEY the suffering of starving families, of farmers driven from their land by mortgage failures. By 1933, one fourth of the entire American labor force was out of work. As similar catastrophes spread throughout Europe, panic paralyzed the governments of many industrial nations, and the masses turned to demagogues who promised jobs and bread.

Job seekers deluge employment office. Federal aid was slow to come (4014)

Apple seller, a common sidewalk sight (4015)

Catholic mission provides bread line relief for the hungry (4016)

Placard bearers protest plight and abuse of the unemployed (4017)

White-collar jobless scan help wanted signs (4018)

Children in "Hooverville" camp of dislodged families (4019)

Congress juggles veteran's bonus issue (4020). Vets came to Washington, were dispersed by troops (4021)

Bread and soup sustain the jobless (4022). One-third of U.S. labor force was unemployed (4023)

Science Advances

Langmuir: Nobel Chemist, pioneered in radio (4024)

T.H. Morgan: genes rule heredity (4025)

Robert Millikan: electron, cosmic-ray research (4026)

Vannevar Bush organized science research (4027)

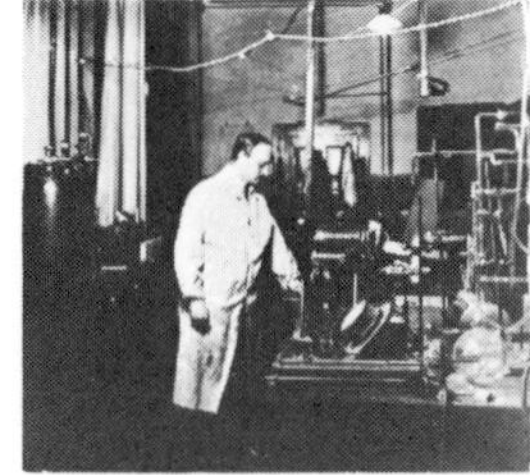

James Franck: new insights into atomic structure (4028)

Franklin D. Roosevelt campaign button expresses his activist creed (4029)

The Roosevelt Age

FRANKLIN D. ROOSEVELT was stricken by polio in 1921 but refused to let it interfere with a promising political career. As governor of New York he tackled the state's economic woes with vigor. This led to his election as President by an overwhelming majority in 1932. This New Deal provided help in the critical areas of unemployment, farming, banking and housing by courageous use of the powers of the government for the welfare of the people. Among the key reforms FDR championed was the Social Security Act of 1935. His charismatic leadership gave new hope to a nation that was forlorn and in distress.

Nominating Al "Happy Warrior" Smith at 1928 Democratic convention (4030)

Inspite of crippling disease, FDR was inaugurated N.Y. Governor, 1929 (4031)

FDR takes oath of office in 1933. The next "100 days" saw vigorous action (4032)

Harry Hopkins, FDR friend and "brain truster" (4034)

Raymond Moley was FDR ally, later his foe (4035)

Felix Frankfurter, liberal jurist (4036)

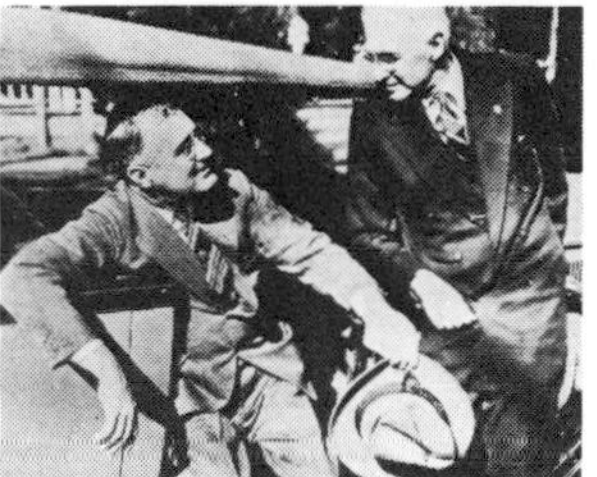

The President and Bernard Baruch, trusted unofficial advisor (4037)

Robert Sherwood, author, was F D R speech writer (4038)

A New Deal generated many agencies, programs (4039)

B Harold Ickes, Interior Sec., public works chief (4040)

C Girls back Natl. Recovery Act, to create jobs (4041)

D WPA artist does mural for Federal Art Project (4042)

E Supreme court ruled NRA was unconstitutional (4043)

F The Spirit of the New Deal. Cartoon by Berryman (4044)

G Social Security Act topped FDR's social reforms (4045)

H Home owners ask Roosevelt for mortgage relief (4046)

I WPA workers protest wages paid for relief work (4047)

J WPA men plant trees to help beautify public park (4048)

K Needed street repairs done by WPA work crew (4049)

L President's fireside chats urged hope, action (4050)

M Federal govt. arranged low cost home loans (4051)

The Dust Bowl

DUST STORMS, the result of drought and poor ground cover (farmers had stripped away protective grass to increase production), destroyed millions of acres of farmland in the Southwest in 1934. As displaced, starving farmers took to the road, their lot as desperate as that of the unemployed industrial workers, the Roosevelt Administration made valiant efforts to resettle them on new land.

Depression squalor. Income was $19.20 per month (4052)

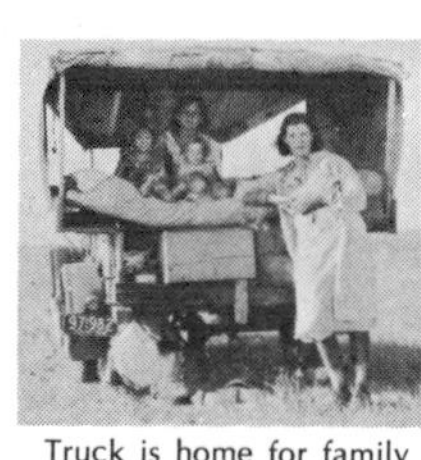

Truck is home for family fleeing dust bowl (4053)

Depression family. Photograph by Dorothea Lange (4054)

Father and son flee from blowing dust storm. Rosenthal photo (4055)

Mother and children wait to move from old shack (4056)

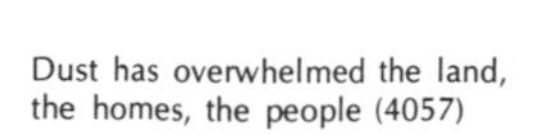

Dust has overwhelmed the land, the homes, the people (4057)

The Turbulent Thirties

THE ATMOSPHERE OF LAWLESSNESS developed during the Prohibition years lent a certain glamour to criminals. In the Depression-wracked thirties, the FBI's "Ten Most Wanted" list nearly became an index of popular fame. Although the most famous crime of the decade, the abduction of the Lindbergh baby, was not the work of professional criminals, it abetted in a perverse way the nation's fascination with crime.

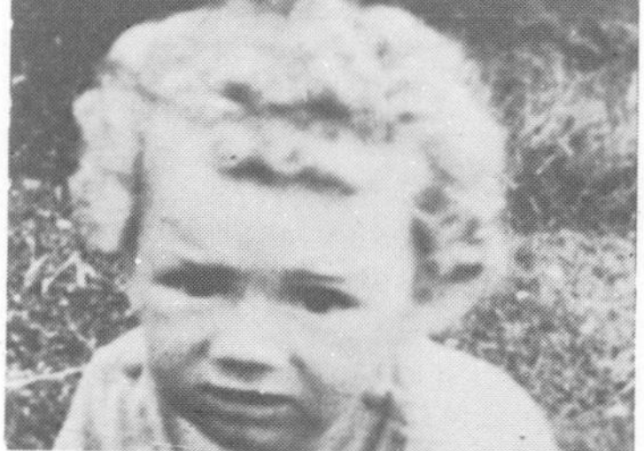
Lindbergh baby found dead near Hopewell, N.J., after a seventy-two-day frantic search (4058)

Bruno Hauptmann (4059), implicated by found ransom, was electrocuted still claiming innocence (4060)

Dillinger, bank robber, escape artist—terrorized midwest in 1933 (4061)

Crime

Bonnie and Clyde went on a murder rampage (4062)

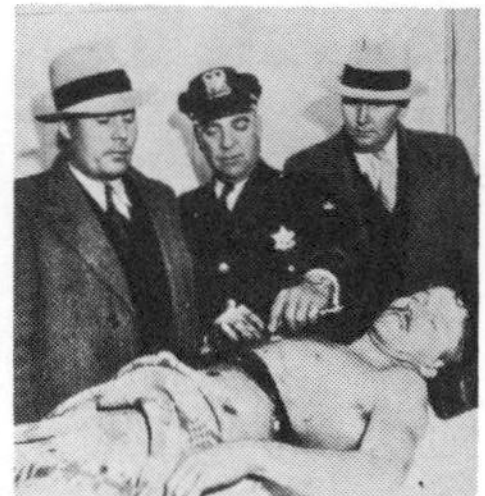
Baby Face Nelson, Dillinger pal, was slain by police (4063)

Convicts breaking rocks on Georgia prison farm (4064)

President signs anti-crime bill as J. Edgar Hoover watches (4065)

Potent Personalities

THE GREAT DEPRESSION bred demagogues and reformers. Promising surcease from want, Dr. Francis Townsend claimed 25 million elderly followers. Huey Long's "Share the Wealth" crusade made him a dictator in Louisiana, while Father Divine wooed blacks with his earthly "heavens." At the same time, right wing Father Coughlin stirred hatred against Jews and FDR in his radio harangues.

Huey Long, Louisiana "Kingfish"(4066), author of *Every Man a King*, was killed in capitol he had built as his memorial (4067)

Ku Klux Klan night session displays cross as warning to blacks of terror to come (4068)

Father Coughlin flayed FDR policy (4069)

Father Divine promised ease, unlimited chicken feasts (4070)

Townsend Pension Plan vanished after Social Security Act (4071)

1936 campaign button for GOP's Alf Landon (4072)

Roosevelt won 532 electoral votes while Landon carried but two states (4073)

Labor

A CLOSE ALLIANCE WITH LABOR was one feature of the New Deal that most annoyed big business. John L. Lewis, who had just formed the powerful CIO, initially backed Roosevelt. The National Labor Relations Act of 1935 was a joint victory. But Lewis, as many other New Dealers, turned bitterly against the President during his second term, and widespread labor unrest followed.

John L. Lewis (4074) forged miners into a powerful labor union (4075)

Other industry groups joined his CIO (4076)

Rising near plants company houses were exposed to pollution (4077)

Labor unrest beset FDR's second term (4078)

Aviation

China Clipper for Hong Kong in 1937 started transpacific flights (4082, 4083)

Howard Hughes greeted by ticker-tape after his around-the-world flight (4079)

Adm. Byrd's "Little America" base approach to South Pole (4080)

In 1937, the *Hindenburg* exploded, burned at Lakehurst, N.J. (4081)

THOUGH TIMES WERE HARD, life in this decade had its charms. Radio dispensed free entertainment, creating such beloved (if mythical) folk heroes as Amos n' Andy. *Information, Please* began an enduring fascination with quiz culture, while Orson Welles with his "War of the Worlds" broadcast frightened millions into believing that the Martians had landed on the planet Earth.

The City

"Great White Way"—Broadway in the mid-thirties (4084)

Chrysler Bldg.—best Art Deco style (4085)

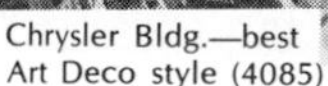

Rockefeller Center, N.Y., rose during New Deal years (4086)

New York's Empire State Building was built during Depression (4087)

Bibulous beauties celebrate the end of Prohibition in a public bar (4088)

Riveter during construction of skyscraper (4089)

Double deck bus: best for travel, sightseeing (4090)

1939 N.Y. World's Fair, "The World of Tomorrow" (4091)

Harlem night-club jitterburg session with men sporting baggy zoot suits (4096)

Country Life

Farmer's wife canning vegetables to feed family in winter (4092)

Barbershop quartet entertains crowd at a Vermont country fair (4093)

Pennsylvania farm home scene. Ma plays parlor organ (4094)

Newspaper boy (4095)

Young couples enjoy a picnic outing (4097)

College fashions of the thirties (4098)

Worker in auto drop-forge plant (4099)

Tobacco farmers in Durham, N.C. await payment for crops (4100)

Store sign for overalls (4101)

Drinking fountains segregated for blacks and whites (4102)

Amos 'n Andy, played by two white actors, Gosden and Correll (4103)

Information Please: Levant, Kiernan, Cedric Hardwick, Adams (4104)

Orson Welles' program triggered panic (4105)

Literature Goes Hollywood

HOLLYWOOD GROUND OUT a thousand features during the thirties, often inviting famed writers to create scripts. Producers also translated popular books into films.

A Producer Laemmle and author Remarque discuss film (4106)

B Hemingway and wife return from Africa (4107). *For Whom*
C *the Bell Tolls:* a classic of Spanish Civil War (4108)

D Louis B. Mayer—producer, Hollywood mogul (4109)

E John Steinbeck (4110) wrote dust bowl epic *Grapes of*
F *Wrath.* Film made the book known worldwide (4111)

G Walt Disney created lovable cartoon characters (4112)

H Prize winner Faulkner (4113) was macabre and morbid. His
I *The Sound and the Fury* was full of violence (4114)

J Eugene O'Neill, the period's greatest playwright (4115)

K *The Hairy Ape:* Man's despair against the machine (4116)

L *Gone With the Wind,* the all time greatest movie (4117)

M Margaret Mitchell produced this one novel only (4118)

The Gathering Storm

Ethiopia

WHILE ROOSEVELT SOUGHT to establish a new order of government in America, Europe's dictatorial regimes moved toward a confrontation with the Western democracies. Already weakened by failure to stop the Second Sino-Japanese War (1931), the League of Nations displayed its lack of power when Mussolini invaded Ethiopia in 1935. Sanctions were voted but not enforced, and the world's demagogues took note.

Haile Selassie asked help of the League of Nations (4119)

Italian troops storm into Ethiopia; only guerrillas resisted them (4120)

Mussolini defied the League, whose embargoes proved ineffective (4121)

Spain

MEANWHILE, A COVERT WAR between the dictatorships and the democracies was staged in Spain. General Franco's attempt in 1936 to overthrow the Spanish Republic met resistance from the Republican working class, supported by voluntary freedom fighters from other lands. But Franco, controlling the army, held the upper hand, and with generous support from Hitler and Mussolini defeated the Republicans after three years of a bloody civil war.

Playboy King Alfonso XIII racing in his Hispano-Suiza car (4122)

Dictator Primo de Rivera, ousted in 1930 by Republicans (4123)

General Franco, leader of anti-republicans (4124)

Women enlisted in the Loyalist army (4125)

A King Departs

WHEN THE ENGLISH GOVERNMENT refused, in 1936, to permit King Edward VII to marry Wallis Simpson, a commoner and a divorcée, King Edward abdicated the throne, marrying her in France while moppets in the dooryards sang, "Hark the herald angels sing! Mrs. Simpson's pinched our king!"

Insurgents prevailed with help from Germany, Italy (4126)

Nationalist troops search captured loyalists (4127)

Prime Minister Baldwin (4128) opposed match of King and commoner (4129)

King Edward VIII in uniform (4130)

Dec. 5, 1937: George VI and Queen Mary after the coronation (4131)

Stalin's Bloody Reign

STALIN, THOUGH DESPISED BY LENIN for his vulgarity, had emerged as party leader after Lenin's death in 1924; in 1928 Stalin's rival Trotsky was expelled. In a massive purge (1933) Stalin exiled or executed nearly one third of his own party members while pursuing a program of rapid, forced industrialization and a brutal mind control.

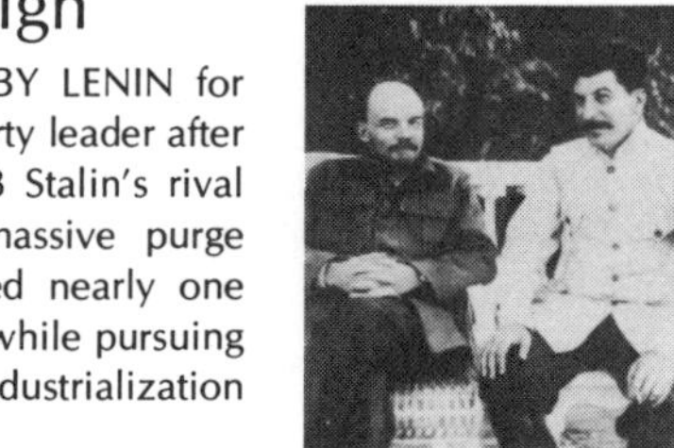

Lenin with his collaborator and successor, Stalin (4132)

Leon Trotsky, loyal to Lenin, strong anti-Stalinist (4133)

Stalin eliminated all rivals, became dictator, purged opposition (4134)

Charting 5–year plan of economic growth (4135)

Trouble in the Orient

JAPAN'S INVASION of China in the 1930s led to a brief period of military cooperation between Chiang Kai-shek's Kuomintang and Mao Tse-tung's Communists. After World War II, Mao's peasant army drove the corrupt Kuomintang from the Chinese mainland and established the People's Republic of China.

Japan stabs peace pact, enters Manchuria (4136)

Chiang Kai-shek, forced to yield to Communists (4137)

Mao Tse-tung, Communist leader, became head of Republic (4138)

Chou En-lai was second only to Mao (4139)

Nazi Nightmare

DISARMED AND BESET by insoluble economic woes, Germany rose again under Adolf Hitler in 1933—to a power status that seemed to defy challenge. Beginning in 1935, Hitler renounced the Versailles Treaty, ended reparations payments and rebuilt the German war machine. In March, 1938 he annexed Austria, and a year later Czechoslovakia. At home he launched a reign of terror that culminated during World War II in the attempted genocide of the Jews. The German people, frightened into submission or caught in a mass hysteria, became the tools of a madman's ambition.

Nationalist anti-Nazi party in 1932 election bid (4140)

Election posters on Berlin kiosk (4141)

Nazi poster proclaims Hitler as country's last hope (4142)

Adolf Hitler, "Der Führer" (4143)

Reichstag fire gave Nazis excuse to persecute Communists (4144)

Youth was taught Hitler's militant gospel (4145)

Nuremberg rallies dazzled Germany with great military might (4146)

Hitler in Munich Bürgerkeller just before attempt on his life (4147)

Rudolf Hess flies to England for mysterious peace bid (4148)

Heinrich Himmler, Gestapo chief (4149)

Nazi boycott of all firms owned by Jews. Their property was confiscated (4150)

After abusive search, non-aryans were condemned to concentration camps (4151)

Wearing Star of David, Jews expelled from home (4152)

Nazi youths watch burning of books condemned by Hitler regime (4153)

Defiant SS Trooper (4154)

Propagandist Joseph Goebbels (4155)

Goose stepping Army backed Hitler (4156)

Return of Saar swelled Germany industry (4157)

Hitler and Mussolini—Rome-Berlin Axis: the great European power base (4158)

Far Eastern and European aims unified by Tri–partite Pact of Axis and Japan (4159)

Hitler's right hand, Goering (4160)

Sudeten crisis. Chamberlain to Czechs: "Give it to him—it is safer!"(4161)

Munich Conference, 1938. Chamberlain signs away Czechoslovakia (4162)

Chamberlain returns to London, "Peace in our Time" (4163)

German troops march into Czechoslovakia; partisans cheer (4164)

Hitler-Stalin pact: "But will it last?" (4165)

Nazi parade saluted by populace with frenetic enthusiasm (4166)

Germany Strikes

SEVEN DAYS AFTER SIGNING the German-Russian Nonaggression Pact, Hitler's blitzkrieg struck Poland from the west while Stalin invaded from the east. Hitler's prophecy seemed fulfilled: "I shall stand on the common German and Russian border, shake hands with Stalin, and carry out with him a redistribution of the world." Stalin then overcame Finland, but only after fierce resistance.

Poland invaded, Sept. 1, 1939, Europe set aflame (4167)

Nazi blitzkrieg crushed Poland in twenty-eight days (4168)

Persecution of Warsaw Jews marked start of genocidal horrors (4169)

Polish anti-Nazis hanged by German troops (4170)

German troops disembark in Oslo, Norway harbor (4171)

Quisling, Norwegian Nazi puppet, traitor (4172)

Germans' lightning move through Belgium trapped 250,000 British at Dunkirk (4173)

France was ravaged in month blitzkrieg (4174)

Hitler, with word of France's fall, does victory jig (4174 A)

German columns pass Arc de Triomphe (4175)

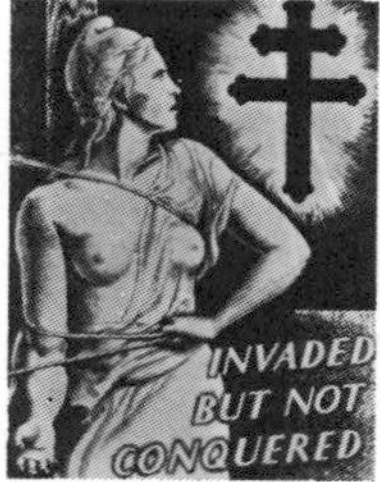

Marianne defies France's surrender (4176)

In England, De Gaulle trained powerful Free French liberation army (4177)

THERE WAS LITTLE ACTION at first on the Western Front, but on April 9, 1940, Hitler moved against Denmark, which fell in a matter of hours. After subduing Norway, the Nazis swarmed through the Low Countries, taking Holland in five days, Belgium in eighteen. Outflanking the Maginot Line, they pressed on to Paris, and France surrendered on June 22. The British Expeditionary Forces, surrounded on the French coast near Dunkirk, were evacuated, making the town a symbol of irrepressible valor.

Air armada unleashed August 1940 (4178)

Battle of Britain

ENGLAND WAS NEXT on Hitler's timetable. To prepare for invasion, his Luftwaffe launched a ferocious bombardment of the British Isles. Though one of every five homes was destroyed, the Battle of Britain was won by the Royal Air Force. As Churchill said: "Never . . . was so much owed by so many to so few."

Churchill, champion of England's unconquerable courage (4179)

Row of houses destroyed in London blitz (4180)

Undaunted British spirit rebounds in London air raid shelter (4181)

Buildings crumble next to St. Paul's Cathedral (4182)

Russia Invaded

ON JUNE 22, 1941, Hitler turned abruptly against Russia. Though the campaign was executed in grandiose style—127 divisions and 3,000 aircraft operated on a 2,000-mile front—Hitler's ambition proved as disastrous as Napoleon's. After losing 330,000 men in the siege of Stalingrad, the Germans were routed, with the Russians in relentless pursuit.

German shock troops in vanguard of surprise attack on Russia (4183)

Red army at Stalingrad gave Nazis crushing defeat (4184)

Marshal Semën Timoshenko, Soviet military hero (4185)

Benghazi Derna El Gazala Tobruk Bardia Sallum El Alamein

Desert Warfare

AS THE WAR EXPANDED, the Axis attacked in North Africa. The Italians surrendered at Bardia, but Rommel's Afrika Korps rolled the British back into Egypt. When Montgomery's counterattack put Rommel's army to flight at Alamein, and Eisenhower's force moved in, the Axis was swept from Africa in 1943.

A North Africa: Germans moved in after Italians. Seesaw battles ensued (4186)

B General Rommel. His Afrika Korps pushed British back to Egypt (4187)

C Open desert war posed problems of strategy. Water was critical (4188)

D Montgomery thwarted Rommel's drive to Egypt at El Alamein (4189)

E Quentin Reynolds, American writer, reported African campaign (4190)

F Luftwaffe plane downed by RAF in dogfight over Libyan Desert (4191)

Arsenal of Democracy

U.S. industry was put on a war footing in 1941 (4193)

First U.S. peacetime draft, October 1940; gradually it reached ten million (4192)

Destroyer deal, Lend-Lease gave Allies backing (4194)

Churchill and Roosevelt meet; Atlantic Charter drafted (4195)

HITLER'S TRIUMPHS OF 1940 finally awakened America to the dangers of Nazism. Prodded by FDR, America became a belligerent "short of war." More than $50 billion in arms and money were raised through Lend-Lease. Even if on the surface the United States still seemed to shy away from overt involvement, war preparations were stepped up during 1940 and 1941, and Congress passed the first peacetime Selective Service Act.

Lend-lease tank (4196)

Roosevelt signs declaration of war against Japan (4199)

YET IT WAS NOT A EUROPEAN but a Pacific threat that abruptly turned the tide. To continue its invasion of China, Japan needed massive sources of supply, particularly oil, to fuel its war machine. While emissaries negotiated the issue in Washington, a surprise attack by Japanese carrier airplanes on the U.S. fleet at Pearl Harbor (December 7, 1941) catapulted the United States into war with Japan, and four days later with Germany and Italy.

(4197)

DAILY NEWS 2
JAPS BOMB HAWAII
DECLARE WAR ON U.S. AND BRITAIN

DAILY MIRROR 2
JAPS DECLARE WAR
HAWAII, MANILA BOMBED; 350 DEAD

Pearl Harbor surprise attack, December 7, 1941, crippled U.S. Pacific fleet, freed Japan for unprecedented conquests of Asia, South Pacific (4198)

General MacArthur: Pacific debacle to victory (4200)

Admiral Ch. Nimitz credited with "island hopping" strategy (4201)

Admiral Halsey crippled Japs at Solomon Islands (4202)

The Pacific War

DESPITE HEROIC RESISTANCE by American forces at Bataan and Corregidor, the Japanese swept over the Pacific in 1942 while the U.S. Navy slowly rebuilt its strength. Japanese dominance soon reached from Wake Island to the Bay of Bengal. The painful process of reconquest began when an American fleet repulsed the enemy in the Coral Sea (May 1942), followed by victories at Midway (June), Guadalcanal (August), Guam (July 1944), and capped by MacArthur's triumphant return to the Philippines in October 1944.

Guadalcanal landing, August, 1942 was followed by six months fighting (4203)

A walking Marine arsenal rests on Tarawa beach (4204)

Machine gun crew in tense lull of fierce New Guinea action (4205)

Blood transfusion on the beach: rifle butt holds plasma (4206)

Black soldiers fight in the Bougainville jungle (4207)

Pacific isle haircut. Barber chair is Japanese (4208)

MacArthur returns, wading ashore on Leyte, Philippine Islands, October 1944 (4209)

The Home Front

D E F G

A

H

B

C

A Poster warns Americans of spies lurking in their midst (4210)

B Flag awarded by War Department for record production (4211)

C War ration book and food stamps issued by rationing board (4212)

D Oveta C. Hobby sworn in as head of WAACs. Gen. Marshall in rear (4213)

E Rosie the Riveter: symbol of female wartime work and dedication (4214)

F Reading the latest war bulletins by the *New York Times* (4215)

G H. V. Kaltenborn: his comments became a fixture of wartime America (4216)

H Conquest of Iwo Jima put Japan into U.S. bombing range (4217)

The Campaign in Italy

WITH AFRICA SECURE, the Allies turned toward Italy itself, taking Sicily in 1943, then moving slowly and painfully up the peninsula. In one of the bitterest battles of the war, German forces near Rome were surrounded and forced to surrender (April 29, 1945) only a day after Mussolini—captured, summarily tried and shot by partisans—had been ignominiously hung by the heels next to his mistress.

In burning town, U.S. soldier on alert to threat of Fascist snipers (4218)

Patton and his troops land in Italy (4219)

Allies welcomed enthusiastically after long Fascist rule (4220)

Mussolini was deposed, rescued by Germans, recaptured, executed by partisans (4221)

Invasion of Europe

Allied commanders confer on D-Day landing: Eisenhower, Tedder and Montgomery (4222)

June 6, 1944—D-Day: 50,000 men, 12,000 vehicles put ashore (4223)

Landing craft and amphibious trucks pour men, materiel ashore (4224)

Paratroopers display flag captured in pursuit of fleeing Nazis (4225)

A SECOND EUROPEAN FRONT, long urged by Russia, was launched in June 1944. Breaching Hitler's Atlantic Wall in Normandy, the Allies gradually reoccupied France, defeating a fierce German counteroffensive in December in the Battle of the Bulge. As the Western Allies marched eastward, the Russians pushed toward Berlin, reaching the city one day after the Führer's suicide. Germany's unconditional surrender followed on May 7, 1945.

Paris liberated: GIs in victory parade (4226)

French underground fighters lead German prisoners amid hostile jeers (4227)

Bradley, Eisenhower, Patton survey damage in Bastogne, Belgium (4228)

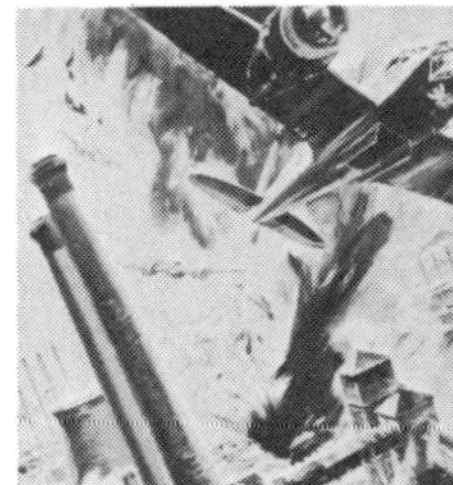

Saturation bombing preceded Allies in Germany (4229)

American tanks rumble through Cologne, gutted by Allied air attacks (4230)

Precision bombing: Ulm Cathedral undamaged; all other buildings demolished (4230 A)

Apollensdorf, Germany: Allies speeding east meet Russians rushing west (4231)

FDR's Fourth Term

WITH THE ALLIED OUTLOOK ever brightening, FDR in 1944 was re-elected for a fourth term. But the strain of world leadership had undermined his health that had always been precarious and, unexpectedly and shockingly, he died on April 12, 1945 at his Georgia home—only weeks before the Allied victory which he had labored so valiantly to attain.

Roosevelt, ill, campaigns for fourth term (4232)

Yalta unity was jolted by Russia's uncomprising demands (4233)

FDR and Churchill in one of their last meetings (4234)

World is shocked by sudden death (4235)

End of the War

Signing of German surrender at Rheims, May 7, 1945 (4236)

New York celebrates the news of Germany's surrender (4237)

Concentration camp horrors discovered by advancing troops stunned the world (4238)

"One man could not simply do it all, and Roosevelt killed himself trying."
—Henry Stimson, Sec. of War

(4239)

The atomic bomb explosion over Nagasaki, August 9, 1945 (4240)

Unconditional surrender of Japan signed Sept. 2, 1945 aboard battleship *Missouri* in Tokyo Bay (4241)

HAVING REGAINED CONTROL of the Pacific, American forces converged on Japan, which refused an appeal for surrender. President Truman now faced an unprecedented, crucial decision: whether to invade Japan with the risk of heavy losses, or to drop the first atomic bomb, destroying hundreds of thousands of Japanese civilians. Opting for the latter, he ordered the destruction of Hiroshima on August 6, 1945, and Nagasaki three days later. Japan surrendered on August 14.

Thus the war ended, with fear and apprehension muting the joy of deliverance. To end the terror started by Hitler's fanaticism, mankind had paid a staggering price: hundreds of cities gutted, tens of millions of civilians and military personnel killed and well over $1 trillion in material cost. And now "The Bomb," which had laid a heavy burden of guilt upon the American conscience, shadowed the peace with fears of annihilation. Recognizing the threat to civilization posed by atomic warfare, the United States, which had failed to join the League of Nations, became the staunchest champion of the new United Nations.

U.S. Delegation signs the United Nations Charter, June 26, 1945. President Truman at left (4242)

The United Nations Building in New York. Its cornerstone was laid in 1949 (4243)

EPILOGUE

Highlights of the Post War Period

Truman after election triumphantly points to headline declaring Dewey winner (4244)

George C. Marshall initiated the Marshall plan (4245)

Berlin Airlift: Allied supplies flown in at cost of millions, after Russians had cut air and land traffic to city (4246)

1950s

War; Space Flight; Cold War Pressures

Korean War: Asia new locus of East-West power struggle (4247)

MacArthur during his farewell address (4248)

Eisenhower: Laissez-faire in U.S. while foreign woes wax (4249)

McCarthy hearings said Army coddled Communists (4250)

Hawaii joins the Union as the fiftieth state (4251)

England's new Queen, Elizabeth II (4252)

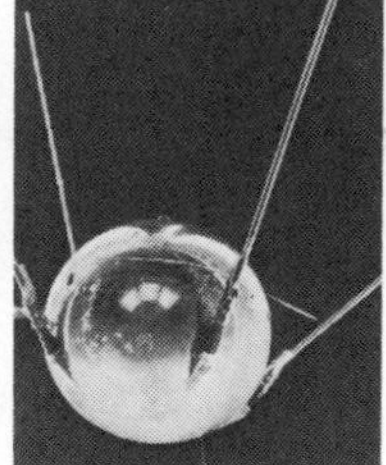

Russia's Sputnik I began the space age (4253)

Pope John XXIII propagated Church reforms, progressive social welfare (4254)

Fidel Castro toppled Batista, became Cuba's ruler (4255)

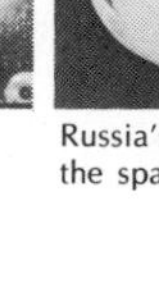

IN THE FIFTIES, as America sought to finance the rebirth of Europe, East-West tensions grew into the Cold War, an ideological conflict held in check largely by the threat of the atom bomb.

With the world split into opposing camps, discontent at home characterized the sixties. Youth, opposing the Vietnam war, defied the conflict as immoral and protested the draft. The blacks, long denied equal rights, followed the nonviolent leadership of Martin Luther King, Jr., to demand them. Ironically, violence stigmatized the decade. Three American leaders—King and two Kennedys—were assassinated.

The mood of disillusionment reached a peak in the seventies as the Watergate scandals forced the resignation of an American President. Yet the experience proved cathartic: a grass-roots appeal to democratic ideals carried Jimmy Carter to the White House.

1960s

Discontent; Vietnam; Social Readjustment

Khrushchev, Kennedy met in Vienna. The reconciliation failed (4256)

J.F.K.'s tragic death (4257)

Lyndon B. Johnson sworn in on flight to Washington (4258)

Immolation: turmoil in S. Vietnam invited Communist thrust (4259)

U.S. deploys troops in Vietnam (4260)

Robt. Kennedy assassinated while campaigning (4261)

Moshe Dayan led Israel in Six-Day War (4262)

Woodstock Festival, height of youth culture (4263)

Jerry Rubin, student leader, in defiant defense at Chicago Seven trial (4264)

1970s

Nixon's Resignation; Carter: A New Order

Nixon visit to China: hope for a new global alignment (4265)

Pentagon Papers trial: victory for free speech, free press (4266)

Nixon resigns to forestall impeachment (4267)

Carter family walks to White House after presidential inauguration (4268)

Emerging Nations

Israel's Declaration of Independence, read by first Prime Minister, David Ben-Gurion (4269)

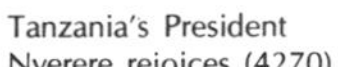

Tanzania's President Nyerere rejoices (4270)

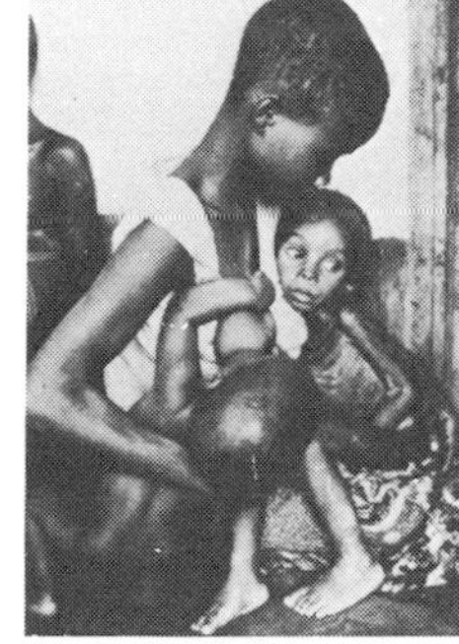

Famine in Biafra during new Nigeria's civil war (4271)

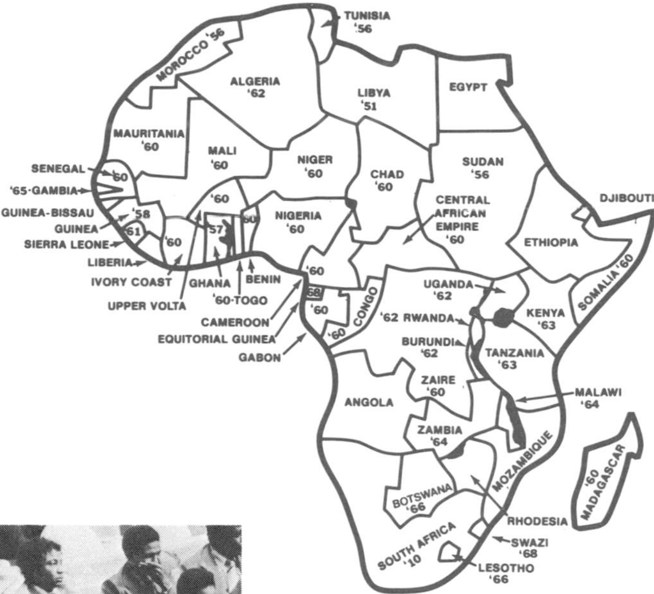

Africa: colonialism replaced by Third World power (4274)

THE THIRD WORLD—the emerging nations in Asia and Africa—rose to challenge the balance of power in the decades after World War II. India, winning independence from Britain in 1947, set the pattern which brought an end to colonialism. More than thirty-five African states achieved independence in the 1960s, seventeen in 1960 alone. These new nations were soon wooed by East and West as the struggle for dominance continued.

THE WORLD-WIDE STRUGGLE for liberation was expressed in the American civil rights movement. Blacks now demanded a greater share of political and social opportunity. Reforms in education, voting laws, housing and employment were enacted. For his "nonviolent" leadership, Martin Luther King, Jr., was awarded the Nobel Peace Prize. Before he fell victim to an assassin, he had begun to bring blacks into the mainstream of American life.

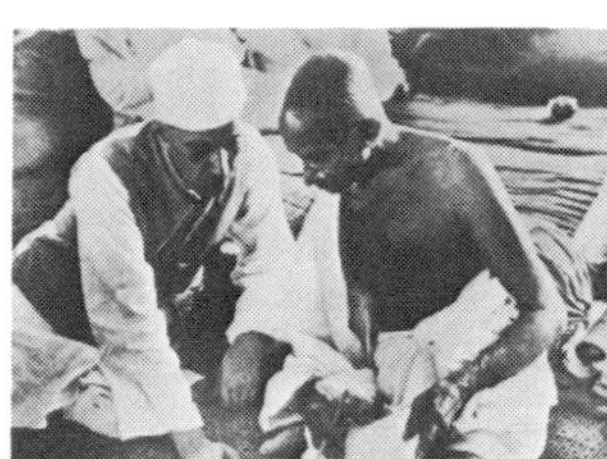

Nehru, Gandhi transformed India into a sovereign Asian power (4272)

Delegates from the Sudan participate in UN General Assembly debate (4273)

Human Rights

Lawyers* celebrate victory in antisegregation trial (4275)

Martin Luther King, Jr., opposed to violence, was its victim (4276)

Little Rock, Ark.: protected black student enters segregated school (4277)

*G. E. Hayes, Thurgood Marshall, James Nabrit

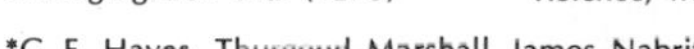

Bus of Freedom Riders who challenged segregation set afire in encounter with Alabama racists (4278)

Voting Rights Act guaranteed blacks ballot; Federal registrar helps new voters (4281)

Rev. Abernathy arrested during protest march on Washington, D.C. (4280)

Plea for legal support to racial minorities (4279)

Posterized demands of civil rights movement (4282)

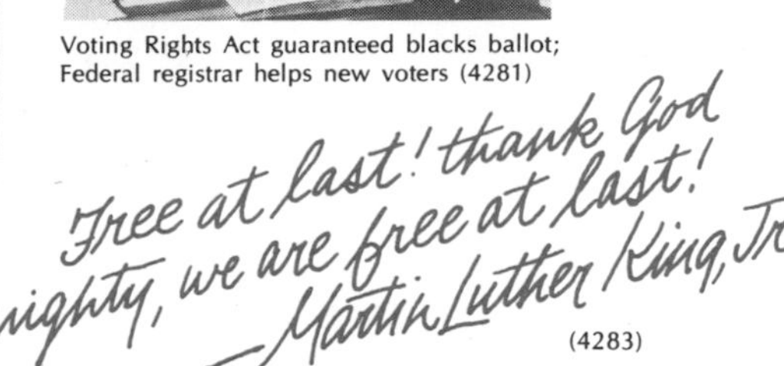

(4283)

TOWARD THE FUTURE . . .

Atomic Energy
Life Sciences
Communications
Space Technology

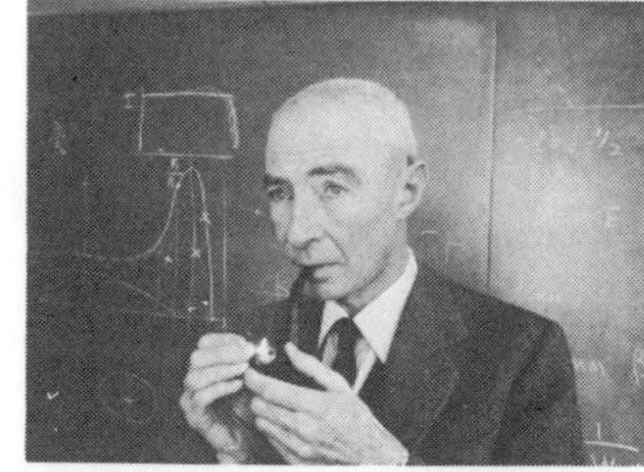

Robert Oppenheimer directed atomic bomb project during World War II (4284)

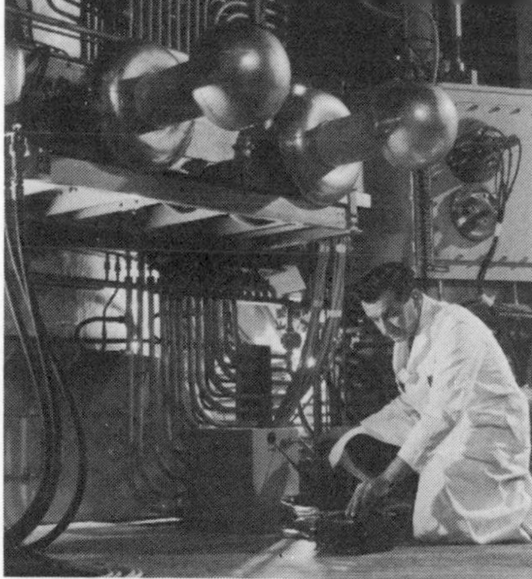

Variable energy cyclatron used for radiation and radio chemistry, radiation damage studies (4285)

Dr. Selman Waksman: antibiotics to counteract infection (4286)

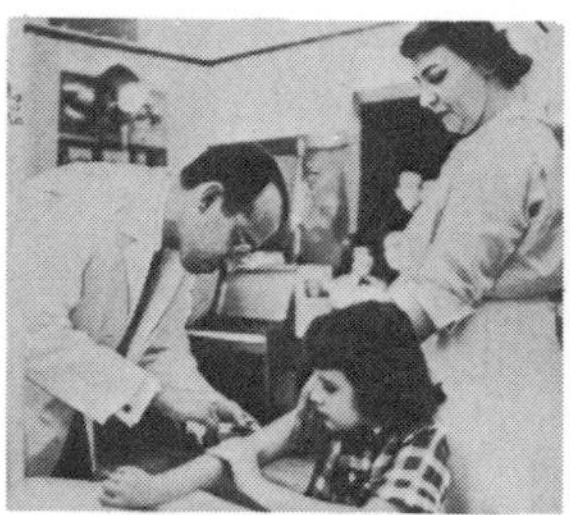

Dr. Jonas Salk developed vaccine against poliomyelitis (4287)

Nobel laureate Wilkins with DNA model (4288)

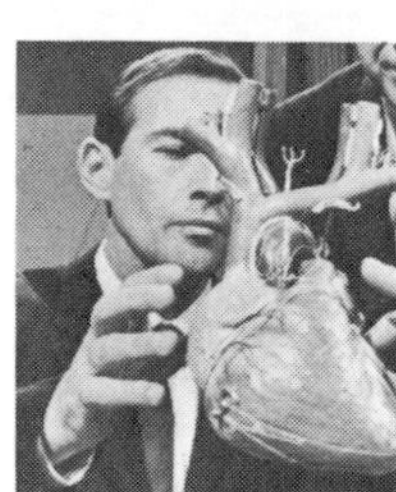

Christiaan Barnard, heart-transplant pioneer (4289)

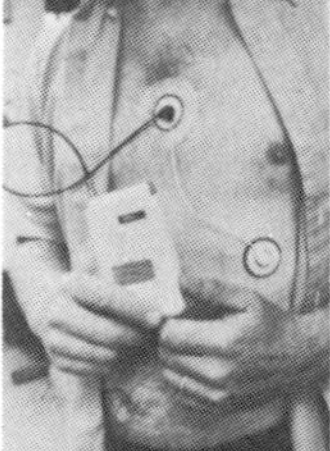

Pacemaker regulates heart rhythm (4290)

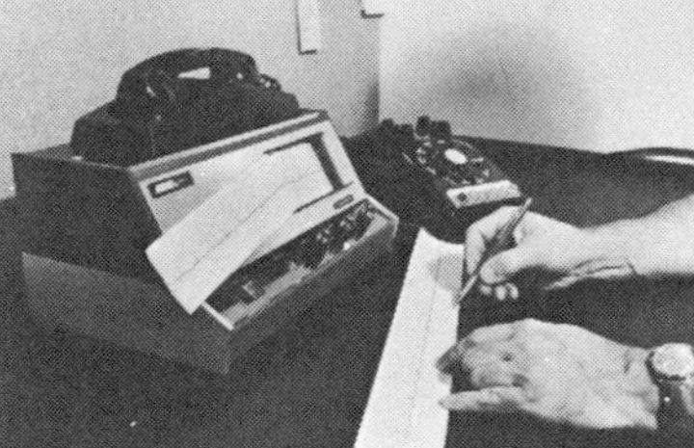

Cardiac diagnosis facilitated by telephone transmittal of electrocardiogram (4291)

Assembly line for television, a revolution in audio-visual communications (4292)

Inventor Carlson and first Xerox (4293)

Computer—an electronic brain of infinite capacity (4294)

Werner von Braun, pioneer in rocket and space technology (4295)

(4296)

HOPES AND FEARS are strangely intermingled as the age of technocracy remodels our world. We are witnessing unprecedented accomplishments and are called upon at the same time to solve unprecedented problems. Progress always creates new troubles to plague mankind: medical miracles with all their benefits have brought us face to face with the problems of the population explosion and the vicissitudes of aging. Technological advances force us to adjust to a new man-made environment; to cope with an unnatural acceleration in the pace of life. And over all our technical breakthroughs there hovers the specter of nuclear war.

Still, there is no reason for despair. Man the problem-solver, seen in historical perspective, has a triumphant record on the whole. If our problems today are enormous in scale, so are our resources to solve them. This thought must strengthen our resolve to face the future without fear. As Faulkner said in his famed Nobel Prize speech: "The basest thing of all is to be afraid. I believe man will not only endure, he will prevail."

(4297)

ACKNOWLEDGEMENTS & CREDITS

Much of my research for this book was done during my winter stays in Boca Raton, Florida, where I have been happily connected with Florida Atlantic University. Its remarkable library offered me rich resources to carry on my studies, while the University's History Department provided a base for fruitful exchange with fellow historians. For guidance and suggestions I am grateful to all of them—as I am to Dr. Jack Suberman, Dean of Humanities, and Dr. John O'Sullivan, Chairman of the History Department, who enabled me to work in an ambiance highly conducive to the development of a pictorial world history.

O. L. B.

While the bulk of the illustrations in this book are from The Bettmann Archive, various organizations and institutions have kindly permitted the use of their material. We are much indebted to the following:

American Museum of Natural History: 32–34, 40, 42, 45; Bibliotheque Nationale: 5, 445; Bibliotheque Royale Albert I: 677; Black Star: 4196; British Information Service: 4129–31; British Library Board: 14, 518, 1126; Bryant Library: 3954; Carnegie Library: 3373; Chicago Historical Society: 2653; Colonial Society of Massachusetts: 1341; Deutsches Museum: 383; Dennis Galloway: 4290–91; Harvard University: 2594; Huntington Library: 2181; Hutchinson and Co.: 139, 1724; Imperial War Museum: 3747; Institution of Electrical Engineers: 3015; Keystone Photos: 4270; Kipling Society: 2982; Kunstmuseum Basel: 904; Mansell Collection: 2448, 2466–67, 3208; Metropolitan Museum of Art: 512, 1130, 1971, 2024; John Morrell and Co.: 1875; Museo del Prado: 1594; National-historiscke Museum på Frederiksborg: 3061; National Portrait Gallery, London: 1783, 1787, 2159, 2162, 3618–19; New York Public Library: 444, 721; New York Stock Exchange: 2005, 2008; Oriental Institute: 64–66; Östereichische Nationalbibliothek: 712; Pennsylvania Academy of Art: 2016; Preussischer Kulturbesitz: 3962, 3969; Science Museum, London: 1155, 2408; Staatsbibliothek, Berlin: 3864, 3971; Sovfoto: 4294; United Kingdom Atomic Energy Authority: 4285; United Nations: 187, 4242–43, 4273; United Press International: 4120, 4125, 4163, 4167, 4203–4, 4226, 4232, 4252, 4258, 4262, 4266, 4277, 4281, 4288; U.S. Army Center of Military History: 4214; University of Pennsylvania: 4294; Walker Art Gallery: 2161, 2425; Westinghouse Corporation: 3209; Wide World Photos: 3899, 4015, 4069, 4126, 4171, 4184, 4194, 4244, 4248, 4250–51, 4253–54, 4256, 4259, 4261, 4263–65, 4267–68, 4271, 4275–76, 4278–80, 4282, 4284, 4289; Wyeth Laboratories: 3494; Zentralbibliothek Zürich: 669.

Entries are followed by two types of numbers: those in regular type identify individual pictures, while those in **bold** type refer to pages offering a series of pictures on the topic listed.

The Index lists in detail historical events, trends and personalities. But it will also serve readers as an "Image Finder," with entries like "wisdom," "valor," and "ruse," which locate graphic illustrations of abstract terms. Included among the entries are colloquialisms ("thumbs down," "handwriting on the wall") and allusions to myth and history which have entered the mainstream of our language ("Gordian knot," "ostracism," "tantalize"). Familiar slogans in America's political rhetoric ("melting pot," "muckraking," "mugwump," "manifest destiny") are also included. As an image finder, the Index points to the origin of such expressions and locates them in historical context.

Although the visual reconstruction of the past is its principal aim, this book also serves as a record of graphic traditions. In this sense it represents an image bank between covers, its thousands of numbered illustrations easily retrievable by those who wish to translate verbal concepts into visual terms.

INDEX AND IMAGE FINDER

B

C

F

G

I

J

K

L

M

N

O

P

Q

R

S

T

Z

CAPTIONS FOR CHAPTER DIVIDER PAGES

Illustrations from editorial pages that are repeated in Chapter Dividers are identified by their regular numbers. All others are captioned below:

CHAPTER 1

A (68)
B (237)
C (66)
D (345)
E (214)
F Chariot race in the Circus Maximus. From a painting by A. Wagner

CHAPTER 2

A Head of Christ. Detail from mosaics, central lunette, Hagia Sophia
B (599)
C (669)
D (458)
E (444)

CHAPTER 3

A Florence: Cathedral dome, Palazzo Vecchio tower, Giotto's campanile
B (908)
C (736)
D (750)
E (734)
F (758)
G Heavily armed 16th cent. vessel; navigator uses magnetic compass
H (753)

CHAPTER 4

A (1283)
B (1170)
C (1143)
D (1167)
E (1137)
F (1085)
G (1359)

CHAPTER 5

A (1402)
B Joseph Hayden composing: symphonies, chamber music, operas, oratorios
C (1514)
D (1462)
E (1447)
F (1434)

CHAPTER 6

A Map of revolutionary America with Ben Franklin and patriotic figures
B Title page of first collected edition of important U.S.A. documents
C (1837)
D (1930)

CHAPTER 7

A (2054)
B (2070)
C (2130)
D (2215)
E (2232)

CHAPTER 8

A (2496)
B (2437)
C (2406)
D (2427)
E (2320)
F (2473)

CHAPTER 9

A (2628)
B (2541)
C (2565)
D (2529)
E (2715)
F "Long Abraham a little longer," Caricature of lanky Lincoln
G (2700)
H (2778)

CHAPTER 10

A (2916)
B (2900)
C (2962)
D (2872)
E (3080)
F (3091)
G Microscope—a prime tool of science for all research and development
H (3026)

CHAPTER 11

A Rounding up the herd—an important and dangerous task for the cowboy
B (3189)
C (3373)
D (3124)
E Corset factory has simple assembly line to gather machine-sewn parts
F (3144)

CHAPTER 12

A (3760)
B (3580)
C (3545)
D (3505)
E V-Day, 1918 in New York City: happy people celebrating in the street
F (3823)
G Near the Marne, France. Artillery barrage destroyed church, village
H (3672)

CHAPTER 13

A (3929)
B (4015)
C (3934)
D (3974)
E Hitler salutes supporters at rally before his ascent to power, 1932
F (4219)
G (4203)
H (4225)
I (4233)
J The insignia of the United Nations

CAPTIONS FOR FRONT ENDPAPERS

a The Sphinx, sculpted from natural rock, and the monumental pyramid at Giza

b Oxen threshing corn, from a harvest scene in the tomb of Menna, Thebes

c Funerary mask of King Tutankhamen, a masterpiece of the goldsmith's art

d The Parthenon, Athens—epitome of Greek architectural perfection

e Terra cotta figurine of woman with parasol. From Tanagra, ca. 300 B.C.

f Greek artifice of the soldier–filled hollow horse led to the fall of Troy

g Death of Socrates, famed thinker and philosopher. Painting by J. L. David

h Struggle between the hero Theseus and the Minotaur. Greek amphora

i "Pont du Gard," major Roman aqueduct near Nimes, France, 158 feet high

j The end of a chariot race in a Roman circus. Nero victorious. Painting

k Perseus and Andromeda. Roman mural painting, house of Dioscuri, Pompeii

l Roman flour mill and bakery, based on finds in the ruins of Pompeii

m Julius Caesar—general and statesman, dictator, orator, writer, reformer

n "The Good Rule of St. Benedict" shown in a miniature painting of 1414

o Medieval tournament: knights proved might is right in colorful panoply

p The Alcazar, Segovia—fortress–castle, medieval residence of Castilian kings

q 15th century banker (l) arranges loan while wife (r) receives gold payment

r Parade armor of Holy Roman Emperor Maximilian I, "Last of the Knights"

s Exquisite tapestry detail shows lady with unicorn reflected in hand mirror

t 8th century Viking trading ship departs on expedition from Norway. Painting

u Michelangelo's tomb of Giuliano de Medici in the church of St. Lorenzo

v Columbus lands in the new world, opens a new era of exploration, exploitation

w Sandro Botticelli's "Birth of Venus," allegory of the Renaissance spirit

x German print shop was a fountainhead for the new art, science, religion

y Martin Luther challenged the Church, began the Reformation, Protestantism

z Nicholas Copernicus, Polish astronomer, revolutionized concept of the universe

aa Stern and firm Lord Protector Oliver Cromwell ruled England for 4 years

bb Louis XIV, the "Sun King," receives a foreign ambassador at his court

cc John Milton visits Galileo, looks through astronomer's telescope

dd Peter Minuit buys Manhattan Island from Indians for trinkets worth $24

ee Captain Kidd, hired to fight pirates, became one, buried his treasure

ff Man's first free ascent from earth in a Montgolfier balloon, Nov. 21, 1783

gg Francois Marie Arouet Voltaire, prime philosopher of the Enlightenment

hh The boudoir of Marie Antoinette in the royal chateau at Fontainbleau

ii Detail, John Trumbull ptg., "Signing the Declaration of Independence"

jj Violinist–composer Leopold Mozart and his children, Wolfgang and Marianna

CAPTIONS FOR BACK ENDPAPERS

a Chemist–physicist Michael Faraday in his Royal Institution laboratory

b Gregor Mendel, discoverer of laws of genetics and heredity, in his garden

c Pierre and Marie Curie investigated radioactivity, discovered radium

d Uncle Sam doffs his hat to Edison's fabulous talking machine. Poster

e French poster extols the new moving pictures for family entertainment

f Louis Pasteur, pioneer in preventative medicine, proved germ theory as fact

g Sigmund Freud developed psychoanalysis and a new therapy for mental illness

h Joseph Lister uses carbolic acid in early antiseptic surgical operation

i Costume proposed by reformer Amelia Bloomer for all liberated women

j Sacajawea guides Lewis and Clark in exploration of Louisiana Purchase

k President–elect Andrew Jackson stops for a speech en route to Washington

l Lincoln at dedication of Gettysburg Cemetery gives his immortal address

m General Sherman leads attack during his famous march through Georgia

n Carpetbagger question: caricature of Carl Schurz as self–willed extremist

o Jesse James, desperado, bank and train robber, killed by one of his gang

p Strike it rich. Miners during the gold rush panning in a stream

q Tragedy strikes the California bound ill–fated Donner party of pioneers

r Cowboy on the trail rounding up the herd to head off a stampede. Litho.

s Overbearing, abusive boss intimidates a garment worker in New York sweat shop

t The steel works. Overwhelming economic might in flames and smoking stacks

u Arriving immigrants pass the Statue of Liberty. Hebrew language poster

v High society couple during the gay nineties leaving the theater loge

w Happy family having a picnic–outing on a summer Sunday in the park

x Colonel Teddy Roosevelt and the Rough Riders charge up Cuba's San Juan Hill

y Henry Ford wheeling out his first automobile on Bagley Ave., Detroit

z Narrow gauge locomotive that hauled ore, goods and people in the West

aa The Wright brothers' first flight at Kitty Hawk. Orville at the controls

bb Fashionable lady and gentleman leave limousine with liveried chauffeur

cc Woodrow Wilson, 28th U.S. President and father of the League of Nations

dd Famous World War I recruiting poster by artist James Montgomery Flagg

ee German U-boat sinks American ship in unrestricted submarine warfare, WW I

ff Franklin D. Roosevelt addresses the nation during a "fireside chat"

gg Natl. Recovery Administration poster from FDR's anti–depression program

hh Adolph Hitler, virulent German leader, threatened existence of western society

ii U.S. Marines plant the flag atop Mt. Suribachi on Iwo Jima in the Pacific

jj Astronaut Edwin Aldrin, Jr. on the moon, photographed by Neil Armstrong

Illustrations on back endpapers are identified on page 223.